Baedeker

W9-CTI-777

Israel

Palestine

www.baedeker.com

Verlag Karl Baedeker

SIGHTSEEING HIGHLIGHTS ★ ★

Judaism, Christianity and Islam have all left impressive buildings and other traces in Israel. But in the Holy Land it would be a mistake to stay merely on the beaten pilgrim track.

Jerusalem – The Jewish Cemetery on the Mount of Olives

De-militarized zone

Golan Heights

1 Acre

2 Tzippori

3 Sea of Galilee

5 Megiddo

6 Caesarea

4 Beit She'an

West Bank

7 Tel Aviv

8 Jerusalem

9 Bethlehem

10 Dead Sea

11 Ein Gedi

Gaza Strip

12 Masada

©Baedeker

13 Mamshit

14 Avdat

15 Makhtesh Ramon

BAEDEKER'S BEST TIPS

Of all the Baedeker Tips in this book, here are some of the most interesting. Experience and enjoy Israel and Palestine from their most attractive side!

🔲 The Bible, live
How did people live in biblical times? Get an answer to this question in Yad Hashmona. To round off a visit, enjoy a biblical meal in the tent made of goat's hide. ▸ **page 171**

🔲 Swimming with a view
Argaman Beach, also known as Purple Beach, is one of the most beautiful beaches in Israel with spectacular views of Akko's harbour walls. ▸ **page 172**

🔲 The early bird...
To enjoy the special atmosphere in the Church of the Nativity in Bethlehem in peace and quiet, get up early. It is best to be there by 6am. ▸ **page 198**

🔲 Diving down
One special feature of Eilat's beaches is Coral Reserve Beach. It is possible to explore the reef and observe the fish from raised walkways or to swim between the coral reefs. ▸ **page 231**

🔲 Golan wine
Anyone wishing to taste and buy this fine wine should visit the Golan wine cellar in Katzrin. ▸ **page 247**

🔲 Beautiful sounds
The Haifa Symphonic Orchestra gives a concert in the Carmelite monastery once a month. ▸ **page 254**

Anyone planning to enjoy the Grotto of the Nativity in peace and quiet should get up early.

❚ Panorama tour
Take line 99 to get to Jerusalem's most important attractions. ► page 287

❚ The Way of the Cross
Anyone unwilling or unable to travel to Jerusalem for Good Friday can still witness

a Via Dolorosa procession, because the Franciscans make their way along the Via Dolorosa with a cross every Friday.
► page 2301

❚ Through the desert
The Mamshit Camel Ranch in Mamshit National Park offers overnight stays in Bedouin tents, and trips through the desert can be enjoyed on the back of a camel or from inside a Jeep. ► page 340

❚ The legend lives on
The history of the fortress is brought to life in the amphitheatre of Masada by an impressive show with lighting effects and music. ► page 348

❚ Rashbi Hilula
Every year in late April or early May thousands of Jews from all around the world come to Meron in honour of Rabbi Shimon bar Yochai – real Jewish »folklore«. ► page 387

❚ Photo Prior
A treasure lies hidden behind the shop windows of this unassuming photo shop in Tel Aviv: Miriam Weissenstein and her husband Rudi have documented Palestine and Israel by camera since the 1930s.
► page 408

Masada's history comes to life with a light and sound show.

Stunning mosaics: the »Feeding of the Five Thousand« in Taghba
▶ **page 88**

BACKGROUND

PRACTICALITIES

Price categories

▶ **Hotels (double room with breakfast**
Luxury: more than NIS 700
Mid-range: NIS 400 – 700
Budget: less than NIS 400

▶ **Restaurants (main course)**
Expensive: more than 135 NIS
Moderate: 65 – 135 NIS
Inexpensive: less than 65 NIS

Night falls over Bethlehem.
► **page 201**

TOURS

SIGHTSEEING FROM A to Z

Herod the Great had the Herodium built as a palace and burial site, but his tomb was not discovered until May 2007.
▶ page 262

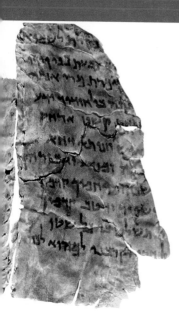

The mysteries of the Dead Sea Scrolls have been revealed.
▶ page 377

Background

THE HOLY LAND AND THE SEARCH FOR PEACE: THE FOLLOWING SECTION EXPLAINS HOW ISRAEL WAS FORMED, HOW ITS PEOPLE LIVE AND WHY IT IS SO HARD FOR THEM TO PUT ASIDE THEIR DIFFERENCES.

SHALOM AND MARHABA!

← *At the Western Wall in Jerusalem*

Israelis who speak Hebrew say »shalom«. Palestinians and Arabs (often including Israeli passport holders) say »marhaba« to greet each other. One thing is clear: everything is a little more complicated in this region. In return visitors are rewarded with an exciting journey through a country that is not just blessed with the sacred sites of three major world religions, but also natural attractions, three seas and Levantine joie de vivre.

The term Israel, also a name by which Jacob was known in the Old Testament, describes the territory of the Jewish kingdom which was created with the First Temple and ended with the destruction of the

Second Temple in AD 70. Palestine was the name that Roman emperors gave to their province in the Levant. The Roman emperors had never heard of countries called Lebanon or Syria, as both of these are 20th-century creations. The »Holy Land« of the crusaders has always been home to both Arabs and Jews. Now the Palestinians are in the process of establishing their own independent state, which is not an easy task. »My land is your land«: conflict among neighbours seems to be the worst sort, especially when both sides have strong claims and nobody can assert sole legitimacy.

The Holy Land must be old, right?
Wrong! Israel is a young country and the new generation longs for peace.

More Than »Holy Land«

Those who visit Israel to see Jerusalem, Bethlehem, Nazareth and Hebron solely with Judaism, Christianity and Islam in mind will see a lot, but for all the churches, mosques, synagogues, crusader castles and excavation sites, they might miss what could be the special appeal of this trip: encountering Israelis and Palestinians, walking through the landscape of Galilee and Golan, bathing in the Mediterranean, the Red Sea and the Dead Sea, trekking in the Negev Desert, staying in a kibbutz, or just dancing the whole night long in the clubs of Tel Aviv, which modestly calls itself the »Big Orange«, the Middle Eastern sister of the Big Apple, New York.

This comparison is definitely true in one regard: with immigrants from more than 140 countries, Tel Aviv is a cosmopolitan and vibrant city, while Jerusalem is more of a spiritual centre, increasingly domi-

Jews
Whether ultra-orthodox or reformed, all Jews are drawn to their most holy site, the Western Wall in Jerusalem.

Christians
Equality rules at the most sacred Christian site: Armenians, Greeks, Catholics, Anglicans and Lutherans all have to share it peacefully.

Muslims
The vast majority of Muslims share a desire for peace in the Middle East with the majority of Jews.

Tourist magnets, controversial symbols
Every visitor to Israel comes here, even though there is conflict between Jews and Muslims regarding the Dome of the Rock and the Temple Mount.

Relaxation
Holidaying in Israel does not just mean exhausting sightseeing. Three seas offer refreshment: the Mediterranean, e.g. near Tel Aviv, the Red Sea near Eilat, and the Dead Sea.

Natural beauties
Places of pilgrimage and ancient excavation sites are one thing, but Israel's landscape is also worth the trip: »mushrooms« in the Negev.

nated by fundamentalist ultra-orthodox Jews. The main attractions in Jerusalem are the Via Dolorosa and the Torah school, rather than nightclubs, and the Old City is definitely the »most oriental« place in the country: scents of cardamom, saffron, caraway and coriander waft up from the spice markets; large shops add a modern touch to the old buildings, selling pirated music CDs, DVDs and T-shirts with slogans, such as »Guns 'n' Moses«.

Waiting for Peace

The people are open and friendly. But when visiting Palestinian territory, if this is actually possible, do not expect too much: this region's economy and infrastructure are underdeveloped and the entire area is ravaged by war and sanctions. The reality of the political situation

will be evident to visitors at the checkpoints, not to mention the wall with which Israel is trying to protect itself from suicide bombers. A number of factors have prevented peace from coming to the region. Many Israelis do not trust the Arabs, and because of the bloody attacks by fundamental militants feel confirmed in their belief that no peace is better than an unstable peace. For the (ultra-)orthodox Jews, who have long since established a parallel society within Israel, peace with the Arabs is treason, and the same thinking can be found among extremists on the Arab-Palestinian side. In this connexion one should not forget that many immigrants come from former communist countries. They tend to support a policy of confrontation rather than reconciliation. Hope rests on better times and on the younger generation, which is less political and more focused on consumerism and entertainment, which only knows of the Holocaust and its survivors from books and television: the young have more courage to compromise and are willing and able to find a more stable peace. The traveller however remains an onlooker, like the painter Marc Chagall (1887–1985): »I came to Palestine to test certain ideas, without a camera, even without a paintbrush. No documents, no tourist impressions, and yet I am glad to have been there. From afar they stream to the Wailing Wall, bearded Jews in yellow, blue, red garments, and fur hats. Nowhere does one see so much desperation and so much joy; nowhere is one so shocked and yet so happy at the sight of these millennia-old heaps of stones and dust in Jerusalem, in Safed, on the mountains where prophets upon prophets lie buried.«

Places of pilgrimage
No other place on earth sees more pilgrims from three major religions than Israel. Christians seek out the Grotto of the Nativity in Bethlehem.

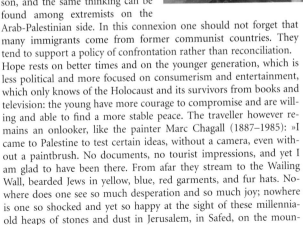

Facts

The over-used expression »both traditional and modern« definitely applies to Israel: the glittering façades of Tel Aviv contrast with the ultra-orthodox Jewish quarter in Jerusalem. On the one hand the Sabbath, on the other a chill-out weekend; here the hi-tech biomedical industry, there oriental bazaars.

Natural Environment

Landscapes

Alternation between mountains and valleys is characteristic of Israel's landscape. The entire southern part of the country is covered by the Negev Desert, while the northern area consists of three regions: the coastal area, the mountains and the Jordan Rift Valley.

Coastal plain

The coastal plain runs for over 180 miles along the Mediterranean, from Lebanon in the north to the Sinai Desert in the south. Gently sloping coastal hills covered in sand dunes alternate with steep cliffs. At Haifa the near-straight coastline is interrupted by a wide bay with the country's main port. This is also where the cape of the Carmel mountains projects into the plain like a wedge. The width of the coastal plain varies: between Rosh Hanikra and Akko it is just 7km/4.5mi, while in the south it is up to 40km/25mi wide. The plain is crossed by two rivers, the Kishon near Haifa and the Yarkon near Tel Aviv and Jaffa.

◄ Central coastal area

The coastal section south of Haifa to Tel Aviv and Jaffa, the **Sharon Plain**, forms the central coastal plain. This region, once forested, then marshland, was transformed into fertile land by drainage. In addition to rural settlements, the towns of Hadera, Netanya, Kefar Sava and Herzliya have grown up here. The continuation of the Sharon Plain to the south, all the way to the Gaza Strip, is the 25–30km/15–18mi **Shefela Plain**.

Mountains

The mountains, largely limestone and dolomite, lie inland from the coastal plain. They are the continuation of the Lebanon mountains: in the north Mount Meron, with a summit at 1208m/3963ft in the mountains of Galilee, south of that the mountains of Samaria, which reach 1018m/3340ft, and the Judaean mountains, which rise to 1020m/3346m and extend all the way to the Negev in the south.

◄ Galilee and Samaria

The mountains of Galilee and Samaria are **broken up by tectonic fault lines**. This phenomenon is clearest at the 20km/12mi-long Jezreel Valley (Emek Yizre'el), which runs perpendicular to the direction of the mountains and forms the border between Galilee and Samaria. The Galilean mountains have large basalt areas in the higher, northern section, where Mount Meron is located. The mountains become lower towards the south and reach a height of 588m/1929ft at Mount Tabor. In the northwest the mountains of Samaria enclose the Carmel range (up to 546m/1790ft), and in the northeast the 518m/1700ft Mount Gilboa. The rivers of Yarkon and Shilo form the border between the mountains of Samaria and the Judaean mountains.

◄ Judaea

The Judaean mountains, the country's largest range, are 80km/50mi long and 15–20km/9–12mi wide. The range runs largely along the

← *Modern Israel: the Azrieli Towers, the country's highest buildings, are lit up above Tel Aviv.*

watershed and is characterized by terraced slopes. The Hebron mountains make up the southern section. They adjoin the Jerusalem mountains to the north. The ridge of the Jerusalem mountains is the site of the Mount of Olives and Mount Scopus. The northern section of the mountain range is made up of the Beit El mountains. Most of the villages of this region are home to Arabs.

Judaean Desert ▶ The Judaean Desert, which is characterized by canyons, valleys and sparse vegetation, is situated between the mountains of Samaria and the Dead Sea and Jordan Valley. It is so arid because it lies in the rain shadow of the mountains.

Jordan Rift Valley In the east the mountains drop off to the Jordan Rift Valley, which is part of the Syrian/African valley system. It begins in northern Israel to the south of the Hermon mountains, with the Hula Valley (Emek HaHula), which is now one of the most intensively exploited agricultural regions of the country. It was created by draining the marshland around a lake, which then also dried out around the mid-20th

Sea of Galilee ▶ century. The Jordan Rift Valley then follows the upper Jordan and reaches the Sea of Galilee (Yam Kinneret), where it is already 210m/690ft below sea level. Now known as Ghor (»that which is hollowed out«), it continues to the Dead Sea where it is the **third-lowest spot on the earth's surface** (cryptodepression): it is approx. 420m/1380ft below sea level at the surface (and still sinking) and the bed of the

The blue of the Sea of Galilee is 210m/690ft below sea level.

Dead Sea lies at up to 796m/2612ft below sea level! The Jordan Rift Valley finally reaches the Red Sea via the depression of the Wadi Arava.

The River Jordan (Yarden), which is not navigable, is the longest river in Israel and Jordan, and also the one that carries the most water. It is formed by the headwater streams of the Banias, Dan and Hasbani in the northern Hula Valley. Several tributaries add extra water on the way to the Dead Sea. The Yarmouk, which flows into the Jordan from the east after the Sea of Galilee, is its largest tributary. The River Jordan marks the border between Israel and Jordan.

◄ Jordan

The Dead Sea (Yam Hamelach), a sea without an effluent river and a surface area of 980 sq km/378 sq mi, measures 78km/48mi from the Jordan inflow to the Wadi Arava, and 18km/11mi at its widest spot. In the west it is bounded by the Judaean mountains, in the east by the eastern Jordanian mountains. The Lisan Peninsula divides it into a northern section, which has a depth of up to 400m/1310ft, and a southern part, which is only 4–6m/13–20ft deep. The high rate of evaporation means the sea's **salt content reaches 33 per cent**. Minerals such as potash and bromine salts are obtained from the Dead Sea; sulphurous and radioactive springs rise at its shores.

◄ Dead Sea

The Negev, the desert in the south of Israel, extends southwards from Beersheba in a wedge shape all the way to the Red Sea; a narrow strip even reaches all the way to the Mediterranean. Artificial irrigation systems in the northern section, which sees around 200mm/8in of precipitation annually, allow large areas to be used for agriculture. Even commercial fish farms can be found here. There are hills further to the south, which reach an altitude of 1035m/3395ft at Mount Ramon. This is also the location of the geological feature typical of the Negev, craters in the chalk known as »makhtesh«. The far south of the Negev, rugged mountainous terrain, is the continuation of the Sinai mountains. Sandstone can be seen at the surface in some places. It often produces curious formations in the shape of mushrooms or columns; in other regions sand and stone deserts are typical. In the east the Negev drops off to the Arava Rift Valley, which is part of the Jordan Rift Valley.

Negev

Climate

Discussions about Israel's climate and weather often include expressions such as scorching heat, sun and aridity. This is largely true, although there can be rainy days on the Mediterranean coast and in the mountains in the winter. The number of annual hours of sunshine is extremely high. Israel is one of the sunniest countries on the planet. The desert in the southeast gets 3500–3600 hours per year (Eilat), which is to 87–90% of the astronomically possible maximum. And even Jerusalem at an altitude of 750m/2460ft still gets 3300 hours, 83% of the maximum possible.

A sunny country

Temperatures of 45°C/113°F are not uncommon in the Negev Desert.

... with a bit of rain ►

While the sky rarely sees any cloud cover during the summer months because of the constant high pressure, there are frequent low pressure areas in the eastern Mediterranean between December and April. The cause of this is the subtropical area of high pressure that moves south over the winter months and the still relatively warm sea. Both promote the development or intensification of bad-weather areas, especially when cold air comes in from the north. Around half of it is unleashed in the form of heavy thunderstorms and precipitation over the Levant coast and the mountainous hinterland.

Three climate zones

From a climate perspective, Israel lies in the transitional area between the semi-humid climate of the Mediterranean and the desert climate of western Asia. The meridional mountains act as distinctive climate boundaries. A distinction can be made between three climatic areas:
the **coastal plain**, which is 15–35km/9–22mi wide and greatly influenced by the Mediterranean, has humid, mild winters and dry, hot summers. Then there is the **mountainous region** above altitudes of 800m/2600ft, which also has a typically Mediterranean semi-humid climate but is significantly cooler and wetter. Finally there is the **Jordan Rift Valley**, which is characterized by long dry periods and significant temperature fluctuations between day and night, as well as

from season to season; the part of the rift valley south of a line from Gaza to the Dead Sea, like the Negev Desert, only receives episodic rainfall.

August is the hottest month, January the coldest. »Sharav« is what the Israelis call the hot southeasterly desert wind that is particularly common in spring and can grow strong enough to produce sand storms and raise the temperature to 50ºC/122ºF. Days like that are rare, but the months from June to September are already hot enough. Temperatures reach around 29–33ºC/84–91ºF on the Mediterranean, 36ºC/97ºF further inland and up to 40ºC/104ºF on the Jordan, the Dead Sea and the Gulf of Aqaba, while temperatures even go up to 45ºC/113ºF in the Negev Desert. As a result it is not surprising that the summer nights are not refreshingly cool in the plains. By the sea the temperatures generally only drop to 23–25ºC/73–77ºF, while the climate remains very sultry; on the extremely muggy Dead Sea the temperature does not drop below 27ºC/81ºF (July–August). The mountainous regions above 800m/2625ft have a pleasant climate. Summer daytime temperature are around 24–29ºC/75–84ºF, and 14–18ºC/57–64ºF at night. The winters on the Mediterranean are mild, in Eilat very mild indeed. Daytime temperatures during the winter are around 18ºC/64ºF (Mediterranean) and 23ºC/73ºF (Gulf of Aqaba), while during the night the temperature hardly drops below 10ºC/50ºF. In the mountains there can be night frosts and the snow line can creep down to 700m/2300ft. This happens on average on two days a year in Jerusalem for example. The winter nights in the Negev and on the Jordan can get quite chilly at -5ºC/23ºF.

Temperatures

Generally speaking rainfall decreases from the northwest to the southeast. Almost all of the rain falls during the winter, largely between December and March, every three to four days on average. The Mediterranean coast gets 400–600 litres per sq m/16–25 inches, the northern mountains up to 1000 litres/40 inches as a result of relief rainfall. The Golan Heights and Upper Galilee secure the country's water supply together with the water from the Jordan. The Jordan Rift Valley, which lies in a rain shadow, gets no more than 200 litres/8 inches of precipitation a year to the north of the Dead Sea and all this falls in fewer than 20 days. To the south of this, all the way to the Gulf of Aqaba and in the Negev Desert, precipitation drops to an extremely low 20–50 litres/1–2 inches per year and in many years even this small amount does not materialize. If rain does fall here in the winter, then usually in connexion with areas of low pressure over the Red Sea, which carry with them humid, warm air to the north. If this air encounters cooler, drier air from the Mediterranean over the Negev, this can result in serious thunderstorms and torrential rainfall. Quantities of more than 100 litres per sq m/4 inches can fall in next to no time, turning dried-up river beds into raging torrents in a matter of minutes.

Precipitation

Climate zones Map

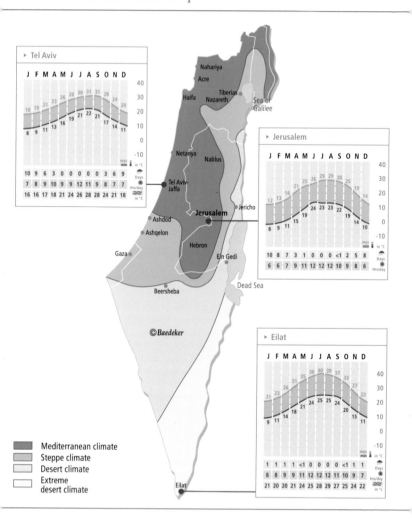

▶ Tel Aviv

▶ Jerusalem

▶ Eilat

Mediterranean climate
Steppe climate
Desert climate
Extreme desert climate

©Baedeker

Wind A humid, not very refreshing sea wind blows on the coast in the late afternoons between May and October. A similar, albeit weaker wind blows around the Sea of Galilee and the Dead Sea in a radius of 5–15km/3–9mi. In the mountains the intense summer sun creates quite pleasant gusts from higher and therefore cooler layers of air from noon onwards.

The water is warmest in August and September: the average temperature is 28°C/82°F for the Mediterranean, 29°C/84°F on the Gulf of Aqaba and more than 30°C/86°F in the Sea of Galilee and the Dead Sea. The water is coldest in February–March, but the temperature still does not drop below 20°C/68°F in the Dead Sea and the Gulf of Aqaba.

Water temperatures

Flora

Large parts of Israel are affected by dry heat and a lack of rain. For this reason, the ability to keep water loss at a minimum and to absorb water is indispensable for plants. Some plants manage to prevent surface evaporation by having a thick layer of wax on the leaves. Others have a highly branching root system with which they can absorb moisture from lower layers, while yet others store waters in bulbs and corms for the summer, then develop quickly after the dry period is over and flower in the wet winter. Some plants grow long wide leaves out of the ground in spring, while the flower only emerges in autumn. One example of this is the sea onion. Most plants adapt their rhythm to the rainy season, during which they do not have to protect themselves from excessive loss of fluids. In the Negev and the Judaean Desert the seeds of some plants often lie dormant in the ground for years, waiting for a wet winter. Then they suddenly germinate, grow, flower and set seed in just a few weeks.

Strategies against the dry climate

> ! **Baedeker TIP**
>
> **Plant a tree!**
> In exchange for US$ 10, the Jewish National Fund, Kren Kayemet LeYisrael, offers the opportunity to plant a tree, as a symbolic gesture and as a small contribution to the afforestation effort (information: www.inisrael.com/kkl; tel. in Israel 02 /658 33 49).

At around the time when Christ was born, large areas of what is now the state of Israel were forested. In order to obtain agricultural land, these forests were cut down, which led to the upper layer of soil being washed away after heavy rainfall. Bare rock emerged as a result and the areas became desolate. Scrubland, maquis and garrigue replaced forests. The settlers who came to Israel in the early 20th century soon recognized the **need for reforestation**. In addition to fast-growing eucalyptus trees, which can also survive in dry areas, undemanding Jerusalem pines, acacias, locust trees, populus trees and tamarisks were planted.

Erosion and afforestation

In the coastal plan and in the mountains of the northern Negev the vegetation is largely Mediterranean. In the central and northern section of the coastal plain and in southwestern Galilee gall oaks, tall trees with wide crowns, were very widespread, but they have been replaced by oleander and myrtle, pines and olive trees. In the hills and

Mediterranean vegetation

mountains above an elevation of 300m/1000ft, decades of afforestation are showing results: today these areas are covered in Jerusalem pines, cedars, gall oaks, bay trees, terebinths, cypresses, Judas trees and carob trees. Lots of flowers bloom in Israel in spring, from tulips and roses to anemones and daffodils. The region around Beersheba is characterized by its steppe landscape; the dominant plant here is wormwood.

Tropical vegetation

In some oases, such as around Ein Gedi and at the Dead Sea as well as around Jericho, there are more than 40 native, tropical and subtropical plant species that need both high temperatures and lots of water. The best-known species is **Christ's thorn**, thus named because Christ's crown of thorns is said to have been made of it.

Desert vegetation

In the Negev, the Judaean Desert, the Aravah and at the Dead Sea, the dominant vegetation is bushes with small, thick leaves or thorns. The hamada regions (rocky desert) are generally completely devoid of vegetation, while thorny bushes flourish in the wadis, most of which have dry river beds. That is because the plants here can obtain water from the ground from time to time. There are some acacias in the desert. They are native to the African savannah. On the dunes along the Mediterranean coast, the water penetrating the sand creates

Every plant species has its own strategy for surviving in the desert.

conditions for plants similar to an extreme desert climate. That is why the same plants grow here as in the Negev, such as wormwood and gorse.

Fauna

Mammals

Since the country is becoming more and more densely populated, the number of mammals living in the wild has fallen significantly. Jackals, hyenas, lions and leopards, all very widespread during biblical times, have become extinct or can only be found in a few locations. Most of the mammals now living in Israel can also be found in other parts of the world. In addition there are many native species such as lesser Egyptian jerboas and different gazelle species, which have become nocturnal as an adaptation to the desert climate.

Reptiles

Because of the high temperatures and the intense solar radiation Israel is home to a large number of reptiles. There are, for example, **three species of tortoise and four of turtles**. Geckos are common, chameleons rarer. The most widespread non-venomous **snakes** are sand boas and the black snake, which grows to more than 2m/6.5ft. The most dangerous of the venomous snakes is the Palestinian viper.

The underwater world of the Red Sea is incredibly colourful.

Birds More than 300 bird species have been recorded. Some of them can be found in Israel not just in summer, but all year round. Hawks and vultures can be seen in remote areas, while seagulls and other water-fowl are at home on the Mediterranean coast. Of the few bird species that live in the desert, the best-known are fan-tailed ravens and coursers. Trumpeter finches prefer bare rock as their coloration blends so well with the desert soil that their presence is often only revealed by their chirping. One interesting occurrence that is also mentioned in the Bible is the appearance of **swarms of quails**, which reach the coasts of the Negev and the Sinai Peninsula in autumn.

Fish and marine animals Sponges, sea anemones, starfish and sea urchins can all be found close to the Mediterranean coast. The somewhat deeper waters are also home to lobsters, crayfish and moray eels. The open water, sometimes right by the coast, is home to squid, rays, hakes, perches and breams. Weeverfish, which are not harmless because of their venomous fin spikes, bury themselves in the sand close to the shore. The Red Sea is famous for its wonderful **coral reefs** and its **diverse underwater world**. Around 150 different stony corals have been recorded in the Gulf of Aqaba alone. The country's largest freshwater lake, the Sea of Galilee, is home to carp, catfish and perciformes, such as St Peter's fish, a mouthbrooding tilapia.

Population · Politics · Economy

Population

Israel is multicultural Israel has an extremely diverse ethnic and religious population. Of the country's 7.8 million inhabitants, around 76% are Jews, 20% Arabs and 4% other minorities. Israelis are largely a people of immigrants, but the majority of the population alive now were born in the country. As a result of the higher birth rate among Jews of oriental origin, Israel is now much more »oriental« than many tourists expect. Immigrants from the former Soviet Union, and their Israeli-born children and grandchildren, form a counterpoint to the oriental majority. They now number more than a fifth of the population. Israel is also **a young country**. The average age is 26. The population of the Palestinian territories (approx. 4 million) are 97% Muslim, 2.5% Christian.

The Jewish majority The declaration of independence in 1948 emphasized the right of every Jew to live in Israel, and invited Jews to move into the country. Holocaust survivors and Jewish refugees from the Arab states with which Israel was at war followed the call, doubling the population in just a few years. Today immigration has declined, but since the early 1990s another one million people have moved to Israel. From a his-

Bar Mitzvah – the acceptance of boys into the community – is celebrated by most Jewish Israeli families, whether they have a strong religious background or not.

torical and religious perspective Jews consider themselves one people, but centuries of global dispersion caused great differences in their religious customs and traditions. Jewish society can be divided into two large groups: Ashkenazi (eastern and central European and American) Jews and Sephardi or oriental (Afro-Asian) Jews.

The Ashkenazi have populated Palestine since the end of the 19th century, shaping Israel's developmental phase and occupying all leadership positions for a long time. Today American and Australian Jews are also included among the Ashkenazi. They **tend to be less religious** and are also more likely to vote for the Labour Party.

◄ Ashkenazi

Originally the term Sephardi was applied to descendants of the Jews driven out of Spain and Portugal in 1492, who then settled around the Mediterranean. Many Sephardi fled to join the »oriental« Jews who had lived in North Africa since the destruction of the Temple. This is why the Sephardi and oriental Jews have much in common now, and also why these two groups are often simply lumped together. Most oriental immigrants came as refugees from Arab countries after the formation of the state of Israel. The Ashkenazi founding elite saw Israeli society as a kind of melting pot and tried to force the new arrivals to give up their traditions in order to turn them into

◄ Sephardi and oriental Jews

»proper Israelis« as quickly as possible. But different backgrounds, whether wealth or level of education, reinforced the divisions in society. The two groups lived side by side, yet practically isolated from each other. However, as a result of political events, the oriental Jews gradually became stronger and more influential.

Russian Jews ► After the collapse of the Soviet Union, Russian Jews began immigrating to Israel en masse, among them many with a university education. With more than 850,000 immigrants since 1989, they are now the **largest ethnic group among Israel's Jews.** 60% of them prefer to communicate exclusively or predominantly in their mother tongue, despite compulsory Hebrew courses. The Russian immigrants opened their own shops and formed their own party, publish their own newspapers and broadcast their own radio and television shows. Because of satellite TV, they still have a link to their old home. The city of Ashdod, 30km/18mi south of Tel Aviv, even has a »Red Square«.

Ethiopian Jews ► Israel is now home to around 65,000 Ethiopian Jews. Most of them were brought to Israel from Ethiopia by the Israeli air force in two spectacular airlifts. For many the flight from Addis Ababa to Tel Aviv resembled a **trip in a time machine**: from village life in an African agricultural society straight into a hi-tech country at the end of the 20th century. For a long time the Ethiopian Jews struggled against prejudice: the rabbinate initially refused even to recognize them as Jews and demanded a new, symbolic conversion to Judaism and a »re-training« of their rabbis. In addition there was racial prejudice and the fear of HIV. The situation has improved, but the Ethiopian immigrants are still socially disadvantaged and significantly under-represented in parliament.

The Arab minority
Israeli Arabs ► When the subject of Arabs and Palestinians is brought up in connexion with Israel, the reference is usually to people who live in the occupied territories, in refugee camps and in exile. However, there are also Arabs who live in Israel, who have Israeli citizenship and the right to vote. They mainly live in Galilee, the Negev and in Jerusalem as well as in places like Akko, Haifa, Lod and Ramla. They now make up **around 20% of the Israeli population**, a minority that seeks equality in Israeli society on the one hand, but is also increasingly identifying itself with the Palestinians in the occupied and autonomous areas. The Israelis like to point out that »their« Arabs enjoy the highest standard of living in the Middle East, but they nevertheless remain second-class citizens: they have lower levels of education, live in more cramped conditions and earn less. The majority of Israeli Arabs are not permitted to serve in the army, because the Israeli state sees them as a security risk. As a result they are denied many opportunities to succeed because they live in a country where a military career is the best way of political advancement. In January 2007 **Ghaleb Majadele** was the first Israeli Arab to become a member of the cabinet; he left the government in 2009.

The »Israeli Arabs« can be subdivided into **several groups of different religions and traditions**: around 75% are Sunni Muslims, while the remaining 25% are Christian, Druze or members of another minority. Travellers will see minarets rising into the sky in northern Israel and Druze people in their black trousers and white caps in the Carmel range, while those travelling in the south will suddenly spot Bedouin tents at the edge of the desert, women shrouded in black veils and children riding donkeys to school.

The 120,000 Israeli Bedouins are not just an ethnic, Arabic-speaking, Muslim minority in a Jewish state: most of them are also inhabitants of the Negev Desert, meaning they live far away from the centre of politics, out of sight and out of mind for most Israelis. Traditionally nomadic, they are now living in a period of change from the old tribal society to a sedentary way of life. They are not required to serve in the army but may do so if they wish. ◄ Bedouins

After the state of Israel was founded in 1948, Israel relocated the Bedouins several times, most recently to an area near Beersheba, where they had to live under military administration until 1966. Since the early 1970s the Israeli government has built several towns for the Bedouins – without industrial estates, parks, community

One fifth of the Israeli population is Arab.

The Bedouins hold on to their traditions.

centres or libraries, but with the highest poverty and unemployment rate in Israel. As a result around half of the Negev Bedouins refuse to live there. The fear of losing their claim to the land they inhabit prevents them from leaving it. As a result the majority live in comfortless camps that are not recognized by the government and therefore do not have running water, electricity, waste removal or a sewage connexion. The Bedouins also have the most catching-up to do when it comes to education and healthcare: the majority of women over the age of 25 are illiterate. Many of them do not speak Hebrew. Medical care for women and children is a problem because in addition to the language barrier there are strict traditions that prevent women from being examined by men, and there are currently almost no female doctors or nurses of Bedouin origin.

Christians The Christians, the second-largest non-Jewish minority after the Muslims, largely come from the Arab part of the population (approx. 140,000). They mainly live in towns such as Nazareth, Haifa, Jerusalem and Tel Aviv-Jaffa. They have a comparatively high level of education (a quarter work in freelance, academic or technical jobs), and the unemployment rate is very low. It is even the case that a third of the women, and therefore a far greater number than among the Jewish and Muslim population, have a job. Since the time of the British

Mandate the percentage of the Christian population has declined greatly. There are more single people among the Christians – they marry later than the Jews and Muslims, and they have fewer children on average – and a lot of them emigrate.

The 70,000 Arabic-speaking Druze mainly live in the Carmel moun- **Druze** tains and in Galilee. Since their faith – rooted in Islam but rejecting Mohammed as the prophet and the Koran as its teachings – only permits them to marry each other, they form a **homogeneous, closed-off group**. In theory the Druze, who have been working with the Jewish population since the 1920s, have possessed Israeli citizenship since 1948, but they too lived under Israeli military administration until 1962, even though they have no separatist or nationalist ambitions and are loyal to the Jewish state. They are among the poorest population groups. Their level of education is very low. As a result of a decision by their leaders, military service is compulsory for them. With the annexation of the Syrian Golan Heights, the Druze living there were incorporated into Israel's Druze society. Many of these have refused to take Israeli citizenship and are instead hoping that Golan will be returned to Syria.

The approximately 1200 **Cherkess people** living in Israel are neither **Cherkess people** part of the Arab nor the Jewish minorities. They are Sunni Muslims from the Caucasus who left Russia in around 1880 and now live in the Galilean villages of Kfar Kama and Rehaniya. Their vernacular, Arabic, is gradually being replaced by Hebrew. The Cherkess people have served in the Israeli army since 1948.

Only around 9% of the population live in rural areas. The popula- **Settlement** tion density fluctuates between 6900 inhabitants per square kilo- **forms** metre (18,000 per sq mi) in Tel Aviv and fewer than 30 (80 per sq mi) in the Negev. Around 300,000 people live in Jewish settlements in the Palestinian West Bank. Because of their detached houses surrounded by gardens and wide streets, many Israeli villages resemble American small towns. In addition two further characteristic settlement forms have developed since 1900: the **kibbutz** (▶Baedeker Special p. 32 / 33) and the moshav. The moshav (plural: moshavim) is a ◀Moshav co-operative settlement in which every family runs its own household (private ownership of home and farm) and works its own land. Machines and larger equipment are acquired together and the products of the co-operative are sold together too. On average, one moshav is home to 60 families. Nahalal in the Jezreel Valley, the first moshav, was founded in 1921. Today the 450 moshavim are home to somewhat more than 3% of the total population. The **moshav shitufi**, like a kibbutz, is based on collective ownership and communal cultivation of the land. However, every family runs its own household. Work and pay are based on individual needs. The first settlement of this kind, Kfar Hittim, was founded in 1936.

THE END OF UTOPIA

The kibbutz, a typically Israeli institution, is at risk. Not much is left of the socialist ideal of the founding generation. Instead, collective communities are being swept up in an atmosphere of capitalism. But necessity is the mother of invention and is leading to an unexpected renaissance.

The word kibbutz comes from the Hebrew word kwuza, meaning »group«. The kibbutz idea played a big role in the creation of the state of Israel. For the founding fathers, returning home from the diaspora meant more than just regaining an independent state. They wanted to create a society that was connected to the soil. The »new Jew« was to be an agricultural pioneer. Many people in public life, such as Golda Meir, Shimon Peres and Teddy Kollek, came from kibbutzim. People living in kibbutzim were soon the most committed members of the unions and the Labour Party and were represented in the government, parliament and army. Today there are around 270 kibbutzim, which are home to almost 130,000 people – approximately 2% of the population.

Change

The kibbutz idea is quite simple to describe: **community, equality and collective property**. All members have equal rights and duties. Men and women share the work, which is distributed on a rota basis. In return a kibbutznik is given accommodation, food and pocket money. Decisions are made in general assemblies, and raising children is a collective affair. However, the kibbutz idea has been subject to constant change right from

חצר
ראשונים

First
Kibbuz

Israel's first kibbutz, Degania A, was founded in 1909. Degania B followed in 1920. Its dining room (far left) has little in common with those days.

the start. The first kibbutzim lived solely from agriculture. Later small industrial enterprises were added, as were service business like supermarkets and petrol stations. The rotation principle for work quickly proved unsustainable because of specialization. In addition many kibbutz members wanted to decide for themselves what work or training they would have. Others, such as nurses and lawyers, started commuting to work in the surrounding area.

The crisis

In the mid-1980s the kibbutz movement fell into a crisis that has now largely been overcome. Economic, demographic and ideological problems all contributed. On the economic front, **the agricultural sector declined in significance** relative to industry and the service sectors. In addition there were efficiency problems, hidden unemployment and poor management. The political change that brought the centre-right Likud government into power in 1977 pushed the kibbutzim onto the defensive: the state subsidies which kibbutzim had been getting were siphoned off to fund the construction of Jewish settlements in the occupied territories. A **fall in prestige** went hand in hand with the economic crisis. The Ashkenazi kibbutzim were increasingly seen as a burden on the state budget and were blamed for the neglect of other groups in society.

The kibbutz crisis also stands for the **increasing level of individualization** in Israeli society: more than half of the young people growing up in kibbutzim now leave for Tel Aviv or Haifa, attracted by universities and city life. The average age of a kibbutznik is 52, and coupled with a below-average birth rate, Israel's kibbutzim are becoming more and more like nursing homes. The hope that new Russian immigrants would bring fresh blood into the kibbutzim came to nothing. Only a small percentage of the Russians, who had after all had practical experience of communism, settled in kibbutzim.

Way out of the crisis

Finally, in 1996, a kibbutz rehabilitation programme was agreed. The kibbutzim had a debt of around 1.6 billion US$, three quarters of which

A typical kibbutz from the pioneer period: Nahalal, founded in 1937

the state and the banks waived; for the remaining sum they had to give to the state land on which it could build new homes. Most kibbutzim have also brought in **management consultants** to examine their economic performance and suggest how they can make savings. The results are clear: chip cards for the dining room, the closure of cinemas, non-viable kindergartens and sick wards, tiered wage systems, premiums for overtime, an increase in private budgets coupled with general cuts and a lot more. This new economic viability often leads to the **dissolution of old kibbutz principles**: the kibbutzim are now home to kibbutzniks and foreign volunteers as well as new immigrants who only want to stay for a certain time, employees from outside and, most recently, also tenants who merely live in the kibbutz. In addition, almost all of them have employed cheap labour from Thailand and Vietnam.

Tourism instead of agriculture

Many kibbutzim now bank on tourism as a source of income. The Kibbutz Hotels Chain has 20 hotels and 17 country lodges, making it Israel's largest hotel group (www.kibbutz.co.il). Some kibbutzim even sell entire holiday homes on 25-year leases, including entertainment programmes such as kayaking trips and Jeep safaris. The fact that the ways out of the kibbutz crisis involve more than just overthrowing outdated utopias is demonstrated by new ideas such as the Kibbutz Yarok movement (»green kibbutz«). These combine an entrepreneurial spirit with modern green thinking and have already worked out a different vision: the creation of green villages and the ecological transformation of urban areas.

Form of Government

The state of Israel (Medinat Yisra'el), created in 1948 for the Jewish **State territory**
people on the basis of a UN resolution, does not have secure borders.
The borders to Lebanon, Egypt and Jordan are recognized by all
countries involved, but this is not the case for the borders to Palestine and Syria. The Golan Heights on the border with Syria were annexed by Israel in 1981 after years of fighting.

In 1950 West Jerusalem replaced Tel Aviv as the capital of Israel. ◄ **Disagreement**
Most states did not recognize this decision and left their embassies in **about the capital**
Tel Aviv. In 1947 the United Nations suggested internationalizing Je-
rusalem.

During the Six-Day War in 1967 Israel occupied Arab East Jerusalem,
which had belonged to Jordan until then, uniting it with West Jerusalem. In response, on 29 July 1980 the UN general assembly demanded that Israel withdraw from all occupied territories, including
East Jerusalem. Israel's response was to declare all of Jerusalem to be
the capital of Israel on 30 July 1980. To this day the status of the city
is disputed.

Israel is a parliamentary democracy based on the Western model. As **Parliamentary**
a result of fundamental conflict about the scope of religious laws, the **democracy**
country **does not have a written constitution**. Instead it has twelve
basic laws, which regulate the various areas of state life. Since Israel
sees itself as the home of the entire Jewish people, Jews who wish to
live in Israel are granted full citizenship. Palestinians who marry Israeli Arabs are not naturalized.

In October 1948 the Provisional State Council declared the Israeli **Flag and**
flag to be the colours blue and white with the Star of David. It cor- **emblem**
responds to the flag designed by the Zionist leader David Wolffsohn
that was raised at the First Zionist Congress in Basel in 1897. The
state emblem depicts the menorah, the ancient symbol of the Jewish
people, surrounded by two olive branches, symbolizing the Jewish
people's longing for place, which are linked by the inscription »Israel« in Hebrew.

The head of state is the president, who is elected by the parliament **Head of state**
for a seven-year term. The president can be re-elected once. He or
she has largely representative and formal tasks. The president ap-
points ambassadors, judges and the state comptroller.

The Israeli parliament, the **Knesset** (in reference to the Knesset HaG- **Parliament**
dola / Great Assembly after the return from Babylonian captivity
mentioned in the Book of Nehemiah), consists of 120 members who
are elected for a four-year term based on the system of proportional
representation. The languages permitted for parliamentary debates
are Modern Hebrew (Ivrit) and Arabic.

Administration Map

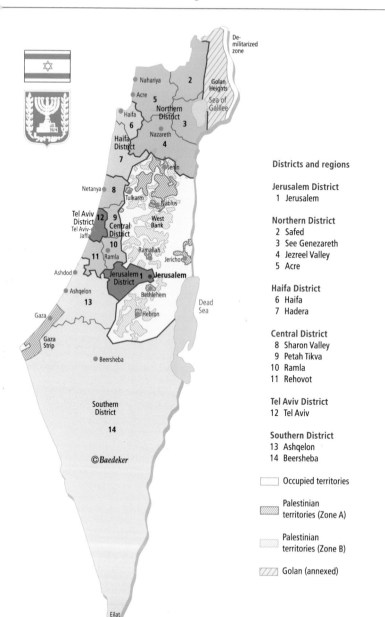

Districts and regions

Jerusalem District
1 Jerusalem

Northern District
2 Safed
3 See Genezareth
4 Jezreel Valley
5 Acre

Haifa District
6 Haifa
7 Hadera

Central District
8 Sharon Valley
9 Petah Tikva
10 Ramla
11 Rehovot

Tel Aviv District
12 Tel Aviv

Southern District
13 Ashqelon
14 Beersheba

☐ Occupied territories

▨ Palestinian territories (Zone A)

▨ Palestinian territories (Zone B)

▨ Golan (annexed)

Facts and Figures Israel

Location
▶ Eastern Mediterranean
▶ 29º30′ – 33º20′ north
▶ 34º20′ – 35º40′east
▶ Neighbour states: Egypt, Jordan, Syria, Lebanon

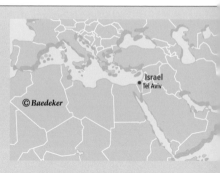

Area and extent
▶ 21,671 sq km / 8367 sq mi
▶ North-south extent: 420 km/260 mi
▶ East-west extent: min. 20km/12mi, max. 116km/72mi

Population
▶ Total: 7.8 million
 • Jews: 5.9 million
 • Arabs: 1.57 million
 • Non-Arab Christians: 0.31 million
▶ Population density: 341 people / sq km (884 per sq mi)
▶ Largest cities:
 • Jerusalem (incl. East Jerusalem): 770,000 (capital)
 • Tel Aviv: 400,000
 • Haifa: 270,000

Economy
▶ GDP (2010): approx. US$ 213.3 billion
▶ GDP per capita (2010): approx. US$ 32,298
▶ Employment figures:
 • Agriculture: 1.6%
 • IIndustry, construction, energy: 21.5%

 • Tourism, trade, finance: 22.2%
 • Public service sector: 33.9%
 • Other: 20.8%
▶ Unemployment rate (2011): 5.6%
▶ Foreign trade (2011):
 • Export: USA 35%, EU 26.3%, Asia 15%
 • Import: EU 34.5%, USA 13%, Asia 23%

Administration
▶ 6 districts
▶ 13 sub-districts
▶ Official languages: Modern Hebrew, Arabic

Religion
▶ Jews: 76.4%
▶ Muslims: 16.9%
▶ Christians: 2.4%
▶ Druze: 1.7%

Government

The government, which is elected for a four-year term, consists of the prime minister and the ministers. All members of government are answerable to the parliament and dependent on its trust. The prime minister is elected by the Knesset and, in contrast to the ministers, also has to be a member of the Knesset. A vote of no confidence is possible.

Electoral system

Everyone aged 18 and over has the right to vote, and candidates must be aged at least 21. The elections operate on a party-list system. There are no constituencies. Every party represented in the expiring

Knesset has the right to participate in the next elections. Other parties can participate if they have collected the signatures of at least 2500 eligible voters and have made a monetary deposit, which is returnable if they obtain 1.5% of the total vote, thereby getting at least one seat. The seats are distributed to the parties proportionally to the share of the vote they receive.

Political parties

The Israeli multi-party system is meant to reflect the society's ethnic, cultural and ideological diversity. Most parties stand for political or religious convictions; others were formed as a reaction to certain issues or represent specific interest groups. There are **two main blocks**: the Labour block Ma'arakh (»groups«), which is centre-left and the Likud (»the consolidation«), consisting of centre-right elements. They are both equally strong and make up two-thirds of the parliament. So far all governments have been coalitions. There are currently around a dozen parties in the Knesset, a circumstance which traditionally has had a paralysing effect on the political system, as it makes large parties dependent on small ones, some of them extremist groups who can be the ones to tip the scales.

Judiciary

The highest instance of the independent judiciary is the Supreme Court in Jerusalem. The separation of religion and state is not total: when it comes to matters regarding a person's marital status, each religious group has its own jurisdiction. For that reason there is **no civil marriage** in Israel, although its introduction has been demanded by many non-religious citizens.

The Knesset – the name of Israel's parliament and also of the place where it meets.

Compulsory military service exists for Jews, Druze and Cherkess **Military**
people (length of service: men 3 years, women 2 years). The army
(Hebrew: Zahal) consists of a small core of conscripts and professio-
nal soldiers. The majority is made up of reservists: men up to the age
of 55 and childless women up to the age of 34 are drafted once a year
for around four weeks to serve in the reserves. Although no other
state in the world demands as much commitment from its citizens as
Israel, there are very few conscientious objectors. A highly controversial position is taken by the ultra-orthodox, who reject the state of Israel in its entirety, and refuse to serve in any of its institutions, including the armed forces.

The Jewish Agency, founded in 1922 as the »Jewish Agency for Pales- **Jewish Agency**
tine« and renamed the »Jewish Agency for Israel« in 1948, plays a
special role. It deals with issues of immigration (organization, transport) as well as settlement problems (assistance with settlement, afforestation and expansion of land used for agricultural purposes)
and mainly receives its funds from donations, interest on its assets,
state grants and loans.

The education system has high standards. It is compulsory for child- **Education system**
ren between the ages of six and 16 to attend school. However, only
95% of all Jewish children and 90% (according to other figures
50%!) of all Arab children are enrolled in the educational system.
Schooling is free. Most children go to state schools. There are also
religious schools or private schools recognized by the state. The Arab
population maintains its own schools in which lessons are held in
Arabic. There are universities in Jerusalem, Tel Aviv, Ramat Gan, ◄ Universities
Haifa and Beersheba. Then there is the Israel Institute of Technology,
the Technion, in Haifa, the Weizmann Institute of Science in Rehovot
and the Bezalel Academy of Art and Design in Jerusalem. Around
25,000 students attend a Talmud school (yeshiva, pl. yeshivot). The
best-known Palestinian university is Birzeit near Ramallah.

The Gaza Strip and the West Bank are the **territories of the future** **Palestinian**
Palestinian state. They have been occupied by Israel since 1967 (Is- **territories**
rael withdrew from the Gaza Strip in 2005), but since 1994 have
been under Palestinian self-administration. The main point of contention in the negotiations for peace in the Middle East and the Palestinian state is East Jerusalem, which was annexed by Israel, but
which Palestine claims is part of its state and its future capital. So far
92 states have officially recognized the Palestinian territories.
The Gaza Strip and the West Bank have been connected by a **transit**
corridor since October 1999. Gaza is the seat of the president of the
Palestinian National Authority, while parliament meets in Ramallah
in the West Bank. The map (see p. 36) reveals the Palestinian territories to be more of a scattered patchwork than a state territory. In ac-
cordance with the 1995 Interim Agreement on the West Bank and

the Gaza Strip, the West Bank is divided into three zones: in Zone A, the larger towns, the Palestinian National Authority has unlimited self-administration; autonomy is limited in Zone B, the village regions, since the Israelis determine security policy; and in Zone C, the Israeli settlements and East Jerusalem, Israel has full sovereignty.

Facts and Figures *Palestinian Territories*

Location
▶ Gaza Strip and West Bank

Area
▶ 6020 sq km/2325 sq mi
  • Gaza Strip: 365 sq km/140 sq mi
  • West Bank: 5655 sq km/2185 sq mi

Population
▶ Total: 4.21 million
  • Gaza Strip: 1.65 million
  • West Bank: 2.56 million
  • approx. 500,000 Jewish settlers in West Bank and East Jerusalem
▶ Population density: 4603 people / sq km (Gaza Strip) and 438 people / sq km (West Bank)

▶ Largest cities:
  • Gaza: 400,000
  • East Jerusalem (claimed by Israel): 465,000 (40% Jewish)
  • Hebron: 165,000 (approx. 500 Jewish settlers)

Economy
▶ GDP (2010): Gaza US$ 11.95 billion, West Bank US$ 12.79 billion
▶ GDP per capital (2010) approx. US$ 2900
▶ Unemployment rate: Gaza Strip 40%, West Bank 16% (2010)
▶ Poverty rate (2010): Gaza Strip 70%, West Bank 46%

Religion
▶ Muslims: 97 %
▶ Christian: 3 %

Reception in Ramallah: Mahmud Abbas and US Vice-President Cheney in March 2008.

Economy

Israel is not blessed with natural resources. Two-thirds of the country consists of desert and mountains. There are almost no mineral resources, there is no coal or oil, and water is in short supply. In addition the country has had to battle with significant, economically burdensome factors since its establishment: the high cost of national security (until the late 1970s Israel spent a quarter of its gross domestic product on defence; today that figure has dropped to around 7.3%) and the economic and social integration of more than 2.6 million immigrants whom the country has taken in since independence. The fact that an »economic miracle« was nevertheless possible is attributed to the large quantities of foreign capital, such as loans from the United States and the World Bank, and reparations payments from Germany, as well as an **extremely high tax rate**. Israel has had one of the highest growth rates since the 1990s and is one of the most developed industrial nations in the world. The price for this impressive economic growth is a **constant balance-of-payments deficit**. The government's goal is therefore to further reduce its dependence on other countries. Long-term economic planning continues to be difficult for Israel. The political developments in the Middle East are shaped by crises and military confrontations, foreign capital and tourists have proved to be cautious and immigration waves are as difficult to predict as the amount of foreign economic and military aid.

Economic miracle despite unfavourable conditions

Israel is nevertheless a research and education giant and spends a greater percentage of its budget on science and research than Switzerland or the United States. The result is an **exceptionally well-educated population** with the highest percentage of university graduates in the world.

◄ *Research and education giant*

The umbrella organization of the Israeli trade unions, Histadrut (approx. 650,000 members), was founded in 1920 and is an eminently important factor in Israel's social and economic life, not just because it represents more than 80% of employees and because it pursues a traditional union remit, but also because it is active on a business level itself and is nothing less than **one of the country's biggest employers**.

The role of the Histadrut

As a small country with a limited domestic market, Israel can only increase its economic growth by expanding what it exports. Israel's ability to compete was strengthened by joining the General Agreement on Trade and Tariffs (GATT) and by signing free trade agreements with the EU (1975) and the United States (1985). The United States and the EU take turns being Israel's most important trading partner year on year. When tensions eased between Israel and Palestine in 1994–95, the extent of foreign investment in Israel doubled, revealing just how important a successful peace process is.

Foreign trade

Energy and natural resources

Israel is poor in energy sources. Although natural gas fields discovered off the Mediterranean coast in 1999–2000 could supply the population and industry for at least 25 years, Israel has had to import almost all of its energy so far. Solar energy is being developed as an alternative, more than ever since there is now the fear that as a result of the 2011 »Arab spring«, Saudi Arabia and Egypt could get together to exert political pressure by turning off the oil and gas tap.

The Negev supplies copper, quartz sand, kaolinite and phosphate. Large quantities of minerals are obtained from the Dead Sea, especially at the **Dead Sea Works** on the southern shore near Sodom, the world's fourth-largest producer of potash (potassium carbonate), which also produces bromine and potassium salts as well as table salt. Some of the asphalt and bitumen from the Dead Sea is exported.

Agriculture

Israel's agriculture is mainly the **chronicle of a constant struggle against the water shortage**. With the help of cutting-edge equipment and new genetic technologies and irrigation methods, Israel has more than doubled its cultivated area since 1948, and the artificially irrigated area has grown no less than eightfold. Irrigation chan-

Only irrigation makes the fields in the Negev green.

nels run from the Sea of Galilee and the Yarkon to the southern coastal plain and the Negev. Precipitation that falls at the edge of the desert is channelled to lower-lying fields. In order to minimize

evaporation, some crops are grown under plastic sheets. Hoses cover the fields where drip irrigation is used. Here the water supplies the roots directly. The water shortage is not just an economic problem. It is also a highly political issue, as it is directly linked to the question of fair distribution, especially between Israelis and Palestinians. In the Negev Israel shows how a rich harvest can be wrung from what was thought to be dead soil. Deep beneath the surface of the desert, there are 30,000-year-old reservoirs of brackish water, unsuitable for drinking, but usable (as a result of new technologies) for growing fruit and vegetables. Even fish are farmed in large quantities these days, including the barramundi (Lates calcarifer), a giant Australian carp.

Israel produces more food than it needs for its own consumption. It only has to import wheat, meat, coffee, cocoa and sugar. A wide range of goods are produced for export: long-stemmed roses, carnations with large flowers, melons, tomatoes, dates, persimmons, avocados, strawberries, mangoes, kiwis and a large number of citrus fruits of course. The wetter climate in the mountainous regions, especially in the Golan Heights, also allows the cultivation of cereals, wine, olives, almonds and peaches.

◄ Typical products

There is not enough grain feed for large-scale cattle farming, and pig farming is not permitted for religious reasons, which admittedly does not prevent several Israeli companies, including a large kibbutz, from producing pork. Fishing in the Mediterranean is not very profitable. Only the fish farms in the north of the country, as well as the Sea of Galilee, produce larger quantities. They do not, however, cover more than the country's own needs.

◄ Animal husbandry, fishing

In order to compensate for the lack of natural resources and to make use of the highly qualified workforce, Israel has focused on the **production of high-end goods**. Initially the country's industrial production was characterized by traditional sectors, such as food processing, textiles, fertilizer, pharmaceuticals, rubber, plastics and metal goods, but from the 1980s Israel also made a name for itself in biomedical engineering, agricultural technology, telecommunications, computer hardware and software, solar energy and diamond cutting.

Industry

Israel's diamond industry is **the largest in the world** with exports worth 7.2 billion euros. It supplies around 80% of the world's total production of small cut stones used for jewellery. The »diamond town« of Ramat Gan is one of the world's leading centres alongside Antwerp and New York. The diamond exchange is based in Tel Aviv.

◄ Diamond industry

Israel owes its ironic sobriquet »Silicon Wadi« to its **hi-tech industry**,

◄ »Silicon Wadi«

which has experienced a boom like no other sector of the economy in the past decade. Its growth rates have meant that the number of jobs in industry has gone up by around 20%, in contrast to the decline in such jobs in most other industrialized countries. The hi-tech boom was originally supported by the interests of the Israeli arms industry. Almost half of the hi-tech products are exported, amounting to almost 80% of total industrial exports. This also includes military technology: Israel ranks among the top ten arms exporters in the world; however, there are no exact figures. The three main purchasers are the United States, Singapore and India.

Tourism Tourism is one of the most important sectors of the economy and Israel's main source of foreign currency. Even though there are regular collapses because of current political events, visitor numbers also recover just as regularly. In 2010 3.14 million visitors came to the country. However, the decline in tourism overall during the Second Intifada clearly shows how crisis-prone tourism in the Middle East is, and just how great the economic potential of a peaceful resolution would be for the region.

Palestinian territories The economy of the Palestinian territories is **more or less completely dependent on Israel** as 90% of the exported goods (agricultural products, textiles) go to Israel and the remaining 10% are sold to other countries via Israel. Since Israel limited the freedom of movement of the Palestinian workforce and Palestinian goods even further, and since the Palestinians started fighting between themselves, the economy has seriously nose-dived. The result is very high unemployment and an increase in the number of people who have to make do on less than two dollars a day. But it could be so different: an Israeli-Palestinian study published in January 2007 predicted a boom for both sides if the conflict were resolved.

Religion

Judaism

Foundations of Judaism The Jewish religion goes back to Abraham. Moses is considered to be the most important prophet, because it was to him that God revealed Himself on Mount Sinai, choosing the people of Israel to take his teachings to the world and preparing it for the Messiah.

The Jewish holy scripture is the **Torah** (the Pentateuch, or the first five books of the Bible) as well as the **Talmud**, which consists of the Mishnah (the parts of the Torah revealed to Moses on Mount Sinai) and the Gemara (commentaries on the Mishnah). The **Sabbath** is celebrated from Friday evening until Saturday evening. The most important site of prayer is the Western Wall of the Herodian enclosure

It does not matter whether Jews wear a tallit or everyday clothes to pray at the Western Wall, but the kippah is a must.

of the Temple District (also known as the **Wailing Wall**) in Jerusalem, which Jews have been able to access again since 1967. Important dates in the life of a Jew are **circumcision** (Hebrew: brit milah) on the eighth day after birth, and the religious coming-of-age at 13 for boys (**Bar Mitzvah**) and at 12 for girls (Bat Mitzvah). From this point on they have to follow the 613 divine commandments (mitzvot).

The synagogue (Hebrew: Beit HaKnesset) is where Jews come to pray, hold their religious services, read and gather. The **shrine with the Torah scrolls** (aron kodesh = holy ark) can usually be found on the eastern wall that faces Jerusalem. Above it is a sanctuary lamp (ner tamid), which symbolizes the pillar of fire that guided the people of Israel during their journey across the Sinai Desert. The Torah scrolls are wound around wooden rods, at the end of which are crowns or caps (rimonim). The Torah is placed on the bimah, a podium or elevated table that is often surrounded by a lattice. In orthodox synagogues, where a service can only take place when at least ten males over the age of 13 are present, women have to go to a gallery or a separate room.

◄ Synagogue

For the morning service, on the Sabbath and on holidays men wear a prayer gown or shawl (**tallit**) with knotted fringes (tzitzit). In addition there are **teffilin**, prayer boxes that contain parchment pieces

◄ Prayer clothes

with excerpts from the Torah. They are attached to the head and arms with prayer strings.

Dietary rules ▶ Of the 613 commandments in the mitzvot, at least 50 deal with dietary issues and table customs. Food has to be **kosher** (pure), in the way the Bible describes in various places. Some of the important commandments include: no consumption of blood (which is why animals are butchered in a specific manner), avoidance of the simultaneous consumption of meat and milk, and no consumption of pork (▶Baedeker Special p. 124).

Jewish institutions
Chief Rabbinate ▶ The highest religious authority of the Jewish people is the Chief Rabbinate, which consists of the chief Ashkenazi rabbi and the chief Sephardi rabbi as well as the Chief Rabbinate Council. The Chief Rabbinate is responsible for questions to do with Jewish law and the ritual purity laws (kashrut); in addition the rabbinical courts are subordinate to it. These courts exists alongside the secular courts (the Supreme Court, the country's highest court, has its seat in Jerusalem) and deal with issues such as marriage and divorce by Jews who are residents of the state of Israel.

Kohanim, Levites, Israel Since the time when the Temple of Jerusalem still stood, the Jewish people has traditionally been **divided into three groups**, which mainly has an effect on Jewish religious life. The Kohanim (singular Kohen), who trace their ancestry back to the sons of Aaron, have privileges in the synagogue, but they also have to fulfil certain duties when it comes to temple service. The Levites, descended from Levi, the son of Jacob and Leah, are lower down in the cult hierarchy and only have an ancillary function in temple service. Israel, the common people, do not have anything to do with the temple service.

? DID YOU KNOW ...?

■ Putting on the straps from the tefillin around the arm is a science in itself: they have to be wrapped seven times around the arm, three times around the hand and three times around the ring finger in order to produce the Hebrew word for God (»shaddai«). Left-handed individuals wear it on the right, right-handed people on the left. Sephardi Jews wrap it in a clockwise direction, Ashkenazi do it counter-clockwise. In addition it **has to** be put on before the tallit and **must** only be worn during the day on weekdays.

When it comes to faith matters, Jews are **by no means a homogeneous group**. It should be pointed out that 49% of the population considers itself secular, and around a third say they are »ordinary believers«. The Chief Rabbinate is orthodox (devout), an orientation it

Orthodox and ultra-orthodox Jews ▶ shares with **around 16% of the population**. Many observant orthodox Jews live in neighbourhoods in which Jewish rules are followed very closely; the external identifying feature for the men is the kippah, the embroidered cap.

The ultra-orthodox Jews (around 4.5%) can be recognized by their black clothes, their payot (sidecurls) and their shtreimel (fur hat).

They mainly speak Yiddish, since they consider Hebrew to be a holy language reserved for religious purposes. **They reject the state of Israel** because in their opinion only the Messiah may establish such an entity. However, that does not prevent them from actively participating in political life, an area they have great influence on, despite their small number. They tend not to use modern technology, newspapers and televisions are frowned upon and the many children only receive a minimum of secular education at the religious private schools they attend. They refuse military service, among other reasons saying that they have to dedicate their whole life to the study of the holy scriptures.

Reform Judaism is a liberal trend that formed in Europe in the 19th century. It has rejected some Jewish traditions as out-dated in order to simplify everyday religious life and integration into a non-Jewish environment. Conservative Judaism emerged from the reform movement. It went back a little on the break with tradition. ◄ Reform Jews

The Samaritans, a small group whose sacred site is Mount Gerizim near Nablus (Shechem), separated from the rest of Judaism after the Babylonian captivity. Their holy scriptures include the Pentateuch and the Book of Joshua in the Old Testament. **Samaritans**

The Jewish year follows the lunar cycle and has 354 days. Over a period of 19 years, seven months of 30 days each are added in order to bring the lunar year in line with the solar year. The Jewish calendar begins with the creation of the world, which expressed in the Christian calendar is the year 3761 BC (►Practical Information, Calendar and Festivals, Holidays and Events). **Calendar**

Muslims, Christians and other religions

Most Arabs living in Israel say they are followers of Islam (»surrender to God's will«), and most of these are of the Sunni persuasion. With the Dome of the Rock and Al Aqsa Mosque, the **most important sacred site of Islam after Mecca and Medina is in Jerusalem**. The canonical book for devout Muslims is the Koran, which is divided into 114 suras containing God's revelations to the prophet Mohammed (571–632). It is supplemented by the collections of the Hadith (tradition) and Sunna (custom). Islam recognizes the Jewish and Christian holy scriptures as precursors to the final revelation; it also recognizes both prophets: Jesus is considered the greatest prophet after Mohammed. The **five duties of a devout Muslim** are: belief in Allah as the only God, prayer five times a day, giving alms, celebrating the month of fasting, Ramadan, and a pilgrimage to Mecca. Friday is the weekly holiday. Qadis are at the top of the Muslim hierarchy. They are judges overseeing religious laws. **Muslims**

The Druze are a religious community named after **Ismail ad-Darazi** (b. 1019) that separated itself from Islam under Caliph al-Hakim **Druze**

Empress Eudocia hands Pope Sixtus III the chains of Saint Peter (detail from the fresco in the church of San Pietro in Vincoli by Jacopo Coppi, 1577).

IT ALL STARTED WITH HELENA

As early as the 3rd century devout Christians went on pilgrimages to Bethlehem and Jerusalem in order to pray at the sites of Christ's birth, passion and resurrection. However, this was not without its controversies in Christianity.

The most important of the Latin church fathers, **Saint Augustine** (354–430), rejected such journeys, since they were of no significance to the faith. His contemporary, **Saint Jerome** (around 347–420), who founded a monastery in Bethlehem and translated the Bible into Latin (the Vulgate) there, considered praying in a place where Jesus had been as an act of faith, and his opinion won through.

Saint Helena

After **Constantine the Great** put Christianity on an equal status with other religions in AD 313, his mother Helena went on a pilgrimage to Palestine in 326, where she became the first successful »archaeologist«. During her trip she had Hadrian's Temple of Venus on the site of Golgotha removed in order to uncover the site of the crucifixion and burial. A wooden cross found in a cistern has been venerated as Christ's cross ever since; it became the most significant relic of Christianity. Helena's son Constantine built the Church of the Holy Sepulchre on this spot.

Relic collectors

After construction of the church, more and more people went on pilgrimages to the Holy Land. They were not even put off by Gregory of Nyssa (d. 394), who bemoaned that Jerusalem was full of adulterers, thieves, idolaters and murderers. In around 400 the **French nun Egeria** went to the Holy Land and up Mount Sinai, where she used the Bible to locate many holy sites. In 438–439 **Empress Aelia Eudocia**, wife of Theodosius II, went on a pilgrimage to Jerusalem with a major entourage. Bishop Juvenalis gave her, among other things, two chains with which Peter is said to have been restrained in prison. She gave one to the Church of the Holy Apostles in Constantinople. The other came to Rome via her daughter, where it can still be seen under the high altar in the church of San Pietro in Vincoli. These and other relics increased the West's interest in the Middle East. Many pilgrims took trading vessels to Palestine, until seafaring became too dangerous during **the period of the Arab con-**

quests in the 7th century and the flood of pilgrims abated. Despite this development, secular and religious dignitaries set off, such as Saint Willibald, born in Wessex in about 700, who went to Rome in 720, and in 723 became possibly the first pilgrim born in England to reach Palestine. Charlemagne, who had an agreement with Caliph Harun al-Rashid, had accommodation built for pilgrims. Spanish nuns took on duties at the Holy Sepulchre for some time.

Official recognition

When the Byzantine Empire pushed back the Arabs in the 10th century, the number of pilgrims went up again. They either went overland via Constantinople through the Byzantine Empire or took a ship via Venice or Bari. Pilgrimages were now recognized by the Catholic church **as atonement for sins** – this was particularly advocated by the Cluniac monastic order. An increasing number of French, German, English and Scandinavian pilgrims visited the Holy Land in this way. However, when the Seljuq Turks expanded their sphere of control to Asia Minor and Palestine, the pilgrims were exposed to such severe hardship that the First Crusade was proclaimed in Europe.

Towards the end of the crusader age (1291) the first literature of pilgrimage appeared. In 1283 Brother Brocardi published a description that was still being printed in Latin in Venice in 1519; it was also translated into other languages. In later times the reasons for travel gradually changed, and from the 18th and 19th centuries the Christian motive declined in significance relative to the research interest.

Pilgrimages today

Despite all the political problems, Christian pilgrims can still be seen at all the holy sites: in Jerusalem especially, but also at the biblical sites around the Sea of Galilee, Bethlehem and Nazareth. Pilgrim tourists are an important economic factor for Israel.

(996–1021). Their esoteric doctrine is described as gnostic mysticism; the basic dogma is the teaching of the unity of the Being of God, which reveals itself in human incarnation, most recently in al-Hakim. The Druze are divided into two groups: the majority, the Juhhal (»the ignorant«), and the Uqqal (»the knowledgeable initiates«), who have been initiated into the religious teachings and who hold services in the »chalwe« on Thursdays. The Druze stronghold is Lebanon; in Israel they are not included among the Arabs.

Christian communities

Israel's Christians belong to **lots of different denominations** . The followers of some have been based here since early Christian or Byzantine days, while others have split from these denominations. In addition to these groups there are Roman Catholics, along with »Uniate« Christians in communion with Rome, and, since the 19th century, Protestants too.

Orthodox believers ▸

The **Greek Orthodox patriarchate** of Jerusalem has been in existence since 451 and now includes around 80,000 believers. **Greek Catholics** are those Orthodox believers who have been in communion with Rome since 1709, i.e. they recognize the pope as their leader in a Greek rite (Melkites). The **Armenian Orthodox church** goes back to the year 451. It is the Armenian national church. Here too, since 1740, there has been an Armenian Catholic church. The Syrian Or-

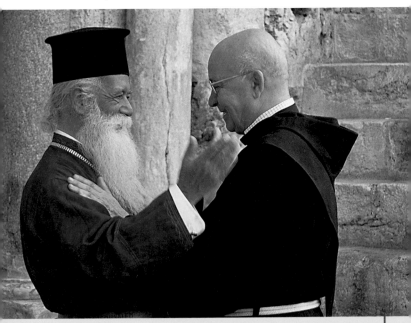

An ecumenical encounter outside the Church of the Holy Sepulchre in Jerusalem.

thodox (Jacobites) also formed in 451. The liturgy is celebrated in old Syriac; its patriarch is based in Damascus.

The Roman Catholic church has a patriarchate in Jerusalem. The holy sites belonging to the Roman Catholic church are under the control of Franciscan friars. ◄ Roman Catholics

Protestants and Anglicans officially only settled in Jerusalem in the 19th century. From 1841 to 1881 there was an English-German diocese; today a provost is responsible for the German and Arab Lutherans; the post was created for the inauguration of the Church of the Redeemer in 1898 and belongs to the Lutheran church in Jordan that was founded in 1959. ◄ Protestants and Anglicans

The humanistic Baha'i faith is mainly encountered in Haifa, which is the centre of this religious community. The tomb of the religion's founder, **Mirsa Ali Mohammed**, who was expelled from his Persian homeland, made Haifa one of the most significant places of pilgrimage for the Baha'i followers, who can be found all around the world. **Baha'i**

History

For almost 10,000 years biblical accounts have mixed with actual events in Palestine. What is true? What is legend? The most recent period – the state of Israel since 1948 – is dominated by a single subject: the hope for peace.

The existence of human life in Palestine has been shown to go back around a million years. The primitive tools of adapted river and pebble stones that were found near Ubeidiya to the south of the Sea of Galilee can be dated back to this time. The first evidence of modern humans was found in the caves of the Carmel mountains in the form of skeletal remains that are believed to be around 92,000 years old. It would seem they had neighbours too, because remains of a type of Neanderthal were also discovered.

Prehistory

From around 8000 BC humans started to settle, planted crops and bred animals: the **Neolithic revolution**, which was completed in this area (oasis of Jericho, upper Jordan Valley, Yarmouk Valley) in around 4000 BC. Important discoveries from that time are the figurines of Sha'ar HaGolan, as evidence of an agricultural fertility cult, and artistically worked skulls from Jericho, expression of an early death cult. The transition phase from the Stone Age to the Bronze Age was the **Copper Age** (Chalcolithic). Between 4000 BC and 3100 BC the metal obtained from copper ores was turned into jewellery, tools and weapons. A Chalcolithic temple was found near Ein Gedi, and not far away, around Nahal Mishmar, a large hoard of copper treasure was discovered, which is now on display in the Israel Museum in Jerusalem.

◄ Humans become settled

Canaanite Period

3100–2100 BC	Canaanite city states
1700–1600 BC	Migration of the Semitic tribes to Egypt
approx. 1250 BC	Return of the Israelites from Egypt

The civilizations that developed from 3100 BC on the Nile and in Mesopotamia between the Euphrates and the Tigris influenced settlements in the land of Canaan, which was to become Israel, and also threatened it. The people, of mixed ethnic origin and religious affiliation, joined forces in city states such as Hazor, Megiddo, Beit She'an, Jericho, Lachish and Arad. Most of them were highly fortified. Every city had its **baal**, meaning a divine owner whom the city king or priest represented on earth.

City states in Canaan

In around 2100 BC, for reasons as yet unknown, Canaan's first city states started to disappeared. From around 2000 BC an increasing number of Amorites came here from the northeast; they reinforced the Semitic element of the population. It seems likely that **Abraham**

Amorites

← *For some it is a stigma, for others it is bitter necessity: the wall separating Israel from the Palestinian territories.*

came into the Holy Land during one of the immigration waves. According to the Old Testament, Abraham, like the other progenitors, came from Ur in Mesopotamia. He cannot be understood as a historical figure and should rather be seen as a symbol. Some of the Amorites were predatory and are said to have been responsible for the destruction of the Sumerian kingdom and its capital Ur.

Hyksos The strong Egyptian influence in Canaan came to an end with the collapse of the Egyptian Middle Kingdom in around 1785 BC. The power vacuum was filled by the Hyksos, an Asian equestrian people who first dominated Canaan and later conquered the whole of Egypt from there. The migration of Semitic tribes from Canaan to Egypt, as recounted in the Old Testament, at the time of Jacob, Abraham's grandson, and his son Joseph presumably coincided with this move of the Hyksos to the Nile in around 1650 BC.

Start of the land seizure After the Hyksos were driven out, the particularly powerful conqueror **Pharaoh Thutmose III** (1490–36 BC) of the New Kingdom regained Egyptian rule of the Canaanite cities. Under Akhenaten (1365–47 BC) Egypt became weaker from a foreign-policy perspective and could not, to any great extent, counter the Semitic nomads entering via the Jordan Valley. This must have been the start of the Israelite land seizures described in the Bible.

19th and 20th dynasties During the reigns of the eleven pharaohs named Rameses, Egypt's power increased again. In 1274 BC Rameses II provoked a confrontation with the powerful Hittites near Kadesh on the Orontes (in modern-day Syria). Both sides claimed victory, but the Egyptian expansionist desires to the north had been stopped. In 1258 BC the two kingdoms made peace in the **oldest surviving peace treaty in the history of humanity**. Canaan continued to be under Egyptian control, but in actual fact it was ruled by the city princes.

Departure from Egypt The event summarized in the Bible as the Exodus was in fact a migration process lasting centuries. It started in the mid-13th century BC. Led by **Moses**, the Israelites set off on a 40-year migration through the desert, as described in the book of Exodus. They crossed the Red Sea, which was parted for them, and camped at the foot of Mount Horeb, where Moses received the tablets with the Commandments. They created the Golden Calf, built the tabernacle for the Ark of the Covenant and finally, after long detours, ended their migration on Mount Nebo in present-day Jordan, where Moses died and his successor **Joshua** organized the land seizure. Neither the story recounted in Exodus, nor the character of Moses, can be taken literally from a historical perspective. Nevertheless they are a valuable source that describes different migration groups at that time and their leaders in an archetypal manner, giving a framework to the actual events, namely ultimately a military seizure of lands occupied by the king-

Family tree of Israel's patriarchs

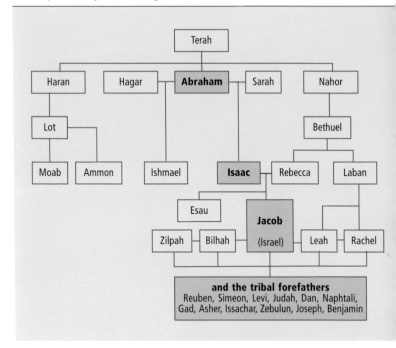

doms of Ammon, Moab and Edom; a further consequence was the conquest of Jericho and Hazor in the 13th century BC.

Israelite Period

1200–1025 BC	Period of the Judges; fighting with the Philistines
1025–587 BC	Period of the Kings
1004–965 BC	King David
965–928 BC	King Solomon: the kingdom flourishes
10th century BC	The kingdom breaks up into Israel and Judah
587 BC	Start of the Babylonian captivity of the people of Judah

In the initial period after the land seizure there was no united king-dom of Israel. At first the Israelites dominated the rural areas, and   **Period of the Judges**

The Philistines – depicted on an Egyptian relief – were tough opponents for the Israelites during the time of the judges.

most of the Canaanite city states continued to exist. Thus in around 1000 BC Jerusalem was one of the last Canaanite cities to fall into Israelite hands. In times of crisis the twelve tribes joined forces. They were all allocated an area under one judge, who can be seen as the precursor to the kings. The major judges, Ehud, Barak, Deborah, Gideon and Samson, are all described in detail in the Bible.

Fighting with the Philistines ▶

From the 12th century BC, the Israelites kept encountering the Philistines, who were already equipped with iron weapons, which made them superior. They were a seafaring nation that had settled on the coast near Gaza, Ashkelon and Jaffa. At the end of the 11th century the Philistines defeated the Israelites near Eben-Ezer, capturing the Ark of the Covenant and destroying the central Israelite temple near Shiloh.

Under the influence of this defeat and lasting oppression, Samuel, the last judge and first prophet, anointed **Saul from the House of Benjamin** king in Gilgal near Jericho in around 1025. This was the beginning of the period of the kings.

◄ Period of the Kings

Saul initially had some success against the Philistines. When he committed suicide after losing a battle against them, his son Ish-bosheth became his successor. However, he was assassinated soon afterwards and succeeded by young **David from the House of Judah** in 1004. David knew the Philistines' tools of war as he had served them as a mercenary. The Israelite victory over the Philistines in the Valley of Rephaim has found its way into the Bible as the **battle between David and the giant Goliath**. David initially ruled in Hebron. After the capture of Jerusalem in around 998 BC he made it the capital of his kingdom, which he significantly enlarged through military campaigns against the Ammonites, Moabites, Aramaeans and Edomites.

◄ Saul

◄ David

David's son and successor Solomon (968–928 BC) had **the Temple for the Ark of the Covenant built in Jerusalem** from 953 BC onwards. Secured by fortifications such as Hazor and Megiddo, the kingdom managed to achieve great wealth thanks to trade with the legendary land of gold, Ophir, presumed to be in eastern Africa, as well as to strict administration.

◄ Solomon

After Solomon's death in around 928 BC, the kingdom fell apart: to the south of Jerusalem, Solomon's son Rehoboam ruled over **Judah** with the tribes of Judah and Benjamin; the ten northern tribes formed the kingdom of **Israel** under Jeroboam I.

◄ Decline of the kingdom

King Omri (878–871 BC) consolidated the state, founded the **capital, Samaria**, and married his son and successor Ahab to the Phoenician king's daughter Jezebel. She restored the cult of Baal, which the prophets Elijah and Elisha opposed. Jehu (842–814 BC), who toppled the Omrides, destroyed the temple of Baal in Samaria, but in 841 had to subordinate himself to the Assyrians. King Hosea in 722 BC refused to pay the tributes, whereupon the Assyrian king Shalmaneser V conquered the entire country, declaring it a province. Many Israelites were displaced by settlers from Babylon. This caused the cultures to become mixed, and so the ten northern tribes came to an end; their successors were known as **Samaritans** from then on.

◄ Israel

The small southern kingdom of Judah was able to remain independent for longer than Israel since it accepted the supremacy of the Assyrians and paid the tribute without complaining. That only changed when the Assyrian empire started to show signs of collapse in the 7th century. Judah sought to profit from this, without success at first. **King Josiah** (639–609 BC) finally stopped paying tribute, cleansed the Temple in Jerusalem from foreign influences and took control of the Assyrian provinces of Israel. Religion became centralized, monotheism was strengthened and the **prophet Jeremiah** took on an advisory function in the background. The new power in Mesopotamia were the Babylonians, who had to confront the Egyptians.

◄ Judah

Judah was stuck between the two sides. In 605 BC it had to start paying tribute to Babylon. King Zedekiah tried to rebel against the Babylonian ruler Nebuchadnezzar II, but after a siege lasting a year and a half, the latter conquered Jerusalem in 587 BC, making sure the Temple and the Ark of the Covenant were destroyed. The surviving population were **taken captive by the Babylonians**.

From Persian Rule to the Hasmonaean Dynasty

539 BC	Palestine under Persian rule; return of the Jews
333 BC	Alexander the Great defeats the Persians near Issus and subsequently conquers Palestine.
323–142 BC	Seleucid reign
166 BC	Start of the Maccabaean revolt

Persian rule   The conqueror of the Babylonian empire, the Persian king Cyrus II (539 BC), allowed the Judaeans to return to their home, which had meanwhile become a Persian province. The returnees rebuilt Jerusalem and also constructed the **Second Temple**, which was inaugurated in 515 BC. Under the Persian-Jewish governor Nehemiah, Jerusalem's city walls were rebuilt in the 5th century BC. A short while later Ezra renewed and reformed the Jewish faith, which is why he is now seen as the actual founder of Judaism.

Hellenistic period   With the subordination of the Persian empire by Alexander the Great between 334 and 327 BC, the provinces of Judaea and Samaria fell to the Macedonians almost without a fight. When Alexander the Great died young in 323 BC, his successors, the Diadochi, divided his empire among themselves. Egypt and Palestine were now ruled by the Ptolemies from 301–198 BC. They practised freedom of religion and only demanded taxes from the high priest, who of course recouped them from the people. This, and the ever stronger Hellenization of society, caused resentment among many sections of Jewish society. As a result, Antiochus III, who ruled in Syria and entered Palestine after his defeat of Ptolemy V at the Battle of Panium, was warmly welcomed by many. The initial tolerance of the Seleucid regime changed under Antiochus IV Epiphanes (175–164 BC) into a policy of Hellenization. The Second Temple in Jerusalem was desecrated in 167 BC and opened to the cult of Zeus. Observing the Sabbath, fasting, the Jewish festivals, the custom of circumcision and even the possession of Torah scrolls were all punishable by death.

The Jewish priest Mattathias, from a Hasmonaean family, gave the **Maccabaean** signal to start a rebellion in the town of Modi'in (near modern-day **revolt** Lod) in 166 BC, when he killed a Seleucid officer during a heathen service. He fled and from his hiding place in the mountains called for armed resistance. After Mattathias's death, his son Judas Maccabaeus (»Judah the Hammer«) took control, occupied the Temple in Jerusalem and opened it up to the Jewish cult again (164 BC). While fighting for political independence against Demetrius I's troops, Judas Maccabaeus fell in 160 BC; his son Jonathan continued the fighting.

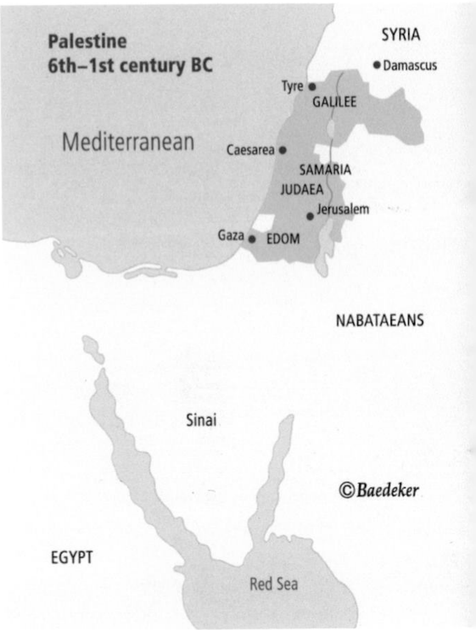

Palestine 6th–1st century BC

SYRIA
● Damascus
Tyre ●
GALILEE
Mediterranean
Caesarea ●
SAMARIA
JUDAEA
● Jerusalem
Gaza ● EDOM

NABATAEANS

Sinai

©Baedeker

EGYPT

Red Sea

The independent **rule of the Maccabees or Hasmonaeans** began in 142 BC with the imprisonment of Jonathan, who had been proclaimed governor by Demetrius I eight years previously, but who fuelled the rivalries between the Seleucids. His brother Simeon managed to get Judaean independence recognized. It lasted until 63 BC and was the **last period of Jewish independence until the state of Israel was founded in 1948**. This period is characterized by power intrigues between the claimants to the throne, who often united the office of high priest and prince or king in one person. Under Alexander Jannaeus (103–76 BC) the kingdom reached a size comparable to its extent under Solomon.

Under the Romans

63 BC	Start of Roman rule
37 BC–4 BC	Reign of Herod the Great
7 BC	Birth of Christ
AD 33	Crucifixion of Christ
66–73	First rebellion against the Romans; destruction of the Temple and start of the diaspora
132–135	Bar Kokhba revolt

A new power factor The Romans, in the shape of Pompey, took advantage of the power struggles among the Hasmonaeans. He conquered Jerusalem in 63 BC and turned the Hasmonaean state into a Roman vassal state. He put Hyrcanus in place as the religious leader, making him high priest. His most important confidant, Antipater, managed to make his sons Phasael and Herod the prefects of Judaea and Perea or Galilee. Escaping from the Parthians, who took Hyrcanus and Phasael captive, Herod managed to get to Rome, where he was proclaimed king of Judaea in 40 BC. Three years later he was able to conquer Jerusalem with Roman help and was confirmed king by Octavian (Augustus).

Herod the Great Under Herod (37 BC – AD 4), who answered directly to Emperor Augustus, the country flourished economically, not least as a result of steady construction work. He built Caesarea. In Jerusalem he had the **Third Temple** built, with the Antonia Fortress for the Roman garrison next to it, and at the western entrance to the city he built a magnificent government palace. However, his reign was ruthless and cruel. In addition the Jews distrusted him because of his links with the Hasmonaeans. The **birth of Jesus of Nazareth** also took place during Herod's reign.

Rebellion against Rome and destruction of Jerusalem After Herod's death Augustus divided Palestine among his sons, Herod Archelaus, Herod Philip and Herod Antipas, but did not make them kings. One event mentioned in the Bible is that **Herod Antipas** had John the Baptist executed in around AD 29 and that he also

Stone with inscriptions from Caesarea, bearing the name of Pilate

mocked Jesus (Luke 23). Little by little Herod's sons were replaced by Roman procurators, who resided in Caesarea. In AD 26 **Pontius Pilate** became one of them. Under him Jesus was sentenced to death by crucifixion in around AD 33.

In AD 66, under Emperor Nero, the Jews, led by fanatically religious »Zealots«, tried to break free from the brutal and corrupt occupying power in the first rebellion against Rome. Titus, son of Emperor Vespasian, put down the revolt in AD 70 and **destroyed the Temple in Jerusalem**, the religious centre of Judaism. The High Council moved the centre to Yavne. But for many Jews this was the beginning of the **diaspora** (»scattering«) that lasted for almost 2000 years.

Around 1000 Zealots were able to hold Masada Fortress on the shores of the Dead Sea for a further three years. During the night before it was stormed, its inhabitants committed collective suicide in order to escape slavery. ◄ Masada

The Jews who remained in the country rebelled again under **Simon bar Kokhba** in AD 132, when, after a string of Roman sanctions, circumcision was prohibited and a temple of Jupiter was built on the Temple Mount. The revolt spread like wildfire across the entire country. The Romans under Emperor Hadrian retaliated with extreme brutality and were victorious in AD 135. Jerusalem was renamed Colonia Aelia Capitolina; Jews were prohibited from entering the city. The entire province was now called **Palestine** in order to eradicate any memory of the former Jewish presence. But in AD 138 Emperor Antoninus Pius allowed the Jewish religion to be practised again.

Bar Kokhba Revolt

> ! **Baedeker TIP**
>
> **Flavius Josephus**
> The events of the First Jewish-Roman War and its dramatic conclusion in Masada were recorded in *The Jewish War* by the Jewish-Roman historian Flavius Josephus (Joseph ben Matityahu) – an exciting read.

Nevertheless Jewish communities were able to continue in the north and especially in Galilee. Beit She'arim, Tzippori and Tiberias as the new seat of the Sanhedrin even developed into new spiritual centres of Judaism, where a large proportion of the Talmud as well as other significant rabbinical texts were written down. At the same time Christianity spread in the 2nd and 3rd centuries. Many places that were once significant Jewish towns, such as Caesarea, became seats of bishops.

Jewish enclaves, spread of Christianity

Byzantines and Arabs

4th century	Church building in Jerusalem under Constantine
636	Palestine under Arab rule
from the mid-11th century	Advance of the Seljuqs

From AD 324 Emperor Constantine ruled alone over the huge Roman Empire from Byzantium (Constantinople). His government produced a crucial change for Palestine, because the insignificant province gradually became **the »Holy Land«**: the first churches were built in Jerusalem and Bethlehem in allegedly historical locations

Byzantine rule

Roman provinces 1st–7th century AD

SYRIA
• Damascus
Tyre •
PALAESTINA SECUNDA
Mediterranean
Caesarea •
PALAESTINA PRIMA
Aelia Capitolina (Jerusalem) •
PALAESTINA TERTIA
Aela ■
Sinai
ARABIA
©Baedeker
EGYPT
Red Sea

(Church of the Holy Sepulchre or Church of the Resurrection, and the Church of the Ascension in Jerusalem, Church of the Nativity in Bethlehem). Palestine was part of the Byzantine Empire that declared **Christianity as the state religion** in 380. At the same time, the significance of Judaism declined further. In 429 the office of the Jewish patriarch came to an end, while the bishop of Jerusalem was elevated to Christian patriarch in 451. In 614 the **Persians**, the second major power of the eastern Mediterranean alongside Byzantium, conquered the country, destroying many Christian churches and removing the Cross from the Church of the Holy Sepulchre. For a short while Jerusalem was under Jewish rule again. Emperor Heraclius managed to reconquer the country in 626 and brought the Cross back to the church.

Arab rule After the death of the prophet Mohammed in 632, the Arabs started spreading Islam. In 634 the Byzantine governor of Jerusalem fell, and in 636 the Byzantine army on the Yarmouk River lost the first crucial battle against the Arabs. Two years later Caliph Omar conquered Jerusalem and had the province, **now renamed Filastin**, ruled first from Emmaus, later from Ramla (near the coast, close to Jaffa). Jews and Christians were treated with tolerance as »peoples of the book«. They merely had to pay a poll tax.

Umayyads, Abbasids and Fatimids ▶ Under the Umayyads the seat of the caliphate was moved from Mecca to Damascus. During their reign (661–750) Filastin also flourished. First the Dome of the Rock (691) was built in Jerusalem under Caliph Abd al-Malik, then al-Aqsa Mosque (715) was built under Walid I. The Abbasids, who replaced the Umayyads, made Baghdad their residence. Filastin, which was now far away from the seat of government, was neglected. At least Caliph Harun al-Rashid made Charlemagne the patron of the holy Christian sites in 807. From 905 onwards the Fatimids ruled the country from Egypt. Caliph al-Hakim (996–1021), a hater of Christians, had most of the churches in the country destroyed.

Turkish **Seljuqs** entered the Arab empire from the north, conquering Baghdad in 1055. They made life difficult for the Christian inhabitants and pilgrims in the whole of western Asia. In Jerusalem, which they conquered in 1071, they closed off the access to the holy sites.

The Age of the Crusades

1085	Call for the First Crusade
1187	Battle of Hattin and reconquest of Jerusalem
1229	Emperor Frederick II takes Jerusalem back by treaty
1244	Turkish troops conquer Jerusalem
1291	Fall of Akko: end of the crusader states

Crusade movement

In 1095 Pope Urban II proclaimed **»Deus lo vult«** (old French: »God wishes it«) at the Council of Clermont, thereby announcing the First Crusade: Catholic Christians from Europe set off to Palestine in several waves in order to gain control of the holy sites. They founded several crusader states, including the Crusader Kingdom of Jerusalem, which existed until 1291.

The crusaders' rule over Palestine, which lasted for less than 200 years, intended to »liberate« and secure the holy sites, but also aimed to seize land for the European nobility and control trade between western Asia and Europe, which frequently led to disputes. The papacy also pursued the goal of uniting with the Byzantine church and establishing itself as the European hegemonial power.

First Crusade

The main participants in the First Crusade were French knights under the leadership of respected nobles (Godfrey of Bouillon, Duke of Lower Lorraine; Raymond IV of Toulouse, Baldwin of Boulogne etc) as well as Flemish crusaders and southern Italian Normans. The army, which was decimated from an original 80,000 to just over 10,000, finally reached Palestine in 1099. After a 39-day siege the crusaders managed to conquer Jerusalem on 15 July. They created a terrible blood bath among the Muslim and Jewish population in the city. **Godfrey of Bouillon** (around 1060–1100) took the title »defender of the Holy Sepulchre« (»advocatus sancti sepulchri«). After Godfrey's sudden death his brother Baldwin made himself King of Jerusalem. He conquered Palestine's coastal towns, thereby further extending the area of influence of the Crusader Kingdom.

The kingdom was organized as a fief based on the French model. In

Crusader era
11th–13th century

Mediterranean

Beirut
Damascus
Tyre
EMIRATE OF DAMASCUS
KINGDOM OF JERUSALEM
Jerusalem
Gaza

FATIMID CALIPHATE

Sinai
Aela

EGYPT

Red Sea

©Baedeker

Saladin captures the Cross at the Battle of Hattin (depiction from the Chronica Majora, around 1250).

addition to the nobility and church dignitaries, other vassals were the military orders – the Knights Hospitallers (founded by Gerhard Tonque in 1099), the Knights Templar (founded by Hugues de Payens in 1119) and the Teutonic Knights (founded in 1190).

Second and Third Crusades

The Second Crusade, proclaimed in 1144 after the fall of the crusader state of Edessa (in the modern border area between Syria and Turkey), failed.

In 1169, a powerful opponent to the crusaders emerged in the person of the Kurdish leader **Saladin** (1137/38–1193), Sultan of Egypt. He signed a truce with them, but when Raynald of Chatillon, Lord of Oultrejordain, broke it in 1187, the decisive battle at the Horns of Hattin (a mountain to the west of the Sea of Galilee) took place on 4 July of that year. Saladin defeated the crusaders completely. That same year he also took the coastal towns and Jerusalem. The response was the Third Crusade, which set off in 1189 and was led by Europe's most important rulers: the Holy Roman emperor **Frederick I** (Barbarossa), the king of England, **Richard the Lionheart** and **Philip II of France** set off for western Asia with a huge army of around

Battle of Hattin ▶

100,000 men. Their success was modest, because the knights only managed to reconquer the coastal towns. Richard the Lionheart managed to get a treaty for Jerusalem in 1192 that allowed pilgrims free access to the holy sites.

The Fourth Crusade did not even get to the Holy Land. The crusaders plundered Constantinople instead. The Fifth Crusade between 1228 and 1229 under the leadership of **Emperor Frederick II** was not bloody. Instead it was marked by successful negotiations. The peace treaty signed in 1229 gave Jerusalem, Bethlehem and Nazareth back to the Crusader Kingdom (an arrangement that did not satisfy the pope). Frederick II crowned himself King of Jerusalem on 18 March 1229. Just 15 years later, in 1244, Jerusalem was taken and destroyed by Turkish troops. They allied themselves with the Egyptian Mamluks and defeated the crusaders on the coast as well.

Fourth and Fifth Crusades

The last two crusades under the leadership of the Louis IX of France produced no successes. The seventh and last crusade did not even reach the coast of Palestine since the ships lost their way, ending up in Tunisia, and the crew and the king died of plague. The last crusader stronghold, the port of Akko, fell to the Mamluks in 1291.

End of the crusader era

Palestine in the Ottoman Empire

1250–1517	Mamluk period
1517–1918	Ottoman rule
1897	First Zionist Congress in Basel
1917	Balfour Declaration

The Mamluks, liberated slaves of Turkish or Cherkess origin, seized power in Egypt in around 1250 and ruled Palestine, now free from crusaders, from Cairo. They improved the road network and constructed several buildings in Jerusalem, but their era is characterized by inner unrest. Nevertheless Sephardi Jews who were driven out of Spain in 1492 came to Palestine.

Mamluks

The Mamluk rule was ended in 1517 by the Ottoman sultan Selim I, who conquered Jerusalem and subsequently also took Egypt. Under Selim's son, Suleiman the Magnificent (1520–66) Palestine experienced a major boom. Trade flourished and Jerusalem was given new city walls. The Islamic temple of the Dome of the Rock was decorated with faiences. Jews were given the unrestricted freedom to move to Palestine. Many did so, since significant Jewish centres of learning

Ottomans

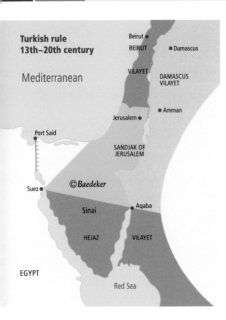

**Turkish rule
13th–20th century**

Mediterranean

©Baedeker

Beirut
BEIRUT
●Damascus

VILAYET

DAMASCUS
VILAYET

Jerusalem●

●Amman

Port Said

SANDJAK OF
JERUSALEM

Suez●

Sinai

Aqaba

HEJAZ

VILAYET

EGYPT

Red Sea

were developing in Jerusalem and even more so in Safed in the mountains of Galilee. Safed became the centre of Jewish mysticism, Kabbala. After Suleiman's death the Ottoman Empire began to decline as a result of misgovernment and corruption. The resulting power vacuum was exploited by local warlords.

One of them was the Bedouin sheikh Daher el-Omar, who ruled the country from Akko between 1730 and 1775. His murderer and successor, the Bosnian **Ahmed al-Jazzar** (the »butcher«) cleverly pitted the European powers against each other in his favour. He got British troops to defeat the attacking French forces under Napoleon Bonaparte. As a result, Napoleon was unable to take Akko, which was the key to Palestine and Syria. In Egypt the Albanian officer Muhammad Ali made himself pasha. His successor, Ibrahim Pasha, seized Palestine and Turkey from the Turks in 1833, but, pressured by Russia, Austria, Great Britain and Prussia, returned the territories to the Turks in 1840.

Immigration waves
Pietists from Württemberg in southern Germany, known as the Templers, immigrated from 1868 onwards, settling in Haifa and Jerusalem. Ten years later Jews from Jerusalem founded the **first Jewish agricultural settlement, Petah Tikva** to the east of the port of Jaffa. In 1882 Palestine saw the first major immigration wave by European Jews (»alijah«, from the Hebrew word meaning »ascent«), triggered by pogroms in Russia and Poland.

Zionism
In 1896, **Theodor Herzl's book *The Jewish State*** was published. It propagated the idea of a Jewish state in Palestine. A year later Theodor Herzl organized the First Zionist Congress in Basel. This was the first time the »creation of a home in Palestine regulated by public law« was openly demanded.

The second alijah between 1904 and 1914 brought numerous eastern European Jews with socialist ideas into the country; the kibbutz movement took shape. Jewish immigrants from Jaffa founded the purely Jewish suburb of Tel Aviv (»spring hill«) in the sand dunes by the Mediterranean in 1909. It is now the country's largest urban area.

During World War I the Ottoman Empire fought on the side of the Central Powers (Germany and Austro-Hungary). In December 1914 Britain declared Egypt a protectorate, and a short while later the British high commissioner guaranteed Hussein bin Ali, sharif of Mecca, the **establishment of an Arabian kingdom** in the event of a victory over the Turks. In 1916 British and French diplomats formulated the **Sykes-Picot Agreement**, which stated that the Arab provinces of the Ottoman Empire were to be divided between England and France, while Palestine was to be put under international administration. Another year later, in 1917, the British foreign secretary, Arthur Balfour, confirmed the decision of his government in the **Balfour Declaration**, saying »His Majesty's government view with favour the establishment in Palestine of a national home for the Jewish people«. Herein lies one of the main causes of the conflict: **the country was distributed to three interest groups in three mutually incompatible declarations**.

British Mandate

1920	Start of the British Mandate
1929	The Jewish Agency is officially recognized.
1939–45	Holocaust in Europe; restrictive British immigration policy in Palestine
1947	UN Partition Plan for Palestine

In 1917 and 1918 the British took Palestine from the Turks. After three years of military administration, Britain was given the mandate over Palestine by the League of Nations at the San Remo Conference of 1920.

That same year **Haganah** (»defence«) formed to protect the Jewish settlements. At first loosely organized and controlled by the Hista-

Formation of Jewish organizations

drut union, its role changed in light of growing tension between Jews and Arabs from the late 1920s until it became a tightly run military organization. The political interests of the Jews were represented by the **Jewish Agency for Palestine**. It was founded in 1923 and, after major immigration waves from Europe, was recognized as the official dialogue partner of the British high commissioner by the League of Nations in 1929. In 1948 it renamed itself Jewish Agency for Israel.

Holocaust in Europe The Jewish persecution that began in Germany in 1933 triggered another major wave of immigration. The British put down an Arab rebellion against the rapidly growing Jewish population in 1936. The British suggestion subsequently made in 1937 in the **Peel Report** of dividing Palestine between the Jews and the Arabs was rejected by the Arabs. In order to solve the conflict, the British government published a **white paper** in 1939, in which Jewish immigration was restricted to 75,000 over the next five years.

From 1940 the British occupation was the target of more and more attacks by Jewish underground groups as a result of this rigorous immigration policy – at a time when the Nazi regime in Europe was already in the process of killing around six million Jews. Nevertheless, European Jews managed to immigrate illegally so that by the end of the Second World War Palestine was home to around 600,000 Jews.

The UN takes over In February 1947 the British admitted that their policy had failed. The **United Nations** was to solve the problem now. In November the General Assembly decided to divide Palestine into a Jewish state (in the areas largely inhabited by Jews) and an Arab state (areas largely inhabited by Arabs were given to Jordan), while Jerusalem was put under international administration. The Jews cheered, but the Arabs resolutely rejected the plan.

War and Peace

14 May 1948	Founding of the State of Israel
1948–49	First Arab-Israeli conflict
1956	Suez Crisis
1967	Six-Day War
1973	Yom Kippur War
1977	President Sadat addresses the Knesset
26 March 1979	Peace treaty between Egypt and Israel
1982	First Lebanon War

On 14 May 1848 **David Ben Guri-on**, the first prime minister, pro-claimed the state of Israel in Tel Aviv, one day later the British high commissioner left the country. One of the immediate consequen-ces of the founding of Israel was that Jordan, Iraq, Syria, Lebanon and Egypt started a **war** in order to prevent the implementation of a Jewish state. They were unsuccess-ful because, although East Jerusa-lem and the West Bank were occu-pied by Jordan, the Gaza Strip by Egypt, contrary to expectations Is-rael conquered other areas instead. The armistice lines set up in the agreement on 15 January 1949 are now considered by Israel to be its borders, which the Arabs do not recognize.

State of Israel
1948/1949

After the war the United Nations refugee organization counted 700,000 Palestinian refugees in the West Bank, which was occupied by Jordan, in the Gaza Strip and in Lebanon; around 200,000 Palestinians stayed in the country. This **re-mains one of the core problems of the Middle East conflict**.

Mass immigration

In the following years Israel had to face its biggest immigration wave to date: 600,000 Jews came from Arab countries alone, where most of them had been driven out after Israel had been founded. Thus, after a constant presence of around 2500 years, the Iraqi Jews finally left Mesopotamia.

Suez Crisis 1956

When President Nasser of Egypt nationalized the Suez Canal Com-pany on 26 June 1956, and also closed off the Straits of Tiran in the Gulf of Aqaba to Israeli vessels, he triggered the Suez Crisis. Great Britain, which did not want to accept this nationalization, France, which wanted to prevent Egypt from supporting the rebels in Alge-ria, and Israel responded by preparing a military operation that started on 29 October 1956 with Israeli troops entering Gaza and the Sinai.

As secretly agreed, British and French troops intervened on 31 Octo-ber and occupied the canal, after the governments of both countries positioned themselves as »honest brokers«, but imposed conditions unacceptable to Egypt. In response to pressure from the United Na-tions and the United States, a truce was signed in November. Israel, France and Great Britain had to withdraw from the territory they

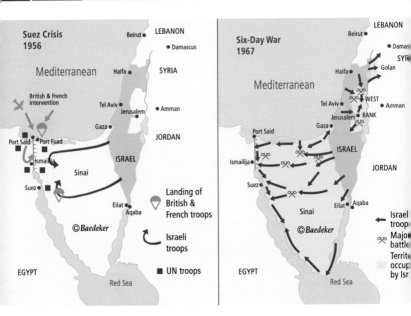

Suez Crisis 1956

Six-Day War 1967

Landing of British & French troops

Israeli troops

UN troops

Israeli troop

Major battle

Territory occupied by Israel

had occupied. The Suez Canal remained Egyptian, the Gaza Strip was put under UN control and the Gulf of Aqaba was internationalized.

Six-Day War When Egypt sent troops to the Sinai in 1967 and once again closed the Straits of Tiran to Israeli vessels, the third Middle East conflict, the Six-Day War, broke out with a pre-emptive attack by the Israelis against the air forces of Egypt, Syria and Jordan. Between 5 and 10 June 1967 Israeli troops occupied the West Bank as well as East Jerusalem and the Gaza Strip, the Sinai Peninsula and the Golan Heights. A truce was signed on 11 June. In November the United Nations Security Council passed Resolution 242, which demanded that Israel withdraw from the occupied territories, and which also understood the need for guaranteeing the territorial integrity and political independence of all the states in the region through appropriate measures.

Yom Kippur War The debacle of the Six-Day War was a thorn in the side of Israel's Arab neighbours. On the most important Jewish holiday, Yom Kippur, the Day of Atonement, 6 October 1973, they made a surprise attack. The Egyptians first advanced far into the Sinai Peninsula, and the Syrians approached the River Jordan and the Sea of Galilee on the Golan Heights, but were soon pushed back by the Israelis, who advanced to the western bank of the Suez Canal and got to within 32km/20mi of Damascus. On 22–24 October the United Nations

LEBANON
Beirut
n Kippur War
'3
Damascus
SYRIA
Haifa
Mediterranean
Tel Aviv
Jerusalem
Amman
Gaza
JORDAN
ISRAEL
Sinai
uez
Eilat • Aqaba

→ Arab attacks
← Israeli attacks
Territory occupied by Israel
–– Ceasefire line 18 Jan 1974

©Baedeker
T
Red Sea

managed to enforce a truce. For Egypt and Syria the war was nevertheless a gain in prestige. During the first half of 1974 Israel signed treaties with Egypt and Syria to disentangle their troops.

Peace with Egypt

The mediating role of US Secretary of State **Henry Kissinger** was successful: in November 1977 **the Egyptian president Anwar Sadat visited Jerusalem** and addressed the Israeli parliament, the Knesset, in a speech that received much attention. After long negotiations in Camp David between the US president Jimmy Carter, the Egyptian president Sadat and the Israeli prime minister Menachem Begin a »Framework for the Conclusion of a Peace Treaty between Egypt and Israel« was agreed on 17 September 1978. The treaty was signed on 26 March 1979. According to the treaty, Israel had to withdraw from the Sinai Peninsula by 1982, and also find a solution for the Palestinian problem in the Gaza Strip and the West Bank. However, the PLO and most Arab states boycotted the treaty. **Sadat and Begin were awarded the Nobel Peace Prize**.

Annexation and withdrawal

On 30 June 1980 the Knesset declared **Greater Jerusalem to be the »eternal capital of Israel«**. Not just the Arab countries, but also the UN condemned this law because it made a solution to the Middle East conflict more difficult.
The Israeli annexation of the Golan Heights in 1981 received just as little approval. Luckily peace with Egypt was becoming a reality: in April 1982 Israel withdrew the rest of its forces from the Sinai Peninsula.

Lebanon conflict

Meanwhile, there were conflicts with Lebanon, from where Palestinians were frequently shooting at Israeli settlements in the north of the country. On 6 June 1982 Israel marched into southern Lebanon, advanced all the way to Beirut and destroyed the power base of the PLO there. A few months later Christian militias, with Israeli endorsement, carried out massacres in the Palestinian refugee camps of Sabra and Shatila in Beirut.

Recent History

End of 1987	Start of the First Intifada
1988	The PLO recognizes Israel's right to exist.
1994	Israelis withdraw from the Palestinian territories
1995	Assassination of Yitzak Rabin
2000	September: start of the Second Intifada
2003	Construction starts on the Israeli West Bank barrier
2009	Israeli government rejects a halt to new settlements and a two-state solution
2010	Israel's army attacks the Gaza Solidarity Fleet in the Mediterranean
2011	Social unrest due to housing shortage and poor educational opportunities

Intifada: The »War of Stones«

Since the start of the 1980s, Israel has engaged in an offensive **settlement policy** in the West Bank and part of the Gaza Strip, which has dramatically reduced Palestinians' prospects and increased their hatred for the occupying power. This tension finally exploded in December 1987 with the start of the Intifada, a rebellion against the Israeli occupiers which the Palestinians mostly fought with stones, burning tyres and Molotov cocktails. A further expression of protest was boycotts and strikes, which did not, however, just affect the Israeli economy. Palestinians too lost their jobs. Since this resistance was largely organized in Palestinian schools and universities, the Israeli military administration closed all educational institutions in the occupied territories until 1989. The universities were only able to reopen in 1991, Birzeit in 1992.

Proclamation of the state of Palestine ▶

On 15 November 1988 the Palestinian National Authority proclaimed the independent state of Palestine, whose president was PLO leader Yasser Arafat from 1989. A short while earlier Jordan relinquished all claims to the West Bank and East Jerusalem. The PLO recognized the right of Israel to exist. Arafat, now internationally respected, denounced all forms of terrorism during a speech to the United Nations.

1991 Gulf War

On 2 August 1990 Iraq occupied the oil state of Kuwait. The Iraqi president Saddam Hussein demanded, among other things, that Israel withdraw from all occupied territories, as one of his conditions for withdrawing from Kuwait. When US troops and their allies attacked Iraq on 17 January 1991, Iraq attacked Israel with missiles. In order to prevent the Arab allies from leaving the anti-Iraq coalition, Israel did not launch any counter-attacks. By the end of the Gulf War on 28 February, Israel had suffered a few deaths and numerous civilian injuries.

Over the years the Intifada turned into a guerrilla war. Fundamentalist Islamic groups such as Hamas organized suicide attacks, and Palestinian »collaborators« were killed in droves. The PLO lost track a little, because Arafat fell into disrepute with his Arab brothers as a result of his support for Iraq. Wealthy Palestinians in Kuwait and Saudi Arabia had to leave both countries, leaving their savings behind. Financial support from the rich Gulf states to the Gaza Strip and the West Bank is no longer given to the PLO, but to the Islamic Hamas.

Fundamentalists appear on the scene

In October 1991 a Middle East Peace Conference, the first of many, was held in Madrid and ended with only minor successes. On 13 September 1993 a completely surprising breakthrough occurred, when the Israeli prime minister Rabin, PLO leader Arafat and US president Clinton signed the **Gaza-Jericho Agreement** in Washington. A first step towards autonomy for the Gaza Strip and the West Bank was taken. The Palestinians saw this as the beginning of the path to their own state. The agreement received great accept-

> ## *i* Rise of the PLO
>
> ■ A young Palestinian engineer, Yasser Arafat, founded the Al Fatah organization in Kuwait in 1959. It was dedicated to the armed struggle against Israel. Fatah grew to become the strongest faction in the PLO (Palestinian Liberation Organization), which was founded during the Arab summit conference in Alexandria in 1964 at the behest of the Egyptian president Nasser. The PLO claimed to represent all Palestinians. It too saw force as the only way of liberating Palestine. In 1968 Fatah, in the person of Yasser Arafat, took over the leadership of the PLO. Terrorist attacks all around the world, especially attacks on Israel from Jordan, started in 1964 and reached their climax in 1967–68.

ance around the world, but was rejected in their own camps by radical factions. Hamas protested with strikes; the Jewish settlement movement was also against it. The protests culminated in the **murder of 29 Palestinians visiting a mosque in Hebron**, shot by the fanatical Jewish settler and doctor Baruch Goldstein in the Cave of the Patriarchs on 25 February 1994. This triggered a spiral of violence, which affected Israel and the Palestinian territories for years. **Suicide attacks by radical Islamists**, targeting bus stops, buses and department stores, claimed many lives. The Israelis often closed off the Gaza Strip and the West Bank for weeks or even months in order to prevent suicide bombers from infiltrating Israel.

Despite all adversity, on 4 May 1994 Israel and the PLO signed a partial autonomy agreement for the Gaza Strip and Jericho in Cairo, which was implemented a few days later. The Israeli army withdrew. That same year Israel **made peace with Jordan**, thereby ending a war that had lasted for 46 years.

Partial autonomy agreement

Despite ongoing violence the negotiations continued: in September 1995 the next agreement to increase autonomy in the Palestinian ter-

Oslo II

For decades the vicious circle of violence and retaliation has kept going, claiming lives on both sides. Is it helpful to pronounce them martyrs, as the Palestinians do in the cemetery of Jenin?

PEACE IN THE MIDDLE EAST?

On 13 September 1993 a picture went around the world: the president of the USA, Bill Clinton, stands behind the Israeli prime minister Yitzhak Rabin and Yasser Arafat, the leader of the Palestine Liberation Organization (PLO), who are shaking hands. The hope for peace finally seemed to be coming true. But it was just an illusion. The only thing that is making any headway is the construction of illegal settlements.

At the start of the 21st century, the optimism of the closing millennium has been overtaken by a sad reality: the signing of the **Declaration of Principles** was of historic significance, but its implementation has proved to be long, difficult and at times impossible, and has also been sabotaged time and again. Nevertheless it was a milestone: after Arafat recognized the right of Israel to exist for the first time ever, Israel accepted the PLO as the Palestinian representation, and both sides committed to dealing in a non-violent manner with the conflict about the Palestinian territories occupied by Israel since 1967. Immediate agreement was also achieved regarding several questions: the newly created **Palestinian National Authority** (PA) was given some power as part of »interim self-government arrangements«. It was limited, however: the Palestinian Authority was given no foreign political competencies and even when it came to domestic politics had to restrict itself to the areas populated by Palestinians, while the majority of the area, including all road connections between Palestinian towns and villages as well as the management of water, remained under sole Israeli control.

The cruxes

However, when it came to the real »hot potatoes«, the positions were so far apart that negotiations about the »final status« did not take place for a long time and the issues have still not been solved to this day: the **status of Jerusalem** (East Jerusalem was to be the capital of Palestine according to the PLO, while Israel did not want to divide Jerusalem), **Israel's withdrawal to the borders as they existed prior to the Six-Day War in 1967** (rejected by Israel), **the question of the Jewish settlements** (which Israel did not want to give up), **the question of Palestinian refugees** (the PLO insisted on having the »right to return«

recognized, while Israel worried its country would be inundated) and **security matters** (Israel demanded active measures to combat the violence coming from the PA from the Palestinian side).

Both parties had hoped that the trust that had been built up would make it possible to agree about the outstanding points of contention. However, it was not long before huge differences emerged regarding the interim self-government arrangements. Israel continued its settlement policy and, not adhering to the agreement, failed to withdraw its army from further parts of the occupied territories, with the justification that the PA was not really working to stop the violence; the PA in contrast emphasized that the Palestinians could no longer be expected to live on small islands of self-government and denounced the Israeli occupation policy as tyranny, explaining that the Palestinians had every right to resist such a thing.

Opponents of peace

The majority of Palestinians and Jewish Israelis are in favour of the peace process, but in everyday political goings-on, well-organized opponents determined what happensd. Fanatical sections of the settlement movement in Israel are in favour of violence against Palestine. The settler Baruch Goldstein shot 29 people in a mosque in Hebron in 1994. They did not even shy away from assassinating Rabin. On the Palestinian side, Islamist groups reject Israel's right to exist and commit suicide bombings and rocket attacks (»acts of resistance«), which ultimately sabotage the peace process.

Whoever wants to win elections in Israel has to take the Jewish opposition into account, because it is the extreme parties who tip the scales when it comes to forming a coalition, and they are well aware of the power that they hold. In the Palestinian territories Arafat set up a system of

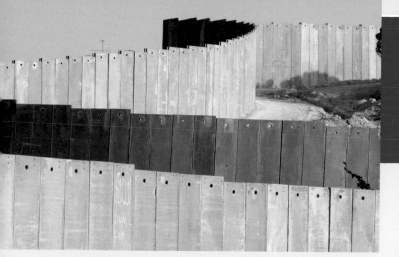

The wall that separates the Palestinians from Israel evokes associations with Berlin and the Cold War in Europe. The Israeli side emphasizes that the number of attacks has fallen significantly since its construction.

nepotism, which, in addition to the weakness of the Palestinian democracy movement, can also be explained by the fact that under the conditions of limited autonomy there is no real chance of economic and social development. In order to keep the situation somewhat stable, the international community supported Arafat even though he proved to be erratic in his behaviour and statements, and put everything into achieving a »sovereign state of Palestine«.

Open future

In 2000 he got closer to this goal than ever before: Israel managed to bring itself to be serious about the negotiations over the »final status«. A meeting at Camp David took place under the auspices of President Clinton, but it failed. This conference has become a legend, as it is regarded as a waste of a historic opportunity. Opinions about this are differ greatly. Did Israel's prime minister Ehud Barak make big concessions regarding ter-

ritorial and political questions? Did the meeting fail because of Arafat's stubbornness? Or were the offers unacceptable to the Palestinians because the state they had been offered would have been territorially non-contiguous and only partially sovereign? Whatever the case may be, Arafat, whom the Arab world believed to have negotiating skills and who was taken completely by surprise by the Second Intifada, returned home from Camp David as a loser. Barak on the other hand gained a political boost from Camp David, but only temporarily, because in early 2001 he lost the parliamentary elections. The real loser was the peace process.

The **Arab League** (with a declaration on the co-existence with Israel including a security guarantee) and then the **»Middle East quartet«** (UN, EU, USA, Russia) tried to get it going again in 2002 by setting out a **»road map«**, which outlined a final solution to the Israeli-Palestinian conflict in three steps by 2005. However, before

One hope less: just four months after Ismail Haniyeh and Mahmud Abbas presented themselves as the new leaders of the Palestinians in February 2007, the »national unity government« failed abysmally.

it could even get going, it was blocked because once again conditions were set, and the violence did not stop. The victory of Hamas in the Palestinian parliamentary elections in 2006 and the subsequent freezing of the West's financial support for the Palestinians, the refusal of Israel and the Western world to talk with Hamas and the refusal of Hamas to recognize Israel, the crazy war between Hamas and Fatah, which divided the Palestinians and led to Hamas seizing power in the Gaza Strip, and finally Israel's military attack on Hamas in the Gaza Strip – all these things stand in the way of a peaceful solution. The Palestinians' attempt in 2011 to get closer to a two-state solution by requesting recognition as a sovereign member state with the UN failed to bring any movement in the stagnating negotiations despite global encouragement. In fact, this caused the situation to become more entrenched. The US announced its veto in the Security Council. Israel threatened to dissolve already extant agreements and defiantly continued its settlement policy, a measure that is controversial even in its own country. As a result, 45 years after the Six-Day War, it is an open question when the conflict will be over, since the political changes in countries such as Egypt and Syria since 2011 have not made the climate any friendlier for Israel in the Middle East. In 2012, the king of Jordan, Abdullah, tried to take on the mediator role that opened up when Hosni Mubarak was toppled.

ritories (Oslo II) was signed in the Egyptian seaside resort of **Taba**. The success of the negotiations was overshadowed by the **assassination of the Israeli prime minister Yitzak Rabin** on 4 November 1995 by a right-wing Jewish student during a major peace demonstration in Tel Aviv. Foreign minister Shimon Peres took over leadership of the interim government. A few days later the Israelis started withdrawing their troops from the Palestinian towns of Jenin, Tulkarm, Nablus, Qalqilya, Bethlehem and Ramallah.

Elections in the autonomous territories ▶
The first free elections in the Palestinian territories took place on January 1996. Yasser Arafat was elected as the president of the Palestinian National Authority in a landslide victory. The peace negotiations continued, but were seriously impaired by further disastrous suicide attacks and missile attacks from Lebanon by the Shiite Hezbollah militia. Israel responded with Operation Grapes of Wrath, launching aerial attacks on the southern Lebanon and the capital of Beirut.

Netanyahu's government
New elections in May 1996 resulted in a strong move to the right and a freeze on the peace process. The new prime minister, **Benjamin Netanyahu** and his Likud party came out on top over a coalition of right-wing and religious parties. As a result of the stagnation of the peace process, tourism dropped dramatically, foreign investors hesitated, and newly opened markets in Arab countries closed themselves off. Netanyahu provoked the Palestinians in autumn 1996 when he allowed a tunnel along the Temple Mount to be opened, and again in 1997 when he gave permission for a new Jewish settlement (Har Homa) to be built to the east of Jerusalem, cutting off the Arab quarters further from their Arab environs. However, even Netanyahu took a small step towards peace by signing an agreement about the partial withdrawal of Israeli troops from Hebron on 15 January 1997. 20% of the city area and therefore 20,000 Palestinians are still subject to Israeli military rule in order to protect around 400 fanatical Jewish settlers in Hebron's city centre.

? DID YOU KNOW …?

■ The fact that even Netanyahu's policies were not able to halt the »train of the peace process« and that something like normalization was taking place was made clear by the election of Miss Israel in March 1999. It was the first time an Israeli Arab won the sought-after title.

Wye River Memorandum ▶
In autumn 1998 the Wye River Memorandum took place as a result of pressure from the United States: Israel was to give more land to the Palestinians, who in turn had to strike from their charter the passages that called for the destruction of Israel. This memorandum was not ultimately implemented: firstly, Netanyahu hesitated; secondly, while the Palestinian National Authority decided to delete the offending sections, there is still no amended version of the charter.

Barak's government
In January 1999 the Knesset voted for new elections. Arafat even postponed the proclamation of the state of Palestine, planned for 4

May, to 17 May, in order not to influence them. They were won by **Ehud Barak** and his Labour Party. He wanted to accelerate the peace process, but was banking on security. In September he and Arafat signed the altered Wye River Memorandum. As promised, Israel withdrew from further parts of the West Bank. In October 1999 the first connecting road between the Gaza Strip and Hebron was opened. In May 2000 Israel withdrew surprisingly quickly from southern Lebanon, which it had occupied for almost 20 years. The Hezbollah militia immediately filled the vacuum. In spring 2000 the final status negotiations with the Palestinians regarding Jerusalem were held, since Arafat had announced the founding of the state of Palestine for 13 September 2000. In July 2000 Arafat, Barak and President Clinton spent two weeks negotiating in Camp David, where they got closer to a solution, but did not ultimately come to an agreement.

On 28 September 2000 Ariel Sharon, accompanied by hundreds of journalists, members of the military and police officers, set off to visit the Temple Mount in Jerusalem. The message was clear: the Temple Mount was and is and will remain Jewish. This led to violent confrontations with the Palestinians. The Israeli security forces responded with live fire. The political situation in Israel was already heated as a result of a bloody series of suicide attacks in the heart of the country. Sharon's visit then triggered the Second Intifada, or at the very least the provocative act made it inevitable. The Palestinians soon used the expression **al-Aqsa Intifada**, which was to become a lot more bloody than the First Intifada. Israel's direct response was to occupy parts of the West Bank and the Gaza Strip, engage in large-scale bombing and the deliberate killing of militant leaders as well as the destruction of missile factories.

Second Intifada

By the end of November 2000, Ehud Barak had announced his resignation in light of continuing Palestinian attacks. On 7 February 2001 Ariel Sharon was elected prime minister of Israel and in 2003 he was confirmed in office. He won with the promise of re-establishing Israel's internal security. He considered his arch-enemy Yasser Arafat as the figurehead of terrorism and categorically refused to talk to him. He went even further: Sharon publicly considered banishing Arafat or having him eliminated. Yasser Arafat in turn, hated in Palestine because of the nepotism and corruption in his family and government, thereby suddenly became the people's hero as in the old days. From 2001 Sharon put Arafat under house arrest in Ramallah several times, and had his headquarters there blown to smithereens.

In 2003 Israel started constructing a 750km/465mi barrier, up to 8m/26ft high in places, which separated Israel from the West Bank and triggered an internationally critical association with the Berlin Wall. Because the barrier has been built in the Palestinian West Bank,

Sharon's government

◄ Israeli West Bank barrier

the latter has lost part of its territory. Many, not least in Israel, worry that this could mark the border of a future state of Palestine.

Arafat's death In October 2004 Sharon's government granted the seriously ill Palestinian president Arafat permission to leave the country for medical treatment and even guaranteed him the right to return. Arafat was flown to Paris, where he died on 11 November 2004.

Nevertheless: attempts to make peace The Arab League tried to get the peace process going again in 2002 by avowing to co-exist with Israel, while the »Middle East quartet« (UN, EU, USA, Russia) created the »Road Map« (►Baedeker Special p. 74).

Israel's unilateral disengagement plan ► In December 2003 Sharon surprised friends and foes alike with the »unilateral disengagement plan«, which stipulates **Israel's withdrawal from Gaza and parts of the West Bank** including giving up Jewish settlements. The implementation led to a government crisis, during the course of which Sharon was able to gain the Labour Party

14 January 2004: after a suicide bombing by a Palestinian woman, Israeli soldiers secure the checkpoint Erez at the Gaza Strip.

as a new coalition partner. The settler movement and right-wing individuals accused him of betraying his own policies. As a reaction to growing resistance, in his Likud party too, Sharon stepped down as prime minister in November 2005, left the party and wanted to stand for election with his newly founded »Kadima« (Forward) party. It looked as if he would win the election, but things turned out differently. After a stroke and coma in April 2006, Sharon was declared unfit for office. **Ehud Olmert**, his second-in-command up until then, became the new prime minister and won the elections in 2006.

»With the military operation Just Price, begun on 12 July, Israel is implementing an act of self-defence in its most fundamental nature«. This is how prime minister Olmert justified a **military operation against Lebanon** in summer 2006. Its goal, after an Israeli soldier was abducted by Hezbollah, was to disarm them and stop northern Israel from being targeted by missiles once and for all. Severely criticized internationally, but tolerated by the United States, the Israeli air force annihilated parts of Beirut and Lebanon, only to accept an almost ignominious truce in the end.

Olmert's government

The elections of 2009 resulted in Benjamin »Bibi« Netanyahu (Likud) taking office as prime minister once more. The formation of a government was made possible by a coalition with, among others, the leader of the ultra-conservative party Beitenu (»Our Israel«), Avigdor Lieberman. Netanyahu and Lieberman reject statehood for Palestine. Lieberman, who worked as a night-club bouncer following his emigration from Moldavia in 1978, is regarded as a man who does not mince his words. In the past he had demanded the execution of members of parliament of Arab descent who had links with Hamas. In the election campaign, he demanded an oath of loyalty from Arab Israelis in return for citizenship. His opponents see this as a sign of racism and fascism. However, his calculation paid off: Lieberman's core voters are immigrants from the former Soviet Union, and in the elections Beitenu won 15 seats, making it the third-largest party in parliament. On his first working day as foreign minister, Lieberman cancelled wide-ranging peace talks with the Palestinians. Netanyahu and Lieberman are doing their best to frustrate the American attempt under Barack Obama to initiate a new peace process, with a halt to the building of settlements, the inclusion of Hamas, and the clear goal of a two-state solution, and they are **turning a blind eye to further illegal settlements**. The relationship with Israel's most important ally, the USA, reached a new low, particularly as a result of the total disconnection between peace rhetoric and actual policy.

Netanyahu again

Israel faced global criticism in 2010 following a military action against the Gaza Solidarity Fleet. In protest against the blockade, activists tried to land 10,000 tons of aid goods in Gaza. In international

Gaza Solidarity Fleet

Since 2003 the barrier seperates Israel from the West Bank

waters, Israel halted the convoy, shooting dead nine people in the process, and wounding dozens. Under international pressure, Israel announced that it would in future facilitate the import of »goods for civilian use« and »materials for civilian projects«. The violent incident in the Mediterranean is symptomatic of the harshness of Netanyahu and Lieberman's actions in their policy towards Palestine, and the way they deployed every diplomatic means at their disposal in autumn 2011 – in the face of opposition from almost the whole of the rest of the world – to frustrate Palestine's application to become the 194th member of the United Nations.

The Arab Spring The **»Arab Spring«**, together with the fall of Egypt's President Hosni Mubarak, one of Israel's most reliable partners, was seen less with pleasure at a flowering of freedom than as a threat, because it involved the destabilization of regimes in the region,. Stable dictatorships, the theory goes, are easier to deal with than neighbours on the threshold of a more or less democratic future. In addition Iran, increasingly seen as a threat, regularly calls for the elimination of the Jewish state, and, it is feared, might acquire the means to secure this end through its nuclear programme. Israel has made clear its readiness to destroy Iranian reactors, by bombing them if need be.

As far as domestic politics was concerned, 2011 was a turning-point for Israel. It began in the summer, with tent demonstrations in Tel Aviv. Hundreds of thousands took to the streets throughout the country. The **protests by students and the middle classes were directed against the dramatically increased cost of living** (European prices, with wage levels 40% less), a housing shortage, and catastrophic health and education policies. In order not to split the movement, no one mentions the causes: the money urgently needed elsewhere is swallowed up by high military spending, state subsidies to the orthodox school system, and the spreading Jewish settlements in the West Bank.

Domestic politics

The start of 2012 was marked by the activities of the ultra-orthodox – only ten per cent of the population, but a powerful and influential minority. Members of the radical Sikrikim group, named after Jewish rebels against the Romans in the 1st century AD, are **demanding an absolute separation of the sexes** more vociferously than ever before: in buses, schools, restaurants, everywhere. These fundamentalists react violently to the smallest deviations from their strict religious norms, and hate everything secular. They shout insults at children whom they regard as indecently clad. They attack women who want to sit at the front of buses in seats reserved for men. They spit at Christians and Muslims in the street. At a demonstration against what they considered to be hostile reporting, some wore the yellow Star of David from the Nazi period, and concentration camp prison clothes. After looking on in the face of all this activity on the part of the ultra-orthodox from the side for a long time, the secular population are starting to protest. »We don't want to become a second Teheran« proclaimed one placard. Israel is bracing itself for a turbulent debate on religion, freedom and democracy.

Ultra-orthodox Sikrikim

Arts and Culture

In a region that has seen so many peoples, rulers and religions over its history, the artistic landscape also resembles a patchwork quilt – which is what makes it so interesting and, from time to time, surprising.

Art History

Early History

Evidence of the first beginnings of urban civilization has been found in Jericho, where round huts and a round tower 8.5m/28ft high that could be climbed via internal stairs and was attached to a thick wall, possibly a city wall, existed as far back at the 8th millennium BC. In the 7th millennium houses were built on a rectangular floor plan. Portrait busts using skulls as their base have been found in them. After a long period during which Jericho and other settlements were abandoned, nomads settled in this region again from the 5th millennium onwards. In the Negev near Beersheba a semi-nomadic people created oval caves that had to be accessed from above (Beersheba Culture).

In the Megiddo region, in the Jezreel Valley, a Canaanite settlement with a temple was built in the 4th millennium. Other Canaanite cities further to the south were Gezer (ruins of Tel Gezer) and Arad. In the north of the country the Canaanites founded Hazor, a large city complex, in the 2nd millennium and Beit She'an with impressive temples. Baal was the foremost of the more than 30 gods of the polytheistic Canaanite religion, and in this **differed fundamentally from the Israelite tribes which migrated to Canaan**. They knew only one god, Yahweh. Yahweh's »residence« was the portable tent that housed the Ark of the Covenant.

First urban civilization
◄ Jericho

◄ Beersheba

◄ Canaanite cities

When the Israelites settled in Canaan in the 13th century BC, they did not have their own architecture or visual arts. However, the making of the Ark of the Covenant as well as its decoration with ornamental gold is described in Exodus 37. According to the Mishnah, **the biblical ban on images** (Exodus 20:4; Deuteronomy 5:8) is intended to prevent idolatry.

King Solomon was an active builder. For example he reconstructed and fortified the city of Megiddo, a place frequently mentioned in the Bible. The most significant structure of this time was the **First Temple in Jerusalem** (953 BC), in which the Ark of the Covenant was kept and for whose construction Solomon brought in Phoenician experts from Tyre.

When the kingdom was divided after Solomon's death in 928 BC, several cities succeeded each other as the capital of the Kingdom of Israel, until King Omri finally founded Samaria as the future capital in 878 BC. The area for the palace and administrative buildings was surrounded by a wall made of smoothly worked stones. This wall is considered to be the **first example of the Phoenician influence in stonemasonry**. In addition ivory carvings have been found in Samaria, which were possibly used for ornamentation on furniture.

Period of the Judges and Kings

◄ Solomon's buildings

◄ Samaria

← *Ornamentation (detail) in the synagogue of Capernaum*

Hellenistic, Roman and Byzantine Periods

Hellenism
After Alexander the Great conquered Judaea, elements of Greek culture in the form of theatres, hippodromes, temples and aqueducts started finding their way into the region from the start of the 3rd century BC onwards. Some of these elements merged with the local construction method, thereby giving them a new character. There are large marble columns that were part of a Greek temple in **Beit She'an**; however, the most impressive ruins there are those of the Roman theatre, the largest and best-preserved in Israel.

Nabataeans
Before Palestine was annexed by Rome, the Nabataean kingdom, which extended from Petra in modern-day Jordan all the way to the Negev, experienced its golden age. The Nabataeans, who settled on the east bank of the Jordan in the 5th and 4th centuries BC, emerged in the mid-2nd century BC with their own culture. Their **wells and water-supply systems** are particularly impressive, but the Nabataeans also knew how to build with clay bricks, work stones and make pottery. They also engaged in far-reaching trade relations. Along their trade route between Petra and the Mediterranean, they built the cities of Avdat, Shivta and Mamshit in what is now Israel.

Herodium Palace

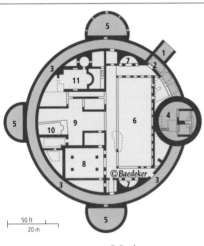

50 ft / 20 m

1 Access ramp
2 Reception room
3 Circular double walls
4 Eastern tower
5 Semicircular towers
6 Garden with columned hall
7 Exedra
8 Triclinium (later a synagogue)
9 Cruciform courtyard (surrounded by bedrooms)
10 Byzantine chapel
11 Baths

With the start of Roman rule in the 1st century BC, the influence of the architectural style characteristic of Late Antiquity also became more pronounced in Palestine. **Herod the Great** covered the land with monumental buildings. Examples of his ambitious construction programme can be found in Hebron, Caesarea, Samaria and Ashkelon, to name but a few. However, the two **fortresses in Masada and Herodium** are the most famous; their location and their adaptation to the topography are just two reasons why they are so impressive. In Jerusalem Herod had the Antonia Fortress built and also commissioned the refurbishment of the Temple. However, the ban on images continued to exist, so depictions of animals in the palace of Herod Antipas in Tiberias were condemned as unlawful and therefore removed at the first opportunity.

The central temple was originally the place of worship for the Jewish community, but after the destruction of Herod's Temple in AD 70, there was no Jewish temple anymore. The turning away from the temple cult, presumably a consequence of the diaspora, caused a different form of religious gathering to become established: **the communal spoken service**, where the focus is on readings from the holy scriptures and prayer. The synagogue became the meeting place and the place where these services were held. The oldest synagogue in Israel dates back to the 2nd and 3rd centuries and stands in Capernaum; the now-ruined synagogue in Chorazin, made of black basalt, dates back to around the same period. These early synagogues were often built following the model of a basilica, in other words the main room is divided into a nave and two aisles by two rows of columns. A forecourt and a vestibule are located in front of the main prayer room. From the 3rd century onwards the Jews **turned away from their total rejection of images**. Depictions of people and animals subsequently appeared in Galilee's synagogues. Greco-Roman and Palmyran influences now emerged in their tombs: sarcophagi with mythological depictions were no longer rejected, as many examples in Beit She'arim confirm.

Development of the synagogue

Emperor Constantine the Great allowed the practice of Christianity with the Edict of Milan in 313. He commissioned the construction of the **Church of the Nativity in Bethlehem** and hired a Syrian architect to draw up plans for the Church of the Holy Sepulchre in Jerusalem, which was completed in around 335 as a basilica with a nave and four aisles as well as an atrium, adjoining which was a round church with Christ's tomb at the centre. Several other churches, monasteries and hospices for thousands of pilgrims were also built under Constantine. The construction of churches and monasteries, entire cities even, reached its climax in the 6th century under Justinian. For the settlements in the arid Negev Desert, the Nabataean irrigation system was used, while the basilica became the dominant architectural type among church buildings. The floors were often decorated with **mosaics**, as can be seen to this day in the basilica in Tabgha. Its floor mosaic features fish and a basket with bread, a reference to the Feeding of the Five Thousand. Christian floor mosaics from the 5th and 6th centuries with depictions of animals and symbols representing the seasons have also been discovered in Beit Guvrin. However, Jewish synagogues from this period were also decorated with mosaics. One outstanding example is the floor of the synagogue near Beit Alfa.

Byzantine buildings

Arab and Ottoman Periods

From the 7th to the 11th centuries, the country was shaped by Arab Islamic culture. The Umayyad caliphs had mosques, palaces and fortresses built. The **Dome of the Rock with its rich mosaic ornamentation and the al-Aqsa Mosque** were built in Jerusalem, and Hisham's

Arab period

The mosaic in the church in Tabgha commemorates the »Feeding of the Five Thousand«.

Palace as the caliphs' winter residence in Jericho. The ban on images, which Islam shared with Judaism, did not yet have an impact in the Umayyad period (until the mid-8th century).

Among further construction projects of this time were the caravanserais (khans), multi-storey buildings, usually around a square courtyard, that provided accommodation, stables and storage space for merchants. Akko is a good place to visit in order to find out what the khans used to look like.

Crusader age Over the course of the crusades (12th–13th century), the crusaders, often French knights, built forts (crusader fortresses), as in Akko, Alit, Belvoir, Caesarea and Montfort, but they also commissioned places of worship such as St Anne's Church, the church at Mary's Tomb and the Chapel of the Ascension in Jerusalem. The crusader church in Abu Ghosh with its wall frescoes is one of the best-preserved in the country. Stylistically, the structures formed a **synthesis of oriental and Western architecture**.

Ottoman period Several buildings also survive from the 400-year period of Ottoman rule (1517–1917): particularly outstanding examples are the mosque of 1781 in Akko and the Mahoumdiya Mosque (1810) in Jaffa. During this period Christian influence became stronger again, so that churches were constructed alongside Islamic buildings, culminating in the Lutheran Church of the Redeemer, which was inaugurated by the German emperor Wilhelm II in 1898.

Arab faience ornamentation on the Dome of the Rock in Jerusalem

Since the 16th century, but especially in the 18th and 19th centuries, **artistic objects** have been made for synagogues. They can now be seen in many museums around the world, but especially in the Israel Museum in Jerusalem. The most attention was lavished on the Torah scrolls and where they were kept: richly ornamented Torah containers carved out of wood, Torah caps embossed with silver and painted and embroidered fabrics made into curtains for the Torah shrine or into Torah covers are usually of high artistic quality.

20th and 21st Centuries

During the British mandate (1920–48) many buildings were constructed in a pseudo-oriental style. The most famous example is the Rockefeller Museum in Jerusalem. While searching for a style the country could call its own, Alexander Baerwald, an architect from Berlin, also used oriental elements for the Technion in Haifa (1914–24). After the Nazis came to power in Germany, many architects also fled to Palestine, among them the Bauhaus student Arieh Sharon, whose workers' flats in Tel Aviv dating from 1935–40 became models of residential construction, as well as Joseph Neufeld, Max Loeb and architects of international fame such as Erich Mendelsohn, Alexander Klein and Johann Ratner. Under their plans, entire neighbourhoods of Tel Aviv and Haifa were transformed into veritable **Bauhaus estates** (▶Baedeker Special p. 406).

Architecture in the state of Israel
Residential construction and town planning ▶

As a result of mass immigration after Israel was founded in 1948, the main aim originally was to create enough homes and focus on town planning, to which end Arieh Sharon created a national plan in the Department of Labour. The implementation of architecturally interesting ideas only played a subordinate role. The result was correspondingly sober and uniform. A change only occurred in the 1960s, when the architecture became more varied and the homes more comfortable. In addition to the home-building programmes on the edge of large cities such as East Talpiot and Ramot in Jerusalem, some cities were also planned from scratch on the drawing board. Arad is one such example. At the same time a start was made on restoring the centres of old cities, such as in Safed and Jaffa and of course Jerusalem.

Public buildings ▶

The new state also manifested itself in prestige buildings, especially in Jerusalem, where the Knesset building was designed by Ossip Klarwein and Dov Carmi. This category of buildings that bestowed national identity includes the Israel Museum in Jerusalem by Al Mansfield and Dora Gat as well as Yad Vashem. Important parts of this memorial were designed by the internationally renowned **Moshe Safdie** from Haifa, who is also responsible for the Yitzhak Rabin Center and Ben Gurion International Airport. The university buildings in Beersheba and Jerusalem (Givat Ram and Mount Scopus) have interesting architecture, as does the Museum of Art in Tel Aviv, designed by Dan Eitan and Yitzhak Yashar. Furthermore, there is the Mann Auditorium in Tel Aviv, which combines monumentality with functionality. The largest place of worship in the Middle East is the Basilica of the Annunciation in Nazareth, completed in 1969 incorporating the work of many artists.

Visual arts

The Tel Aviv Museum of Art and the Israel Museum in Jerusalem are the best venues to explore contemporary Israeli art. Painting and sculpture can be seen in many public places in Israel. Unusual and sometimes confusing at first glance is the presentation of modern art on ancient excavation sites, between Roman ruins or under medieval pointed arches. Art and handicraft galleries are mainly based in Tel Aviv, Jerusalem and Haifa. A tip for art-lovers is the Tel Aviv art fair Fresh Paint, first held in 2008, and now an established fixture. It presents works of art in different places each year, many of them by newcomers to the scene. Those who prefer to see art in a studio should go to Safed or to the artists' village of Ein Hod near Haifa, where visitors can view the works in the place of their creation. The sculptor **Dani Karavan** (b. 1930) has achieved international fame. He has created highly regarded monuments in France, Germany, Spain and Japan, as well as in Israel. Another globally-known artist is **Micha Ullman** (b. 1939) who created the Memorial in Remembrance of the Burning of the Books in Berlin. Helen Bermann (b. 1936), who left the Netherlands for Israel in 1978, has become famous as a painter.

Many young artists focus on the fate of the Palestinians. A video work by **Sigalit Landau**, who was born in Tel Aviv in 1969, shows an endless loop of the artist's gyrating hips on which there is not a hula hoop but barbed wire leaving wounds – violent »threshold experiences« can, in their simplicity, be carried over on to experience of political thresholds. The pictures painted by **David Reeb** (b. 1952, Rehovot) also address the history of the occupation of the Palestinian territories, the »green line« and the Intifada. He based them on press photographs depicting everyday, almost banal scenes – the main actors are not the political protagonists, but events and people of everyday life. The documentary filmmaker **Eyal Sivan** (b. 1964, Haifa) now lives in Paris. In *The Specialist* (together with Rony Braumann) he processed and manipulated more than 350 hours of footage relating to the 1961 trial of Adolf Eichmann. Eichmann is portrayed not as a criminal, but as a German bureaucrat, who dutifully followed the orders of his regime – a mechanism latent in all modern states.

◄ Young scene

Palestinian art is far less known in Europe than Israeli art. Ramallah, the unofficial capital of the Palestinian territories, is the best place to experience young Palestinian art as well as traditional folk art, which in contrast to the fantastical works of foreign-based artists such as

◄ Palestinian art

Anyone in search of modern Israeli art will find it in the Israel Museum.

Palestinian literature

Mona Hatoum and Fareed Armaly, draws on daily experience of the depths of the everyday life. One painter known in Europe is **Osama Said**.

It is easy now to enjoy Palestinian literature, which only really began in 1948. Its themes (expulsion, exile, injustice, powerlessness, the lack of a homeland) are dominated by the conflict with Israel, the occupation. For a long time, a ban on publication drove authors underground. Under Israeli rule, there was no right to free expression in book form either on the West Bank on Gaza. Thus the works of Emil Habibi, Ghassan Kanafani, Jabra Ibrahim Jabra, and Sahar Khalifa were mostly published abroad, for example in Cairo or Beirut. If there was a voice of Palestine, then it belonged to the poet **Mahmoud Darwish**, who was born in Galilee in 1941, fled with his family to Lebanon in 1948, and died in 2008. Although he returned to Galilee, he went into exile after being arrested on several occasions. With increasing age, he abandoned his initial sympathy for armed resistance and martyrdom. In 1996 Darwish was allowed back and went to Ramallah. A year before his death, he even appeared in Israel. Tirelessly, he berated the Arab world's half-hearted solidarity with the Palestinians, by complaining for example that the Palestine was only a »land of words«.

Language

A multilingual country

The primary official language in Israel is **Ivrit** (Modern Hebrew), and the second is Arabic. Use of English is widespread. Since Israel is a country of immigrants, lots of other languages are also spoken here: French, German, Russian, Polish, Spanish, Hungarian and Yiddish.

Hebrew (see p. 130)

Hebrew is a western Semitic language, related to Assyrian and Aramaic. **Aramaic** was the administrative language of the Persian Empire, and from the 6th century BC until the 6th century AD it was the lingua franca throughout the Middle East. It became the vernacular of the Jews (as did Greek during the Hellenistic period), replacing Hebrew. Hebrew however was still used in religious services, by scholars and in literature. The Mishnah, completed in around AD 200, is largely written in Mishnaic Hebrew, which was supplemented by words taken from Greek and Latin.

Hebrew experienced a golden age from the 11th century until 1492 in Moorish Spain, and a revival during the Jewish Enlightenment

? DID YOU KNOW ...?

■ Israelis have no trouble reading the Bible in Hebrew, whereas someone who only learned biblical Hebrew will have difficulty reading an Israeli newspaper.

(Haskalah) in Germany in the late 18th century, spreading to Italy, Poland and Russia. Along with the start of the Zionist movement in the 19th century a trend developed that sought to release Hebrew from the confines of the religious sphere and instead aimed to turn it into the popular language, an aim which was actually achieved in Israel, not least because of **Eliezer Ben Yehuda** (▶Famous People).

Arabic

Arabic is also a Semitic language. Northern Arabic became dominant with the spread of Islam and is now spoken in many dialects all over northern Africa and in Western Asia. The most important dialect that is also spoken by the Arab population in Israel is Egyptian Arabic. The Palestinians speak their own Arabic dialect, which is similar to that of Syria and Lebanon.

Famous People

People from Israel: an underground fighter and a general who both managed to become prime minister, an agent who became the mayor of Jerusalem, and a successful singer who is as unpopular with orthodox Jews as with devout Muslims.

Samuel Josef Agnon (1888–1970)

Shmuel Yosef Agnon was the first Hebrew author to receive the **No-** **Writer**
bel Prize for Literature (1966). Agnon, born in Galicia in 1888 and
resident in Germany from 1913 to 1924, finally settled in Jerusalem
in 1924.

In a large number of legends, novellas and novels he mainly described eastern European Judaism, but also modern Israel, as in *Yes-
teryear*, published in 1936, where he describes the lives of young pioneers in Israel at the start of the 20th century. Characteristics of
Shmuel Agnon's works are the combination of an archaic-sounding
language with modern narrative techniques and the inability of his
protagonists to implement their plans.

Yasser Arafat (1929–2004)

The keffiyeh, the black and white Palestinian headscarf, a badly fit-   **Palestinian**
ting uniform, and a gun in his belt – that is how Yasser Arafat turned   **president**
up at the General Assembly of the UN in 1974 and that is how the
world knew him. For more than 35 years, Arafat, born on 27 August
1929 in Jerusalem according to his own claim, in Cairo according to
his birth certificate, was the leader of the Palestinian liberation
movement. In 1959 he founded the militant organization **al Fatah**
(Movement for the Liberation of Palestine), which started attacking
Israel in 1965, at first from Jordan and later also from Lebanon. It also launched terrorist attacks around the world. After Fatah had been
incorporated into the PLO group, the tactician and strategist Arafat
became its leader too in 1969.

Arafat managed to transform the PLO from an underground organization into the internationally recognized representative of Palestine,
thereby promoting the idea of the foundation of an independent
state of Palestine. For his role in the peace process he, the prime
minister of Israel, Yitzhak Rabin, and the Israeli foreign minister Shimon Peres were awarded the **Nobel Peace Prize** in 1994. That same
year he became the president of the Palestinian National Authority.
In this office he got more and more enmeshed in a network of corruption and nepotism. With the outbreak of the Second Intifada in
autumn 2000, Arafat entered the last phase of his life. Put under
house arrest in Ramallah by the Israeli government, where he was
the target of bombings several times, he was politically incapacitated
and stripped of all power. In addition his already poor health deter-
iorated. In 2004 he had to be flown to Paris for treatment. He died
there on 11 November. The Israeli government did not grant him his
wish of burial on the Temple Mount in Jerusalem and so he was laid
to rest at his headquarters (Mukataa) in Ramallah.

← *Israel's first prime minister:*
  David Ben Gurion

Menachem Begin (1913–92)

Prime minister and recipient of the Nobel Peace Prize

Menachem Begin achieved what his predecessors as prime minister had not: he **made peace with Egypt**, the most powerful of Israel's Arab neighbours. For that he was awarded the Nobel Peace Prize in 1978, together with the Egyptian president Anwar El Sadat, who was assassinated in 1981. Begin, who was born in Brest-Litovsk in 1913, witnessed the murder of his parents when the Nazis arrived in Poland. He himself was able to flee to the Soviet Union, where he was arrested and sent to a camp in Siberia because of underground activities. In 1942 he came to Palestine as a member of the Polish liberation army. After leaving the army, he ran the terrorist underground organization Irgun Zevai Leumi from 1943 to 1948. After the state of Israel was founded, Begin was one of the founders of »Herut« (freedom) and the right-wing Likud. Even as prime minister (from 1977 onwards) he pursued the goal of asserting a state of Israel within the borders of biblical Palestine. During his time in government, Israel annexed the Golan Heights and Israeli forces entered Lebanon, which brought him increasing national and international pressure. In August 1983 Begin stepped down and lived a reclusive life in Jerusalem until his death in 1992.

David Ben Gurion (1886–1973)

Israel's first prime minister

Israel's first prime minister was born David Gruen in Poland. He came to Palestine via Constantinople and the United States. In Palestine he co-founded Histadrut, an organization whose secretary-general he was between 1921 and 1935. Ben Gurion was also responsible for the creation of the socialist labour party Mapai. In 1935 he became head of the Jewish Agency and in 1944 of the World Zionist Organization. As prime minister of a provisional government, he proclaimed the independent state of Israel on 14 May 1948. In his diary, he cautiously commented about this event: »Everywhere in the country there is boundless joy and cheering, but once again I feel ... like someone suffering among all these happy people.« Over the following years as head of government, Ben Gurion managed to assert Israel's existence against the opposition of its Arab neighbours. However, worn down as a result of cabinet crises and feuding within his own party, he stepped down as prime minister in 1953 and joined the kibbutz Sde Boker. His withdrawal from politics only lasted for 14 months, as the diplomatic situation forced him to return to political office: first as minister of defence, and then, until 1963, as prime minister again. The statesman spent the last years of his life largely in Sde Boker, where he was buried.

Eliezer Ben Yehuda (1858–1922)

»Inventor« of Hebrew

The Lithuanian-born linguist Ben Yehuda is considered the »inventor« of modern Hebrew (Ivrit). In 1881 he started work as a teacher and journalist and was one of the leading minds of the Zionist movement in Jerusalem. His main concern was **to revive Hebrew as a popular language**. To do that, he constructed a modern language from biblical and other classical sources and recorded it in a dictionary containing both ancient and modern Hebrew. In addition he founded the Committee of the Hebrew Language in 1890, from which the Academy of the Hebrew Language later developed.

Dana International (b. 1972)

When it comes to music in Israel, most people think of Ofra Haza **Artist** (see p. 99) and Dana International, who used to be a man called Yaron Cohen. In the 1980s the boy, inspired by Madonna and Ofra Haza, discovered his musical talent and his increasing desire to be a woman. Yaron quickly made a name for himself as a drag queen in the clubs of Tel Aviv, already using the female name Sharon. When he had enough money, the star had a sex-change operation in London. His first record, *Dana International*, released in 1992, was a huge success. The techno dance scene had found a new star.

Hostility rose along with his success. The Arabic version of the title was banned in Egypt, but it was sold a million times under the counter. In Israel orthodox Jews were irate, as according to Dana they believe transsexuality is a »sign of darkness«. The singer's breakthrough occurred in 1998 when she won the Eurovision Song Contest for Israel with the song *Diva*. The artist is involved in human rights groups that fight for the rights of lesbians and homosexuals: »I represent liberal Israel, an Israel that accepts human life, never mind what you're like, what you look like, what sex you are or what race you are.«

David (reigned 1004–965 BC)

The Bible describes him as the epitome of a god-fearing ruler, a **King** statesman, poet, general and musician in one. The former shepherd boy, who became a hero when he defeated the giant Philistine warrior Goliath (Samuel 1:17), was anointed King of Judah after the death of the first king of the Israelites, Saul, and recognized as king of the entire realm by the twelve tribes. David **made Jerusalem the political and spiritual centre of Israel**, since the constant tensions between the two realms, Israel in the north and Judah in the south, required him to choose a neutral place of residence: he conquered the hitherto undefeated Jebusite city of Jebus (Jerusalem), but did not dispel its inhabitants in order to avoid losing their support. The Jebusite acropolis called »Zion« was renamed »David's City«. It was soon extended, fortified, and made the new home of the Ark of the Covenant, whereby it became the capital.

However, this much-praised ruler was also guilty of misconduct, when he watched **Bathsheba**, the wife of his former comrade-in-arms Uriah, bathing, sent for her and made her pregnant. He ordered Uriah to be sent into battle, where he died. David regretted his actions and obtained forgiveness from Yahweh. After the period of mourning he married Bathsheba, who bore the heir to the throne, Solomon.

Moshe Dayan (1915–81)

Military strategist

The myth of the invincibility of the Israeli army is largely associated with the name of Moshe Dayan. The general and politician who was born in the kibbutz of Degania Alef near the Sea of Galilee and wore an eye patch following the loss of his left eye, was significantly involved in several military campaigns in the war of 1948. In 1953, as a 38-year-old, he was made chief of staff of the Israel Defence Forces by David Ben Gurion. After his five years in office were up, Dayan studied politics and in 1959 became minister of agriculture in Ben Gurion's government. But when the diplomatic situation came to a head in 1967, the experienced soldier Dayan took on the office of minister of defence, helping his country to achieve a clear military

Moshe Dayan in conversation with Golda Meir

success in the Six-Day War. As foreign minister he made a crucial contribution to the Israeli-Egyptian peace treaty. However, because of significant differences with Menachem Begin regarding settlement and foreign policy, he stepped down from this office just two years later in 1979.

Batya Gur (1947–2005)

Writer

With her character **Inspector Ohayon**, a detective of the thoughtful and intellectual kind, the writer Batya Gur created a character who, as the »Maigret of Jerusalem«, won over the hearts of crime fiction fans in next to no time. Batya Gur was born in Tel Aviv and studied Hebrew literature in Jerusalem. She taught at the Hebrew Academy in New York in the 1970s, and was almost 40 years old when she published her first crime fiction. She quickly reached top spots on bestseller lists. *I Didn't Imagine it Would Be This Way* was translated into twelve languages. A characteristic of her crime fiction was the exploration of human relationships within a closed world – a group of psychoanalysts in *The Saturday Morning Murder: A Psychoanalytic Case*, a kibbutz in *Murder on a Kibbutz: A Communal Case*. Gur rarely made political statements, but after 2001 she made no attempt to hide her critical attitude to the Sharon government and its policy regarding Palestine. On 19 May 2005 she died in Jerusalem following a serious illness.

Ofra Haza (1958–2000)

Singer

Often imitated, never matched. What made the Israeli singer Ofra Haza different from many other performers is that many of her vocal pieces, consisting of elements of Arabic-Jewish folklore and pop music, are now sampled by hip hop and rap bands. At the same time the ninth child of a Yemenite migrant family is considered the forerunner of world music, which mixes native traditions with Western sounds. The charming singer achieved her breakthrough in Europe in 1983, when she took second place at the Eurovision Song Contest in Munich, where the medieval Yemenite prayer *Im Ninallu*, underscored by modern rhythms, became a global success. By the time of her death in February 2000, she had managed to produce 16 gold and platinum albums and obtained one Grammy nomination.

Herod the Great (around 73–4 BC)

Hated king Herod I was probably the most hated and ambivalent of the country's potentates and at the same time the only one to be given the sobriquet »the Great«. After the murder of Antipater, the Roman triumvir Mark Antony appointed him tetrarch in 42 BC, but the fighting for the Jewish throne that was thus triggered forced him to flee to Rome. There the senate proclaimed him King of the Jews in 40 BC, and in 37 BC, after the conquest of Jerusalem, he began his reign. His policies were marked by close imitation of Rome and the constant attempt to implement the Roman concept of Pax Romana in combination with Hellenistic thought. The country experienced an incredible economic boom and more than 30 years of peace. The Jewish cult remained almost untouched, but orthodox Jews were unhappy about Hellenization. All opposition was radically suppressed. Herod extended Caesarea and Jerusalem and constructed fortresses such as Masada. Despite his achievements, he went down as a bloodthirsty, raving despot in Christian tradition, being the one who ordered the Massacre of the Innocents. Herod died in Jericho. His body was brought to the Herodium near Bethlehem. The tomb, which was considered lost for a long time, was discovered in spring 2007.

Theodor Herzl (1860–1904)

Founder of Zionism Theodor Herzl was the founder of political Zionism, without which there would be no state of Israel today. Born in Budapest, he obtained his PhD in Vienna in 1884, at a time when anti-Semitic outbursts were an everyday occurrence at the university. In 1896 Herzl published the Zionist manifesto, ***The Jewish State – Proposal of a Modern Solution of the Jewish Question***, in which he demanded the creation of a sovereign Jewish state, because, he claimed, Jews were not just a religious community, but also a people. At the First Zionist Congress in Basel in 1897, which he organized, this demand was adopted in a programme of Zionism. Herzl commented in his diary: »I founded the Jewish state in Basel. Maybe in five years, but definitely in 50, everyone will see that.« He was not able to witness his success, since negotiations about the founding of a Jewish state failed. After the founding of the state of Israel, his body was brought to Mount Herzl in Jerusalem, where the opening ceremonies for Israel's national holiday are held every year.

Ephraim Kishon (1924–2005)

Satirist Ephraim Kishon, born Ferenc Hoffmann, is one of the most-read Israeli authors in Europe. After graduating from university in the city of his birth, Budapest, he survived the war years in Hungarian, German and Russian camps. In 1949 he emigrated to Israel, where he

1898: Theodor Herzl travelled to Palestine to meet Emperor Wilhelm II of Germany.

earned a livelihood as a fitter and mechanic and learned Hebrew. He started publishing political satire in 1952, and wrote a column for Ma'ariv, Israel's most-read daily newspaper, for 30 years. Kishon humorously mocked human weaknesses and political as well as bureaucratic absurdities. The easy and humorous writing style of books such as *Look Back Mrs. Lot* (1960) gained him a world-wide readership thanks to translations into almost 40 languages. His second wife Sara, referred to in his writing as »the best wife of all«, died in 2002. In 2003 he married Austrian author Lisa Witasek, 32 years his junior. In 2005, aged 80, he suffered a heart attack in Switzerland, where he had chosen to live.

Teddy Kollek (1911–2007)

Teddy Kollek made a name for himself far beyond the confines of his city as mayor of Jerusalem. He was considered to be **one of the most popular and progressive Jewish politicians**. Born in Hungary, he emigrated to Palestine in 1935, where he founded the kibbutz of Ein Gev on the eastern shore of the Sea of Galilee. After various missions for the Zionist movement, including his work for the secret service in Istanbul during World War II, Kollek started preparing the found-

Legendary mayor of Jerusalem

Teddy Kollek

ing of the state of Israel in New York in 1947 by purchasing weapons, smuggling, and collecting money from American Jews. Between 1952 and 1964 he ran the prime minister's office of the new state. However, it was as mayor of Jerusalem that he achieved fame. It was an office he held for almost 30 years (1965–93). No other politician contributed more to turning a provincial administrative town into a flourishing city. In 2002 he caused a stir when he spoke out in favour dividing Jerusalem, for the sake of peace. Teddy Kollek died on 2 January 2007.

Golda Meir (1898–1978)

Female prime minister

One of the few women to play a significant role in Israel's history was Golda Meir, who was **prime minister from 1969 to 1974**. After early years in poor circumstances in Kiev, Meir went to the United States in 1906, where she worked as a librarian and was involved in the Zionist movement. Together with her husband Morris, she emigrated to Palestine in 1921. Politically, she emerged as a member of Mapai and the trade union organization Histadrut. Further stations in her political life were her work as Israeli ambassador in Moscow in 1948–49, then the running of the labour ministry and her eleven-year term as foreign minister. In March 1969 she was elected by the Knesset to head the government. She announced her resignation in April 1974 as a result of domestic confrontations regarding the Yom Kippur War.

Amos Oz (b. 1939)

Writer and peace activist

He is Israel's most famous writer and one of the strongest critics of his country. He has followed the development of the state of Israel with an ironic and at times satirical perspective. His novels and short stories, including *A Perfect Peace* and *Where the Jackals Howl* (translated into more than 20 languages), address the issue of Arabs and Jews living together. The son of Russian immigrants, he is never short of answers. The co-founder of Israeli peace movement Peace Now always has a clear opinion. In Israel he tirelessly expresses his »position of compromise and the Palestinian right to their own state«. When once the view was expressed that Oz would make a good foreign minister for Israel, his response was: »I have discussed

this question with Vaclav Havel, but it's damaging to civilization when writers get involved in politics, leaving it to politicians to write the novels.«

Yitzhak Rabin (1922–95)

It was not just the Israeli people who were deeply shocked when, on 4 November 1995, the prime minister Yitzhak Rabin was assassinated at one of the most peaceful rallies in the history of Israel. Rabin was the son of Russian-Jewish immigrants. Born in Jerusalem, he joined one of Haganah's elite units in 1941. With his participation in the Six-Day War in 1967, the chief of staff ended his military career as a national hero, whereafter he represented his country for five years as ambassador to Washington. As the successor of Golda Meir, he was prime minister for the first time in 1974. He became prime minister for the second time in 1992. His appeal to give up the »illusion of a Greater Israel« as well as his efforts in the Arab-Israeli conflict earned Rabin, along with foreign minister Shimon Peres and Palestinian leader Yasser Arafat, **the Nobel Peace Prize in 1994**. A man who had a reputation for doing as he said and letting other people know where they stood, he died at the zenith of his political life at the hands of a fanatical Jew.

Prime minister and recipient of the Nobel Peace Prize

A time of hope: Yitzhak Rabin and Yasser Arafat with President Clinton in September 1993 in Washington D. C.

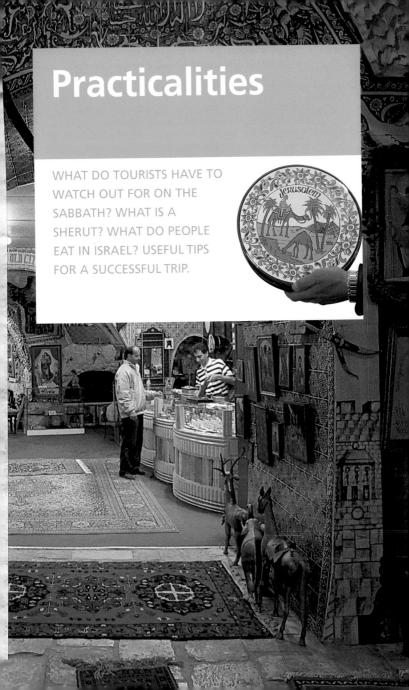

Practicalities

WHAT DO TOURISTS HAVE TO WATCH OUT FOR ON THE SABBATH? WHAT IS A SHERUT? WHAT DO PEOPLE EAT IN ISRAEL? USEFUL TIPS FOR A SUCCESSFUL TRIP.

Accommodation

Hotels
Israel has hotels for different requirements and budgets, from luxury accommodation to mid-range hotels and basic options in dormitories. Prices are comparatively high, but they vary significantly depending on the season. The most expensive times are around Christmas and Easter as well as around the Jewish New Year and the summer months. Weekends can be more expensive than weekdays. Generally speaking, it is cheaper to book a hotel as part of an all-inclusive deal via a travel agent. Information and a directory are available from the Israel Hotel Association.

> **i** Price categories
>
> - Luxury: more than NIS 700
> - Mid-range: NIS 400–700
> - Budget: less than NIS 400 for a double room with breakfast

Kibbutz hotels
Around 60 of the approx. 270 kibbutzim run modern guesthouses, which often have beaches, pools and other sporting facilities. Their standard corresponds to three or four-star accommodation, but the atmosphere is often more familiar and personal. These hotels also offer trips and excursions to the surrounding area as well as lectures about life in a kibbutz and other cultural events.

Pilgrim hospices
Pilgrim hospices are a special and comparatively cheap form of accommodation in Israel. Originally set up exclusively for pilgrims, they are now open to everyone. The selection is greatest in Jerusalem and Nazareth, but they can also be found in other places of religious significance. Generally speaking these pilgrim hospices have the same standard as mid-range hotels, with minor differences such as the absence of a television or the emphasis on simplicity in the rooms, which make do without unnecessary creature comforts. Most hospices have double rooms and multi-bedrooms as well as dormitories (sex-segregated). Those planning to spend a night in a pilgrim hospice should book the room before leaving home: they are quickly booked out, since it has become well known that they offer good value for money. The Pilgrimage Promotion Committee provides information. Several hospices are also listed in the hotel recommendations in the »Sightseeing from A to Z« section.

← Shop in Jerusalem's Arab quarter

Bed & Breakfast
In several holiday destinations, especially in Jerusalem (where there are currently more than 20 such establishments), private individuals run bed & breakfast establishments. The ATG finds accommodation for travellers wishing to stay with Palestinian families.

Camping
The number of campsites in Israel is relatively small. Getting information is difficult, because there is no camping association anymore.

▶ INFORMATION ADDRESSES

HOTELS

▶ **Israel Hotel Association**
29 Hamered St., P.O.Box 50066
Tel Aviv 61500
Tel. (03) 517 01 31
Fax. 510 01 97
www.israelhotels.org.il

KIBBUTZ HOTELS

▶ **Kibbutz Hotel Chains**
90 Ben Yehuda St.
Tel Aviv 61031
Tel. (03) 560 81 18
Fax 527 80 88
www.kibbutz.co.il

PILGRIM HOSPICES

▶ **Israel Hotel Association**
see above

▶ **Pilgrimage Promotion Committee**
23 Hille St
Jerusalem
Tel. (02) 623 73 11, fax 625 34 07

BED & BREAKFAST

▶ **The Home Accommodation Association of Jerusalem**
P. O. Box 7547
Jerusalem 91074
Tel. (02) 645 21 98
www.bnb.co.il

▶ **ATG (Alternative Tourism Group)**
P. O. Box 173
Beit Sahour
Tel. (02) 277 21 51
Fax 277 22 11
www.atg.ps

HOSTELS

▶ **Israel Youth Hostel Association**
Jerusalem International
Convention Center
P.O.Box 6001, Jerusalem 91060
Tel. (02) 655 84 00 / 655 84 06
Fax 655 84 32, www.iyha.org.il/
eng/

Nevertheless it is possible to pitch a tent in rural regions, as long as you ask locally about a suitable place to spend the night.

All hostels have dormitories and kitchens for guests to use. Most of them also serve meals. Some hostels also have family rooms for parents travelling with children. Apart from the hostels run by the Israel Youth Hostel Association, there is are a large number of similar privately operated establishments. *Hostels*

Arrival · Before the Trip

There are direct flights between **Ben Gurion International Airport near Tel Aviv** (Lod) and many European and intercontinental destinations. From the United Kingdom El Al and British Airways fly *By air* from London Heathrow, while Easyjet has direct flights from Luton and Manchester. Flying time is around 4.5 hours. From the United States, El Al and Delta fly from New York to Tel Aviv, flying time 11 hours. For those who are travelling from the European continent, or are willing to change at a European hub to get a better price than with a direct flight from the UK, it is worth looking at the current offers of Czech Airlines (via Prague), Air France (via Paris), Malev (via Budapest) or Austrian Airlines (via Vienna). KLM, Alitalia and Lufthansa also have scheduled flights to Tel Aviv. The Israeli airline Israir flies from Berlin, Milan, Nice and Rome.

El Al, Arkia and Israir fly from Tel Aviv to Eilat on the Red Sea. During the summer season there are also charter planes to Eilat.

By land   It is possible to enter Israel by land from Jordan and Egypt. Private vehicles are allowed to cross the borders (except for those licensed in Israel or Jordan), but hired cars are not.

Most visitors come and go via Ben Gurion International Airport.

ARRIVALS INFORMATION

AIRLINE COMPANIES

► **El Al**
Office in New York
15 East 26th Street
Tel. (1) 800 223 6700
Office in London
16 Upper Woburn Place
Tel. (20) 712 114 00

Reservations in Israel:
Tel. (03) 972 23 33
Tel Aviv:
Tel. (03) 526 12 22
Jerusalem:
Tel. (02) 677 02 07
Haifa:
Tel. (04) 861 26 70
Eilat:
Tel. (07) 637 15 15

► **British Airways**
www.britishairways.com
Tel Aviv office:
Tel. (03) 606 15 55

► **Delta Airways**
 www.delta.com
In Israel: tel. (800) 241 41 41
Ben Gurion International Airport:
tel. (03) 972 77 64

► **Easyjet**
www.easyjet.com

► **Israir**
www.israirairlines.com
Tel. in Israel: (03) 795 40 38

► **Arkia**
www.arkia.com
Tel. (02) 98 64 44 44

AIRPORT

► **Ben Gurion International Airport**
Information: tel. (03) 88 11 11

Transfers to Jerusalem: sherut taxis around the clock at fixed prices (tel. 02 / 531 95 50); Egged Bus Lines to the central bus station. Current timetable and further information: tel. (03) 694 88 88 or www.egged.co.il

By rail: connections to the line Tel Aviv–Haifa – Akko –Nahariya

BORDER CROSSINGS

► **From / to Egypt**
Eilat / Taba: crossing to East Sinai, open daily 24 hrs

► **From / to Jordan**
Allenby Bridge
(King Hussein Bridge):
40km/25mi east of Jerusalem near Jericho; Sun–Thu 8am–midnight, Fri and Sat 8am–3pm

Jordan River Crossing
(Sheikh Hussein Bridge): east of Beit She'an; use not permitted with an Israeli hired car or private vehicle. There is a shuttle service to the border crossing; Sun–Thu 6.30am–10pm, Fri and Sat 8am–8pm, closed on Yom Kippur and on the first day of the Muslim year.

Arava: north of Eilat; Sun–Thu 6.30am–10pm, Fri and Sat 8am–8pm, closed on Yom Kippur and Id El Adha

Travel Documents

Identification To enter Israel, travellers need a passport that is valid for at least six month from the start of the journey. A free visa is then issued at the point of entry. Anyone wishing to stay for longer than three months will require a visa from an Israeli embassy (▶Information). All visas will be stamped on a loose sheet of paper if requested, since no Arab state apart from Jordan and Egypt will accept a passport containing an Israeli visa.

Children Children's passports need to have a photograph, even for those under the age of 10. Young people (under the age of 18) travelling alone must have an officially confirmed statement from their legal guardian giving them permission to travel.

Vehicle papers Israel recognizes driver's licences and vehicle papers from other countries, and travellers must bring them. Third party personal injury insurance is a legal requirement in Israel. The international green card motor insurance is recognized as long as the issuing insurance company has declared it valid for Israel. Travellers who do not possess a valid green card must take out an insurance policy upon arrival.

Vaccinations and travel insurance There are no required vaccinations. Travellers should take out private medical insurance.

Pets Anyone wishing to take their pets (cats, dogs) to Israel will need a certificate of health issued by an officially recognized vet as well as two copies of a certificate showing that the animals have been vaccinated against rabies. Cats and dogs under the age of three months cannot be brought into Israel.

Customs and Departure Regulations

Entry Items intended for personal use may be imported into Israel duty-free. These items include 250 cigarettes or 250g of tobacco in a different form, 2 litres of wine, 1 litre of spirits (for travellers over 17), 250ml of perfume or eau de toilette and gifts worth a total of US$ 200.

Return to the EU Travellers returning directly to the EU may import souvenirs up to a value of EUR 430/£ 390 duty-free; travellers over 15 may in addition import 500g of coffee or 200g of instant coffee, 100g of tea, 50ml of perfume and 250ml of toilet water, while persons over 17 may in addition import 200 cigarettes or 100 cigarillos or 50 cigars or 250g of tobacco, and 1 litre of spirits with alcohol content of more than 22% by volume and 2 litres of beer. Also medication for personal use.

Travellers entering the USA from Israel have a duty-free allowance once every 30 days of $800 of accompanied baggage, including not more than 200 cigarettes, 100 cigars and one litre of alcoholic beverages (travellers above the age of 21). For full details, see www.cbp.gov.

Flights should be confirmed at least 72 hours prior to departure with the tour operator or the airline company to make sure that there have not been any changes. Because of the strict security checks it is best to be at Ben Gurion International Airport **at least three hours prior to departure**. 45–60 minutes should be allowed for returning a hired vehicle.

Before departure

Those departing Israel for Egypt must be in possession of an Egyptian visa (available from the Egyptian embassy in Tel Aviv, Basel St. 54, tel. 03 / 546 41 51 or from the Egyptian embassy in the home country). Exception: when departing via Taba to the Sinai Peninsula, travellers are issued a special visa only valid for East Sinai (including Saint Catherine's Monastery), but travellers with this visa must also return via Taba.

Departure by land

◄ to Egypt

Travellers need a visa to enter Jordan. These are issued at the border, but not when departing via Allenby Bridge.

◄ To Jordan

Beaches

Israel possesses both a Mediterranean coastline and a coastline on the Red Sea and can therefore lay claim to lots of wonderful beaches for swimming. There are also many places to go swimming in the Sea of Galilee, whereas the Dead Sea is unsuitable for bathing because of the high salt content, but it is good for a health cure. However, floating around in the water without sinking is also fun! Most public beaches are well appointed with showers, bars and restaurants. Beach loungers and parasols can be hired. All beaches, including those around the Sea of Galilee, are patrolled by life guards.

A destination for beach holidays

Nude swimming is completely foreign to Israel, as is going topless; this applies both to hotel pools and beaches.

Nude bathing

▶ THE BEST BEACHES

▶ Achziv
Long, well-tended sandy beach north of Nahariya. Area adjoins a national park and has good places for picnics and restaurants.

▶ Nahariya
Wide beach several miles long to the north and south of the seaside resort – one of the best in Israel.

▶ **Shavei Tzion**
Beach of the moshav Shavei Tzion to the south of Nahariya with showers, changing rooms and refreshment stalls.

▶ **Haifa**
The beaches to the south of the city are particularly well kept and extensive, with every amenity.

▶ **Dor**
Comparatively quiet, attractive beach with four offshore islands (bird sanctuaries). Popular with underwater archaeologists.

▶ **Caesarea**
Appealing beach to the north of the national park near the aqueduct. Usually ideal conditions for windsurfers.

▶ **Netanya**
The central beach is very well looked after, but also very busy during the peak season. The sections to the north and south are quieter.

▶ **Herzliya**
Popular destination among Israelis. As a result it gets very busy on Saturdays.

▶ **Tel Aviv**
The beaches and beach promenade of Tel Aviv are popular. Surprisingly clean for a city beach.

▶ **Ashqelon**
The section at the excavation site is one of the nicest beaches: extensive green areas, bathrooms, picnic sites and restaurants.

▶ **Eilat**
The north beach is usually crowded. The beaches to the south are more appealing, especially Coral Reserve Beach, a paradise for snorkellers and divers.

Netanya has some of Israel's most beautiful beaches.

Calendar

The Jewish calendar begins with the Creation, which is dated to the year 3761 BC. The calendar is based on the lunar year with 353, 354 or 355 days. It is divided into twelve months of 29 or 30 days. Over a 19-year cycle there are seven leap years in order to keep up with the solar year.

The Islamic calendar starts its first year with the flight of the prophet Mohammed from Mecca to Medina (AD 622). It is based on a purely lunar year with months of 30 or 29 days, so that there are 354 days a year. Over the course of 32 and a half years, the Islamic calendar goes through the Gregorian calendar backwards once.

Jewish calendar

 Jewish months

- Tishri (Sept / Oct)
- Cheshvan (Oct / Nov)
- Kislev (Nov / Dec)
- Tevet (Nov / Dec)
- Shvat (Dec / Jan)
- Adar (Feb / Mar)
- Nisan (Mar / April)
- Iyyar (April / May)
- Sivan (May / June)
- Tammuz (June / July)
- Av (July / Aug)
- Elul (Aug / Sept)

Children in Israel

▶ ACTIVITIES FOR CHILDREN

IN JERUSALEM

▶ **City of David**
Information/reservation:
Tel. 02 626 87 00
www.cityofdavid.org.il
The most exciting thing in Jerusalem is probably the City of David (see p. 316) and the exploration of one of the tunnels; one involves wading through water with a torch. For three-year-olds and up, there's a workshop where they can make things with pine-cones.

▶ **Biblical Zoo – The Tisch Family Zoological Gardens**
HaAron Shuluv, near Malcha Mall
Tel. 02 675 01 11,
www.jerusalemzoo.org.il
Sun–Thu 9am–5pm, Fri/before holidays 9am–2.30pm, Sat/holidays 10am–5pm
A zoo that only biologists with a good biblical knowledge could have dreamt up: everything that walks, creeps or flies and is mentioned in the Pentateuch, and, if endangered, released to its proper habitat having been successfully raised. There's a road-train through the lovingly laid-out complex, while the visitor centre is housed in a reconstruction of Noah's Ark. Children love the night-time tours of the zoo which are put on in summer.

► **Time Elevator**
37 Hillel St, Agron House
Reservation needed,
Tel. 02 624 83 81
www.time-elevator-jerusalem.co.il
Sun–Thu 10am–6pm, Fri
10am–2pm
»Edutainment« is how the operators describe this virtual trip on
the Time Elevator. It takes place in
a cinema auditorium of the sort
familiar from Disneyland. From
the comfort of your chair, you can
watch the temples being built and
destroyed, and experience the birth
of Christianity. The seats shake, it
creaks and roars at all ends of the
hall in the interests of authenticity,
and water is splashed around too.
To accompany the Babylonian
Captivity, there's the Slaves' Chorus
from *Nabucco*. Empress Helena
parades along the Via Dolorosa to
the strains of Mozart's Requiem.
Chaim Topol, the famous »Fiddler
on the Roof«, is the lead player in
this cinematic journey through
3000 years of Jerusalem's history.
Sound and commentary (incl.
English) on headphones.

► **Israel Museum**
Boulevard Rupin
Tel. 02 2 670 88 11
www.imjnet.org.il
Children can take an active interest in art in the Ruth Youth Wing
for Art Education. That may
sound dry, but it's fun for older
children, who might also work up
some enthusiasm for the Pop Art
section of the museum.

► **Bloomfield Science Museum**
Rupin Blvd, Hebrew University,
Givat Ram
Tel. 02 654 48 88, www.mada.org.il
Mon–Thu 10am–6pm, Fri

10am–2pm, Sat 10am–4pm, 40 NIS
What do roller-coasters in leisure
parks have to do with physics?
How does electricity work? How
can the human brain be tricked,
and what have scientists at the
Hebrew University found out
about its function? What makes
Albert Einstein so unique? But
also: what links war and peace and
stereotypes? The Science Museum
leaves no questions open. Thanks
to its interactive exhibits and
demonstrations, it is a fascinating
experience for the whole family,
worth setting aside half a day for.

► **Train Puppet Theater**
Liberty Bell Park
Tel. 02 561 85 14
www.traintheater.co.il
Internationally renowned puppet
theatre housed in a disused railway
coach in Liberty Bell Park. There
are performances in Hebrew and
English, but the language is not
really important for children.

► **Go-Karting**
Lev Talpiot Mall, 17 Haoman St.
Tel. 077 503 05 66,
www.teamkarting.co.il
Sun–Thu 10am–2am, Fri
10am–5pm, Sat from the end of
Sabbath
In the Mall, part of the underground car park has simply been
cordoned off, with tyres as crash
barriers – and there's your go-kart
track.

► **Botanical Garden**
Burla St, Givat Ram Campus of
the Hebrew University
Tel. 02 679 40 12,
www.botanic.co.il
Sat–Thu 7am–sunset, Fri
7am–3pm; tickets for Sat and

holidays must be bought in advance.

Swans swim on the lake, more than 6000 plants flourish in the gardens, many of them mentioned in the Torah and the Talmud. The Botanical Garden in the southwest of Jerusalem is a magnificent park to look at and to relax in. Particularly worth seeing are the tropical and butterfly houses. A miniature train for children makes its way through the garden hourly between 10am and 2pm.

BETWEEN JERUSALEM AND TEL AVIV

► **Mini-Israel**
Near Latrun, between Jerusalem and Tel Aviv
Tel. 08 913 00 00,
www.minisrael.co.il
Sat–Thu 10am–7pm, Fri 10am–2pm
In this park you can see 385 of the sights of Israel on 3.5ha/8.5 acres (scale 1:25); the figures are 7cm/4in tall. In addition, numerous games and karaoke events. There is a dedicated taxi service to hotels in Tel Aviv and Jerusalem.

► **Nazareth – Nazareth Village**
Tel. 04 645 60 42,
www.nazarethvillage.org
Mon–Sat 9am–5pm
This open-air museum gives an idea of life in Christ's time. The inhabitants wear the clothes usual at that time in Galilee, carpenters and weavers demonstrate how their crafts were carried out 2000 years ago, while during the season children can harvest olives.

► **Negev – Alpaca Farm**
Mitzpe Ramon
Tel. (08) 658 80 47, 658 81 04
www.alpaca.co.il
You live on a curious ranch. Children can help to feed the llamas, ride on them, and even join little tours of the moonscape of the nearby crater.

► **Eilat – Swim with Dolphins**
Dolphin Reef, Coral Beach
Tel. 08 6 30 01 00,
www.dolphinreef.co.il
On Dolphin Reef (see p. 231) you can if you like simply observe the dolphins. Children from the age of 10 who are good swimmers can also, equipped with goggles and snorkel, swim with the dolphins. Duration approx. one hour, price approx. 300 NIS.

Israel is a very good place to travel with children. There are nearly always substantial discounts for children (as well as students and pensioners) in museums. In hotels **children can usually sleep free** (or at a minimal charge) if they share a room with their parents. Given 24 hours' notice, most larger hotels will organize a babysitter. Those holidaying by the sea in Eilat, Tel Aviv or Haifa or exploring the Galilean landscape will have no trouble finding something for children to do (the Dead Sea by contrast is positively dangerous for children on account of its high salinity). The question to ask, though, is: **what sort of cultural experience have the parents planned for Jerusalem?**

Those who have planned an intensive sightseeing programme should think long and hard about whether their children will go along with all these churches, synagogues, mosques, museums, excavations, fortresses and bazaars. The younger the children, the greater the whinge-factor. Even so: all over Israel there's a lot for children to do. Here is a selection, with a concentration on Jerusalem, where it's most difficult to devise a balanced, child-friendly programme.

Electricity

The electricity grid in Israel supports 220 volts AC. Most sockets require plugs with three pins, but these are not the same as the UK standard. Adapters can be purchased in Israel.

Emergency

▶ IMPORTANT NUMBERS

EMERGENCY NUMBERS IN ISRAEL

▶ **Police**
Tel. 100

▶ **Emergency Doctor**
Tel. 101

▶ **Fire Brigade**
Tel. 102

INTERNATIONAL AIR AMBULANCE SERVICES

▶ **Cega Air Ambulance (world-wide service)**
Tel. +44(0)1243 621097
Fax +44(0)1243 773169
www.cega-aviation.co.uk

▶ **US Air Ambulance**
Tel. 800/948-1214 (US; toll-free)
Tel. 001-941-926-2490 (international; collect)
www.usairambulance.net

Etiquette and Customs

Behavioural tips
On the Sabbath ▶

It is particularly important to pay attention to pay attention to the country's customs on the Sabbath and on major holidays. This includes not smoking. At the Western Wall in Jerusalem, one of the most sacred Jewish sites, it is not permitted to take photographs on this day. The ultra-orthodox quarter of Mea Shearim is not a place to visit on the Sabbath.

Churches, synagogues and mosques should only ever be visited in appropriate clothes (not in shorts, short sleeves, short or low-cut dresses) and not during services. Devout Jews cover their heads in the synagogue and tourists should do the same. Shoes have to be taken off before entering a synagogue and women should cover their hair and shoulders.

◀ Visiting sacred sites

Taking pictures and filming at important military facilities (includes airports, stations, bridges and border crossings) is prohibited. Even though Israelis are not generally shy of having their picture taken, it is best to ask before taking a close-up of someone. This is particularly true for the ultra-orthodox neighbourhoods such as Mea Shearim in Jerusalem, but also in the Arabic locations. A telephoto lens might help those intent on capturing an image.

Taking pictures and filming

Festivals, Holidays and Events

To understand the Israeli and Palestinian holiday calendar is a science in itself, but one that the traveller needs to master in order to plan journeys in a region where religion plays a large role. Jewish, Christian and Muslim holidays affect everyday life more than almost anywhere else. True, on Yom Kippur, when all of Israel is in mourning and everyone stays at home, you can go rollerblading down the motorways, and some people do. However, in your ignorance you may find you get stuck somewhere without the slightest chance of getting away. And Yom Kippur is just one holiday among many.

Confusing

On other holidays it may be that the whole country is out and about, and every flight and hotel room is sold out. The matter becomes totally complicated because the Christian denominations celebrate their major festivals according to their own different church calendars, while the Jewish and Muslim festivals follow the lunar calendar and fall each year on a different day of the Gregorian calendar.

And talking of calendars: even the years are different. 2014/15 of the Gregorian calendar is the Jewish year 5775, and 1436/37 in the Islamic calendar. Luckily everyday life is dominated by our familiar Gregorian calendar, but remember the Sabbath.

Calendars

The Sabbath (Saturday) is a weekly **Jewish holiday and national day of rest**. Most Jewish shops, museums, institutions and businesses, as well as many restaurants, close not only on the Sabbath but from Friday afternoon onwards, and there is no public transport. According to Jewish beliefs, the day and therefore **the holiday begins with the**

Sabbath

evening, and ends with sunset the following evening. The justification for this comes from Genesis 1:5: »And the evening and the morning were the first day.«

▶ HOLIDAY CALENDAR

NON-RELIGIOUS HOLIDAYS

Holocaust Remembrance Day (Yom Hashoah) on 27 Nissanal (March/April)
Remembrance of the Fallen (Yom Hazikaron) on 4 Iyar (April/May)
Independence Day (Yom Ha'atzmauth) on 5 Iyar (April/May)

JEWISH HOLIDAYS

▶ **Rosh Hashanah**
New Year on 1/2 Tishri (September) is also the first of ten days of fasting with which the year begins. During these days people blow on the shofar, a ram's horn, and wear wide gowns as a symbol of the transience of humans and faith in God. The Tashlikh ceremony, in which sins are symbolically thrown into the water, takes place at the Pool of Siloam.

▶ **Yom Kippur**
The most solemn holiday in the Jewish calendar is at the end of Rosh Hashanah on 10 Tishri: the day of atonement and reconciliation between God and man.

▶ **Sukkot and Simchat Torah**
15 days after the New Year's celebrations, on 15 Tishrei (Sept/Oct), Sukkot, or the Feast of Tabernacles, is celebrated for eight days. During this time, huts are set up in gardens, courtyards and on balconies to commemorate the fact that the Israelites had to live in such basic huts during their exodus from Egypt. Meals are then eaten in these huts. The orthodox also sleep in them. The festival ends with the »rejoicing of the Torah« (Simchat Torah), where the Torah is carried around in processions.

▶ **Hanukkah**
The Festival of Lights is observed on 25 Kislev (Dec). Hannukah means rededication, meaning that of the Second Temple, after it had been re-taken in 165 BC during the Maccabean revolt. When the people wanted to light the menorah, they only found a small amount of oil and yet the candelabra burned for eight days. As a result Hannukah is an eight-day festival; every day a new candle is lit on the nine-branched Hanukkah candelabra.

▶ **Purim**
Purim, meaning »lots« (14 Adar, February/March) is the most joyous of the Jewish holidays. It is based on the deliverance of the Persian Jews from an attack by vizier Haman, as described in the Book of Esther. Esther, the Jewish wife of the Persian ruler Xerxes I, revealed that she too was Jewish, thereby preventing the planned persecution of the Jews. The festival is celebrated with colourful processions, while children dress up. There is dancing, singing and gift giving.

During Sukkot pious Jews commemorate the exodus from Egypt.

▶ **Passover**

Passover (Pesach), one of the most important feasts in the Jewish calendar, is celebrated in the month of Nisan (March/April) to commemorate the exodus of the Israelites from Egypt and their liberation from oppression – Pesach means »leaving out, sparing«. During the seven-day holiday unleavened bread is eaten and there must not be any leavened foodstuffs anywhere in the home.

▶ **Shavuot**

The festival of Shavuot, which is also the harvest festival, marks the end of the 50 days of mourning after Passover.

CHRISTIAN HOLIDAYS

Christian shops are closed on Sundays.

New Year's Day (Western churches: 1 Jan; Eastern churches: 14 Jan),
Epiphany (6 Jan)
Palm Sunday/Good Friday/Easter
Ascension Day
Whitsun
Christmas (Western churches: 24/25 Dec; Eastern churches: 7 Jan)

MUSLIM HOLIDAYS

Muslim shops close on Fridays.
Ramadan: month of fasting,
2013: July 9–Aug 7,
2014: June 28–July 27
Id el-Fitr: the last three days of Ramadan (Oct/Nov)
Eid al-Adha: Festival of Sacrifice during the month of pilgrimage to Mecca (Dec/Jan)
Ras as-Sanah al-Hijriyah: New Year

Events and Festivals

Israel's event calendar is full throughout the year and across the country. The programme ranges from spectacular events such as the Gay Pride parades in Jerusalem and (even bigger and more spectacular) in Tel Aviv, all the way to concert evenings and fashion shows in the amphitheatre in Caesarea. There are marathons both in Jerusalem (March) and Tel Aviv (March/April). Information can be obtained from the magazine *Time Out* (print and online editions) or the Israel Tourist Office (see p. 128)

Concerts   The country's most famous orchestra is the **Israel Philharmonic Orchestra**, which is based in the Frederic R. Mann Auditorium in Tel Aviv (tickets from tel. 03/621 17 77; www.ipo.co.il). Classical music concerts are also given by the orchestras of Haifa, Ramat Gan and Beersheba as well as by the Israel Chamber Orchestra. Tel Aviv is the best recommendation for all current music trends.

The Israel Festival (May to the end of June/beginning of July, www.israel-festival.org.il) provides a stage for newcomers and established artists in the fields of dance, jazz, world music and classical music.

Opera   The stage of the Jerusalem Masada Dead Sea Opera Festival at the foot of Masada Fortress is often referred to as the world's »lowest-lying« opera venue (June, www.opera-masada.com). The programme comprises popular works such as *Aida*, *Nabucco* and *Carmen* performed by Israeli Opera Tel Aviv, and also gala concerts by Andrea Bocelli.

Theatre   The best-known theatres play in Jerusalem and Tel Aviv. One top address in Jerusalem is the **Khan Theatre** (Remez St.), while in Tel Aviv theatre lovers tend to go to Israel's national theatre, **Habimah**, (Habimah Square) or the Cameri Theatre (Dizengoff St., www.cameri.co.il). These theatres also put on performances with live translations into English. The International Puppet Festival (August, www.traintheater.org.il, see p. 114) in Jerusalem is devoted to an almost forgotten art. Puppet theatres from all over the world come here to perform.

Art fair   Contemporary Israeli art is on the up, and is slowly conquering Europe too. The best overview is provided by the art fair Fresh Paint (www.freshpaint.co.il), started in 2008 and held every summer since.

Ballet   Tel Aviv has an interesting ballet and dance scene. Classical ballet is performed by the **Israel Ballet**, while modern ballet, dance theatre and other modern dance performances can be seen in the **Bat Dor Theatre** (Ibn Gvirol St.) and especially in the **Suzanna Dellal Centre for Dance and Theatre** in the district of Neve Tzedek (6, Yechiely St., tel. 02/510 56 56, www.suzannedellal.org.il).

Jewish humour is well-known; Jewish comedians hardly know any taboos. In Off the Wall (34 King George St, tel. 050 875 56 88, www.israelcomedy.com), Jerusalem's first comedy club, stand-up comics (immigrants from Britain or America) give regular shows in English. For all their Zionist enthusiasm, they make fun of Israel as it actually is: the orthodox community, bureaucracy, rude compatriots, sexism. The founder of Off the Wall was the comedian David Kilimnick, himself the son of a rabbi, who immigrated in 2003 (www.davidkilimnick.com).

Jewish comedy

At the Jerusalem Book Fair (February, every two years: 2013, 2015, www.jerusalembookfair.com) in the Jerusalem International Conference Center, more than 800 publishers from all over the world display their wares. The fair is boycotted by the Arab states.

Book fair

The acclaimed Jerusalem Film Festival (July, www.jff.org.il) presents shorts, avant-garde, retrospectives, animations and documentaries. A prominent place is traditionally given to films dealing with human rights and peace in the Middle East. The Cinematheque in Tel Aviv is responsible for the programme of a top-class festival of documentaries, the Tel Aviv International Documentary Festival (www.docaviv.co.il).

Film festivals

▶ HOLIDAYS AND EVENTS CALENDAR

EVENT TIPS

Magazines and internet: *Helloisrael* (www.helloisrael.net), *Time Out Jerusalem, Time Out Tel Aviv, This Week in Palestine* (www.thisweekinpalestine.com), the Friday edition of the *Jerusalem Post*, and *International Herald Tribune* with an English-language Haaretz supplement.

MARCH/APRIL

▶ **Akko**
Concerts for Passover in the crusader fort

▶ **Ein Gev**
Passover is celebrated in a particularly elaborate manner here with music, dance and entertainment.

▶ **Jerusalem**
Good Friday procession along Via Dolorosa. Magnificent procession from the village of Bethphage on the Mount of Olives to the Church of the Holy Sepulchre on Palm Sunday. Easter is celebrated separately by the Christian denominations. The most spectacular celebrations are held by the Armenian and the Greek Orthodox churches, with the »appearance of the holy fire« in the Church of the Holy Sepulchre. There is also a marathon through Jerusalem and around the Old Town.

IN MAY/JUNE

▶ **Throughout the country**
The three-week Israel Festival is the cultural highlight of the year. Jerusalem in particular has a lot

going on, hosting concerts, plays, and ballet performances and seeing international participation.

▶ **Jerusalem**
International Film Festival, held in the Cinemathèque

▶ **Tel Aviv**
DOCAVIV, international documentary film festival

MAY AND DECEMBER

▶ **Tiberias**
The Jacob's Ladder Festival in Tiberias (www.jlfestival.com) has been an institution since 1967, when it began with the Folk Club set up by an immigrant couple. Today fans of bluegrass, country, Irish music, rock and blues flock to the spring festival, which lasts several days, and to the weekend festival in December for concerts in the kibbutz Ginosar Inn Hotel, north of Tiberias. Tickets tel. 04 685 04 03

JULY

▶ **Tiberias**
Festival with music, dance and theatre in the old quarter and on the water

JULY/AUGUST

▶ **Eilat**
Musicians from all around the world come together for the jazz festival (www.redseajazzeilat.com).

SEPTEMBER/ OCTOBER

▶ **Abu Ghosh**
Festival of vocal music in the crusader church

▶ **Jerusalem**
Tens of thousands come for Sukkot, to take part in this colourful festival with street parades and picnics in parks.

DECEMBER

▶ **Sea of Galilee**
Tiberias Marathon along the Sea of Galilee

DECEMBER/JANUARY

▶ **Jerusalem and Bethlehem**
Christmas: Jerusalem does not have much of a Christmas atmosphere. Believers go to midnight mass in the Church of the Nativity in Bethlehem on Christmas Eve; the mass held there is broadcast on Manger Square.

Food and Drink

Culinary treats from around the world

The cuisine is like the country: multicultural through and through. Immigrants from the Middle East, North Africa, central and eastern Europe, Asia, South America and elsewhere have imported delicacies from all over the world. Israel's gastronomy unites nouvelle cuisine, Californian new wave and fusion.

Israelis eat hearty breakfasts, and serve them to hotel guests too. The buffet groans under the weight of eggs, cheese, yoghurt, fresh salads, olives, fish salads, marinated and smoked fish. What you won't find is sausage of any description: this is due to the regulations of kosher cuisine. The Jewish religious authorities also discourage cooked breakfasts on the Sabbath.

For **lunch and dinner**, there is a huge choice: couscous, moussaka, kebabs (with lamb), »**gefilte fish«** **(fish rissoles of pike or carp)**, spicy Ethiopian chicken ragout. At every street corner there's someone selling shawerma, a kind of grilled lamb or chicken in pitta bread: you can choose the side-dishes (cole slaw, hummus, peperoni, onions, spicy sauces etc.) from a buffet counter. Another tasty snack available at every street corner is falafel, deep-fried vegetarian rissoles. Israeli and Arab cuisine are similar in numerous respects: **the popularity of hummus, chick-pea soup and falafel knows no bounds**.

Price categories

- Expensive: more than 135 NIS
- Moderate: 65–135 NIS
- Inexpensive: less than 65 NIS

For one main course

Supper is the largest and most important meal of the day among *Supper* Arabs. For starters (mezze) thick sauces are served into which you dunk your flatbread; tehina (tahini) is a tasty and filling sesame cream. Aubergines are fried in oil and puréed as babaghanough, accompanied by labnah, a spicy yoghurt salad. The main dishes are less imaginative. Chicken, lamb, beef and fish are served grilled, accompanied by rice with raisins and nuts or saffron.

Desserts are not for slimmers: **honey-sweet bakhlava, or kanafa, a** *Desserts* **pastry with cheese and honey**, or halvah, a sesame confection, and mutabak, a light flaky pastry stuffed with cheese and served with syrup. The meal is rounded off with tea, preferably flavoured with mint, or Turkish coffee. A hookah can be smoked at the same time: tobacco flavoured with mint, apple, strawberry, or other fruits is available. Alcohol can be obtained throughout the country, and in parts of the Palestinian territories too. The two most popular beers in Israel are Goldstar and Maccabee, but the Palestinian Taybeh beer (www.taybehbeer.com), developed by Bavarian brewers, tastes better.

Israel produces some very good wines.The region's viticulture started *Alcohol* in 1870 with financial assistance from Baron Edmond de Rothschild. ◄ *Wine* The entire growing region of around 3000ha/7400 acres is distributed across **five recognized regions**: Galilee in northern Israel (including the Golan Heights), Samaria (upper central Israel, including the Carmel mountains), Samson (Judaean lowlands to the coast), Judaean Hills and the Negev. Grapes grown here include Carignan, Grenache, Semillon and Muscat, and, especially in the cooler regions of Galilee, Cabernet Sauvignon, Merlot, Sauvignon Blanc, Riesling and Chardonnay. The largest and oldest vineyard is the co-operative of Richon LeZion and Zikhron Ya'akov, which supply 60% of the domestic market.

An ultra-orthodox Jew in Jerusalem's Mea Shearim quarter checks meticulously whether all the cooking equipment was cleaned correctly.

EVERYTHING KOSHER?

For visitors in Israel there is no avoiding kosher food. More and more restaurants display the kosher seal. This becomes particularly clear during the week of the Passover festival, when the entire country, with the exception of the Arab areas, consumes nothing but unleavened bread, matzah.

Matzot commemorate the flight from Egypt, when there was no time to leaven the dough. The writer Ephraim Kishon once characterized matzot as follows: »If anyone has ever tried living off cardboard for eight days straight, he will understand why we care to eat only leavened bread for the rest of the year.«

Dietary rules from the Bible

Kosher cuisine is based on the dietary laws of the Bible, which can be found in the Torah and in their interpretation in the Talmud. It says, for example, that only mammals that are both ruminants and even-toed ungulates may be eaten, which means camels, hares, pigs and horses are not allowed. The same section also states that the only permitted marine animals are those that have both fins and scales, which excludes crustaceans and molluscs: so no mussels, shrimps, lobsters or crayfish.

Mammals have to be butchered in a specific way, to ensure that all the blood drains from the carcass. The chef is also expected to treat the meat to make thoroughly sure that all remaining blood is gone, because the consumption of blood, which is considered part of the soul, is strictly prohibited.

Meat and milk

The most difficult biblical commandment to observe in the home is the one that says: »Thou shalt not seethe a kid in his mother's milk« (Exodus

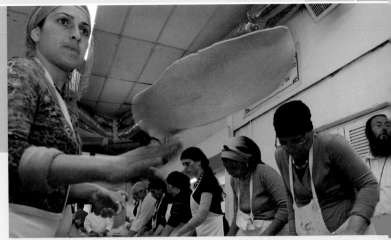

Women make unleavened bread for Passover. A rabbi makes sure all the rules are adhered to. The women have to wash their hands every 15 minutes.

23:19). This sentence could be a matter of interpretation, but the rabbis settled on the strict interpretation that dairy products must not come into contact with meat. This holds not only for the stomach but also for the plate, the fridge, the sink and the shopping bag. A kosher household and every kosher restaurant therefore has to have two of everything as well as separate storage facilities: there are two sets of plates and cutlery, two sets of pots and bowls, and separate compartments in fridges and sinks.

Coffee without milk

Many dishes and drinks familiar to Europeans are absent from the traditional Jewish menu: meat with cream sauce or covered in cheese, cheese after meat dishes, desserts containing cream after eating meat, or milk in coffee. Since tourist hotels often serve meat dishes in the evening, breakfast is a good time to enjoy milk-based treats. Most restaurants in Israel are kosher. That's not a legal requirement and it does not say anything about the quality of the food, but it has been recognized that many Israelis stick to the dietary laws. Family celebrations generally only take place in kosher restaurants; it is legally required that public facilities such as office canteens, schools and prisons prepare kosher food. This law was pushed through by orthodox parties who never had the majority, but who were often necessary to give the government in power the majority.

Passover

Some highly imaginative dishes are served during Passover, such as tasty versions of lasagne where matzah replaces the pasta, or cake made of grated matzah. According to the interpretation in the Talmud, the bread is only unleavened when no more than 18 minutes pass between the mixing of the water with the flour and the end of the baking process. That is why shelves with products made of flour such as pasta, cake and biscuits are covered up during the Passover week.

His pride and joy: a red wine from the Carmel mountains.

Restaurants and cafés
While most Israeli hotel kitchen prepare kosher food, there are many restaurants that do not follow Jewish dietary laws, particularly in cities with many foreign visitors.

Restaurant opening times ▶
Most restaurants are open around lunchtime and during the evening hours and often close at around 11pm or midnight. However, it can be a bit more tricky on a Friday evening or Saturday to find an open restaurant, because most close for the Sabbath. But don't worry: there will always be some bars and restaurants open, even in Jerusalem.

Business lunch ▶
Many restaurants, especially in the higher price categories, offer a business lunch, at which complete menus are served at considerably lower prices than in the evening. For many restaurants this is a main selling point, while others simply indicate it with signs in Hebrew: if in doubt, ask.

TYPICAL DISHES

Baklava	Sweet pastry with honey and nuts. Served as a dessert or at street stalls, particularly in Arab towns and in the Old Town of Jerusalem.
Blintzes	Pancake with a sweet curd-cheese mixture
Bourekas	Pastry filled with either cheese, potatoes or spinach
Challah	Traditional braided bread eaten on the Sabbath

Something for those with a sweet tooth: baklava

Falafel	Deep-fried dumplings made of ground chickpeas and spices. They are an ideal snack and are served by many street stalls in round flat breads with salad.
Gefilte fish	A typical Jewish dish, consisting of ground fish, mixed with onions, matzo flour, eggs and spices, which is then (if done in the proper fashion) shaped into the form of a fish. It is all boiled in fish stock or baked or fried.
Gilderne joch	Chicken soup, traditionally eaten on the Sabbath
Hamantashes	Small triangular pastry filled with a walnut, poppy or apple mix (other variants possible)
Holishkes	Minced beef in cabbage leaves, cooked in a sweet and sour sauce. Traditionally eaten at Sukkot.
Hummus	Pureed chickpeas seasoned with garlic, oil and lemon juice. Often served with pita bread.
Kebab	Well-seasoned beef or mutton mince, made into meatballs and grilled or fried on a skewer.
Kanafeh	Pastry with syrup, almonds, pistachios and walnuts
Knishes	Dough filled with potatoes, onions and meat
Latkes	Potato pancakes. Often served with cinnamon sugar, apple sauce and/or sour cream. Traditionally eaten at Hanukkah.
Mahallebi	Rice pudding with rose oil, sugar and nuts

Matzot	Unleavened bread
Of sum-sum	chicken covered in sesame seeds and fried in oil
Pita	Round, flat bread made of wheat, water, yeast and salt
Seniya	Beef or lamb with tahini
Shawerma	Meat from a spit, similar to a doner kebab
Tahini	Sesame seeds pureed with oil, lemon juice and garlic
Cholent	Stew made of beans, potatoes and fatty meat. It is eaten on the Sabbath and prepared on Friday.

Health

Medical care Adequate medical care is available throughout the country. Almost all doctors can speak at least one foreign language. Common drugs are available everywhere, but it is best to stock up on specialist drugs before going.

▶ MEDICAL EMERGENCIES

► **Magen David Adom**
(Red David Star)
Tel. 101 (24 St.)

► **Dental/
Medical emergency service**
Medical Center Tel Aviv
18 Reines St.
Tel. (03) 527 00 20 (24 hours)

Information

▶ INFORMATION ADDRESSES

IN CANADA

► **Israeli Government
Tourist Office**
1800 Bloor Street West, Suite 700
Toronto, ON M5S 2V6
Tel. (416) 964 37 84
www.goisrael.ca

IN THE UNITED KINGDOM

► **Israeli Government
Tourist Office**
80 Oxford Street.
London, W1D 1NN
Tel. (0207) 299 11 00 80
www.thinkisrael.com

IN THE USA

▶ **Israeli Government Tourism Office**
800 Second Avenue
New York, NY 10017
Tel. (212) 499 56 50
www.thinkisrael.com

IN ISRAEL

Local tourist information offices:
▶ »Sightseeing from A to Z«

DIPLOMATIC REPRESENTATION

▶ **Israeli Embassies and Consulates**
Israel Consulate in Canada
180 Bloor Street West, Suite 700
M5S 2V6 Toronto
Tel. (416) 640 85 00
www.embassyofisrael.ca

Israeli Embassy in Ireland
Carrisbrook House
122 Pembroke Road
Ballsbridge Dublin 4
Tel. (01) 230 94 00
http://dublin.mfa.gov.il

Consulate of Israel in UK
15a Old Court Place
London W8 4PL
Tel. (020) 79 57 95 00
www.embassyofisrael.co.uk

In the United States
Israel Consulate General
800 Second Ave.
New York NY 10017
Tel. (212) 499 50 00
www.israelfm.org

▶ **Embassies and Consulates in Israel**
Canadian Embassy
3/5 Nirim Street
Tel Aviv 67060
Tel. (03) 636 33 00
E-mail: taviv@international.gc.ca

▶ **Embassy of the Republic of Ireland**
Rehov Daniel Frisch, 3
Tel Aviv
Tel. (03) 50 696 41 66
E-mail: telaviv@iveagh.irlgov.ie

▶ **British Consulate-General**
19 Nashashibi Street
Sheikh Jarrah Quarter
East Jerusalem 97200
Tel. (02) 541 41 00
http://ukinjerusalem.fco.gov.uk

▶ **US Consulate General**
18 Agron Road
Jerusalem 94190
Tel. (2) 622 72 30
http://jerusalem.usconsulate.gov

INTERNET ADDRESSES

All the following websites are in English.

▶ **www.infotour.co.il**
Very informative website with lots of further information, especially about practical travel issues and about attractions

▶ **www.timeout.com**
Up-to-date tips on leisure, shopping, culture, restaurants, bars etc. can be found in *Time Out Israel*; the monthly free sheet can be picked up at airports etc.

▶ **www.inisrael.co.il**
Relatively well suited as a source of information to plan a trip, especially to find out about the current hotel situation

▶ **www.visit-palestine.com**
Website of the Palestinian ministry of tourism, with information on accommodation, travel and sightseeing.

▶ **www.alternativenews.org**
Alternative Information Centre (AIC). Politically and socially committed website of the non-governmental organization that works for Palestinian-Israeli understanding

▶ **www.thisweekinpalestine.com**
An overview of events in the Palestinian Territories

▶ **www.bibleplaces.com**
In-depth overview of the biblical sites in Israel and Palestine

▶ **www.imjnet.org.il**
The English-language version of the website of the Israel Museum in Jerusalem introduces all of the country's significant museums. One great feature are the virtual tours through the Shrine of the Book and through the model of Jerusalem during the time of the Second Temple.

Language

Communication   The official languages are Modern Hebrew (Ivrit) and Arabic, both of which are Semitic languages. However, it is possible to communicate in almost all European languages, especially English, French and German. English is the business language.

Ivrit   Ivrit is based on the Hebrew of the Old Testament but deviates from it significantly. The Hebrew alphabet has 23 letters. Since the words are formed from a more or less rigid consonant framework, while the vowels can vary, writing was limited at first to the consonants, which embody the general sense of the words. In later development the vowels were indicated by vowel symbols that are written below the consonants they follow when spoken. Their phonetic value varies. Every consonant has a corresponding numerical value, which has played a big role in Kabbala numerology.

Script   Like Arabic, Hebrew is written from right to left. Because of the tendency to fit all symbols into imaginary squares, it is also known as »square script«.

Arabic   Modern Arabic has developed from the language spoken in northern Arabia in Antiquity. Together with Islam it spread across large parts of the southern and eastern Mediterranean. In Arabic, long vowels are denoted by the signs alif, waw and ya, while short vowels are either left out or marked by special symbols above or below the consonant. The pronunciation of the short vowels changes significantly depending on the consonants on either side, and on the level of education of the speaker.

LANGUAGE GUIDE

Greeting

English	*Hebrew*	*Arabic*
Good morning	Bóker tov	Sabach el-cher
Good day	Shalóm	Es-salamu'alekum
Good evening	…Érev tov	Misa el-cher
Goodbye	Lehitraót	Ma'as-salama

At a glance

I can't understand you	Ani lo mevín/a	A'na mish fahmak
Excuse me	Slach li	A'sif
Yes/No	Ken/Lo	Aiwa/La
Please	Bevakashá·	Min fadlak
Thank you	Toda·	Shukran
Yesterday	Etmól	Embarich
Today	Hajóm	En-nahar-da
Tomorrow	Machar	Bukra
What time is it?	Ma hasha'a·?	Es-sa'a kam?
When is … open?	Matái potchím …?	I'mta jiftach …?
When is closing time?	Matái sogrim …?	I'mta jiqifil …?
I would like …	Ani mevakesh/et…	Urid …

While travelling

Departure	Jeziá·	Safar
Arrival	Bi·	Wusul
Bus	Otobás	Otobis
Station	Tachanát harakévet	Macha'tta
Train	Rakévet	Qatr
Airport	Sde teufá·	Mata'r
Taxi	Monít, táksi	Taxi
Toilet	Beit kise	Mir'chad
Post office	Beit dóar	Ma'ktab beri'd
Hotel	Malón	Funduq
Single	Chéder bishvil ben	Ghurfa bisirir
Room	adám echád	wachid
Double room	Chéder kafúl	Ghurfa bisiririn
Restaurant	Mis'ada	Mat'am
Town	Ir	Balad
Square	Kikar	Sahat
Road	Derech, rehov	Shari'
Castle	Metsuda(t)	Qasr, qalaat
Tower	Migdal	Burj
Tomb	Kever	Kaber

Alphabet

Hebrew Alphabet

Letter	Name	Pronunciation (Iwrit)	Num. value
א	Alef	standard vowel	1
ב	Bet	b, v	2
ג	Gimel	g	3
ד	Dalet	d	4
ה	He	h	5
ו	Waw	v	6
ז	Sajin	z	7
ח	Chet	ch (as in Scots »loch«)	8
ט	Tet	t	9
י	Jod	y (as in »yes«)	10
כ	Kaf	k, ch	20
ל	Lamed	l	30
מ	Mem	m	40
נ	Nun	n	50
ס	Samech	s	60
ע	Ajin	glottal stop	70
פ	Pe	p	80
צ	Zade	ts	90
ק	Kof	k, q	100
ר	Resch	r	200
ש	Sin	s	300
ש	Schin	sh	
ת	Taw	t	400

Arabic Alphabet

Letter	Name	Pronunciation
ا	Alif	standard vowel
ب	Ba	b
ت	Ta	t
ث	Tha	th (as in »thing«)
ج	Dschim	j
ح	Ha	h (strongly aspirated)
خ	Cha	ch (as in Scots »loch«)
د	Dal	d
ذ	Dhal	th (as in »the«)
ر	Ra	r (rolled)
ز	Saj	z
س	Sin	s
ش	Schin	sh
ص	Sad	s (emphatic)
ض	Dad	d (emphatic)
ط	Ta	t (emphatic)
ظ	Za	ts (emphatic)
ع	Ain	glottal stop
غ	Ghain	gh, r (velar fricative)
ف	Fa	F
ق	Kaf	k, q (velar)
ك	Kaf	k (palatal)
ل	Lam	l
م	Mim	m
ن	Nun	n
ه	Ha	h (never silent)
و	Waw	w
ى	Ja	y (as in »yes«)

Vowel sign	Name	Transliteration
◌ַ	Patach	a
◌ָ	Kametz	ạ
◌ָ	Kametz Chatuf	ọ
◌ֶ	Segol	ẹ
◌ֵ	Sere	e
◌ִ	Chirek	i
◌ֹ	Cholem	o
◌ֻ	Kibutz	u
◌ֲ	Chatef Patach	ả
◌ֱ	Chatef Segol	ẻ
◌ֳ	Chatef Kametz	ỏ
◌ְ	Schwa (indefinite vowel, as -er in »other«)	ẻ

©Baedeker

Most letters of the Arabic alphabet have four different forms, depending on whether they stand alone, are joined with the following letter, or the preceding one, or with both.

Bridge	Gesher	Jissr
Mountain	Har	Jebel
River	Nahar	Nahr
Sea	Yam	Bahr
Valley	Emeq	Wadi
Market	Shuk	Souk

Food and Drink

Water	Majim	Majja
Tea	Te	Schaj
Coffee	Kaffe	Ahwa
Milk	Chalav	Laban
Fruit juice	Miz	Asir
Bread	Lechem	Esh
Eggs	Bejza	Bed
Meat	Bassar	Lahm
Fish	Dag	Samak
English	*Hebrew*	*Arabic*
Vegetables	Jerakot	Chudar
Breakfast	Aruchat boqer	Fitar

Illness

Pharmacy	Beit merkáchad	Agsacha'ne
Doctor	Rofé klali	Tabib
Dentist	Rofé shinájim	Tabib asna'n

Numbers

zero	effes	sifr
one	echád, achát	wachid, wachda
two	shnájim, shtájim	itnen
three	shloshá, shalósh	talata
four	arba'á, arbá·	arba'a
five	chamish·, chamésh	chamsa
six	shishá, shesh	sitta
seven	shivá, shéva	sab'a
eight	shmoná, shmoné	tamanja
nine	tishá, tésha	tis'a
ten	asará, éser	ashara
a half	hachézi	nuss
a third	shlish	tult
a quarter	réva	rub
a tenth	asirít	'oshr

Literature

Literature

Novels and essays

James A. Michener: *The Source.*
Historical novel, a global success since its publication, and a classic. A team of archaeologists excavates a tell in Galilee in 1964. Using the settlement layers as a timeline, the entire cultural and religious history of Israel is vividly recounted.

Leon Uris: *Exodus.* Corgi, 1970
A bestselling novel, translated into many different languages, about the fate of the persecuted Jews and the »birth of a nation«, i.e. the founding of the state of Israel.

Israeli authors

SY Agnon: *Only Yesterday,* Princeton 2002, first published in 1945. By a founding father of modern Israeli literature, a major work about Zionist immigration in the late 19th century by Israel's only winner of the Nobel Prize for Literature.

Batya Gur: *The Saturday Morning Murder,* HarperPerennial, 1993
An exciting crime fiction novel in Jerusalem's psychoanalytical milieu.

Amos Oz: *My Michael.* Vintage Classics 2011
Novel about the fate of a young woman set in the political and social changes that took place in Israel in the 1950s and 1960s.

Meer Shalev: *The Blue Mountain,* Canongate 2002. A novel about life on a kibbutz in days of early Zionist settlers.

A.B. Yehoshua: *The Lover,* Halban Publishers 2004.
The storyline, of a man who searches for his wife's lover in the aftermath of the Yom Kippur War, is the background for an exploration of social, religious and ethnic tensions in Israeli society.

Palestinian authors and subjects

Mahmoud Darwish: *Unfortunately, It Was Paradise: Selected Poems,* University of California 2003. By giving his people a literary voice, the Palestinian poet Darwish has become a popular figure.

Elias Khoury: *Gate of the Sun,* Vintage 2006
Set in the Galilee Hospital in Shatila refugee camp in Beirut. Khalil tells his sick, comatose friend Yunus, a former resistance fighter, his own story and therefore the story of the Palestinians since 1948.

Matt Beynon Rees: *The Collaborator of Bethlehem/A Grave in Gaza.* Mariner, 2008
The crime fiction novels by Welsh author Matt Rees have as their central character the Palestinian history teacher and reluctant sleuth

Omar Yussef and depict Palestinian reality as a mixture of hopelessness, violence and corruption.

Thomas Asbridge: *The Crusades: The War for the Holy Land*, Simon and Schuster 2012.
The book to accompany the author's BBC documentary series. Lucid and easy to read, but based on solid scholarship, and marked by an ability to tell the story from both the Christian and the Muslim point of view.

History of the region

Daniel Hillel: *The Natural History of the Bible*, Columbia 2007.
The influence of the natural world of the Holy Land on the events and people of the Bible.

Amin Maalouf: *The Crusades Through Arab Eyes*, Saaqi Books, 1984.
An alternative view by the Lebanon-born French novelist, retelling the story of the crusades on the basis of Arab historical sources.

Simon Sebag Montefiore: *Jerusalem: The Biography*, Phoenix 2012.
Erudite and entertaining, a vivid account that is worthy of its exciting and moving subject-matter.

Father Jerome Murphy O'Connor: *The Holy Land*, Oxford Archaeological Guides 2008.
A thorough scholarly survey of the archaeology of the region by a professor who teaches at the Ecole Biblique in Jerusalem.

Steven Runciman: *History of the Crusades*, first published in the 1950s, still available in various editions e.g. Peregrine Books, Folio Society.
A three-volume classic of history writing, highly readable and informative but somewhat dated.

David Ben Gurion: *Israel, A Personal History*, New English Library, 1972
Memoirs of the first prime minister of Israel.

Non-fiction books about politics and society

Matthew Levitt: *Hamas: Politics, Charity and Terrorism in the service of Jihad*, Yale 2006.
A highly critical analysis of Hamas from its beginnings as terrorist group to its current status.

Edward W. Said: *Out of Place: A Memoir*, Granta Books, 2000.
The work of Said, a leading post-war intellectual of international ranking, who came from a dispossessed Palestinian family and died in 2003, was eminent as a literary theorist, especially as the author of the controversial work *Orientalism*, but his writings span the fields of music and philosophy.

Tom Segev: *One Palestine, Complete: Jews and Arabs Under the British Mandate*, Abacus 2001
A detailed and thoughtful account by a leading Israeli journalist and historian of a subject which is far from being history as it still ignites heated debate.

Zeev Sternhell: *The Founding Myths of Israel*, Princeton University Press 1999
The author, a political scientist, undertakes a controversial and fascinating examination of the accounts of the founding fathers of Israel and the versions of Israeli history offered by Zionists.

Media

Radio and TV

Israel's media have been under greater pressure since the Netanyahu government took office, especially since the premier himself has often been the subject of reports concerning corruption. The Knesset passed a law allowing anyone who regarded himself as having been insulted by the media to demand approx. 300,000 NIS in damages without having to prove anything. The intention was to nip critical reporting in the bud. Almost all television programmes are broadcast exclusively in modern Hebrew and Arabic, but many feature films are shown in their original language with subtitles. Hotels generally have televisions in the rooms as standard, so that guests can at least receive an English-language news station (BBC or CNN) as well as satellite programmes.

Newspapers

All daily newspapers in Israel are published in Tel Aviv or Jerusalem. The papers with the highest circulation are the Hebrew *Yediot Acharonot* and *Ma'ariv* (conservative), the Hebrew and English *Ha'aretz* (more left of the centre) and the English *Jerusalem Post* (more to the right), one of the country's most respected newspapers. The latter two also publish very good online editions (www.haaretz.com; www.jpost.com). The *International Herald Tribune* produces an English-language supplement for *Ha'aretz*. In addition there are newspapers in Arabic and almost every European language as well as several daily newspapers in Russian. European dailies and magazines are generally available one day after their publication date but they tend to be relatively expensive.

Money

Currency

The currency is the Israeli New Shekel (NIS), which is divided into 100 agorot (singular: agora). Notes are issued in 10, 20, 50, 100 and 200 shekels as well as coins of ½, 1, 2, 5 and ten shekels.

The shekel exchange rate depends on US dollars and is subject to frequent fluctuations. For that reason it's a good idea to wait to get to Israel before changing money. The cheapest places to change are post offices and large tourist information offices, such as the one at Jaffa Gate in Jerusalem, since they do not charge a commission. It is possible to change money back, up to a value of US$ 500, but for higher sums proof of the original exchange is needed.

Changing money

i Exchange rates

- 1 NIS = 0.17 £;   1 £ = 6.00 NIS
- 1 NIS = 0.21 €   1 € = 4.75 NIS
- 1 NIS = 0.27 US$ 1 US$ = 3.70 NIS

The import and export of foreign currency is not subject to any restrictions. Israeli currency can be imported in unlimited quantities, but exporting can only be done after consulting a bank.

Importing and exporting foreign currency

Credit cards are accepted almost everywhere. They and debit cards can be used to get Israeli shekels at many bank machines. A PIN will be needed; there may be charges, depending on card.

Credit cards
Cash machines

Banks are generally open Sun–Thu 8.30am–12.30pm, on Sun, Tue and Thu also 4pm–5.30pm, Fri only 8.30am–noon.

Banks

❯ CONTACT DETAILS FOR CREDIT CARDS

In the event of lost bank or credit cards you can contact the following numbers in UK and USA (phone numbers when dialling from abroad):

► **Eurocard/MasterCard**
Tel. 001 / 636 7227 111

► **Visa**
Tel. 0800 / 811 84 40

► **American Express UK**
Tel. 0044 / 1273 696 933

► **American Express USA**
Tel. 001 / 800 528 4800

► **Diners Club UK**
Tel. 0044 / 1252 513 500

► **Diners Club USA**
Tel. 001 / 702 797 5532

Have the bank sort code, account number and card number as well as the expiry date ready.

The following numbers of UK banks can be used to report and cancel lost or stolen bank and credit cards issued by those banks:

► **HSBC**
Tel. 0044 / 1442 422 929

► **Barclaycard**
Tel. 0044 / 1604 230 230

► **NatWest**
Tel. 0044 / 142 370 0545

► **Lloyds TSB**
Tel. 0044 / 1702 278 270

Museums

Watch out for the Sabbath! Most museums, excavation sites and other attractions are open Sun–Thu from 9am or 10am until 4pm or 5pm. Many places close early on Friday and remain closed entirely on Saturdays for the Sabbath.

National Parks · Nature Reserves

National parks Places designated as national parks (currently 66, www.parks.org.il) in Israel are those of archaeological, historical or scenic interest. Almost all the significant excavation sites are therefore national parks.

Nature reserves An area of around 20,000ha/50,000 acres is designated nature reserve, from marshland to desert and oases with lavish vegetation, home to 3000 different plant species (of which around 150 are endemic), 430 bird species, 70 mammal species and 80 reptile species.

Green Card It is a lot cheaper to visit the country's national parks and nature reserves with a Green Card, which is available from the large parks.

SPNI The Society for the Protection of Nature in Israel (SPNI) runs seminars and nature trails, very informative guided tours in areas that have a particularly interesting landscape.

▶ NATIONAL PARKS

▶ **National Park Authority**
3, Am VeOlamo St.
Givat Shaul, Jerusalem 95463
Tel. (02) 500 54 44
Fax 538 34 05
www.parks.org.il

▶ **SPNI / Nature Trails**
4, Hashfela St.
Tel Aviv
Tel. (03) 537 44 25, fax 687 76 95
www.aspni.org/aspni_israel_
trail.html

Organized Tours

A wide choice Lots of travel companies offer trips to Israel and Palestine, be it study trips focusing on archaeology, art history or politics, pilgrimages, spa holidays (▶Spas) or through working holidays in a kibbutz or at excavations (▶Working Holiday). Pilgrimages are also offered by lots

TOUR OPERATORS

TRIPS TO PALESTINE

► **www.visit-palestine.com**
Lists a whole number of addresses
for Palestinian tour operators

► **Alternative Tourism
Group (ATG)**
Beit Sahour, Palestine
Tel. (02) 277 21 51
Fax 277 22 11
www.atg.ps/index.php

of religious institutions. Round trips and excursions lasting one or
more days can also be booked in Israel – particularly in Jerusalem –
with local bus companies and travel agencies.

There are also specialized local tour operators for trips to the Palesti-   ◄ Into Palestinian
nian territories. One company offering interesting trips is the Alter-   territories
native Tourism Group, which runs round trips with various focal
points and bed & breakfast with Palestinian families.

Post and Communications

Most of the main post offices are open continuously Sun–Thu   Post
8am–6pm, Fri 8am–1pm or 2pm. Branches are usually open
8am–12.30pm and 3.30pm–6pm. Letter boxes are red or yellow and
marked with a white deer; letters to other countries must be posted
in the red letter boxes.

A postcard to Europe currently costs NIS 4.20, letters and larger cards   ◄ Postage
cost NIS 5.60. Apart from in post offices, stamps can be purchased in
stationery and souvenir shops, bookshops and the large hotels.

Landlines: the most expensive place to make calls is from international   Telephone
hotels, which charge around 15 NIS per minute to Europe. The
cheapest way is to use a phone card (Telecard, available in all post offices and many newsagents) at one of the many public payphones.

Mobiles and Air Cards: using the GSM mobile phone, you can regis-
ter to use roaming services to get into the Israeli network. Your service provider at home will tell you the cheapest option. The alterna-
tives: pre-paid cards are very cheap (e.g. from Orange, www.orange.-
co.il); they can be got from newsagents, markets and tobacconists.
Rental cellphones and Air Cards for the laptop are available as soon
as you get off the plane at Ben Gurion Airport. Prices are dependent
on the precise contract (timed, flat rate, data options). Cheapest:
ATS Telecom Systems, tel. 050 571 39 72, www.ats.israel.com; Travel
Cell, tel. 1800 72 11 11, www.travelcell.com

▶ DIALLING CODES

INTERNATIONAL DIALLING CODES

▶ **To Israel**
from the United Kingdom and New Zealand: 009 72
from the United States and Canada: 011 972
from Australia: 0011 972

▶ **From Israel**
to the United Kingdom: 00 49
to the United States and Canada: 00 1
to Ireland: 00 353

to Australia: 00 61
to New Zealand: 00 64
Remember to drop the zero for the local dialling code!

LOCAL DIALLING CODES

Jerusalem: 02
Ashqelon: 07
Beersheba: 07
Eilat: 07
Haifa: 04
Netanya: 09
Tel Aviv: 03
Tiberias: 06

Prices and Discounts

Tipping | Israel is not a cheap country, but to attract more tourists, the government is hoping to reduce holiday costs by an average of 25% in the next few years, focusing on the cost of accommodation. For budgeting, you must factor in typically Israeli features. A service fee is usually always included in the bill, unless there is a clear indication that this is not the case. Those satisfied with the service usually give an additional tip of 10–15%, while the practice of rounding up the amount is usually only for taxi drivers.

VAT
Exceptions and special rules ▶ | VAT, value added tax **(17%)** is included in the price. Flights with an Israeli airline, regular tours and charter tours, accommodation costs and rental cars are all exempt as long as these were paid in a foreign currency (US$, etc). **There is no VAT in Eilat**. The third special rule is that tourists who purchase goods worth more than US$ 50 in a shop

▶ WHAT DOES IT COST?

PRICE OVERVIEW

Cup of coffee
NIS 10.00

Simple meal
from NIS 15.00

Double room
from NIS 300.00

»recommended by the Ministry of Tourism« (the emblem is a blue bow, men carrying grapes in the middle) can claim a discount of at least 5% and a VAT refund on departure. All tobacco goods and electronic items are excluded.

To get a refund, show the receipt(s) at a counter of the Leumi bank at Ben Gurion International Airport.   ◄ Refunds

Security

Israel is one of those countries where safety and security is an on-going issue. The violent confrontations between Palestinians and Israelis in the Palestinian territories and the attacks in Israeli cities or at holy sites are dangers that necessarily affect tourists when they occur, although the attacks are not specifically targeted at tourists. Anyone wanting to rule this out entirely only has one option, and that is to not visit the country at all. On the other hand, there are probably not many countries where so much is done to protect citizens and tourists as in Israel. The drawn-out luggage inspections and questioning upon arrival in Israel alone are enough to give an idea of what Israel means by security measures. Even within the country, bags are checked and body searches are performed in places where people congregate or institutions need protecting, especially in Jerusalem's Old City and at the checkpoints. Armed civilians are either inhabitants of the West Bank or members of the **Mashas** militia. The constant military presence takes some getting used to, regardless of whether it is perceived as comforting or as a constant reminder of the danger.

A continuing issue

Current situation

- To get up-to-date information about the security situation, visit www.fco.gov.uk/en/travel-and-living-abroad/

There is no way to be completely safe from attacks, but in times of political unrest it is best to avoid places where violent conflicts have occurred in the past. They mainly include the Gaza Strip and the Palestinian cities in the West Bank, such as Hebron, Ramallah and Nablus. Anyone wishing to visit those places should do so with a tour operator or in a Palestinian taxi.

Some security precautions

Shopping · Souvenirs

Don't be put off by the huge shopping malls which are spreading in Israel as elsewhere both in town centres and on green-field sites, all

Clothes and shoes

Come in: these men with their trustworthy appearance are Druze antique and souvenir dealers.

with the same chains and selling the same brands. Fashion is dominated by the large, in some cases global retailers, so if you're looking for Gap, Zip, Nautica, Renuar, Mango or Lord Kitsch, you'll find them. However, Israel also caters for discriminating shoppers, not just with **excellent wines and olive oil**.

The most numerous clientele with the most money for young and hip fashion and accessories is in Tel Aviv. Sheinkin Street is one of the top addresses for the sort of boutiques and designer shops catering to this group. Jerusalem, the capital of the »men in black« with its much stronger orthodox presence, cannot really compete where fashion is concerned, except on Emek Refa'im Street in the somewhat more chic German Colony.

Judaica To make up for this, you'll find the Holy City has more to offer if it's Judaica you're looking for, e.g. in King David Street. Here you can find a choice of menorahs, candles etc. in unusual shapes and colours.

Bazaars Unique to Jerusalem is the oriental bazaar. There's no better one in Israel and Palestine than the souk in the old city. Candles, rosaries, figurines of saints and many other devotional accessories are on sale here alongside clothes, spices, electronic equipment and leather goods. It is the done thing to **haggle over every shekel**. Typical souvenirs also include ceramics (Armenian products are famous), carved handicrafts (olive wood and mother-of-pearl), copper and silverware, embroidered tablecloths, and kelims. Some shops specialize in historic photographs. Among the goods from Palestine are crafts, including hookah pipes and carvings. The only comparable bazaar is in Akko, which has a similar atmosphere but is a hundred times smaller.

Those searching for art (pictures, sculptures etc.) are bound to come up with something. There are **a number of artists' colonies** in the country. In Jerusalem's Hutzot Hayotzer, between the Jaffa Gate and Yemin Moshe, some three dozen studios and workshops sell Judaica, paintings, ceramics and jewellery. Similar wares can be found in the Jerusalem House of Quality (12 Hebron Rd, tel. 02 671 74 30, www.art-jerusalem.com), which plays host to galleries and craft shops in an historic building with a picturesque interior courtyard. For Palestinian crafts (including jewellery, ceramics and carpets) visit Sunbula's Shop in Sheikh Jarrah (7 Nablus Rd, tel. 02 672 17 07). Further colonies include the artists' village of Ein Hod (www.ein-hod.info) near Haifa, which is picturesque in itself, or the artists' quarter in Safed, where prices are definitely lower than in Jerusalem. *Art*

And finally cosmetics: those marketed as »Dead Sea products«, **obtained from the Dead Sea's minerals**, are said to serve health and beauty. There are creams, soaps, bath salts, cures for skin problems of every kind. A range of skincare products for men also sells well. These wares can be bought everywhere, not least in the duty-free shop, where they're cheaper. *Cosmetics*
Incidentally, it is not so easy to exchange or return goods in Israel as elsewhere. In particular where crafts (e.g. Judaica) are concerned, you can forget it. Many shops have signs to this effect, but often only in Hebrew.

Shops are generally open from 8am or 8.30am to 1pm and from 4pm to 7pm, while smaller food shops open earlier and larger department stores do not close for lunch. Jewish shops observe the Sabbath, meaning they are open on Fridays from 8.30am to 2pm, but then remain closed until Sunday morning. Christian shops are closed on Sundays, Muslim ones on Fridays. *Shop opening times*

The products of the diamond and jewellery industry can be purchased in certified shops. **Tel Aviv and Netanya** are centres of the diamond industry. Typical Israeli products include **Nativity figures made from olive wood**, the greatest selection of which can naturally be found in Bethlehem. The best place to purchase **wine** is Zikhron Ya'akov, the wine-growing region of the Carmel mountains (▶Food and Drink). The souvenir trade is particularly lively around the biblical sites and especially of course in Jerusalem. The selection ranges from sentimental, over-the-top devotional objects to hand-painted *Typical Israeli souvenirs*

ceramics, **cosmetics from the Dead Sea**, embroidered blankets and crocheted skull-caps to alabaster vases and lamps made of hand-blown coloured glass, known as Hebron glass... the list is endless. There is a **very large selection of leather bags and shoes** on offer in Jerusalem's Old City and depending on the purchaser's bartering skills, they can be obtained for good prices.

Antiques In Israel, archaeology, especially »archaeology in search of the Bible«, has become something of a popular hobby. Of course there are also people who try to turn this into a profit and therefore **most antiques are fakes**, which is why it is best to be on your guard. Shops »recommended by the Ministry of Tourism« are better options. They can be identified by the emblem in the shop window featuring a blue bow with two people carrying grapes.

Spas

Sea of Galilee and the Dead Sea The centres of Israel's spa tourism are the ►Dead Sea and ►Tiberias on the ►Sea of Galilee. The main spots around the Dead Sea are Ein Bokek and Neve Zohar, but other good options include Ein Gedi and, somewhat further north, Mitzpe Shalem.

The healing power of the unique climate at the Dead Sea, the special composition of the water and the black mud are controversial. The unique combination of high air pressure, intense sunlight and dry air is particularly helpful with skin problems (psoriasis and eczema), muscle and joint problems as well as with psychosomatic complaints (information: **www.deadsea.co.il**).

There are 17 springs in Tiberias on the Sea of Galilee with a temperature of around 60ºC/140ºF, whose water contains a rare and complex combination of minerals. A spa holiday here would benefit those with muscle and joint problems, chronic sinusitis, physical rehabilitation and psychosomatic complaints.

Sport and Outdoors

Israel is a decidedly outdoor country. Especially in Tel Aviv, where the body cult is most pronounced, joggers can be seen at all times of the day and night. Training in gyms is de rigueur for anyone who's anyone. Israelis are a sporty nation, in other words, although sweating and tanning on the beach is also regarded as a summer »sport«. **The varied landscape provides a stage for many sports**: windsurfing, kite surfing, sailing, swimming, diving, riding, kayaking, hiking in Galilee and on the Golan, desert tours in the Negev. Holidaymakers have plenty of choice.

Various tour operators offer special hiking holidays. Day hikes and multi-day trips are also organized by the Society for the Protection of Nature in Israel (SPNI; ▶National Parks and Nature Reserves). Of course it is also possible for travellers to explore the country on foot without being part of a guided tour.

Hiking

For more demanding hikers, there's the challenge of the magnificent 965km/600mi Israel National Trail (www.israelnationaltrail.com). It runs from the Syrian/Lebanese border in the north via the Sea of Galilee and the Mediterranean coast to Eilat. It passes through the Negev, to towns and kibbutzim. This demanding trail is only suitable for experienced hikers. On the stretch through the Negev it additionally requires climbing experience, and everywhere it demands stamina. In order to experience Israel's flourishing natural scenery at its most intense, it is best to **walk the trail between mid-February and mid-May**. Until the website provides more facts and maps in English, an English trail-guide describing each of the 25 sections as daily stretches is indispensable.

Hiking on the National Trail

Jacob Saar's *Hike the land of Israel – A Complete Guide to the Israel National Trail* (ISBN 9789659124909) can be obtained from bookshops in Israel, online, or from Eshkol Publishing Ltd., tel. 08 690 90 70, info@eshkol-b.co.il.

Windsurfing off the coast of Eilat

Golf Israel's oldest golf course is by the excavation site in Caesarea and has 18 holes (Caesarea Golf and Country Club, www.caesareagolf.-com). The course is open to tourists via a special membership scheme. The country's other golf course belongs to the Gaash kibbutz (www.golfgaash.co.il) near Tel Aviv.

Cycling As in all countries of the Middle East, **cycling is not widespread in Israel**, either as an environmentally conscious mode of transport or as a sport. There is no cycle network, and do not expect drivers to be very considerate of cyclists. That does not mean, however, that Israel cannot be explored by bike. Following the international trend, special cycle tours around the country are being established, both for sporty and lazy cyclists: information from www.bikeisrael.com. Mountain bikers can get information from the International Mountain Bicycling Association (www.imba.com). The official cyclists' association is the Israel Cycling Federation www.ofanaim.org.il). Not exactly suitable for cyclists, but at least friendly towards them these days, is Tel Aviv, where almost 40 per cent of the population possess a bike. A total of 1500 luminous green bicycles (»rent-o-bikes«) are available for hire for 30 minutes and up at so-called »docking stations« all over the city. You pay by credit card when you pick the bike up. If there are none to be had, cycles are available for hourly hire from Cycle (www.cycle.co.il) or O-fun (www.o-fun.co.il) in Ben Yehuda St.

Riding Not only countless riding clubs, but also holiday resorts and kibbutz hotels (such as Beit Oren in the Carmel mountains) run excursions on horseback as well as guided tours, while others hire out horses. The region of Upper Galilee is particularly attractive for riding.

Kayak trips One good area for kayaking trips is the Banias, one of the headwater streams of the Jordan. Tours are organized by the kibbutz Kfar Blum (tel. 06/694 36 66).

Sailing Sailing boats can be hired in the marinas of Eilat, Haifa, Tel Aviv, Jaffa and Tiberias.

Skiing Israel's winter sports resort is on Mount Hermon in the north of the country. There is a ski school and a ski rental in the moshav Neve Ativ, founded in 1969. The runs on Mount Hermon are not very challenging from a skill or endurance perspective, but are nevertheless popular with Israelis. The season begins in December or January and lasts until around mid-April.

Windsurfing Windsurfing is possible along the entire Mediterranean coast, and is especially good at Nahariya and Caesarea. There are also good windsurfing opportunities near Eilat on the Red Sea and on the Sea of Galilee.

Eilat on the Red Sea is known as a **year-round, top-class diving area** (visibility 40m/45yd) because of its rich fish stocks and wonderful coral banks. The options range from snorkelling at the beach to diving at the coral reef or diving in caves and grottoes and participating in special archaeological diving expeditions. Diving schools run courses for beginners and the more advanced. It is generally possible to hire diving and snorkelling equipment. The diving season on the Mediterranean lasts from September to December and March to May (visibility approx. 10m/10yd). This is particularly exciting for amateur archaeologists.

Diving, snorkelling

Time

Israel follows Israel Standard Time (GMT + 2 hrs). From mid-April to the beginning of October it follows Israel Summer Time (GMT + 3 hrs). Note that this summer time is thus shorter at both ends than summer time in Europe.

Transport

Israel's road network covers more than 4000km/2500mi and is densest in the coastal region around Tel Aviv. Almost all passenger transport and a majority of freight transport is by road.

By car

The most important arteries are Route 1 between Jerusalem and Tel Aviv, and Route 2 (close to the coast) between Rosh Hanikra (in the far north) and Ashqelon. Both are of motorway standard. Between Ben Gurion Airport and Tel Aviv there is a toll lane on the motorway; hire cars are generally not registered to use it. Driving in Israel is comparatively stress-free compared to other countries in the Middle East. One thing that takes a little bit of getting used to is that although Israelis are very friendly in their day-to-day lives, some do succumb to road rage quite quickly.

◀ Main roads

◀ Driving in Israel

Israel's official road maps do not usually distinguish between Israel proper and the Palestinian territories. But there is no need to worry about venturing into Palestinian territory by mistake; the signage is adequate.

◀ Road maps

For a small surcharge you can hire a sat-nav when you pick up your hired car. The problem is that the equipment often has trouble deciphering addresses which are not entered in Hebrew. When you hire the device, have hotels etc entered, e.g. by GPS 4 Rent, tel. 03 975 45 00, www.gps4rent.co.il, Ben Gurion Airport, office at the main car-hire centre in Airport City.

▶ TRANSPORT ADDRESSES

BREAKDOWN SERVICE

▶ **MEMSI (Automobile and Touring Club of Israel)**
Tel. (03) 564 11 11 (24 hrs.)

BUS COMPANIES

▶ **Egged Tours**
Tel. (03) 920 47 77
www.eggedtours.co.il

▶ **Dan Tours**
Reservations:
Tel. (03) 693 32 43
www.dan.co.il

RAIL TRAVEL

▶ **Israel Railways**
Tel. (03) 611 700
www.rail.co.il

AIRLINES

▶ **Israir**
Reservations:
Tel. (03) 613 65 64
www.israirairlines.com

▶ **Arkia Israel Airlines**
Reservations:
Tel. (03) 690 22 22
www.arkia.co.il

Traffic regulations ▶ Israel's traffic regulations are not wildly different from those of other countries that **drive on the right**, and the traffic signs largely correspond to the international norms. Larger towns and cities as well as other destinations are almost always signposted in Hebrew, Arabic and English. Within towns, the **maximum speed** is 50kph/30mph; while outside urban areas the speed limit for cars is 80kph/50mph unless it expressly says 90kmh/55mph. Cars with trailers can only go at 60kph/38 mph and motorbikes are restricted to 70kph/44mph. The speed limit on highways is 100kph/60mph (or 110kph/70mph where signs indicate). Even though hardly any Israeli driver sticks to the legal speed limit, especially on the rural roads in the south, it is best to remember that exceeding the speed limit by just 20kph/ 12mph will incur a fine of NIS 100! Coloured curbs indicate the **parking regulations**: red and white means no parking and no stopping, red and yellow means that only buses are allowed to stop, while blue and white means vehicles are allowed to park with a parking ticket.

Car rental Travellers wishing to hire a car will need a national or EU driving licence, a passport and an international credit card; the minimum age is 21. All international hire-car companies have branches in Israel's larger towns; there are also local companies. The agencies in Israel generally close on Friday afternoons and Saturdays; the offices at Ben Gurion International Airport are open every day, 24 hours. Those hiring a car from home will often pay less.
It is not permitted to cross the Israeli-Jordan border or the Israeli-Egyptian border, or to enter the Palestinian territories, with a car hired in Israel.

Public transport (buses and sherut taxis) **does not operate on the Sabbath, on Friday evenings or during Jewish holidays**, or even during the preceding evenings. The only modes of public transport in operation at this time are taxis, buses driven by Palestinians and sherut taxis (such as in East Jerusalem and Nazareth).

◄ Public transport

The most important form of public transport, both within urban areas and for overland trips, is the bus. 90% of trips are run by the co-operatives Egged and Dan. It is quick, convenient and inexpensive to take a bus from the central bus stations in Jerusalem (224 Jaffa St), Tel Aviv (Harakevet St) and Haifa (2 Hahagana St) to every part of the country. Overland buses have air-conditioning.

◄ By bus

The seven-seater **group taxis** known as sheruts are somewhat more expensive than the bus (around 20%), but cheaper than travelling by taxi. The journeys are fixed, but there are no set stops except for the start and finish location.

◄ By sherut taxi

Taxis can be booked over the telephone or flagged down. There are official prices for journeys between towns (the driver is required to show the price list). Within towns taxis use their taximeters; for night trips the fee is 25% higher. Take a taxi with an Arabian number plate for trips to the West Bank.

◄ By taxi

A bit of adventure is part of it …

By rail ▶   Israel Railways basically just operates one line: from Nahariya along the coast via Haifa to Tel Aviv (also to Ben Gurion International Airport) and onwards to Jerusalem / Beersheba.

By air ▶   Domestic flights, operated by Arkia and Israir, are not of any great importance. Arkia runs scheduled flights between Tel Aviv and Rosh Pinna, Kiryat Shemona, Haifa and Eilat, while Israir runs scheduled flight between Tel Aviv and Eilat and Haifa.

Travellers with Disabilities

Many public institutions and hotels as well as the Ben Gurion International Airport cater for the needs of disabled travellers. The charitable organization Yad Sarah has a network with good coverage for travellers with disabilities. The nationwide branches hire out wheelchairs and other aids; in addition there is a transfer service from Haifa, Tel Aviv and Jerusalem to the Ben Gurion International Airport.

▶ ADDRESSES FOR DISABLED TRAVELLERS

▶ **Yad Sarah**
Kiriat Weinberg, 124 Herzl Blvd.
Jerusalem
Tel. (02) 644 45 55, fax 644 45 08
www.yadsarah.org.il

▶ **Access Israel**
www.aisrael.org
Information on accessible tourism sites and accommodation, tours, transport, cultural events, restaurants, festivals, etc

When to Go

Too hot   From June to October the climate, except at higher altitudes, is difficult to cope with given the great heat, the intense sunlight and/or the very muggy atmosphere (Mediterranean and inland seas). This is true for the Dead Sea from May onwards. Since air temperatures rarely drop below 23ºC/73ºF at night, while the relative humidity goes up to 85%, nights in cities are particularly tough.

Travelling with the weather   From a weather perspective, the best time to go for all of Israel is spring and late autumn, starting from October. June to September are only for those who can stand the heat, unless travelling to higher-altitude locations. This is particularly true for the Dead Sea, where the high evaporation rates cause unbearably muggy conditions from May onwards. Since the wintertime rainy season in the eastern

Mediterranean only really gets going in December, an autumn sea-side holiday can be extended until the end of November, with late summer warmth and water temperatures of more than 20°C/68°F. The Gulf of Aqaba is a real winter destination. Sunshine, hardly any rain, as well as air and water temperatures of around 22°C/72°F (maximum: Eilat 32°C/90°F) mean that beach visits are lovely, even in January.

Those who are not travelling to Israel for religious reasons should avoid the main Christian holidays. Jerusalem in particular gets incredibly crowded with believers around holy sites. During the Jewish ▶ holidays, festivals and events expect lots of the seaside resorts to be very busy. The same is true for the Israeli school holidays from mid-June to the beginning of September.

Watch out for holidays

Working Holidays

Those interested in a working holiday in a kibbutz (young people between the ages of 18 and 32) should have at least three weeks to spare. Free bed and board, as well as pocket money, are provided in return for work six days a week, at least six hours a day. Working holidays in a kibbutz are arranged by various operators. A complete overview is available from the Israeli tourist offices (▶Information).

Working in a kibbutz

Amateur archaeologists may participate in a dig under scholarly supervision. Previous experience with digs is not usually required. Volunteers have to pay for their own accommodation and meals. Depending on the excavation site and individual preferences, volunteers stay in tents, youth hostels or hotels. At weekends it is common for excursions to be put on to attractions in the surrounding area. Current information about excavations and registration formalities: **www.mfa.gov.il/mfa** under »History of Israel / Early history«.

Participating in excavations

▶ WORK ON A KIBBUTZ

▶ **Kibbutz Program Center**
www.kibbutz.org.il/eng/
6 Frishman St.
Tel-Aviv 1030
Tel: 972-3-5246154/6

▶ **Kibbutz Program Center in New York**
www.kibbutzprogramcenter.org
114 West 26th St.
New York, NY 10001
Tel. (212) 462 27 64

Tours

TO MAKE SURE YOU ALWAYS
FIND THE WAY, DESPITE THE
CURIOUS SIGNPOSTING, HERE
ARE FOUR TOURS THROUGH
THE HOLY LAND.

TOURS THROUGH ISRAEL

None of the tours suggested in this book are overly long. Nevertheless it is best to take plenty of time for them because there is lots to see: holy sites, ancient excavations, modern cities, wonderful beaches, impressive landscapes, and, from time to time, political realities.

The Sea of Galilee
two of the recommended tours touch the Sea of Galilee between the Golan Heights and the Galilean mountains.

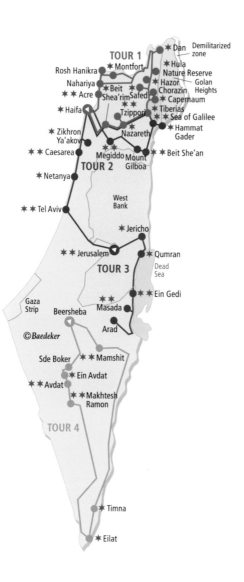

©Baedeker

Travelling in Israel

Seaside, culture and adventure holiday

Israel is a country where round trips are convenient. This is due in part to the fact that Israel and Palestine are quite small, geographically speaking. It is possible to travel from Tel Aviv to the Lebanese border and back in a day, or from Jerusalem to the Dead Sea and back in half a day. Israel is also the Promised Land, where there are plenty of public transport options. Every part of the country can easily be reached by bus, group taxi, plane or (less commonly) by train. The most convenient way of exploring the country is to hire a car. Hire cars are very cheap in Israel, especially as competitors try to outdo each other with attractive flat rates for week-long hires. Visitors will be most appreciative of this option when exploring Galilee and the Golan. Then it becomes possible to stop anywhere on a whim in the national parks and go on outdoor adventures (mountain biking, hiking, camping). Domestic flights within Israel are only worthwhile to and from Eilat.

All-inclusive or independent travel?

Those looking for a pure beach holiday on the Mediterranean, in Eilat or on the Red Sea, or even just a spa vacation on the Dead Sea, should book a package tour, as this is the cheapest way to get such holidays. Those who want to explore the highlights of the Holy Land in the most comfortable manner, accepting that this involves being part of a group most of the time and travelling in an air-conditioned bus with tinted windows, will also benefit from a package. Independent travellers will not have it quite so easy. Although they will experience more of the country and its people and can visit sites for as long as they wish, the cost is the time-consuming nature of making travel plans.

Those travelling during peak season are well advised to fix their route well in advance and book their hotels. Doing this in situ can be tiresome during the busy period.

Time budget

Israel's tourist diversity suffices for several exciting holidays. Among the country's highlights and a must for everyone is **Jerusalem**, the city of the three monotheistic religions. One day is enough for a merely superficial visit. Anyone wanting to get to know the city in more depth, should take three to six days. That gives enough time to visit the Old City, the Temple Mount, the Wailing Wall, the museums and, of course, Yad Vashem, which is worth at least half a day on its own. The **Dead Sea** is best explored in conjunction with Masada from Jerusalem. This can be done in a day. **Tel Aviv** is worth two to four days. Haifa can be visited in one full-on day (two are better), while it takes three to seven days to visit the northern Mediterranean coast, Galilee and the Golan as well as Nazareth, Tiberias and the Sea of Galilee. During peaceful times visitors can travel to the West Bank (with Ramallah and Jericho) and Bethlehem.

Israel's security problem is well known and will exist for as long as there is no comprehensive peaceful solution to the Israeli-Palestinian conflict. Attacks by radical Palestinian groups are, as recent history has shown, unfortunately possible at any place and time. Avoiding buses may reduce the risk, but will not eliminate it entirely, because attacks have been directed at shopping centres, markets and café boulevards (►Practicalities, Security). ◄ Security

Travelling into the Palestinian West Bank and the Gaza Strip is sometimes prohibited from the Israeli side depending on the current situation. There are regular taxis, sherut taxis and buses to Bethlehem, which is very close to Jerusalem. A sensible alternative to taking a hire car or public transport (►Practicalities, Transport) would be to join organized bus tours (usually one-day trips), which are run by many Palestinian operators. Travel agencies and hotels in Jerusalem are happy to help pick an operator (►Practicalities, Organized Tours). ◄ Into Palestinian territory

Tour 1 From the Sea to the Mountains

Start and finish: Haifa　　　　**Distance:** approx. 320km/200mi

This round trip through the north is particularly suitable for those who want to see a lot of Israel's diverse natural landscape. For part of the tour you'll be following in Christ's footsteps.

Travellers who merely wish to go for a few walks and visit the most important attractions can do this tour in three days. Starting point is Haifa. Accommodation options are Tiberias on the Sea of Galilee and a kibbutz hotel in the far north (such as Kfar Giladi and Kfar Blum).

Instead of taking the direct route from ❶✳ **Haifa** to ✳ **Nazareth** why not take the longer detour through the ✳ **Carmel mountains**, which is far more impressive. Leave Haifa via its attractive district of Central Carmel and take Moriah Road in a southeasterly direction. It makes its way past the university and then climbs to the highest elevation in the Carmel range. There are a number of opportunities for a photo stop. The sparsely wooded landscape, with many trees reduced to blackened stumps, recalls the disastrous forest fires that raged here in 2010. Just beyond the Druze village of Daliyat a road branches off to Mount Muhraka with the Carmelite monastery of St Elijah. Back on the main road, travel another 7km/4mi southbound to reach Route 70 from Zikhron Ya'akov. Follow this road in a northeasterly direction, bearing left after 6km/3.5mi and turning right shortly afterwards to ❷✳ **Beit She'arim**. The sizable catacombs with tombs of Sanhedrin members are surviving evidence of its former significance as the seat of the high council (Sanhedrin) in the 2nd–4th centuries AD. From Haifa to Beit She'arim

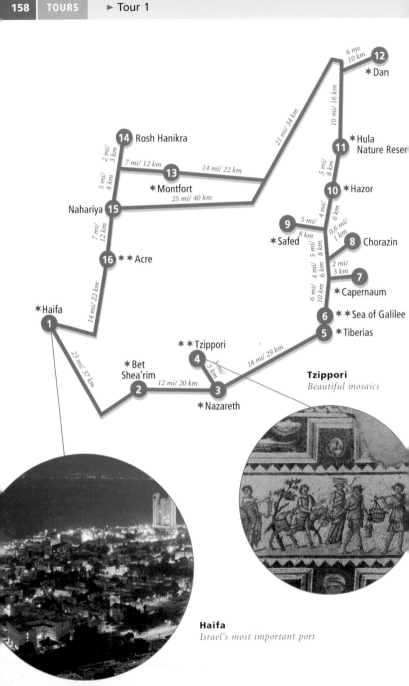

6 mi/ 10 km
12 ✳ Dan

21 mi/ 34 km

10 mi/ 16 km

14 Rosh Hanikra
2 mi/ 3 km

11 ✳ Hula Nature Reser

7 mi/ 12 km

5 mi/ 8 km

13 ✳ Montfort
14 mi/ 22 km

5 mi/ 4 km

10 ✳ Hazor

25 mi/ 40 km

6 km

Nahariya **15**

9 ✳ Safed
5 mi/ 8 km

0.6 mi/ 1 km

8 Chorazin

7 mi/ 12 km

5 mi/ 8 km

2 mi/ 3 km

16 ✳ ✳ Acre

6 mi/ 10 km

4 mi/ 6 km

7 ✳ Capernaum

✳ Haifa
1

14 mi/ 22 km

6 ✳ ✳ Sea of Galilee

5 ✳ Tiberias

✳ ✳ Tzippori
4

23 mi/ 37 km

18 mi/ 29 km

✳ Bet Shea'rim

3 mi/ 5 km

Tzippori
Beautiful mosaics

2
12 mi/ 20 km
3

✳ Nazareth

Haifa
Israel's most important port

Just beyond Beit She'arim is Route 75 from Haifa to Nazareth. Crossing the plain, it is around 20km/12mi to ❸ ✳ **Nazareth**, site of the famous Church of the Annunciation. Up hill and down dale, one approaches the town in mostly heavy traffic. It is not a particularly pretty place. The whitewashed houses cling to the slopes, between them the unfinished shells of buildings, dark vegetation, and a distant view into the valley. A worthwhile detour would be to visit ❹ ✳✳ **Tzippori National Park** 5km/3mi to the north. One of the archaeological compound's most impressive sites is the Nile mosaic, with a depiction of the Egyptian river.

Nazareth and Tzippori

The next destination, 9km/5.5mi to the northeast, is the village of Cana, the site of the Wedding at Cana. Continuing towards Tiberias, the Horns of Hattin can be seen on the left-hand side of the road. This is where the crusader army was decisively beaten by Saladin in 1187. After that the tour continues to ❺ ✳ **Tiberias** on the ❻ ✳✳ **Sea of Galilee**, where visitors ought to try the region's speciality, St Peter's fish (tilapia), in one of the waterfront restaurants, and go to the spa centre as well as the old synagogue in the Tiberias Hammat district. Those who wish to stay the night here can schedule a boat trip on the Sea of Galilee in the afternoon. There is regular ferry traffic to the kibbutz En Gev on the opposite bank.

Sea of Galilee

Continuing northbound along the shores of the Sea of Galilee (Route 90), one good option would be to stop at one of the beaches for a swim or to have a waterside picnic. An interesting place to stop is the kibbutz of Ginosar on the lake, which exhibits a fishing boat from the time of Jesus. Next along the road are sites related to Christian tradition: Tabgha, the site of the miracle of The Feeding of the Five Thousand, and ❼ ✳ **Capernaum** with a partially rebuilt synagogue and other excavations. At Tabgha the road leaves the lake and climbs northwards into the mountains. On the right-hand side there is a church on the Mount of Beatitudes. Soon afterwards, also on the right-hand side, is the access road to the ruins of ❽ **Chorazin**. Further north, in Rosh Pinna, a winding roads turns off to the left. It makes its way up to the elevated town of ❾ ✳ **Safed** (8km/5mi). Straight on, on the left-hand side is ❿ ✳ **Tel Hazor**, where 23 layers of settlement have been uncovered. Just beyond, on the right, is the kibbutz of Ayelet Hashahar with a guesthouse and a museum, which exhibits discoveries from Tel Hazor.

From Tiberias Hule Plain

The road now runs along the Hule Plain, which was once marshy but is now used for agricultural purposes. The ⓫ ✳ **Hule Nature Reserve**, just a few miles beyond the kibbutz Ayelet Hashahar, gives a good idea of what the landscape here used to look like.

To the far northeast

Pass through the small town of Kiryat Shemona and then carry on eastbound. ⓬ ✳ **Dan** Nature Reserve is worth visiting. There are

Golan Heights

waymarked circular trails leading through dense vegetation to the Dan springs and the remains of Tel Dan. Another picturesque spot is ✴ **Banias**, a few miles to the northeast, where one of the Jordan's three headwaters rises. A winding road makes its way up the Golan Heights from here and past Israel's winter sports resort of Neve Ativ, to Nimrod Fortress. The drive alone is worth it for the stunning views of this medieval fortress.

✔ **DON'T MISS**

■ Haifa and the Carmel: Israel's largest port city and Israel's largest wine-growing region
■ Sea of Galilee: The place where Jesus grew up is also a great place for a wonderful vacation.
■ Akko: famous Crusader city with an Oriental touch.

Leave Banias, driving back to Kiryat Shemona. There, follow the road to Metula on the right, then turn left and drive past Tel Hay. The tomb of Joseph Trumpeldor, a leading Zionist who defended the settlement during an Arab attack in 1920, is located here. A museum commemorates the event in the building where the inhabitants barricaded themselves in. The road quickly climbs up and then runs in a southerly direction, parallel to the Lebanese border. There are lots of good views of the fertile Hule Plain.

Bar'am

Beyond the kibbutz of Yiftah stay on Route 899. Carry on driving along the border all the way to the left-hand turning to Bar'am, whose synagogue dates back to the 2nd or 3rd century. From Bar'am the road now heads southwest towards Sasa. Those wishing to save time and make quick progress should follow the main road from now on. It runs via Hurfeish to Nahariya (approx. 40km/25mi).

Alternative route via Montfort

The more picturesque option is the very winding, narrow road from Sasa to the northwest. It goes past the remote settlements of Netu'a, Even Menahem and Shomera and then reaches Goren Natural Forest by the kibbutz of Elon, where a footpath to the crusader castle of ⓭ ✴ **Montfort** 3km/2mi away begins.

Rosh Hanikra

A few miles beyond Elon the road meets the north-south axis on the Mediterranean. Take this road to get to the village of ⓮**Rosh Hanikra** on the Lebanese border. The limestone caves there are a popular destination among Israelis. Just beyond the top station of the cableway and the restaurant-bar, a barbed-wire entanglement blocks the way; the other side is enemy territory, southern Lebanon. From the carpark there is a magnificent view of the coast.

Nahariya, Haifa

For the return journey to Haifa, choose Route 4, which runs along the Mediterranean. It first passes the excavation site and recreational area of Tel Achziv and shortly afterwards, having paid a brief visit to the free republic of Ahziland (»Eli Avivi« says the sign, recalling the name of the founder), reaches the pretty seaside resort of ⓯ **Naha-**

riya. There is a floor mosaic of an early Christian basilica in Moshav Shave Zion. Next along the road is the kibbutz of Lohamei Hageta'ot. The exhibition in the local museum, both interesting and harrowing, commemorates the saddest chapter in Jewish history.

Visiting ⑯ ✶ ✶ **Akko** (Acre) is an unforgettable experience. In addition to a number of interesting buildings from the time of the crusaders and the Ottomans, it has a fascinating oriental atmosphere by the picturesque harbour and in the narrow streets of the bazaar. Those who buy nothing here only have themselves to blame. It's worth spending the night in the Old Town. Beyond Akko (the modern city is rapidly spreading along the coast) the road makes its way around Haifa Bay before finally reaching the port again.

Akko

Tour 2 Central Israel and the North

Start and finish: Jerusalem / Haifa   **Distance:** approx. 365km/225mi

Culture, archaeology, nightlife, swimming: this tour touches on the most interesting places and some particularly beautiful landscapes in central and northern Israel. Those who have a little more time could also combine it with Tour 1.

The round trip through central and northern Israel begins in ❶ ✶ ✶ **Jerusalem**. Start very early to avoid the daily traffic chaos. After around 15km/9mi on Route 1 towards Tel Aviv, there is a right-hand turn towards Abu Gosh. This picturesque mountain town is worth visiting for its interesting crusader church.

Starting point Jerusalem

At ❷ ✶ ✶ **Tel Aviv** this tour has reached the Mediterranean coast, where the skyline is dominated far and wide by the Azrieli Tower. The lovely beach of this young city is an enticing addition to city sightseeing between May and October. Tel Aviv is also the major hotspot for nightlife in Israel. Those for whom Tel Aviv has too much big-city feel will probably prefer Jaffa, with its picturesque harbour, many cosy restaurants and small shops.

Tel Aviv and Jaffa

Take Route 2 northwards. At times it runs very close indeed to the Mediterranean coastline. The prosperous town of Herzliya has nice, well-kept beaches as does the seaside resort of ❸ ✶ **Netanya** around 20km/12mi further north. The coast road offers constant glimpses of wonderful beaches, and a stop for a quick dip is tempting. Netanya itself is modern and rather disappointing, but an excellent place to go swimming. Poleg Beach, surrounded by high sand dunes around 5km/3mi south of Netanya, is considered one of the most beautiful beaches for swimming and surfing on Israel's Mediterranean coast.

Along the coast

6 ✶ Haifa
12 ✶ Tiberias
✶✶ Sea Galilee
10 · 11
14 mi/ 22 km
19 mi/ 30 km
19 mi/ 31 km
34 mi/ 55 km
12 km
7 mi/ 12 km
5 mi/ 8 km
2 mi/ 4 km
8 mi/ 13 km
19 mi/ 30 km
✶ Hammat Gader
9 mi/ 15 km
5
7
19 mi/ 31 km

Jaffa
Modern life in Tel Aviv
oriental traditions in Ja...

✶✶ Caesarea 4
✶ Zikhron Ya'akov
✶✶ Megiddo
8
6 mi/ 10 km
9 ✶✶ Beit She'an
12 mi/ 20 km
Mount Gilboa

3 ✶ Netanya

21 mi/ 34 km

2 ✶✶ Tel Aviv

40 mi/ 65 km

1 ✶✶ Jerusalem

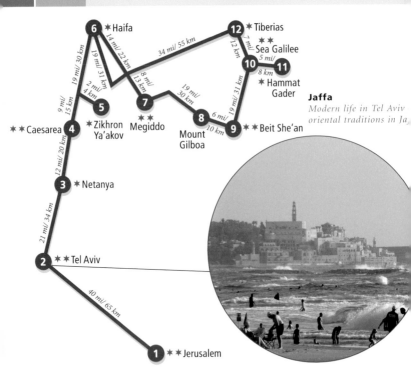

In summer, the search for somewhere to park demands a great deal of patience. Get there early!

Caesarea   Another 20km/12mi to the north between the coastal road, which is a highway here, and the sea, the excavation site of ❹ ✶✶ **Caesarea** is particularly appealing, not least thanks to its splendid location on the water. For the onward journey, leave the highway and take Route 4, which runs parallel to it across the fertile Sharon Plain. Potato fields, orange and lemon groves and banana plantations line the road to the left and right.

Zikhron Ya'akov   The excursion to ❺ ✶ **Zikhron Ya'akov** leaves the coast behind around 15km/9mi beyond Caesarea and makes its way up into the ✶ **Carmel mountains**. Visiting this famous wine region is a pleasure not just for wine connoisseurs, as it also has lots of pretty restaurants and cafés, as well as wineries of course, in which visitors can sample the local produce.

Haifa   ❻ ✶ **Haifa** is considered to be one of Israel's most beautiful cities, not least because of its stunning location at the foot of Mount Carmel. One of Haifa's most visited attractions is the domed mausoleum that the Baha'i sect built for its founder in the middle of lavish terraced gardens on the slopes of Mount Carmel.

There are two ways to get to the next destination, ❼ ✳ ✳ **Megiddo**: directly along the Route 75 (but to use it, it is necessary to first cross Haifa's eastern industrial suburbs), or the scenically much more attractive road across Mount Carmel (► Tour 1). After around 35km/ 22mi, located on an elevation on the right-hand side of the road, is the excavation site of a settlement that dates back to Canaanite times.

Megiddo

Leave Megiddo and head east through the agricultural Jezreel Valley to Afula, then continue east. Around 10km/6mi outside Beit She'an, turn right to Beit Alfa, a kibbutz at the foot of ❽ **Mount Gilboa**. There is a well-preserved floor mosaic in the 6th-century synagogue in the neighbouring kibbutz of Heftziba. After this detour, continue onwards to ❾ ✳ ✳ **Beit She'an**, one of Israel's largest and most significant excavation sites. The town itself is of no great interest.

From Megiddo to Beit She'an

Route 90 runs north from Beit She'an. After approx. 10km/6mi, take the winding road to the crusader fortress of Belvoir, situated 500m/ 1650ft higher up. Back on the main road, drive a further 20km/12mi to get to the southern tip of the ❿ ✳ ✳ **Sea of Galilee**, not far from the historic site where the River Jordan leaves the lake and John the Baptist performed baptisms. One destination near the lake, 8km/5mi to the east in Yarmouk Valley, is equally popular with locals and tourists: ⓫ ✳ **Hamat Gader**, a large water park set in lavish green, with a swimming pool, hot springs and ancient ruins. Another place to find hot springs is the spa quarter of ⓬ ✳ **Tiberias**, the tourist centre on the lake's western shore. The way back from Tiberias to Haifa is described in Tour 1.

Sea of Galilee

✔ **DON'T MISS**

- Jerusalem: holy city of three religions
- Tel Aviv: Israel's ýongest city
- Poleg Beach: one of the most beautiful beaches in the country
- Caesarea: city of the Greeks, Romans, Byzantines and Crusaders
- Haifa and the Carmel: see Tour 1
- Beit She'an: the best preserved Roman theatre in Israel

Tour 3 To the Dead Sea

Start and finish: Jerusalem / Dead Sea   **Distance:** approx. 280km/175mi (there and back)

The highlight of this trip, which begins in the holy city of Jerusalem, is undoubtedly the Dead Sea. However, on the way the route passes several historic places in Palestine and not least the world's oldest city, Jericho.

Before setting out, make sure you have a spare wheel. The stretch along the Dead Sea is notoriously hard on tyres. Also, take a good supply of drinking water. Those who wish to take some time over the individual attractions or go on a longer hike in Ein Gedi National Park should plan to spend at least two days doing this tour. Accommodation options here are the kibbutz guesthouse of Ein Gedi or one of the rather expensive hotels in Ein Bokek on the Dead Sea.

It is advisable to inquire about the security situation beforehand because this tour also goes through the West Bank.

Wadi Qelt   There is a good highway leaving ❶ ✶✶ **Jerusalem** in an eastbound direction. Follow the signs towards Jericho. The hot climate will not allow anything to grow here anymore. All that can be seen are a few

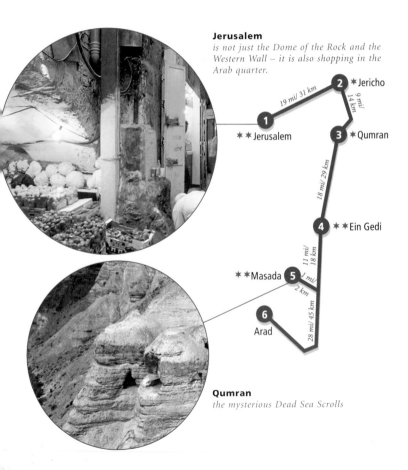

Jerusalem
is not just the Dome of the Rock and the Western Wall – it is also shopping in the Arab quarter.

❷ ✶Jericho

19 mi/ 31 km

9 mi/ 14 km

❶
✶✶Jericho

✶✶Jerusalem

❸ ✶Qumran

18 mi/ 29 km

❹ ✶✶Ein Gedi

11 mi/ 18 km

✶✶Masada ❺ 1 mi/ 2 km

❻
Arad

28 mi/ 45 km

Qumran
the mysterious Dead Sea Scrolls

Bedouin tents. After approx. 20km/12mi a turning to the left goes to St George's Orthodox Monastery in ✳ **Wadi Qelt**. The views of Qelt Valley from the car park are splendid.

The next destination is the city of ❷ ✳ **Jericho**, located in the West Bank, and the oldest known settlement in the world. Here the ascent of the Mount of Temptation can be done on foot or by cable-car. Leave the city in a southbound direction to get to the ✳✳ **Dead Sea**. The road runs southwards, right along the shore. The next destination, ❸ ✳ **Qumran**, owes its fame to the Dead Sea Scrolls, which were discovered in the caves near the monastic complex of the Essenes and can now be seen in the Israel Museum in Jerusalem.

This section of the tour runs along the Dead Sea shore. Approx. 20km/12mi beyond Qumran an access road on the right-hand side leads to the kibbutz of Metzoke Dragot. At ❹ ✳✳ **Ein Gedi** palm trees and green spaces break up the scenery somewhat – it is very easy to spend a day in the lovely national park. Around 20km/12mi further south is ❺ ✳✳ **Masada**, Herod's famous fort. It takes absolutely no effort to get to the top of the rocky plateau as a cable car runs to the top. This is not just a highlight for those with an interest in archaeology, but also a must for the fantastic views of the Dead Sea up here.

From Qumran to Masada

Return to the road on the Dead Sea, to get first to Ein Bokek and a little while later to Neve Zohar, where most of the spas and bathing facilities on the Dead Sea are located. By this point at the latest get into the water and drift around almost weightlessly, while reading the paper of course for the souvenir photo.

Dead Sea

It is worth going on an excursion to Arad from Neve Zohar, which is situated 24km/15mi to the northwest. The road that heads inland from Neve Zohar towards Arad climbs rapidly and soon passes two viewpoints in quick succession; the first has particularly lovely views of the Dead Sea and the mountains of Moab in the evenings, while the second looks out on magnificent mountain landscape and down to the Nabataean, then Byzantine, castle of Mezad Zohar, which guarded the old valley road from Judaea to Edom. ❻ **Arad** is an ideal place for those suffering from asthma because of its altitude and its desert location. Those wishing to see the Masada son-et-lumière show held every evening must also go via Arad. Around 10km/6mi beyond the town a road branches off to the Tell Arad excavation site.

Detour to Arad

Tour 4 Discovering the Negev Desei

Start and finish: Beersheba   **Distance:** approx. 490km/305mi

During a trip through the Negev Desert there are not many attractions and the landscape does not change much either. Nevertheless, it does not get boring. The many faces of the desert landscape, which glows in warm colours in the evening hours, are what makes this route special.

Via Sde Boker to Avdat

Since the roads are good, it just takes two days. Eilat on the Red Sea has a wide choice of accommodation. The tour begins in ❶ **Beersheba**, the less than exciting regional centre. Depart in a southeasterly direction to Yeruham, then follow the road that heads southwest. After 19km/12mi it reaches the famous kibbutz of ❷ **Sde Boker**, founded in 1952 and home of the first Israeli prime minister, David Ben Gurion. After 3km/2mi, on the left-hand side, is the »School of the Desert« (Midreshet Sde Boker) founded by him. He is buried in front of its library, at the edge of a park. The complex lies above the Wadi Zin. There is a road leading into it from here. From the car park it is just a short walk to the springs of ❸ ✳ **Ein Avdat**, not to be confused with the neighbouring Nabataean, then Byzantine, town of ❹ ✳✳ **Avdat**, whose impressive ruins lie 5km/3mi to the south, to the left of the road to Eilat on a hill with plenty of views.

From Makhtesh Ramon to Eilat

After a drive around of 30km/20mi through the Negev plateau, the road reaches Mizpe Ramon. Directly beyond the small town is one of the largest depressions in the world, ❺ ✳✳ **Makhtesh Ramon**. From the viewing platform of the visitor centre on the steep edge, the views of the huge crater are breathtaking. Set out on your hike very early in the morning to avoid the searing heat later. Ideally, stay in Mitzpe overnight, for example on the Alpaca Farm; the local SPNI Field School also organizes astronomical expeditions into the desert. The onward journey southwards on Route 40 is also characterized by wonderful landscape. This is particularly true of the last part of the journey: around 85km/53mi south of Mitzpe Ramon leave Route 40 and turn right onto Route 12 (just outside of Shizzafon). Approx. 10km/6mi outside of Eilat there is a signposted turning to the spring of Ein Netafim, which can be reached after a short walk. Finally the route reaches ❻ ✳ **Eilat**, a tourist hotspot on the Red Sea and Israel's southernmost town, where the conditions for sunbathing, swimming, snorkelling and diving are perfect.

Through the Arava Depression

To head back north, take Route 90 through the Arava Depression, along the Israeli-Jordan border. The depression reaches a height of 200m/655ft and then drops gradually northwards to 398m/1306ft below sea level at the Dead Sea. After 25km/15mi this road passes the

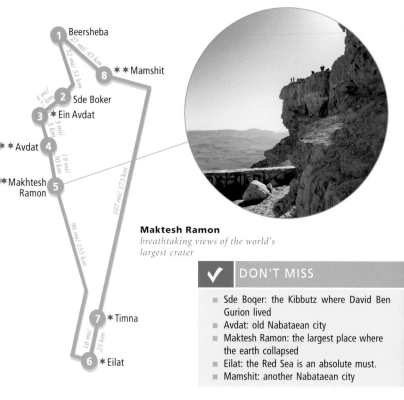

Beersheba
27 mil/43 km
32 mil/51 km

✶✶Mamshit 8

4 mil/7 km 2 Sde Boker
3 ✶Ein Avdat
3 mil/5 km
✶✶Avdat 4
19 mil/30 km
107 mil/173 km
✶Makhtesh Ramon 5
96 mil/155 km
7 ✶Timna
16 mil/25 km
6 ✶Eilat

Maktesh Ramon
breathtaking views of the world's largest crater

✔ **DON'T MISS**

- Sde Boqer: the Kibbutz where David Ben Gurion lived
- Avdat: old Nabataean city
- Maktesh Ramon: the largest place where the earth collapsed
- Eilat: the Red Sea is an absolute must.
- Mamshit: another Nabataean city

track to the copper mines of ❼ ✶ **Timna**, which turns off 2km/1.25mi further to Timna Park with its bizarre rock formations. Continuing northwards, after approx. 17km/11mi the road reaches the wildlife park Hai Bar, home to antelopes, onagers, ostriches and other desert animals. The neighbouring kibbutz of Yotvata, founded as an army settlement in 1951, is known for its outstanding dairy products, which can be bought all over Israel.

At Gerofit, 8km/5mi beyond Yotvata, the road rejoins Route 40 to Beersheba, but the tour continues to the Dead Sea. At the town of Paran, after around 45km/28mi the road passes the wide Wadi Paran and later the Wadi Zin, which begins at the spring Ein Avdat. A short while later there is a turning to the left to Beersheba. Take this road (no. 25). After a further 27km/17mi it reaches the impressive remains of the Nabataean settlement of ❽ ✶✶ **Mamshit** in the desert landscape above a wadi. Return to Beersheba via Dimona.

Via Mamshit to Beersheba

Sightseeing
from A to Z

SACRED SITES OF THREE
WORLD RELIGIONS,
EXCAVATIONS OF
SETTLEMENTS THOUSANDS O
OVERWHELMING SCENERY:
ISRAEL IS PACKED FULL
WITH ATTRACTIONS.

ויאה דולורוזה

طريق الآلام

VIA DOLOROSA

The security situation As this book went to press, the Foreign Office said tensions remained high in the country, and advised against all travel to Gaza. Check the current situation in the country beforehand at **www.fco.gov.uk/en/**.

Abu Ghosh

F 4

District: Jerusalem
Population: 5500

Altitude: 600–700m/1900–2300ft

The Arab village 12km/7mi west of Jerusalem above the highway is worth visiting for its lovely crusader church.

Crusaders and Bedouins The small town is named after Abu Ghosh, a Bedouin sheikh from the Hejaz, who moved here with his four sons in around 1800 and was given the right by the Ottoman government to secure the pilgrimage road between the sea and Jerusalem, as well as to levy a toll for the service. Even before the Bedouins arrived, Abu Ghosh was inhabited, as there was a spring here. In the 1st century, the Romans built a castle with two cisterns for parts of the Legio X Fretensis, the legion that was probably involved in the crucifixion of Christ. During the Islamic period a caravanserai formed and a further cistern was built. In 1099 the crusaders gathered in the location they believed to be the **biblical Emmaus** (Luke 24:13) because of the spring. Emmaus is the Greek translation of the Hebrew name Hammat (hot spring). The crusaders built Château Fontenoide here in order to secure the road to Jaffa and in 1142 constructed a church over the spring.

What to See in Abu Ghosh

✴
Crusader Church The Crusader Church, whose architect adopted the pointed arch as a design element from the existing caravanserai, stands out as a mighty structure. Since 1956 the church, next to which a mosque had been built centuries earlier, has belonged to the Lazarist Fathers. There is a stone next to the entrance in the church's northern elevation with the inscription »Vexillatio Leg(ionis) Fret(ensis)«, a reminder that the church was built on the site of the Roman fort. The basilica is, like St Anne's Church in Jerusalem (▶ p. 300), an outstanding example of the crusaders' monumental early Gothic architecture. From the outside the church, with its walls 3–4m/10–13ft thick, has a fortified feel. The interior is simple but atmospheric. The spring rises in the crypt (Mon–Wed, Fri, Sat 8.30am–11.30am and 2.30pm–5.30pm).

← *Masada Fortress*

🕐

Notre Dame de l'Arche d'Alliance Our Lady of the Ark of the Covenant stands above the town and is of interest because of its statue of Mary. It was built in 1924 above the remains of a Byzantine church and belongs to the French Sisters of St. Joseph (same opening times as the Crusader Church).

Around Abu Ghosh

Driving from Abu Ghosh towards Jerusalem, look out for a side street just outside town that goes to Kiryat Anavim, the Village of Grapes. The **first kibbutz in the Judaean hills**, it was founded in 1920 above a valley in a stunning setting. The spacious guesthouse with a pool in a well-tended garden is a tranquil place to stay before or after visiting Jerusalem.

Kiryat Anavim

Kiryat Ye'arim, the Village of the Forest, lies 1km/0.5mi west of Abu Ghosh and was founded in 1952. It bears the name of the biblical Kiryat Ye'arim (Joshua 9:17), which was probably located on the hill 3km/2mi to the northeast. The town's name is mentioned in the Old Testament in connection with the **Ark of the Covenant**: the Israelites had carried the Ark of the Covenant with them during their battles against the Philistines in the 11th century BC, and lost it to their enemy at Ebenezer. The Philistines brought it to Ashdod, then to Gat and Ekron (1 Samuel 4 f.). Since the Philistines believed the Ark of the Covenant would bring them misfortune, they returned it to the Israelites, who brought it to Kiryat Ye'arim. It stayed there for twenty years in the house of Abinadab (1 Samuel 6 f.). When David became king of the whole of Israel and took Jerusalem, he had the Ark of the Covenant brought there.

Kiryat Ye'arim

 Baedeker TIP

Bible live

How did people live in biblical times? In Yad Hashmona, 2km/1.25mi north of Kiryat Ye'arim, this question is answered vividly. Everything that made up a biblical village is there: the synagogue, oil-presses and the mint. To conclude a visit, why not enjoy a biblical meal in a tent made of goat's leather; there is a guest-house (tel. 02/5 94 20 000, www.yad8.com).

✷ Acre · Akko

F 2

District: Northern
Population: 60,000

Altitude: 20m/65ft

The town of Akko, historically known in English as Acre, which protrudes into the sea on a fortified headland, was Palestine's most significant harbour from Antiquity to the 19th century and is now one of the liveliest and most visited towns in the country. From its time as the capital of a crusader kingdom, several interesting structures remain. The old town was declared a UNESCO World Heritage Site in 2001.

Oriental flair Mosques, caravanserais, fortifications, crusader buildings and the old harbour that is now used by fishing boats and sailing yachts give the old town, inhabited by Arabs, its unique atmosphere. A good place to experience Akko's market life is its souk, where fresh fish, vegetables and spices are for sale. Small street stalls all over the town sell freshly pressed juices, ice cream or pastries sweetened with honey.

5000 years of history A Canaanite settlement, which was probably inhabited as early as 3000 BC, was located in the spot that is now Tell el-Fukhar to the east of the old town. Because of its **strategically favourable location** Akko was occupied by the Egyptian pharaohs Thutmose III and Rameses II. From 532 BC until the Greek conquest exactly 200 years later, Akko was Persian. In 261 BC it was given the name Ptolemais, after Ptolemy II, but in 219 BC it fell to the Seleucids, under whom it was able to achieve independence as a city state. In AD 67, Emperor Nero awarded it civic privileges, from AD 190 the town was the seat of a bishop and during the Byzantine period it was a flourishing centre of trade.

! **Baedeker TIP**

Swimming with a view

Argaman Beach, also known as Purple Beach, is one of Israel's most beautiful beaches. It has spectacular views of Akko's harbour walls (coast road Haifa–Akko).

Capital of the crusader kingdom ► The crusaders conquered the port in 1104, calling it St Jean d'Acre and making it the economic centre of the crusader kingdom and the headquarters of the Order of Saint John. Genoa, Pisa and Venice founded trading posts in Akko, Emperor Frederick II landed here in 1228 during his crusade, and the French king Louis IX stopped in the port after his unsuccessful crusade in 1250. For a few years the different religions lived peacefully side by side in Akko, until Christian soldiers murdered a number of Muslim citizens in 1290. When the Mamluk sultan al-Ashraf Khalil took Akko on 18 May 1291, this marked the end of the crusader state. The derelict port remained uninhabited for more than 300 years, until the Druze emir Fakhr al-Din had it rebuilt in the 17th century.

Ahmed al-Jezzar ► The most beautiful Arab buildings and the old town in its current form were built under the violent Ahmed al-Jezzar, known as the Butcher, who ruled as pasha from 1775 to 1805. With British help he prevented Napoleon from establishing himself in Akko in 1799. During the late 19th century Beirut and Haifa succeeded Akko as significant ports. When British forces took Akko from the Turks in 1918, the town had a population of 8000, the majority being Arabs. The Brit-

? **DID YOU KNOW ...?**

■ Over the course of its history, the town has seen many illustrious visitors, not all of whom came with peaceful intentions. A small selection includes King Solomon, Alexander the Great, Julius Caesar, St Paul the Apostle, Francis of Assisi, Emperor Frederick II, Louis IX (Saint Louis) and Napoleon.

ish held Jewish guerrillas captive in the citadel in 1920 and during the Second World War. On 17 May 1948, the town was taken by Israeli troops.

Tour of the Old Town

Walk along Weizmann Road from the central bus station to a wide opening in the town wall. It got its current appearance in the 18th century under Ahmed al-Jezzar. For a good view of the entire town, it is worth climbing up the ramp and walking along the wall all the way to the land gate. En route, at the northeastern corner, is the imposing tower of Burj el-Kummander, which Napoleon failed to take in 1799. It stands on the foundations of the so-called Cursed Tower, from which Richard the Lionheart had the banner of the Duke of Austria taken down in 1191. The land gate was the only way into the old town from the landward side until 1910, when a large breach, now Weizmann Road, was made in the fortification.

Town wall and land gate

To get to Jezzar Pasha Mosque, the **largest and most beautiful mosque in Akko,** follow Saladin Road. Its tall, slender minaret, the only one of its kind in Israel, towers above the roofs of the old town. Ahmed al-Jezzar had it built in 1781 on the site of the crusader cathedral, based on the pattern of Ottoman domed mosques (daily 8am–noon, 1.15pm–4pm, not during prayer times). The mosque's courtyard, with palms, olive and citrus trees as well as fragrant flower beds, is accessed via a staircase next to the delicate Rococo kiosk. The courtyard is surrounded by arcaded halls on three sides; in the past pilgrims and believers were put up in the neighbouring rooms.

★ **Jezzar Pasha Mosque**

? DID YOU KNOW ...?

■ The oath »by the beard of the prophet« is well known. In Jezzar Pasha Mosque (in the extension with the sarcophagi) there are indeed three hairs of the prophet, which are venerated as relics.

The eye-catcher in the courtyard is an ablution fountain, whose copper roof is supported by delicate columns. The mosque's domed prayer room, ornamented with plenty of marble, is considered to be a particularly beautiful **example of the Turkish Rococo style.** The sarcophagi of the man who commissioned its construction, Ahmed al-Jezzar (d. 1805) and his successor Suleiman Pasha (d. 1819) can be found in a small annexe to the right of the prayer room.

◄ Prayer room

From the left (eastern) arcade of the courtyard, there are steps down to an underground cistern from the time of the crusaders. After partially collapsing, it can no longer be accessed, however.

Cistern

The crusader town within the citadel is the main attraction of Akko. The enormous complex of buildings, constructed and used by the Order of Saint John as an administrative centre, was covered and

★ ★ **Citadel and crusader town**

► Knights' Halls

filled in after 1291 and is now 4m/13ft below street level. Ahmed al-Jezzar had his citadel built above the crusader town in the 18th century. Definitely take advantage of the audio guide that is included in the entrance fee. Seven vaulted halls were uncovered in the northern part of the complex. They are known as the Knights' Halls, and probably correspond to the order's seven »tongues« or national divisions. They served as accommodation for the order's soldiers. A further hall, known as Grand Munir, covered by a groin vault, adjoins the other halls to the south. The impressive spatial impact of the Knights' Halls is exceeded by the refectory, incorrectly also known as the crypt: massive round columns support the early Gothic vaulted ceiling of this huge, dark hall, which was »modernized« in the 13th century, meaning it was given cross ribs. The coats-of-arms with lilies on two corbels recall the stay of the French king Louis VII in 1148.

● VISITING AKKO

INFORMATION

Akko Visitor Centre
1 Weitzman St., P.O. Box 1181
IL-Old Acre
Tel. 1-700-708020
www.akko.org.il

TRANSPORT

There are regular buses from/to Haifa (no. 262, 271, 272) and towards Nahariya (information tel. 04/954 95 55).

WHERE TO EAT

Wherever there are tourists, there are plenty of shawerma stalls, particularly around Jezzar Pasha Mosque.

► Expensive

① *Uri Buri*
At the lighthouse
Tel. (04) 955 22 12 The speciality of this much-praised restaurant is anchovy fillet in lime juice and pepper.

► Expensive/Moderate

② *Abu Christo*
Marina

Tel. (04) 991 00 65 Popular tourist restaurant on the marina; mainly grilled fish and meat dishes.

WHERE TO STAY

► Mid-range

① *Palm Beach*
Acre Beach (south of the Old Town)
Tel. (04) 987 77 77
Fax 991 04 34
www.palmbeach.co.il
125 very nice and generously-sized rooms; the country club, a pool landscape in a lovely green setting, is pleasingly extensive. 15 minutes' walk to the old town. There is a beach with different times for women and men nearby.

② *Akkotel*
1 Salahuddin St, Old Town, Tel. (04) 987 71 00, www.akkotel.com This boutique hotel on the old fortification wall of the Old Town still possesses a crusader atmosphere. The restaurant has a vaulted ceiling, while the roof terrace has a first-rate view. Double rooms from 500 NIS

Acre · Old Town *Map*

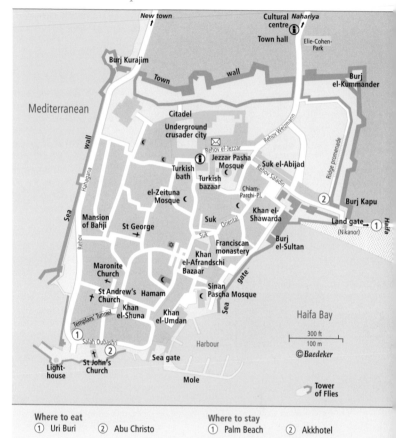

Mediterranean

New town
Cultural *Nahariya*
centre
Town hall
Elie-Cohen-Park
Burj Kurajim
Town wall
Burj el-Kummander
Citadel
Underground crusader city
Rehov el-Jezzar
Rehov Weizmann
Ridge promenade
Jezzar Pasha Mosque
Suk el-Abijad
Turkish bath
Rehov Saladin
Turkish bazaar
el-Zeituna Mosque
Chiam-Parchi-Pl.
Burj Kapu
Mansion of Bahji
Suk
Khan el-Shawarda
Land gate
(Nikanor)
St George
Suk Oriental
Franciscan monastery
Burj el-Sultan
Haifa
Maronite Church
Khan el-Afrandschi Bazaar
St Andrew's Church
Hamam
Sinan Pascha Mosque
Sea gate
Haifa Bay
Templars' Tunnel
Khan el-Shuna
Khan el-Umdan
Salah Oubashri
Harbour
300 ft
100 m
©*Baedeker*
St John's Church
Light-house
Sea gate
Mole
Tower of Flies
Rehov Hahagana
Wall
Sea
Burj el-Kummander

Where to eat
① Uri Buri ② Abu Christo

Where to stay
① Palm Beach ② Akkhotel

Leave the refectory down a flight of stairs and follow a low **underground corridor**, which was originally 350m/380yd long – not for those who suffer from claustrophobia. It dates back to the Persian period and was used by the crusaders as a secret passage to the town wall to the north and the harbour in the south. Today the corridor can only be accessed as far as the **Bosta**, a caravanserai (11th century), later a hospital run by the Order of Saint John. From the Bosta there is a trellised door, on the other side of which lies the »Beautiful Hall«.

Baha'u'llah and his family were incarcerated for two years in the **northwestern citadel tower**; his son died here. Many Bahai followers come here on a pilgrimage.

Underground Crusader City

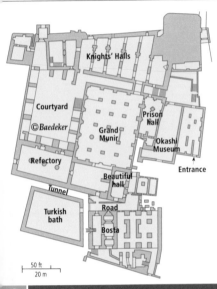

Knights' Halls

Courtyard

© Baedeker

Prison hall

Grand Munir

Okashi Museum

Refectory

Entrance

Beautiful hall

Tunnel

Turkish bath

Road

Bosta

50 ft
20 m

> ## ! *Baedeker* TIP
>
> ### Exploration
> Discover the Old Town of Akko away from the well-trodden paths and dare to enter the labyrinth of streets where Arab boys play football and old men sit outside cafés, chatting and smoking pipes.

Turn left at the Bosta to enter a (very touristy) **Turkish bazaar** or visit the **Turkish bath** (Hammam el-Pasha), created by Ahmed al-Jezzar.

Akko's **picturesque Old Town** was made a **UNESCO World Heritage Site** in December 2001. In the narrow streets to the south of the crusader town, some of which are roofed in corrugated iron, is the souk, a lively marketplace that gives an impression of everyday market life. There are also several former caravanserais (khans) dotted throughout the old town, but only **Khan el-Umdan**, which completes the harbour square to the south, still gives an idea of how these trading posts, built around a large square courtyard, may have once looked. The oldest is Khan el-Afranji, which means khan of the Franks (or Europeans), was built by Fakhr al-Din in around 1600.

The **harbour** of Akko was an important port of call in Antiquity and the Middle Ages. During the time of the crusades around 80 ships anchored here at any one time. Today colourful fishing boats and yachts bob up and down in the water and the waterfront is always very busy during the summer months.

Templar tunnel The town-side entrance to the aforementioned Templar tunnel, which runs from the crusader town to the southwestern sea wall, is located in Khan el-Shuna, a few metres west of Khan el-Umdan. A stretch of around 100m/100yd of the tunnel is open; it is significantly wider than the section in the crusader town, so no claustrophobia here. Leave the tunnel again on the western sea wall, in which an earthquake tore a huge hole in 1837.

Burj Kurajim The northern end of the sea wall is marked by Burj Kurajim (Tower of the Vine), which the Turks built to protect themselves from attacks from the sea.

From the town wall running inland, a lane leads to the entrance to Ahmed el-Jezzar's 18th-century citadel. It was used as a prison for a long time. A small museum exhibits photographs and documents commemorating the Jewish underground fighters who were imprisoned or executed here during the British mandate (Sun–Thu 9am–5pm).

Citadel

Around Akko

Around 3km/2mi north of Akko, on the road to Nahariya, are the Persian Gardens of Bahji. Amid this wonderful green space is the shrine with the mortal remains of Baha'u'llah (1817–92), the founder of the Bahai religion, who was banished from Persia to Akko in 1868 and spent his final years in the manor house in the park.

Gardens of Bahji

Louis VII, King of France, spent time in Akko's great halls.

✳
Ghetto Fighters'
House

Another 2km/1.25mi further, just outside Regba, is the striking museum building of the Lohamei Hageta'ot kibbutz, the Ghetto Fighters' House, founded by survivors of the Shoah (Holocaust) and former Jewish partisans. Apart from a cultural centre and a documentation centre named after the poet Beit Katznelson, who was murdered in Auschwitz in 1944, the building houses a museum about the different concentration camps and Jewish resistance to the Nazis in Poland and Lithuania.

Yodfat

Yodfat (ancient Jotapata) in Galilee is situated at the foot of the 548m/1798ft-high Azmon, almost 25km/16mi south of Akko. The town played a role during the Jewish rebellion in the years AD 66–70 and is also known as the **»Masada of the North«**. As **Josephus** wrote, it is located »almost entirely on a steep rock, whose sides drop away so steeply that anyone looking down will feel dizzy before his gaze reaches the bottom«. The town is only accessible from the north, where it is built straight across the flattening mountain ridge.

Jotapata was perfectly suited, being easy to defend, and thus it was occupied by many rebellious Jews in AD 67 under the leadership of the young priest Josephus, the same Josephus who later penned two of the most significant histories of Antiquity, *The Jewish War* and *Antiquities of the Jews* (in Latin). They defended Jotapata so fiercely against the Romans that Vespasian came himself. On the 47th day of the siege the Romans managed to breach the defences with a battering ram and take the town. They killed many of the inhabitants and took 1200 prisoners. Josephus hid in a cistern, from which he emerged a few days later to give himself up. He predicted that Vespasian would become emperor (which indeed he did a short while later), which is why he was spared.

Arad

F 5

District: Southern
Population: 22,000

Altitude: 640m/2100ft

Arad is a town designed on the drawing board and built in 1961 just a few miles to the southwest of the ▶ Dead Sea. Because of the extremely dry and warm climate, asthma sufferers come here to improve their health. The desert town is also known for the significant excavation site Tel Arad.

✳ Tel Arad

Excavation site

Approx. 10km/6mi west of Arad a road branches off from the Beersheba road, and leads to the Tell Arad excavation site, which consists of two larger complexes: the Canaanite settlement and the citadel.

On the site, which has been inhabited since the 4th millennium BC, a Canaanite settlement formed in the 2nd millennium along the important trade route between Syria and Egypt. Its king beat back the Israelites when they sought to enter the Promised Land from the south (Numbers 21:1). After Joshua had taken the site (Joshua 12:14), the Kenites, who were related to Moses, settled here (Judges 1:16). The extension and fortification of the town were probably the work of King Solomon, who also had a new temple built here for Yahweh on the site of a Kenite shrine.

The excavated settlement dates back to the second millennium BC. The royal palace and the temple are in the northwest, the residential quarter in the southwest.

Canaanite settlement

The buildings on the citadel date back to the post-Canaanite period. It was built between the early Israelite and Roman times. The massive fortification walls of the citadel were constructed from the original material. Enter the complex through the eastern gate, which is framed by massive defensive towers.

Citadel

The most important building here is the Jewish temple in the northwest of the citadel. Smaller rooms surround the courtyard, with the altar for burnt offerings, made of rubble and clay tiles, to the right.

✶ ◀ Temple

▶ VISITING ARAD

INFORMATION
28 Elazar Ben Yair St.
Tel. (08) 995 44 09
Sat–Thu 9am–5pm,
Fri 9am–1.30pm

GETTING THERE
There are several buses a day from Beersheba.

WHERE TO EAT
All the hotels serve full lunches and dinners.

WHERE TO STAY
▶ Mid-range
Margoa
87 Moav St.
Tel. (08) 995 12 22
Fax 995 77 78
www.margoa.com
Spa hotel with extensive grounds, rooms with views of the desert, ideal for trips to the Negev Desert and the Dead Sea

Inbar Hotel
38 Yehuda St.
Tel. (08) 997 33 03, fax 997 33 22
Building located on the edge of town with generously sized, nice rooms and pools (fresh and saltwater)

▶ Budget
Nof Arad
Moav St.
Tel. (08) 995 70 56, fax 995 40 53
Clean hotel with a pleasant pool

Arad Hotel
6 HaPalmach St.
Tel. (08) 995 70 40
Fax 995 72 72
Basic hotel, clean rooms

Towards the sanctum the bases for two cult columns have been discovered, which, under the names of Jachin and Boaz, also stood at Solomon's Temple in Jerusalem. Two low horned altars flank the entrance in the small rectangular room of the sanctum, with two cult stones in situ. The channels cut into the rock in the temple area served to bring water to the area and store it; there is for example a man-high channel that penetrates the walls of the settlement to the left of the sanctum. The temple is the **only Jewish religious building of its kind uncovered by excavations** and therefore of particular significance to the world of archaeology and religious history. The complex is considered evidence of the decentralization of the cult in the first centuries after the Israelites took possession of land in Canaan, when there were temples in Shiloh as well as in Bethel and Dan, and also in Arad. This state of affairs ended with King Josiah of Judah, who focused the temple cult on Jerusalem as part of comprehensive reforms of religious life.

Ashqelon

E 4

District: Southern   **Altitude:** 0–10m/33ft
Population: 105,000

For the local population the national park in Ashqelon (Ashkelon), a port 56km/35mi to the south of Tel Aviv, is primarily an excellent recreational area with a nice Mediterranean beach; however, the archaeological sites within the park are also of interest.

Residence of the Philistine princes — Excavations confirm that Ashqelon was already inhabited between 7000 and 4500 BC. One of the five residences of the Philistine princes from around 1200, Ashqelon became Phoenician in the 6th century BC. Four centuries later, under the Seleucid ruler Antiochus IX, it was given the right to be autonomous as well as its own calendar. In around 73 BC **Herod the Great** was probably born in Ashqelon. He gave the town »monumental baths and elaborate fountains as well as colonnades of incredible size and workmanship« (*The Jewish War* 21:11). Under the Romans, Ashqelon, in an advantageous position because of its location on the important north-south road (Via Maris), developed into an affluent trading town. The crusader king Baldwin II took the town in 1135. It remained in the hands of the crusaders until conquest by the Mamluk sultan Baibars in 1290. In place of the decaying port the Arab village of Migdal (tower) was

? DID YOU KNOW ...?

- In 1999 the oldest shipwrecks ever discovered were found off the coast of Ashqelon. Phoenician ships were on their way from Tyre to Carthage with a cargo of wine when they capsized in a storm in around 750 BC.

built here later. Jews from South Africa founded the settlement of Afridar (now the commercial centre) to the east of Migdal in 1952, from which the modern town of Ashqelon developed.

Until the time of the Jewish rebellion against Rome, Ashqelon and the Israelites were enemies. This is reflected in the biblical account of Samson: » For, lo, thou shalt conceive, and bear a son; and no razor shall come on his head: for the child shall be a Nazarite unto God from the womb: and he shall begin to deliver Israel out of the hand of the Philistines.« (Judges 13:5). Samson, who was married to a Philistine woman, killed 30 Philistines in Ashqelon during an argument. When the Philistines burned his wife, Samson, who was as strong as a bear, is said to have slain a thousand men (Judges 14–15). He revealed the secret of his strength to Delilah: he was invincible as long as his hair was not cut. After the Philistines cut off seven of his locks, they were able to capture him and blind him. But when his hair grew back, so too did his strength, and when he was presented at a festival in honour of the god Dagon to amuse the people, he pulled down the Temple of Dagon on top of himself and large numbers of Philistines.

Samson and the Philistines

Ashqelon *Map*

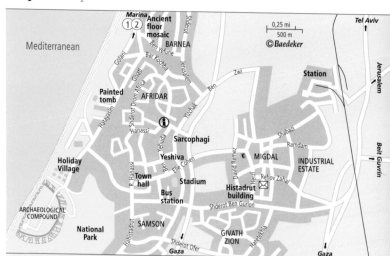

Where to stay
① Holiday Inn   ② Dan Gardens

▶ VISITING ASHQELON

INFORMATION

Town Hall, Afridar Center
Tel. (08) 673 24 12
Sun, Tue 8.30am–1pm, 4pm–6pm,
Mon, Wed, Thu 8.30am–2pm
In Ashdod:
Municipality Building
Tel. (08) 854 54 81

GETTING THERE

Buses and sherut from Tel Aviv and
Jerusalem to the central bus station

SHOPPING

There is a busy market in Migdal on
Mondays and Thursdays. The *pedes-
trian zone in Migdal* is a lovely place
to stroll; larger shops can be found in
Lev Ashqelon Mall in the Samson
Quarter, which has almost 100 stores.

WHERE TO EAT

Lovers of fast food will find plenty of
options here. Exception: the restaurants on the beaches are usually a good
tip for fish.

WHERE TO STAY

▶ Expensive

① *Holiday Inn*
9 Yekutiel Adam St.
Tel. (08) 674 88 88
Fax 671 88 23
www.afi-hotels.com
Comfortable rooms, spa, large pool,
garden, good restaurants; this is an
excellent option. The two buildings
are also interesting from an architectural perspective, and all of the rooms
have sea views.

▶ Mid-range

② *Dan Gardens*
56 Hatayassim St
Tel. 520 25 52
Fax 548 01 11
www.danhotels.com
248 rooms, nice swimming pool, the
hotel is also quite imaginative with
ideas for entertaining younger guests.

What to See in Ashqelon

Bearings Ashqelon consists of five neighbourhoods, which lie relatively far apart: Migdal, Givath Zion, Samson, Afridar and Barnea. The town is trav- ersed by wide streets. The huge **green spaces** stand out. Turn off the north-south road between Tel Aviv and Gaza, seaward into Shderot Ben Gurion, which leads into town. To the north of it and to the west of the railway line are the industrial area, where the Eilat pipeline ends, and the town of Migdal, Arab until 1948, which was incorporated into the young town in 1955. Past Histadrut House is the town centre.

Roman sarco- phagi Diagonally opposite the information office in the Afridar neighbour- hood there are two magnificent Roman sarcophagi under a protec- tive structure. They were discovered during excavation works in 1972. While one depicts battle scenes, the other shows the abduction of Persephone by Hades.

The Painted Tomb, which dates back to the Roman period (3rd century), near Ganei Shulamit hotel, is also worth seeing. Four steps lead down into the barrel-vaulted room with **frescoes**. The fresco on the wall opposite the entrance depicts two nymphs in a stream between trees and animals. The ceiling fresco shows Demeter, a dog chasing a gazelle, the head of a Gorgon, a boy with a basket of grapes, and Pan with his shepherd's flute.

Painted Tomb

Around 2km/1.25mi to the south of the town centre, embedded in a national park with a camp site, picnic sites, restaurants and a nice beach, is the **excavation site of ancient Ashqelon**. An impressive semicircular town wall, built by Baldwin III and Richard the Lionheart, surrounds the area and the discoveries, which range from the time of the Philistines to the Middle Ages. There is a path to a large car park from the entrance in the north of the complex. Just to the south of it are remains from the Roman period – large Corinthian capitals, bases and other remains of the extensive 100-column stoa,

National park

> ! **Baedeker TIP**
>
> **For water lovers**
> Ashqeluna Water Park, with pools, flumes, cafés, restaurants and a picnic area, is located on Delilah Beach, tel. (08) 673 99 70.

built by Herod the Great. The apse at the southern end of the stoa was refurbished several times at later dates, most recently as the prayer niche of a mosque. There is a large-format relief in it: a winged goddess of victory above a kneeling Atlas, supporting the world. A different relief depicts the goddess Isis with her son Horus. The **settlement hill of the Philistine town** is located at the old harbour in the far south. The remains of the Hospitaller tower and the foundations of the Church of St Mary from the crusader period stand on the site of the biblical Ashqelon.

Around Ashqelon

Around 20km/12mi to the north of Ashqelon is Ashdod, the country's second-largest port after Haifa. So far the town, with its population of 160,000, is mainly characterized by industrial activity, but there are plans to make tourism more important in the future. Around **10km/6mi of Mediterranean beach** and good bus and sherut connections to Jerusalem and Tel Aviv are the main attractions of Ashdod, which is why it could be considered as a place to stay.

Ashdod

> ! **Baedeker TIP**
>
> **Miami or Lido**
> The residents of Ashdod go to Miami Beach; that is where most of the cafés and evening meeting places are. But Lido Beach is also pleasant and on Wednesdays there is also a flea market here.

The kibbutz 10km/6mi to the south of Ashqelon, **Yad Morde-**

khay, was founded in 1943 and **named after the leader of the Warsaw Ghetto Uprising**. During the 1948 War of Independence the members of the kibbutz were able to hold off the Egyptian troops for five days, which allowed the Israeli armed forces to regroup in Tel Aviv. The battlefield has been rebuilt, true to the original. There is also a memorial hall commemorating the Warsaw Ghetto uprising.

★★ Avdat · Horvot Avedat

E 6

District: Southern   **Altitude:** 625m/2050ft

The extensive complex of ruins of the town of Avdat (Arabic = Avda) is among the most significant sites in the Negev Desert.

Significant Nabataean town

The excavation site (archaeological national park) with buildings from the Nabataean, Roman and Byzantine periods, is situated 65km/40mi south of ►Beersheba, immediately south of the road to Eilat. It is conspicuous from afar, located on top of a hill. Excavations proved that the town was founded in the 3rd century BC. At that time, the Nabataeans, who came here from northwest Arabia, switched from a nomadic to a sedentary lifestyle. The Nabataean caravan leaders and merchants secured the trading connections between Petra (in modern-day Jordan), their capital, and the Mediterranean port of Gaza through several bases, such as Nitzana, ►Shivta, Obodas (Avdat) and Mampsis (►Mamshit) as well as through guard posts along the way. These settlements are among the more than 2000 Nabataean settlements in southern Jordan, in the Negev and on the Sinai Peninsula.

i **Illustrious origins**

▪ The Nabataeans claimed to be descended from Nabat, a grandson of Abraham.

Golden age ►

At the end of the 1st century BC the town was named after the Nabataean king Obodas II (20–9 BC), from which the modern name Avdat derives. King Obodas was buried in Avdat and worshipped as a god. Under him and his significant successor Aretas IV (9 BC–AD 40) the town experienced its first golden age.

Roman rule ►

The Romans conquered the region of Nabataea in AD 106 and incorporated it into the empire as Provincia Arabia Petraea. They built a road from Eilat to Damascus which avoided Avdat. This led to its decline. When a military camp was built north of Avdat in the late 3rd century and a Temple of Jupiter was built in the site of the Temple of Obodas on the acropolis, the town recovered again. At the end of the 4th century, the Nabataeans were Christianized. In the 6th century Emperor Justinian moved monks to the acropolis, who extended the irrigation systems and worked the land. A new golden age began.

However, when Avdat was conquered by the Persians in AD 614 and by the Islamic Arabs in AD 634, it declined. It was abandoned in the 10th century and the irrigation systems fell into ruin.

✱ Excavation Site

The **entrance**, with a large car park, a ticket office, a visitor centre, a kiosk, and a petrol station, is situated below the excavation site near Route 40 from Beersheba to Eilat. A road leads up to two further car parks.

🕐 Opening hours: April–Sept daily 8am–5pm, otherwise until 4pm

Burial site

Half way to the upper car park, turn right to the Nabataean burial site. From a vaulted anteroom made out of ashlar blocks, a door, whose lintel features a relief of a horned altar flanked by the moon and a star (left) and the sun (right) as well as two columns, leads into the actual burial chamber, which is carved into the rock. It had room for 22 double-storey tombs.

Roman quarter

Shortly before the upper car park, on the right-hand side, are the remains of a Roman villa, now a restored residential building, which was arranged around a square courtyard with a cistern.
From the upper car park, walk through a **residential quarter** that dates back to the Roman period. Next there is a Nabataean **wine press** with a semicircular upper and rectangular lower section, which was used until the Byzantine period.

Byzantine fort

The route now makes its way through the south gate of the acropolis into the Byzantine fort on the plateau (61 x 41m/67 x 45yd). From the watchtower it is possible to see the entire extensive compound with its partially restored walls and towers, the large cistern in the courtyard as well as the ruins of a late Byzantine **chapel** by the north wall. An opening in the east wall leads to the 90 x 90m/100 x 100yd Roman army camp and to the former **Nabataean pottery**. The Nabataeans were famous in ancient times for their painted clay vessels with extremely thin walls.

Religious district

Go back to the Byzantine fort and turn west. Adjoining the fort on this side is the religious district, which also dates back to the Byzantine period. There are two churches, which were built on the sites of Nabataean and Roman temples. To the left is a church named after a 4th-century Greek martyr, Saint Theodore's Church, also the South Church, a basilica with three apses. The central portal is adorned by two Nabataean horned capitals. In the southern aisle there is a panel depicting the seven-armed candelabra next to the cross; another says that Zechariah, son of John, was buried here »in the martyrdom of Saint Theodore«. The chancel is two steps higher. On the right-hand side of the main apse, as well as in front of the side apse, parts of the templon survive. The templon separates the nave from the chancel.

◄ Saint Theodore's Church

Avdat Map

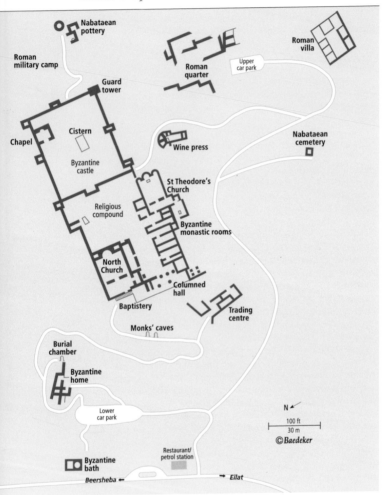

Nabataean pottery

Roman military camp

Guard tower

Roman quarter

Upper car park

Roman villa

Chapel

Cistern

Wine press

Nabataean cemetery

Byzantine castle

St Theodore's Church

Religious compound

Byzantine monastic rooms

North Church

Columned hall

Baptistery

Trading centre

Monks' caves

Burial chamber

Byzantine home

Lower car park

N

100 ft
30 m
©*Baedeker*

Byzantine bath

Restaurant/ petrol station

Beersheba ←

→ Eilat

Monastic quarters from the Byzantine period adjoin the church to the west. Bordering the steep drop at the western side of the religious district is a wide **terrace**, which opens up into the courtyard through columns. The gate to the terrace is – like the central entrance to Saint Theodore's church – fitted with Nabataean capitals. At the northern section of the terrace, the **baptistery**, there is a cruciform font. Next to it is the entrance to the atrium of the complex's oldest church, the **North Church**, whose dedication is not known. It too is a

One of the best-preserved parts of Saint Theodore's Church is the sanctuary.

basilica (nave, two aisles) with three apses. Two steps lead into the chancel with its square altar.

The route from the lower car park to the acropolis first leads past the remains of a Byzantine residential quarter. Then, after a picture of a saint with a Greek inscription, there are the saints' burial chamber as well as two cave tombs. To get to the terrace, take the steps by the font. Below the lower car park is a **Byzantine bath**, which was still in use during Arab times.

Byzantine quarter

Anyone who feels like a little bit of nature and wants to cool off after visiting the ruins of Avdat should drive via ►Sde Boqer to the nearby spring of Ein Avdat. Walk down a steep gorge, where the cool water rises up from the rock. Swimming is not permitted, but that hardly bothers anyone. Beware! The water is not for drinking.

★
Ein Avdat springs

Banias

G 1

Area: Golan   **Altitude:** Sea level

From the source of the Jordan River an excursion leads to the country's far north. The Banias, the second-largest headwater stream of Israel's longest and most significant river, rises at the foot of the Hermon massif.

National park The area, occupied by Israel since 1967, has since been declared a national park. At the spring, 13km/7mi east of the small town of Kiryat Shmona, situated in stunning scenery, a town with the same name developed. It is a popular destination for Israeli and Druze families (Hermon National Park; daily 8am–4pm, in summer until 5pm, same times for Nimrod Fortress, see below).

History The name Banias, Arabic Baniyas, Hebrew Hermon, comes from the Greek Paneas. A significant temple dedicated to the shepherd god Pan stood at the source from the Hellenistic period. The worship of Pan had emerged from an older cult of Baal. Augustus gave the area to Herod I, whose son Philip declared Paneas the capital of his kingdom and renamed it Caesarea Philippi in honour of the Roman emperor.

This is the spot where Jesus called his disciple Simon **Peter** the rock on which he would build his church (Matthew 13:13–20). Agrippa II (AD 53–94) built himself a magnificent palace here, the remains of which were only recently discovered. In the 4th century Caesarea was the seat of a bishop, and in the 7th century it was conquered by the Arabs. For around 40 years it was part of the crusader kingdom and subsequently was an Arab village until 1967.

What to See in and around Banias

Banias spring The Banias (Baniyas) spring rises from a reddish-grey rocky wall and gathers in several pools. The niches of the caves above once contained statues of Pan. The river originally appeared from the large grotto of the Pan temple, until an earthquake blocked this route.

Weli Further left, on a hill, is the tomb (weli) of the Islamic saint and Druze prophet Sheikh el-Khidr (the Green One), which is a site of pilgrimage for members of the Druze religious community.

Waterfall A pleasant trail leads from the spring past a water mill and to a 10m/30ft waterfall, 1km/0.6mi to the west. It can also be reached by car. A road to the car park branches off from the road to Kiryat Shmona (on the left).

The second-largest headwater stream of the Jordan rises in this cave.

Around 3km/2mi to the east, to the left of the road to the Hermon region, is Nimrod Fortress, on top of an elongated mountain ridge (Subeiba). According to Druze tradition, the Babylonian king Nimrod, great-grandson of Noah, built this huge fortress. It gets its second name, Subeiba, from a legend that says that God sent the boastful Nimrod a fly (Hebrew: zebub), which killed the king in a gruesome manner by creeping into his brain and eating it. The fortress often changed hands in the Middle Ages. For three years it was the base of the Assassins. It was extended by the crusaders, who took the peak in around 1130, and then again in the 13th century by the Muslims. Even as a ruin, the extensive complex, fortified by towers, still presents an impressive picture. It is also worth a visit because of its stunning views.

★
Nimrod Fortress

Beersheba · Be'er Sheva

E 5

District: Southern
Population: 200,000

Altitude: 240m/790ft

Anyone travelling to southern Israel will almost inevitably pass through Beersheba (Be'er Sheva), which has developed within just a few decades into a proper transport hub and the »capital of the Negev«.

»Gateway to the Negev«
The industrial and university town located around 85km/53mi southwest of Jerusalem is unmistakably also the »gateway to the Negev«, because the extensive fields that determine the landscape to the north here give way the arid steppe, which cannot be used for anything other than grazing, and which in turn gives way to desert. Beersheba does not have any outstanding attractions. Tourists mainly come here in order to visit the large Bedouin market that is held every Thursday.

History
The earliest settlement in the Beersheba area (Tell Beersheba) dates back to the 4th millennium BC and was inhabited by semi-nomadic people who built cisterns and caves on the riverbank. In the dry period they left these dwelling places and followed their herds northwards. Several discoveries from their settlement are on display in the Negev Museum in Beersheba. After the land seizure by the Israelites the town formed the southern border of their domain.

Beersheba Map

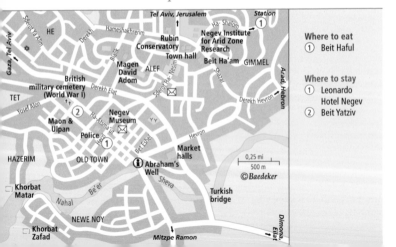

Where to eat
① Beit Haful

Where to stay
① Leonardo Hotel Negev
② Beit Yatziv

► VISITING BEERSHEBA

GETTING THERE
Good bus connections and sherut taxis from Jerusalem, Tel Aviv (duration: approx. 90 mins) and Eilat

SHOPPING
The much-praised Bedouin market is worth a short visit at best. Those who are looking for electronic goods, clothes, shoes and the like will enjoy it. The Canion Mall is a popular place to go shopping.

ENTERTAINMENT
Beersheba's night owls meet around Trumpeldor St. and Hasimita St., for example in the branch of Tel Aviv's Punchline (same name), where the waiters not only serve, but also sing and dance.

WHERE TO EAT
The Spaghettim pasta factory, known around the country, a lot of fast food chains, countless restaurants – Beersheba lacks culinary highlights.

► Inexpensive
① *Beit Haful*
15 Ha-Histradut St.
Tel. (08) 627 04 25
Lovers of ful, a dark bean mash, swear by this basic restaurant, which also serves shawerma.

WHERE TO STAY
► Mid-range
① *Leonardo Hotel Negev*
4 Henrietta Szold
Tel. (08) 640 54 44
Fax 640 54 45
www.leonardo.hotels.com
Guests stay near the Ben Gurion University and the shopping malls; the hotel also helps with organizing tours to the Negev Desert.

► Budget
② *Beit Yatziv*
79 Ha-Atsma'ut St.
Tel. (08) 627 74 44
Fax 627 57 35
Very clean hostel with a more comfortable guesthouse for those guests who are not quite so young anymore.

The town only became more significant when the Turkish rulers set up the **administrative centre for the Bedouin tribes** of the Negev in Beersheba in around 1900, creating what is now the old quarter as well as a Bedouin market. Beersheba was the first town in Palestine to be occupied by the British in 1917. The Jewish families who had moved to Beersheba left the town during the 1929 Palestine riots. After Israel's independence in 1948, Beersheba once again saw Jewish settlers moving in.

What to See in Beersheba

Beersheba still has a little bit of the »wild west character« of its founding years. Life is concentrated around the **old quarter**, created   Orientation during the Turkish period, with its grid-pattern street layout, many shops, basic restaurants and snack stalls as well as the cultural centre Bet Ha'am. Extensive residential quarters were built to the north of the old town, while industry is located to the east. This is where the Negev's resources are processed.

Negev Museum

The main axis of the old town is HaAzmaut St., also the location of the Negev Museum. It was set up in a mosque dating back to the Turkish period and exhibits, among other things, discoveries from the settlement of Tell Beersheba from the 4th millennium BC.

Abraham's Well

Follow HaAzmaut St. in a southerly direction. At the junction with Hebron St. (Derekh Hevron) there is an old, restored well. Although known as Abraham's Well, it was probably only built during the Turkish period.

i Etymological matters

■ When Abraham forged an oath of allegiance with King Abimelech and signed a treaty that gave him the right to use the well he had dug himself, he gave Abimelech seven lambs just for the well and called the place Beersheba: »Be'er = well, shewa = seven« (Genesis 21:22–32).

At the southern end of Beersheba, at the road to ► Eilat, a large **Bedouin market** is held on Thursday mornings. Items of interest to tourists are rugs, artistically embroidered cushions and camel saddles as well as copper containers and many other traditional handicraft objects. Those expecting a picturesque oriental scene will be disappointed; nevertheless a visit to this market will provide an insight into Bedouin life.

Around Beersheba

Tell Beersheba

4km/2.5mi northeast of Beersheba, at the monument to the Negev Brigade, which distinguished itself in the war of 1948, lie the remains of ancient Beersheba, Tell Beersheba (national park). The remains from different settlement phases have been uncovered on the excavation site, including an ancient fortress, a well as well as casemates. Most of the walls date back to the 8th–10th centuries.

Kibbutz Lahav

✱

Bedouin Museum ►

🕐

The Lahav kibbutz, around 20km/12mi northeast of Beersheba, has a Bedouin museum that was opened in 1985. Just like the Daroma Museum, which informs visitors about daily life from the Stone Age to the Iron Age, it is part of the Joe Alon Center. The well-selected exhibits, particularly the traditional clothes, household items, tools and jewellery, provide insights into the everyday life and culture of the Bedouin tribes of the Sinai and the Negev Desert (daily 9am–5pm, Fri until 2pm).

Israeli Air Force Museum

Around 10km/6mi west of Beersheba, near the kibbutz of Hazerim, the Israeli Air Force Museum was opened next to the Hazerim base.

The Bedouin market of Beersheba is practical rather than picturesque.

Original aircraft, a photographic exhibition and film screenings document the history of the Israeli Air Force (tel. 08 990 68 53 daily except Sat 8am–5pm, Fri until 1pm). ⊕

✳ **Belvoir**

District: Northern   **Altitude:** 312m/1024ft

High above the Jordan Valley are the imposing ruins of the large crusader castle that was appropriately called Belvoir by the French Templars because of its view of the valley. In Hebrew it is called »Kokhav Hayarden« (»Star of the Jordan«).

The castle built after 1168 by the Knights Hospitallers was one of the strongest border fortifications of the French kingdom and was even able to resist Saladin's attack in 1187. Two years later, however, the knights had to abandon the fort in exchange for being allowed to retreat to Tyre in safety. When the danger arose that the crusaders would try to repossess the castle, the Arabs razed it in 1219. The Christians, who retook the fort in 1241, elected not to rebuild it.

History

✳ **Belvoir Castle**

🕐 Opening hours:
Daily 8am–4pm, in
summer until 5pm

The complex, made out of dark basalt and measuring 100 x 140m/
110 x 155yd, is surrounded by a deep moat on three sides. The outer walls, in the shape of a pentagon, are strengthened by seven towers. To the east of the castle complex the mountain drops off steeply
to the Jordan Valley. This side
was fortified by a tower that pro-
jected very far was destroyed the
last time Belvoir Castle was besieged. The castle walls surround
an inner (square) fort, which
could still be defended even in
the event that the outer castle was
captured. On the ground floor of
this inner castle there were store
rooms, the kitchen and, adjoining
it, the dining hall. Upstairs were
the knights' living quarters as well
as a church. Today a pedestrian
bridge in the west crosses the
trench where once there was a
drawbridge.

Belvoir Crusader Castle

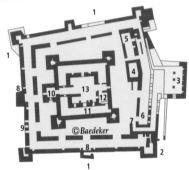

1 Moat
2 Southeastern tower
3 Eastern tower
4 Cistern
5 Bathhouse
6 Warehouses, stables etc.
7 Inner eastern gate
8 Escape gate
9 Western gate
10 Main gate of
   the inner fortress
11 Dining room
12 Kitchen
13 Inner courtyard

The **kibbutz of Neve Ur**, around
4km/2.5mi south of Belvoir, is
home to Jews from Iraq, which is
why it is named after the Mesopotamian home of Abraham.

Bet Guvrin · Maresha · Lachish

E/F 4

District: Southern   **Altitude:** 275m/900ft

**Beit Guvrin Maresha National Park comprises the ruins of the sites
of Beit Guvrin and Maresha. The special feature of Maresha are
the caves, around 60 of them, all around the tell. There is another
excavation site not too far away: the Canaanite settlement of
Lachish.**

Getting here   The extensive national park grounds are located to the south of
Route 35 from Ashqelon to Hebron, near the kibbutz of Beit Gubrin,
which was founded in 1949 on the ruins of an Arab village. Coming
from ►Ashqelon the entrance to the national park is to the right before reaching the entrance to the kibbutz.

In the 6th century BC, Beit Gubrin was just a suburb of the Edomite capital of Maresha 2km/1.25mi away. In the 2nd century BC both were conquered by the Maccabees. Under Roman rule it developed into a significant fortified settlement, to which Emperor Septimius Severus gave the name of Eleutheropolis, meaning city of the free.

Capital of the Edomites

Maresha was considered part of the area of the Kingdom of Judah in the Old Testament (Joshua 15:44) and covered an area of around 2.4 ha/6.25 acres – just a third of the neighbouring Lachish (see below). Solomon's son Rehoboam, King of Judah, fortified Maresha in around 920 along with Lachish and 14 other places: »These were fortified cities in Judah and Benjamin« (2 Chronicles 11:8–10). The town destroyed by the Babylonians in 587 BC was not re-occupied by Jews after the Babylonian exile. In the 4th century BC the Phoenicians founded a colony here, which went against their habit, as it was not by the sea but in the interior. In the 3rd century the town was Hellenized and was the main town of the province of Idumaea. In around 160 BC Judas Maccabaeus captured it on his way from Hebron to Asdod, and under the Hasmonean leader John Hyrcanus I it was Judaized by force. Its final destruction occurred in 40 BC.

Beit Guvrin Maresha National Park

Almost nothing is left of the former Beit Guvrin. Excavations 1km/ 0.5mi south of the current village have brought to light two floor mosaics from 5th/6th-century churches. They depict hunting scenes, wild animals and the symbols of the seasons. In addition a 3rd-century synagogue was discovered. Both the mosaic floors as well as the synagogue's most important interior pieces are now in the Rockefeller Museum in ▶Jerusalem.

Excavations

The well-signposted route to the individual caves and other attractions can be covered on foot or by car. There are several car parks in the park. Picnic tables, toilets and a kiosk are located at the Bell Caves northeast of Tell Maresha.

Bearings

Drive from the park entrance to the car park at the foot of Tell Maresha. The views make the climb worthwhile. On the tell's western slopes is a kind of **burial cave** from the 2nd century BC. It is 32m/ 35yd long and 2.3m/8ft wide. The walls have, like Roman necropolises, more than 2000 niches in them. There is still no agreement as to whether urns were kept in them or whether they just served as nesting sites for pigeons. In any case, the name that has stuck for the largest of the approximately 60 caves discovered in the surrounding area is Columbarium (dovecote).

Tell Maresha

◀ Columbarium
◀ Bathing Cave

The next stop on the tour is the Bathing Cave with pools carved from the rock, and the neighbouring cave with an **oil press**. Continue towards the car park to get to a house with a large cistern dating back to late Antiquity. The caves to the south of the tell, which are

This burial chamber with 44 niches was discovered in the eastern part of Tell Maresha.

all interconnected, were used for various purposes.

Bell Caves ▶ Even more impressive than the burial caves are the Bell Caves to the northeast of the tell, which are interconnected via underground passages. The individual caves were bell-shaped structures that received light through openings in their ceilings. The »cave builders« struck holes into the hard surface rocks in order to exploit underground quarries. The caves were probably made between the 7th and 10th centuries.

St Anne ▶ The Church of St Anne to the east of the road connecting Maresha and Beit Guvrin was built by crusaders in the 12th century. The nave is still well-preserved.

Lachish · Lakkish

Getting here Take road 35 from Beit Guvrin towards Kiryat Gat. After 7km/4.5mi, a road turns off to the left and leads 3km/2mi to Tell Lachish.

Site of the Lach-
ish letters In the 2nd millennium BC Lachish was a Canaanite town which was conquered in the 13th century BC by Joshua along with the neighbouring Maresha (Joshua 10). The palace was rebuilt by either David or Solomon in the 10th century BC. Solomon's son Rehoboam fortified the town in around 920 BC (2 Chronicles 11:11). The Assyrian Sanherib conquered Lachish in 701 BC (2 Kings 18:13–17) and depicted this event in reliefs in his palace in Ninveh. In 588 BC, two years before the conquest of Jerusalem, the Babylonian Nebuchadnezzar conquered the town. The time immediately preceding this is documented in the 21 Lachish letters, which are now kept in the

British Museum in London and in the Rockefeller Museum in ►Jerusalem.

A total of nine settlement layers from the 3rd millennium BC until the 3rd century BC as well as the remains of a town wall to the north of modern-day Moshav were discovered during excavation works. The fortification, consisting of an interior and exterior wall, has a powerful gateway, in whose tower (to the right behind the outer gate) the **Lachish letters** were found: **clay tablets with ink, in ancient Hebrew**. A palace, the seat of the governor, a well tunnel and a temple to the sun from around 1480 BC were discovered on the excavation site. `Tell Lachish`

✱ Bethlehem · Bait Lahm

`F 4`

Area: West Bank (Palestine)

Altitude: 750m/2460ft
Population: 50,000

The Hebrew name of Christ's birthplace refers to the region's fertility because it is translated as »house of bread« (Hebrew »lehm« = »bread«), while the Arabic name means »house of meat« (Beit Lahm). Christians from all around the world come to pray at the Church of the Nativity.

The town was mentioned for the first time in a report about the death of Jacob's wife **Rachel** (Genesis 35:19). Centuries later the widowed **Ruth** left Moab with her mother-in-law Naomi for her home town of Bethlehem. It was there that Ruth married Boaz and gave birth to Obed, »... the father of Jesse, the father of David« (Ruth 4:17). David was anointed king in Bethlehem (1 Samuel 16:13). According to tradition it was from his line that **Jesus** was descended. According to the gospel (Luke 2:1–7), he was born in Bethlehem after Mary and Joseph left their home town of Nazareth to come here for the census. `Christ's birthplace`

From 1967 to 21 December 1995 Bethlehem, situated around 10km/ 6mi to the south of ►Jerusalem in a fertile landscape, was occupied by Israel. Now the city is **under Palestinian administration**. Bethlehem's Arab population is half Muslim, half Christian. A majority of the population live from tourism. The manufacture and sale of figurines and Nativity sets are particularly prevalent, but tourists can also buy jewellery as well as mother-of-pearl and embroidery. Those who do not work in tourism have found work processing the local white limestone into building material. A lot of men from Bethlehem also work in hotels in Jerusalem, in the construction industry or as farmers. `Bethlehem today`

✷✷ Church of the Nativity

Opening hours:
Daily 6am–6pm

After the Bar Kokhba revolt was put down, in AD 135 Emperor Hadrian built a Temple of Adonis over the Grotto of the Nativity, which Emperor Constantine replaced by a church in AD 325. This church was probably a basilica with a central nave and four aisles, with an atrium in the west and an octagon in the east. The grotto was below it and pilgrims were able to look down into it through an opening. In AD 386 **St Jerome** travelled to Bethlehem, settled in a cave next to the Grotto of the Nativity and wrote the Vulgate, his now famous translation of the Bible into Latin. Even in those days pilgrims came from many countries.

> ! *Baedeker* TIP
>
> **Early morning**
>
> Those who wish to enjoy the special atmosphere in the Church of the Nativity without lots of other visitors around will have to get up early, preferably to arrive when the basilica opens its doors at 6am. This is particularly true in the turbulent Christmas period.

Rebellious Samaritans destroyed the church in 529. Sabbas, who lived in the nearby monastery ►Mar Saba, persuaded Emperor Justinian to reconstruct it. Justinian's architect took over the concept of the nave and four aisles from the old church, but replaced the octagon with a three-apse arrangement, forgoing the atrium.

This church still stands today, which is nothing short of a miracle. The Persians. who were at war with Byzantium, spared the church in 614 because they believed that the Three Magi in oriental clothes on the relief above the entrance were their fellow countrymen. On Christmas Day 1100 the crusader Baldwin I was crowned the first king of Jerusalem here. From 1161 to 1169 Emperor Manuel had the church thoroughly restored.

In the 18th and 19th centuries there were more and more confrontations between the Greek Orthodox believers, Catholics and Armenians, which became even worse through the involvement of Russia and France. In 1757, the Sublime Porte tried to address this problem by imposing a **usage regulation**, which is still in effect today.

Entrance through the Door of Humility

The fort-like Church of the Nativity stands in the eastern corner of Manger Square, squeezed between a Franciscan monastery and the Church of St Catherine in the north, a Greek Orthodox monastery in the southeast and an Armenian monastery in the southwest. It originally had three entrances but the two at the sides have been walled up. At the central entrance the original door frame with the architrave of Justinian's building from the 6th century is still extant. The crusaders reduced the size of the entrance by adding a pointed arch portal and walling up the upper portions. It was later reduced in size yet again, so that it is now only 1.2m/3.9ft high, forcing those entering the building to bend down, hence the name Door of Humility.

Bethlehem *Map*

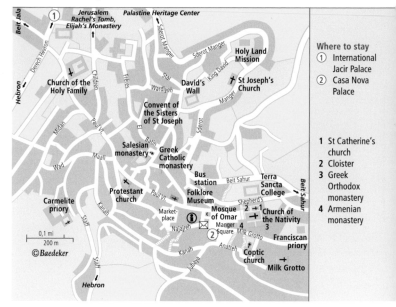

Beit Jala

Beit Jala
Jerusalem
Rachel's Tomb,
Elijah's Monastery

Palastine Heritage Center

Sderot Manger

Holy Land
Mission

King David

Church of the
Holy Family

Children

Freres

Star
Wardiyeh

David's
Wall

St Joseph's
Church

Manger

Convent of
the Sisters
of St Joseph

Sderot

Paul VI

Batin

Salesian
monastery

Greek
Catholic
monastery

Maali

Wad

Bus
station

Beit Sahur

Terra
Sancta
College

Beit Sahur

Carmelite
priory

Protestant
church

Paul VI

Folklore
Museum

Shepherd's

Kanah

Market-
place

Najajreh

Mosque
of Omar

Manger
Square

Church of
the Nativity

Milk Grotto

Franciscan
priory

0,1 mi
200 m

© Baedeker

Staff

Kanah

Anatreh

Coptic
church

Milk Grotto

Jibaja

Hebron

Where to stay
① International
   Jacir Palace
② Casa Nova
   Palace

1 St Catherine's
   church
2 Cloister
3 Greek
   Orthodox
   monastery
4 Armenian
   monastery

Interior

The interior still possesses the monumentality of Justinian's basilica. Four rows of eleven columns each, topped by Corinthian capitals that were originally gilded, support the clerestory in the nave and the roof of the aisles. Two openings in the floor of the nave allow visitors to see the floor mosaics of Constantine's church from AD 325, which lie 60cm/24in below the current floor level. The font is in the right aisle.

Some of the 13th-century wall mosaics commissioned by the Byzantine Emperor Manuel can still be seen on the walls of the nave. Depicted above the architrave on the north side are Christ's ancestors according to Luke and on the south side those according to Matthew. Shown above them are the first seven ecumenical councils (well preserved: Nicaea 325, Constantinople 381, Ephesus 431 and Chalcedon 451) with their doctrinal pronouncements. The paintings from the time of the crusaders are preserved on the shafts of the columns. They show pictures of saints and the helmet of Baldwin I with a swan decoration – Baldwin was considered the descendant of the knight of the swan, Lohengrin.

The church ends in the east in three apses. The Armenian altars of the Virgin Mary and the Three Magi can be found in the northern section, while the Altar of the Circumcision is in the southern section. Like the main altar behind the iconostasis, it belongs to the Greek Orthodox Church.

▶ VISITING BETHLEHEM

INFORMATION

Palestine Tourist Information
Old Municipal Building, Manger St.
Tel. (02) 274 15 81, 274 37 53
www.travelpalestine.pa

Manger Square
Tel. (02) 276 66 77

GETTING THERE · SECURITY

The best way to get to Bethlehem from Jerusalem is by taxi or sherut taxi (from the Damascus Gate) or by making arrangements with one of the many tour operators in Jerusalem.

EVENTS

Midnight mass on Christmas Eve, often broadcast on television around the world, is the biggest event of the year. In a moving ceremony, the Latin patriarch leaves the sacristy of the church next to the Church of the Nativity, in which the Greek Orthodox believers celebrate their mass, carrying a statue of the Christ Child, which he places in the middle of the altar.

SHOPPING

The way to get to the lively food souk is from Manger Square at Peace Fountain.
Palestinian Heritage Center
Manger St.
Tel. (02)-274 23 81, www.phc.ps
The aim of the Heritage Center is to preserve traditional crafts, provide work for Palestinian women, and secure their families' livelihoods. On sale are clothes with fine embroidery, jewellery, lamps, jugs, carpets and Palestinian cloths.

ENTERTAINMENT

Cosmos Club
Beit Jala, Olive Tree Village Mall

The only West Bank night club with a bar and a dance floor is near Bethlehem in the middle of Hamas territory. The bar is well-stocked, which is also a minor miracle. This place gets really crowded on Saturdays, political circumstances permitting.

WHERE TO EAT

Grilled chicken, falafels and shawerma (meat from a spit) are standard dishes in the small restaurants around Manger Square such as St George, Afteem, or in the street to the left of the mosque, in Al Andaluz. Its Arab salads or the meat-filled pastry koubbeh cannot be beaten as starters.

WHERE TO STAY

▶ Mid-range

① *Intercontinental Jacir Palace*
Hebron Rd
Tel. Tel. (02) 276 67 77, fax 227 67 70
www.ichotelsgroup.com
The imposing Arab-style building dates from 1910, and is just a few minutes' walk from the Church of the Nativity. Elegant rooms, good service; particularly attractive is the restaurant in the interior courtyard.

▶ Inexpensive

Casa Nova Palace
Manger Sq.
Tel. (02) 274 27 98
www.casanovapalace.com
The Casa Nova is a basic, clean and cheery pilgrims' hostel, very central, and booked out on feast days.

There are stairs leading down into the 12 x 4m/40 x 13ft Grotto of the Nativity. These stairs can be accessed from both transepts via a finely worked pointed arch portal with bronze doors dating back to the time of the crusaders. The **site of Christ's birth** is marked by a silver star with the inscription »Hic de virgine Maria Jesus Christus natus est« (»Here Jesus Christ was born of the Virgin Mary«). In a niche above it is an altar with a very faded mosaic from the 12th century. Opposite, three steps down, is the Chapel of the Manger, where the shepherds worshipped Jesus (Luke 2:16–19); the Altar of the Three Magi is nearby. The rear part of the grotto is not accessible – the door leading to the branching cave system is only opened during processions.

Grotto of the Nativity

The access to the neighbouring Catholic Church of St Catherine, built in 1881 by Franciscans on the site of an earlier church, is located in the north transept of the Church of the Nativity. Every year on 24 December the famous **Midnight Mass** is celebrated here. Stairs in the right aisle lead to the northern section of the cave system, to

Church of St Catherine

A destination for pilgrims from around the world: the city of Christ's birth.

PLACE OF CHRIST'S BIRTH

✶ ✶ **The Church of the Nativity now stands where the manger is said to have stood: a fortress from the outside, a labyrinth on the inside, and strictly separated by denomination.**

🕐 Open:
daily, 6am–6pm

① Door of Humility
The entrance to the Church of the Nativity is just 1.2m/4ft high, probably in order to protect it better from intruders.

② Mosaics
The nave contains the mosaic floor of Constantine's church built in 325.

③ Sanctuary
Fairly divided among the churches: the Armenians in the north (left) with the Altars of the Three Magi and the Virgin Mary, the Greek Orthodox church in the south and at the centre with the main altar and the Altar of the Circumcision.

④ Nativity altar
Below the Nativity Altar, in the grotto of the Nativity (Greek Orthodox), is a silver star donated by Sultan Abdul Mejid I in 1842. It marks the spot where Jesus is said to have been born.

⑤ Grotto of the Nativity
This is where the Three Magi are said to have worshipped the child. The grotto now belongs to the Catholics.

⑥ Chapel of Saint Joseph
Fitted out in 1621.

⑦ Chapel of the Innocents
Commemorates the Massacre of the Innocents.

⑧ Arcosolia and Altar of the Innocents
These arched burial niches (»arcosolium«) were a typical burial method in early Christianity.

⑨ Grotto of Eusebius of Cremona
Eusebius was the pupil of Jerome. Paula and Julia, Roman women who ran charitable foundations in Bethlehem, have also found their final resting place here.

⑩ Chapel of St Jerome
Saint Jerome lay buried here until his remains were translated to the church of Santa Maria Maggiore in Rome at the end of the 13th century.

⑪ Cell of St Jerome
This is where the saint worked on the Vulgate, his translation of the Bible.

Every pilgrim wants to get as close as possible to the place of Christ's birth.

the
ivity

© Baedeker

①

The only way to access the Church
of the Nativity is in a »humble«
manner, i.e. bowing.

Until the 13th century St Jerome
(d. 420) lay buried at this spot.

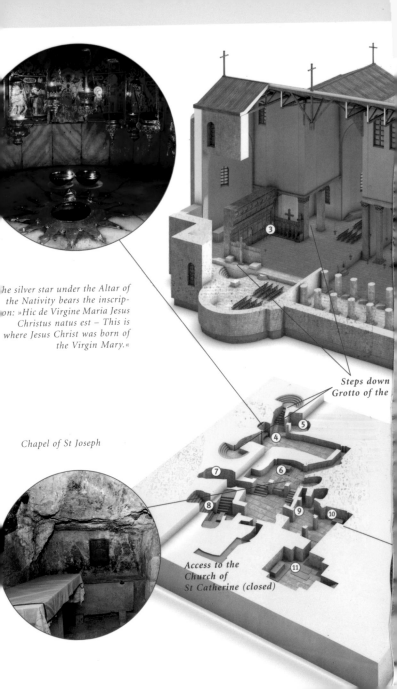

The silver star under the Altar of the Nativity bears the inscription: »Hic de Virgine Maria Jesus Christus natus est – This is where Jesus Christ was born of the Virgin Mary.«

Chapel of St Joseph

Steps down
Grotto of the

Access to the
Church of
St Catherine (closed)

Church of the Nativity Plan

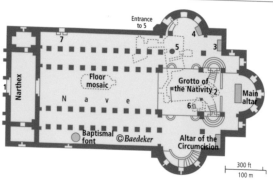

Entrance
to 5

7
4
5
3

Narthex

Floor
mosaic

Grotto of
the Nativity 2

Main
altar

N a v e

Baptismal
font ©Baedeker

Altar of the
Circumcision

300 ft
100 m

1 Entrance
(Door of Humility)
2 Ikonostasis
3 Altar of the
Three Magi
4 Altar of the Virgin
5 Chapel of the
Innocents
6 Altar of the Nativit
7 Access to the Chur
of St Catherine

Opening hours:
Daily 5am–noon,
2pm–6pm

the Chapel of the Innocents commemorating the children killed in Bethlehem by Herod (Matthew 2:16) and to the Chapel of Saint Joseph.

Pass the Chapel of Jerome and the tombs of Saint Paula and her daughter Eustachium on the right to get to the tomb of Saint Jerome, who had come to Bethlehem with the two women. It is possible to see the stone slab at the rear wall where the deceased (AD 420) saint lay until he was buried in the Papal Basilica of Santa Maria Maggiore in Rome. It is said that Saint Jerome wrote the Vulgate in the room to the north of this slab.

Cloister Adjoining the Church of St Catherine is a cloister dating back to the time of the crusaders. It was uncovered in the mid-20th century and rebuilt using the original material. The statue in the cloister's courtyard depicts Saint Jerome.

Further Sights

Manger Square The heart of Bethlehem is Manger Square. Formerly a car park for buses and cars, it has now undergone traffic-calming measures. All around the square there are cafés and restaurants as well as souvenir shops, a police station and the tourist information office. It is worth strolling along the surrounding streets, such as towards the Milk Grotto or to the Christmas Lutheran Church to sense the town's charm away from the hubbub around the pilgrimage sites. The Arab market for example is still very traditional. It sells everything from food to plastic tableware to jewellery to hand-woven rugs.

Milk Grotto, Grotto of the Lady Mary From the forecourt of the Church of the Nativity a street leads southeast to the Milk Grotto or Grotto of the Lady Mary, a cave (turned into a chapel) where the Holy Family are said to have taken refuge on their flight to Egypt. According to legend, Mary lost a drop of her milk while she was nursing, whereupon the limestone turned bright white. Finely ground, it is said to help nursing mothers produce more milk.

A few metres to the northwest of Omar Mosque is the Bethlehem Folklore Museum. It was founded in 1971 by the Arab Orthodox Women's Union with the goal of preserving local traditions and the **cultural heritage of the Palestinians**. Life in 19th-century Bethlehem comes to life with furniture, traditional clothes, handicrafts and documents.

Bethlehem Folklore Museum

To the west of the northbound Sderot Manger, not far from St Joseph's Church, are King David's Wells, a set of cisterns cut into the rock. The site commemorates the place where David's soldiers broke through the enemy lines to get water for their king (2 Samuel 23:15f.).

David's Wells

Around Bethlehem

The small town of Beit Jala to the west of Bethlehem has almost merged with the city. The most interesting of the town's four churches is the one dedicated to Saint Nicholas. The road continues to the 923m/3028ft Har Gillo 2km/1.25mi away. The view of Jerusalem from the summit is splendid.

Beit Jala Har Gillo

Rachel's Tomb is located in the north of the town, just at its exit. She died giving birth to Benjamin. The domed building of the Jewish place of pilgrimage largely dates back to the 18th and 19th centuries.

Rachel's Tomb

The 6th-century Monastery of Elijah, which was renewed by the crusaders in the 11th century and by the Greek Orthodox in the 17th, is located around 2km/1.25mi north of Bethlehem, on the main road to the right leading to Jerusalem.

Monastery of Elijah

1km/0.5mi further towards Jerusalem is the settlement of Ramat Rahel, founded in 1926, whose name refers to Rachel's Tomb. A palace belonging to the kings of Judah from the 9th and 8th centuries BC was excavated on a hill near the kibbutz of the same name. It was inhabited until around 600 BC and was probably destroyed by the Romans in AD 70.

Ramat Rahel

The village of Beit Sahour lies 3km/2mi southeast of Bethlehem. Sites of interest here are the field of Boaz, who married Ruth from Moab, and the **Shepherds' Field** where the angles announced the birth of Christ (Luke 2:8–14). The frescoes in the Angels' Church by the Italian architect Antonio Barluzzi (1953–54) depict the message of the angels to the shepherds, their homage and their return home. In ad-

Beit Sahour

dition to the remains of a Byzantine church there is also a modern Franciscan church. In 1972 archaeologists discovered a place of worship from the 4th century with a nice mosaic floor next to the Greek Orthodox church.

The road forks at the outskirts of Beit Sahour: the left-hand road passes the Monastery of Theodosius and reaches, after 8km/5mi, the desert monastery of ▶Mar Saba, while the right-hand one passes the village of Za'tara, set up in the 1960 for Bedouins from the Taamara tribe, and reaches the ▶Herodium (11km/7 mi).

Solomon's Pools

In a southwesterly direction, following the road to ▶Hebron, are Solomon's Pools, three large, open cisterns, which according to tradition were built in the 10th century BC by King Solomon to supply Jerusalem with water. »I made me pools of water, to water therewith the wood that bringeth forth trees« (Ecclesiastes 2:6). Even though water from this area blessed with springs has always been used, the current cisterns do not date back to Solomon, but to the time of Herod the Great.

✷✷ Beit She'an · Bet She'an

District: Northern
Population: 16,000

Altitude: 115m/377ft below sea level

It is written in the Talmud about Beit She'an: »If the Garden of Eden is in the land of Israel, then its gate is at Beit She'an.«

Small town with a big past

The small town is situated 26km/16mi south of the ▶Sea of Galilee in the fertile and water-rich Beit She'an Valley, the southern continuation of the Jezreel Plain towards the Jordan Valley. Since 1986, excavations have brought to light the ruins of an ancient settlement (3rd century BC–8th century AD). During Byzantine times it is said to have been larger than Jerusalem and is now a national park, being **one of the largest and most significant archaeological sites in Israel**. Theatres, baths, temples and colonnaded streets grouped around the high tell of Beit She'an. It has more than 20 settlement layers that are thousands of years older. The new approach to the monuments is badly signposted. It is near the Beit She'an Shopping Center. From the visitor centre a horse-drawn cart takes visitors to the monuments.

Millennia of history

Israeli archaeologists discovered in the 1980s and 1990s what is so far the oldest evidence of settlement from the 4th millennium BC. Beit She'an is first mentioned in Egyptian documents from the 19th century BC. After the conquest of Canaan in the 15th century BC, Pharaoh Thutmose III turned the town into a fortress. In the 11th century BC the Philistines took the place over. When they defeated King Saul and his sons in the battle at Mount Gilboa in around 1004 BC, »… they put his armour in the house of Ashtaroth: and they fastened his body to the wall of Beth-shan« (1 Samuel 31:10). Saul's successor David captured the Philistine town, which was abandoned in the 8th century BC during the Assyrian conquest.

It was not until the 3rd century BC that it became the home of Scythian veterans from the Iranian area. It was renamed Scythopolis and became Greek. Pompey declared it a free town in 63 BC. Under Roman rule Scythopolis flourished once more, thanks to its high-yielding agriculture and textile industry, a fact to which many buildings still bear witness.

During the Byzantine period the town was home to more than 40,000 people. Most of them were Christians, but there was also a Jewish community. In 363 an earthquake destroyed large parts of the Byzantine town, but a short while later it had been rebuilt in its former glory. The Islamic conquest in 639 was the beginning of the end, but many inhabitants stayed. It was not until another earthquake destroyed Beit She'an in 749 that the town was abandoned.

After the state of Israel was founded in 1948, the Arabs left Beit She'an. In the following years the main new arrivals were Jewish settlers from Arab countries. Towards the end of 1994, shortly after peace was made with Jordan, the new border crossing, the Jordan River Crossing (Sheikh Hussein Bridge) between Israel and Jordan was opened near Beit She'an.

> ### ? DID YOU KNOW …?
>
> ■ »Pecunia non olet (money does not stink)« was something the Romans used to say, even though they did many a deal while sitting next to each other on the toilet. Indeed, a sophisticated sewer system constantly washed away the deposits, so that the nuisance to the nose was probably kept to a minimum during such negotiations.

Excavation site

The **best-preserved Roman theatre in Israel** was built in the 1st century BC, expanded under Septimus Severus in the 2nd century AD and altered under Justinian in the 6th century AD. It was originally able to seat 6000 spectators over three tiers. The lowest tier made of white limestone was incorporated into the terrain; its 14 rows are still well preserved. The second and third tiers, made of black basalt, were supported by a strong foundation. There were nine entrances leading into the interior here; behind these entrances were short, narrow corridors, at the end of which there are small rooms that used to be covered by domes. Their purpose is unknown, but they could have had something to do with improving the theatre's acoustics. The stage and the proscenium, once 21m/65ft tall, are still extant in parts, and have been partially reconstructed. Today operas are performed here during the summer months.

** **
Roman theatre
◷
Opening hours:
April–Sep daily
8am–5pm, Oct–
March until 4pm

Beit She'an was inhabited for more than 1000 years.

Palladius Street
Between the theatre and the tell is the centre of the Greek-Roman-Byzantine town. The shortest connection between the theatre and the tell is one of the town's main roads, named Palladius Street after one of the town's 4th-century governors. The original basalt herringbone pavement, still extant in parts, covers the town's main sewer. There are shady colonnades to the left and right of the street.

Byzantine baths ▶
The extensive complex of the Byzantine baths lies to the west of Palladius Street. This significant facility in the town's cultural and social life stands on the foundations of a Roman bath. The outdoor gym (palaestra), surrounded by columns on three sides, still has remains of ancient floor mosaics. Inside there were several rooms with pools of cold, warm and hot water where visitors could relax. The rooms were heated with the Roman hypocaust technology, the ancient system of underfloor heating.

Exedra ▶
On the west side of Palladius Street, towards the tell, a semicircular open space from the 6th century marks the site of an exedra, which used to be something like a shopping centre with exclusive shops. The **floor mosaic** in one of the rooms shows a female figure with a mural crown on her head, holding a cornucopia. These were the symbols of Tyche, the Greek goddess of fate and the Roman patron goddess of the town.

Beit She'an • Excavation Site *Map*

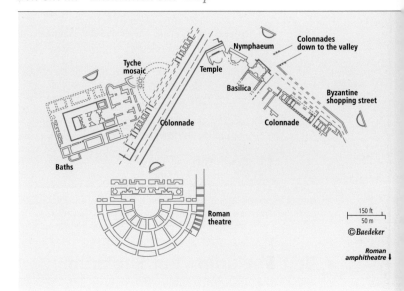

Wide steps once led up to the urban Temple of Dionysus from the square with white paving stones at the end of Palladius Street.

◄ Temple of Dionysus

Along the town's second main road, at the base of the tell, Sylvanus Street, which runs from northwest to southeast, there used to be more public buildings: a nymphaeum, an elaborate foundation from the 2nd or 4th century next to the temple, then the basilica, the multipurpose Roman market and assembly hall in which legal matters were also addressed. From there the valley road, once lined by colonnades, turns off to the northeast, crossing the river Harod on the remains of an imposing Roman bridge and leading to the neighbouring hill complex, which has not yet been investigated much. To the south of the basilica a number of Roman columns and the remains of a Byzantine row of shops have been uncovered.

Sylvanus Street

◄ Basilica

The highest elevation is the 40m/130ft Tell Beit She'an, which towers above the Roman-Byzantine ruins. From here there is an impressive view over the excavation site; the climb is strenuous, especially in the heat of the day. More than 20 identifiable layers are evidence of the **busy settlement activities over a period of more than 6000 years**. The Romans, Byzantines and Arabs were all at work here, as the remains of a Temple of Zeus, a Byzantine church and a mosque confirm. In the 1920s the main items uncovered were steles, sculptures and objects from the period of Egyptian rule. Most of the discov-

Tell Beit She'an

eries, such as a stele of Pharaoh Seti I from 1318 BC and a stele of the goddess of war Anat (1250 BC), are on display in the Rockefeller Museum in ▶ Jerusalem. Parts of the temple and the administrative buildings have been reconstructed.

Monastery of Lady Mary

On the neighbouring Tell el-Mataba are the remains of the Monastery of Lady Mary, founded in 567 by a noblewoman of that name. The mosaics, now roofed over for their protection, are noteworthy.

Outside the archaeological park, near the main road through Beit She'an, are the **ruins of the oval amphitheatre**, which was also used as a hippodrome (horse track) and which, like the theatre, had space for around 6000 spectators.

The **ruins of the eastern bath house** near the ancient theatre are not so well preserved as those of the western bath house, but still provide an impressive view of a confusing system of pipes and furnaces. In addition a large **public latrine** with 40 seats has been uncovered.

★ Beit She'arim · Bet She'arim

F 2

District: Northern   **Altitude:** 138m/453ft

Beit She'arim was a centre of Jewish rabbinical learning between the 2nd and 4th century and one of the most important burial sites in the country. The impressive catacombs lie in an attractive hilly landscape below the ruins of the Jewish town.

Getting there

To get to the excavation site (now a national park), located 20km/12mi southeast of ▶ Haifa, turn right towards Beit She'arim shortly after Kiryat Tiv'on, if travelling towards Nazareth. The signposting is very good.

Seat of the supreme court

During the second half of the 2nd century the recognized religious leader of the Jews, **Yehuda Hanassi** (also known as Judah the Prince), moved the highest religious body of his people, the Sanhedrin (supreme court), to Beit She'arim. As head of the Sanhedrin, he gathered the leading Jewish scholars around him. He wrote parts of the **Mishnah** in Beit She'arim. These stories and commandments known from Moses, which had hitherto been passed down as oral tradition, were to be written down out of fear that the Jewish people, largely living in a diaspora, might forget them. Several members of the Sanhedrin are buried in Beit She'arim. Judah the Prince himself wanted this to be his final resting place even though he spent the last 17 years of his life in Tzippori. However, his tomb has not yet been discovered.

Built while Judah the Prince was still alive: the entrance to catacomb 20

Many pious Jews had themselves interred here from the end of the 2nd century to the mid-4th century out of veneration for the many scholars buried here. Another factor that contributed to this development was that the old cemetery on the Mount of Olives in Jerusalem was inaccessible to Jews for many years after the Bar Kokhba revolt in 135. Funeral services became a lucrative business for the people of Beit She'arim: they did not just bury Jews from their own country, even the embalmed bodies of pious Jews from other countries were brought here.

Excavation Site

Before the entrance to the national park, to the left of the access road, is the ruin of a large synagogue from the 3rd century whose portal, like the one on the synagogue in Capernaum, is oriented towards Jerusalem. A few metres further, also on the left-hand side of the road, is an old olive press.

From the excavation site of the town there is a tight bend down to the necropolis in the middle of old holm oaks and Judas trees. 26 catacombs were carved out of the soft limestone rock for the necropolis between the 2nd and 4th centuries. They vary in size and house between 20 and 400 tombs, which had **all been robbed** by the time of the excavations. Neither bones nor any burial gifts worth mentioning were found. Only the inscriptions on the sarcophagi and the walls, the reliefs of animals and people, and many Jewish symbols (seven-armed candelabra, Torah shrines etc.) remained. The depictions are not overly artistic. Most of the sarcophagi were made of the

🕐
Opening hours:
April–Sept daily
8am–5pm
Oct–March until
4pm

★
Necropolis

local limestone, and the few marble imports were later destroyed or removed by grave robbers.

Catacomb 20 The large Catacomb 20, built during the lifetime of Judah the Prince, has a partially reconstructed façade with three stone gates under three arches. Several corridors of varying lengths and rooms lead off from a wide central corridor. 130 limestone sarcophagi and 200 recessed tombs (arcosolia) were found in this »underground palace«. The back part of the first side corridor on the left has the Hunting Sarcophagus (a lion hunting a gazelle), the Lion Sarcophagus and the Sarcophagus of Gates. The Eagle Sarcophagus stands in a side room near the entrance, the second room on the right has the Mask Sarcophagus with a bearded male mask on the front, while the Shell Sarcophagus stands in the third side corridor on the right.

Catacomb 14 Catacomb 14 to the east of Catacomb 20 also has a façade consisting of three arches. Enlightening inscriptions in Hebrew, Greek and Aramaic were found in it, for example on the sarcophagi of a Simon and a Gamaliel, probably the sons of Judah the Prince.

Museum To the southwest of Catacomb 20, on the way towards the kiosk and the car park, is the small museum, housed in what was once a water cistern. A few burial objects are on display here, as well as wall reliefs and information about the Sanhedrin, the Jewish burial rites and the menorah.

✶✶ Caesarea · Hefar Qesari

E 3

District: Haifa   **Altitude:** 20m/65ft

The ancient town of Caesarea, attractively situated in the dunes right by the sea, halfway between ►Tel Aviv and ►Haifa, is one of the top attractions on the Israeli Mediterranean coast.

National park The national park is made up of the area of the former crusader town and a part of the Byzantine town, as well as the Roman theatre and Herod's palace 1km/0.5mi to the south. Among the monuments outside the national park boundary, the imposing aqueduct is particularly worth viewing.

From seat of the Roman prefect to diocesan town The first settlement goes back to the Phoenicians, who created a harbour here in the 4th century BC. In 22 BC Herod the Great started building a large city, which he named Caesarea in honour of Emperor Augustus. With its Temple of Augustus, theatre, hippodrome and advanced water supply, it was an important port, home to Jews and non-Jews alike.

After Judaea became a Roman province, Caesarea was the residence of the procurators, including **Pontius Pilate** (AD 26–36) and Felix (AD 52–60), who imprisoned Saint Paul here for two years. It was probably still under Pilate that Peter baptized the centurion Cornelius (Acts 10), which created a big stir. Confrontations between the Jewish and Greek population led to the outbreak of the Jewish revolt in AD 66. **Vespasian**, who put down the revolt four years later, was proclaimed emperor in Caesarea in AD 69, elevating the town to Roman colony. After the failure of the second Jewish revolt against Rome, its spiritual leader, **Akiva ben Joseph**, was tortured to death in Caesarea in AD 135.

◄ Seat of the procurators

In the 1st century the apostle Philip founded a Christian community and from the end of the 2nd century Caesarea was the seat of a bishop. The crusaders came in 1101, but Caesarea was only given additional fortifications by the French king Louis IX in 1254. Just 21 years later the Mamluk sultan Baibars conquered the town, whose harbour silted up completely. The Turks moved Muslim refugees from Bosnia to the area of the crusader town in the late 19th century. Further settlement occurred in 1940 with the founding of the kibbutz Sdot Yam. The archaeological exploration of the area is still not complete.

! *Baedeker* TIP

Archaeological dive

Herod's harbour is a unique underwater archaeological park. Snorkellers and divers can view underwater relics close up. Bathing beach, craft and souvenir shops, and right at the end of the long pier, beyond the restaurant, is the Old Caesarea Diving Center. Here you'll find everything you need for snorkelling and diving in the harbour basin, and also tickets for underwater tours. You can descend to the depths from the beach in the company of a guide, either alone or in groups. Amphorae, columns, and the remains of wrecks can be seen. Old Caesarea Diving Center, tel. (04) 626 58 98, www.caesarea-diving.com

✴ Excavation Site

Three entrances lead into the national park: two at the crusader town (East Gate and South Gate) and a further one to the south, at the Roman theatre. The following round trip starts at this latter gate. Here stands a cinema tent with a multimedia Caesarea, a trip by Time Trek through the millennia, where you can experience Herod's ancient harbour, meet Romans, Arabs, crusaders and the first Jewish immigrants. Time Trek can also be seen on the pier among the restaurants and shops.

🕐 Opening hours: Sat–Thu 8am–5pm, in winter until 4pm, Fri always until 3pm

The Roman theatre, one of the main attractions, had room for around 4000 spectators. It is possible to see the sea from the seats, looking over the orchestra and the remains of the proscenium. The building, constructed under Herod, had its proscenium removed and, a second semicircle was added to the original semicircle of the

Roman theatre

► VISITING CAESAREA

INFORMATION

Caesarea National Parks Authority
Tel. (04) 626 70 80
Apr–Sep 8am–5pm, Oct–Mar
8am–4pm

GETTING THERE

The best way to get here is by hire car
or taxi. All bus connections to and
from Haifa and Tel Aviv stop at the
main road, but the connecting bus
service to the excavation site more
than 3km/2mi away is irregular.

EVENTS

Caesarea, especially the amphitheatre,
is often used as a backdrop for fashion
shows, concerts and similar events.

WHERE TO STAY

► **Luxury**
Dan Caesarea Golf Hotel
Tel. (04) 626 91 11, fax 626 91 22

www.danhotels.com
The unrivalled Dan Caesarea near the
national park is a very elegant and
smart hotel with an 18-hole golf
course.

► **Mid-range**
Kef Yam Resort
Kibbutz Sdot Yam
Tel. (06) 636 44 44
Fax 636 22 11
www.kef-yam.co.il
Wonderful resort on the sea, ideal for
sports and other activities, including
organized day trips (book in advance).

BEACHES

Beaches can be found by the harbour
of the crusader town (entry fee
required: small but well looked-after)
and at the aqueduct to the north,
outside the national park.

orchestra, resulting in an elliptical amphitheatre. In the 4th century
the area of the orchestra was transformed into a large basin that
could even accommodate ships. Today the restored theatre is used
for events again. The wall fragments on the headland to the west of
the Roman theatre probably belong to **Herod's Palace**.

Amphitheatre
A waterfront route runs north from the palace to the crusader town.
A U-shaped arena with space for 10,000 spectators, which was used
for horse racing and other events and was called an amphitheatre
during King Herod's time, has already been excavated. To the east of
the area archaeologists have uncovered a Byzantine street system.
The main buildings excavated so far are warehouses with high
vaulted ceilings. One of these vaulted rooms was later transformed
into a **Temple of Mithras** – the only one known in Israel to date.

Crusader town
Next up is the southern entrance to the crusader town. A town was
built here under Arab rule. Louis IX of France fortified it no later
than 1254 with walls reinforced by bastions and a deep trench.
Within the fortified area, turn right and climb up to the plateau cre-

ated by Herod. This is the ancient forum, from where it is possible to get a good overview of the town. He had a temple built here in honour of Augustus, while the Byzantines built a church on the octagonal foundations and the crusaders built **St Paul's Cathedral**. This is the best-preserved structure: three semicircular apses. The remains of the **Temple of Augustus** can still be made out next to the cathedral.

From the plateau on which the cathedral stands, visitors can look down on the **mosque** of the Bosnian settlers (end of the 19th century) and some **warehouses** of the **ancient harbour**. The current harbour basin was built during the time of the crusaders. The harbour built by Herod has been completely flooded by the sea. It consisted of two harbour basins, one mole and a 400m/450yd breakwater. The **crusader citadel** once stood on the headland projecting into the sea. There is now a restaurant on its remains.

The Holy Grail?

- A famous object now kept in the church of San Lorenzo in Genoa was acquired by King Baldwin I during the conquest of Caesarea on 17 May 1101: the »sacro catino«, which was believed for a long time to be the Holy Grail, in other words the cup or chalice of the Last Supper, in which Christ's blood was also collected. William of Tyre, chronicler of the First Crusade, describes it as a fairly shallow bowl cut out of a large emerald. Baldwin had to hand over the precious treasure to the Genoese for their support. It has now been determined that this is merely a glass bowl dating from the 9th century.

As can still be seen in some parts of the southern section of the crusader town, the medieval builders used material such as column segments, capitals and cut stones from the ancient and Byzantine town for the road and houses of the residential quarter near the East Gate. Walk through the pretty Byzantine **pointed-arch arcade** to get to the southern corner, where it is possible to climb onto the wall and get good views of the expansive complex. A vaulted gateway from the 18th century marks the eastern entrance hall to the crusader town.

◄ Residential quarter

Outside the National Park

A few remains of the Caesarea from the days of Herod and the Byzantine rule can be found outside the national park: for example the remains of the Byzantine shopping street at the car park outside the east gate of the crusader town. The surviving floor mosaic with a Greek inscription states that Flavius Stategius built the complex under the governor Flavius Entolius.

Byzantine shopping street

Even further out of town, also on the left of the road to Tel Aviv, is the former hippodrome (race track), 230m/250yd long and 80m/90yd wide with a capacity of 20,000.

Hippodrome

A further relic from Herod's time, which is covered by sand dunes in part but nevertheless remains impressive, is the aqueduct with which

✴ **Aqueduct**

Caesarea Map

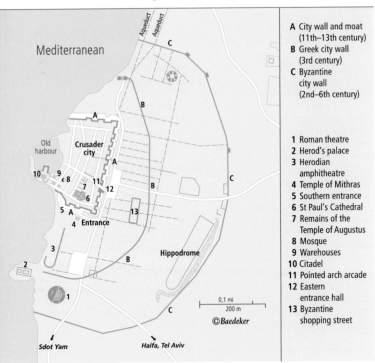

A City wall and moat
(11th–13th century)
B Greek city wall
(3rd century)
C Byzantine
city wall
(2nd–6th century)

1 Roman theatre
2 Herod's palace
3 Herodian
amphitheatre
4 Temple of Mithras
5 Southern entrance
6 St Paul's Cathedral
7 Remains of the
Temple of Augustus
8 Mosque
9 Warehouses
10 Citadel
11 Pointed arch arcade
12 Eastern
entrance hall
13 Byzantine
shopping street

0,1 mi
200 m

©*Baedeker*

Mediterranean

Old harbour

Crusader city

Hippodrome

Entrance

Sdot Yam

Haifa, Tel Aviv

Aqueduct

water was brought to Caesarea from a spring 6km/3.5mi north of the town. A second aqueduct was built further inland in around AD 100.

Sdot Yam The small museum in the kibbutz of Sdot Yam, 1km/0.5mi south of Caesarea, exhibits a few discoveries from the excavation site.

Around Caesarea

Dor and Nahsholim Dor and the neighbouring kibbutz of Nahsholim have good facilities for a relaxing holiday with a resort right on the water and a wonderful beach. Immigrants from Greece founded Moshav Dor in 1949 on the ruins of the Arab village of Tantura, around 15km/9mi north of Caesarea.

Dor was one of the 31 city states that Joshua conquered in around 1200 BC (Joshua 12:23). Solomon made the husband of his daughter Tafat, after whom one of the four offshore islands is named, the governor. After conquest by the Assyrians in the 8th century BC, Tan-

A venue that is just as sunny today as it was in Antiquity: the theatre of Caesarea

tura temporarily belonged to the Phoenician kings of Sidon; from the 4th century AD the town was inhabited by Christians. In the 12th century the crusaders built a castle, named after de Merel, which was destroyed in 1291 by the Mamluks.

✳ Capernaum · Kfar Nahum

District: Northern   **Altitude:** 205m/673ft below sea level

Capernaum on the northern shores of the ►Sea of Galileeis among the most important sites of Christ's ministry.

According to tradition, Capernaum (Hebrew: Kfar Nahum, Nahum's village; Arabic: Tell Num), along with ►Tabgha was one of the places where Jesus temporarily lived during his time as an itinerant preacher. It was here that he called his first disciples: Peter and his brother Andrew, James and his brother John (Matthew 4:18–22 and Mark 1:16–20). He preached in the synagogue there (John 6:26–59) and

Christ's ministry

performed several miracles (e.g. Mark 1:21 ff., 2:1–12, Luke 6:6–11). The excavation site, managed by Franciscans, is now a **much-visited site of pilgrimage**. Visitors are expected to wear appropriate clothing, in other words short skirts, shorts and uncovered shoulders are not acceptable. The excursion boats on the Sea of Galilee also dock at Capernaum during the high season.

History   Capernaum was built in the 2nd century BC and initially lay between the synagogue and the Sea of Galilee. During Christ's lifetime it possessed a fishing port and a customs office. From the 2nd century AD, Jews who had been driven out elsewhere came to the town. Gradually new quarters were added to the east and north of the synagogue.

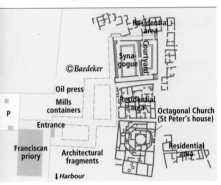

Capernaum Map

It is evidence of the inhabitants' affluence that the 4th-century synagogue was not built out of the richly abundant black basalt, but out of limestone, which had to be brought here especially. The number of Christians also soon increased, and thus an octagonal church was built above older homes in around AD 450 in commemoration of Saint Peter, who is said to have lived on that site. Urban life came to an end with the arrival of Islam; Capernaum was nothing but a poor fishing village with seven huts, as the pilgrim Burchard noted during his travels in the 13th century. In 1894 the Franciscans acquired the ruins. A short while later the first excavation works began, with the friars participating themselves.

✳ Excavation Site

Small but important ⏱   The excavation site, which is partially shaded by old trees, is not very extensive. The most important sites are the octagonal church and the partially reconstructed synagogue. Residential areas have been uncovered to the north and east of the synagogue (daily 8.30am–4.15pm).

Octagonal church   The octagonal church has had a modern concrete dome supported by low pillars since 1990. The purpose is to protect the excavation site, but unfortunately this greatly impairs its impact. The site contains remains of walls from a residential quarter. The oldest houses date back to the 1st century BC. They were meagre – narrow rooms and small courtyards with hearths – and probably belonged to fishermen, as fish hooks were discovered there.

The synagogue in Capernaum is one of the oldest Jewish places of worship.

One of the houses was plastered at least three times. The archaeologists found 131 inscriptions on the plaster, in which the names of Jesus and Peter appear several times. It is thus believed that this was the **house of Saint Peter**, in which Jesus stayed and whose mother-in-law he healed (Matthew 8:14–17; Mark 1:29–31; Luke 4:38–41).

In around 350 the house got a new enclosing wall and a new ceiling. The Spanish pilgrim Egeria noted at the end of the 4th century that the house of the Prince of the Apostles in Capernaum had became a church and that its walls remained unchanged.

In 450 a church was constructed above this building. It had an octagonal floor plan. The floor mosaic has a peacock at its centre as a symbol of immortality. The semicircular apse in the east served as the baptistery.

★ **Synagogue**

The partially reconstructed synagogue, the most imposing monument on the excavation site, is regarded as one of the oldest and most attractive synagogues. Steps lead up to the porch, from where three doors open into the nave and two aisles, while two further doors lead into the adjoining courtyard to the east. The central door features corbels with palm trees. Inside, the aisles are separated from the nave by rows of columns topped with finely worked Corinthian capitals. On the north wall the columns, which once also supported the matroneum (gallery for women), have been rebuilt together with the entablature. Stone seats can be made out on the left wall. Architectural fragments from the synagogue, including columns, a relief with vine laves, grapes and palm leaves and a cornice with a seahorse and two eagles can be seen in the garden.

Around | There are further sites of religious historical interest near Capernaum, such the Church of the Multiplication at ► Tabgha, the ► Mount of Beatitudes, the biblical site of Bethsaida in Hayarden Park (►Sea of Galilee) and the basalt ruins of ►Chorazim.

✳ Carmel · Har HaKarmel

E / F 2

District: Haifa   **Altitude:** 546m/1791ft

Carmel (Hebrew Har HaKarmel) means »God's vineyard«, and the region does its name justice with its fertile slopes and valleys.

National park | The Carmel range is a rugged ridge 23km/14mi long and 8–10km/5–6mi wide. The peaks here are the foothills of the mountains of Samaria. The Carmel range rises between the Jezreel and Sharon Valleys in the southeast and runs all the way to the bay of ►Haifa in the northwest, where it drops steeply towards the coast. Because of the pristine, beautiful landscape, large areas around the 598m/1962ft summit of Mount Carmel have been declared a national park. The pine forests with their picnic sites and many lovely viewpoints are popular destinations, as are the Druze villages.

Centre of Baal worship | Discoveries from caves confirm that the Carmel range was inhabited as early as 150,000 years ago. The skeleton of the »**woman of Tabun**« was found in Tabun Cave for example. It is around 10,000 years old. Baal was worshipped here from at least Canaanite times. King David annexed the Carmel region in around 1000 BC, but it was not until the 9th century that the prophet Elijah asserted the Yahweh cult over the Baal cult in a kind of contest of the gods (1 Kings 18:17–40). The rocky cave of Muhraka in the southeast of the Carmel range is believed to be the site where this event occurred. Nevertheless Baal worship remained very popular in this area. Baal was equated with Zeus by the Greeks, while the Romans called him Deus Carmelus.
During the time of the crusaders, Christians settled on Carmel for the first time. The **Carmelite order** was founded near Haifa in 1155.

What to See in the Carmel Range

✳ Landscape | The Carmel range consists of hard limestone and dolomite. Thanks to plentiful precipitation in the lowlands, various plants and bushes flourish here. Wine, oranges, bananas, figs and other fruits are cultivated in the valleys. This produce can be bought from stalls at the side of the road. Leaving Haifa to the east in the direction of Carmel, the road goes through scenery known by some as Little Switzerland, by others as Israel's Tuscany. In 2010, during the worst forest fires in Israel's history, 42 people died and more than four million trees were destroyed, almost half the total. Probably for some time to come, the route will lead via many hairpin bends for miles through a ghost landscape of leafless, blackened trees, with a few green shrubs in between. In a major reforestation programme, pines, carobs, oaks, olive trees, eucalyptus and pistachio trees have been planted.

Road 672 leads southeastwards from Haifa, across the Carmel range. After a 15km/9mi drive the road reaches **Isfiya**. Druze families from Syria as well as some Christian ones have lived here and in the village of **Daliyat** al-Karmel, around 4km/ 2.5mi away, since the 18th century. Altogether, the settlements, which stretch across several elevations, have a population of around 15,000.

Druze villages

These towns are not overly picturesque, but it is interesting to encounter the lifestyle of a religious minority, something which is not possible almost anywhere else in Israel. The people of Isfiya and Daliyat mainly live from selling souvenirs. The Saturday market is a popular local destination. Vendors in the bazaar streets in the centre sell Druze handicrafts and Arab snacks. The **traditional Druze people** can be recognized by their clothes: the men still often have striking moustaches and wear wide, baggy trousers as well as a kind of fez, while the woman are shrouded in long, black dresses and cover their head and shoulders in white tulle.

> ! **Baedeker TIP**
>
> **On horseback**
>
> There are other outdoor pursuits besides bathing, surfing or diving. One of the holiday activities on offer in the kibbutz Beit Oren (»house of pine«, destroyed in the 2010 forest fires, but rebuilt) are trips on horseback. The lovely scenery around the kibbutz in the middle of the national park is perfect for hacks. To get to Beit Oren, take road 721, which winds its way through the national park to the coast.

2km/1.25mi beyond Daliyat a road turns off to the Horn of the Carmel (Arabic: place of burning), a hill on which stands the Carmelite monastery of Saint Elijah. This place is believed to have been the site where Elijah erected the two altars during his dispute with the priests of Baal, which is why the Carmelites founded a monastery here at the end of the 19th century. There is a statue of Elijah in the courtyard. The prophet is the Carmelites' patron saint. The **views** of the bay of Haifa and Jezreel Valley from the roof of the monastery are lovely.

Horn of the Carmel (Dir el-Muhraka, Keren Hacarmel)

Drive back a little bit towards Haifa to get to Beit Oren. The kibbutz lies in the middle of a pine wood, hence its name. Just 6km/4mi from the sea, it offers visitors a varied stay.

Beit Oren

The **artists' colony** of Ein Hod (www.einhod.info) lies on the western slopes of the Carmel mountains, near the no. 4 coast road, embedded in lavish green. There is a footpath to the idyllic village beyond the

Ein Hod

artistically crafted entrance gate. The village gets its special charm from the lovingly tended, sometimes slightly overgrown gardens. Ein Hod was founded by the Dadaist Marcel Janco on the site of an abandoned Arab village in 1953. Today it is home to around 100 artists and craftsmen and their families, who run their galleries (many galleries and studios are closed on the Sabbath). During the summer the villagers organize cultural events in the small amphitheatre. One of the village's attractions is the small Dadaism museum.

Zikhron Ya'akov ►Zikhron Ya'akov

Chorazin · Qazrin

G 1/2

District: Northern **Altitude:** 270m/885ft

The ruins of the small Jewish town of Chorazin are among the worthwhile archaeological sites in the vicinity of the Sea of Galilee.

A doubting place Chorazin (or Korazim) is mentioned in the New Testament as one of the sites that Jesus described as being unrepentant (Matthew 11:21). The excavation site, declared a national park, around 4km/2.5mi north of the ►Sea of Galilee, incorporates a town that was built on an older settlement in the 2nd century AD.

Excavation Site

Opening hours: Daily 8am–4pm, in summer until 5pm

The first impression of the excavation site, even in bright sunshine, is sombre because the town's houses were made of black basalt. Most of the 2nd-century residential homes only remain as foundations. The bath is better preserved and the paved market square can also be made out quite well.

Synagogue The most impressive structure in Chorazin is the partially restored synagogue from the 3rd and 4th centuries. Just as in ►Capernaum and Beit Alfa (►Mount Gilboa) it has a nave and two aisles, and the entrance is in the south. Parts of walls of the rectangular prayer room, the floor and the plinths of ten of the originally 14 columns that separated the nave from the aisles are extant. The synagogue was decorated with architectural sculpture, as can be seen on the pediment, for example. However, the brittle basalt did not permit very fine working, of the kind of which can be seen in Capernaum for example. One special discovery from Chorazin is an artistically produced **stone chair with a Jewish-Aramaic dedication inscription** (now in the Israel Museum in ►Jerusalem). Such chairs were set up in ancient synagogues as the honorary seat of the religious leader.

✱ Dead Sea · Yam Hamelah

F/G 4?5

Area: Southern district and West Bank (Palestinian territory)

Altitude: 398m/1306ft below sea level

A trip to the Dead Sea is one of the most scenic tours in Israel. Located around 30km/18mi from Jerusalem, the inland sea measures around 600 sq km/230 sq mi and is surrounded by a barren desert landscape and air that shimmers in the heat.

The number-one characteristic of the Dead Sea is its high salt content, which makes all plant and animal life impossible. The **salinity of around 33%** is almost ten times higher than that of the Mediterranean, which is why the Dead Sea is called **Yam Hamelah** (Salt Sea) in Hebrew. Lots of bizarre rock salt formations can be found in the southern part of the Dead Sea where the salt content is even higher than in the northern part. They have an eerie quality in the way they rise out of the water. Along the shoreline they form a white line. While spas and bathing are the main activities around the northern part of the Dead Sea, the southern section is dominated by huge industrial facilities in which potash and bromine are obtained.

Salt Sea

Bizarre salt formation on the banks of the Dead Sea

VISITING DEAD SEA

INFORMATION

Dead Sea Tourist Information Center
Ein Bokek
Tel. and fax (08) 997 50 10
www.deadsea.co.il

Dead Sea Research Center
European Medical Center
Dead Sea Gardens Hotel, Ein Bokek
Tel. (08) 658 43 38
www.deadsea-health.org

Further information offices
see Ein Bokek, Ein Gedi

BATHING

In the north (near ►Qumran): Einot Tsukim, Neve Midbar, Siesta and Atraktzia water park; further south: Mineral Beach near Mitspe Shalem and near ►Ein Gedi.
In the south: ►Ein Bokek and Neve Zohar

World's lowest dry point

The Dead Sea is part of a huge trench that was formed millions of years ago and runs from Turkey to eastern Africa. The sea, situated between Israel and Jordan, and its shores lie at **423m/1388ft below sea level**, making them the world's lowest elevation on land. A peninsula projecting into the water at the eastern shore divides the sea, whose total length is 76km/47mi, into the smaller southern part, which only has a depth of 4–6m/13–20ft, and the larger northern part, which reaches a depth of 366m/1201ft.

The Dead Sea's most important feeder river is the ►Jordan, and even though it does not have an effluent river, the water level remained almost constant for a long period of time. The reason for this is the hot climate. The average annual temperature is more than 25°C/77°F, which causes a lot of evaporation. Because of increased water extraction from the River Jordan and the ►Sea of Galilee in order to supply Israel and Jordan with drinking water, the amount of water flowing into the Dead Sea via the Jordan is decreasing all the time. As a result of a decreased water level, the peninsula now almost divides the Dead Sea in two; in addition the lack of fresh water flowing into the sea is causing increased salinization. The situation is worsening because of the Unity Dam on the Yarmouk River in Jordan, which was built with Israeli agreement. The situation is growing stranger all the time. While the north is becoming drier and in some places jetties are now several metres above the surface, water levels are rising in the southern half of the Dead Sea. The cause is rampant uncontrolled industrialization. Because of the evaporation tanks of the chemical industry (asphalt and potash extraction), thousands of tons of salt remain behind each year, which leads to a rise of 20 centimetres annually in the water level. The consequences are dramatic: tourist spots like Ein Bokek are threatened with flooding in the foreseeable future. It is said that it will cost over 1 billion dollars to remove the existing salt from the south and create a permanent solution. There have even been suggestions to move the resort somewhere else.

The Arabic name for the Dead Sea, **Bahr Lut**, means »Lot's Sea« and refers to the fate of the biblical cities of Sodom and Gomorrah, both of which are believed to have been located in the salt landscape at the southern end of the Dead Sea.

Sodom and Gomorrah

God destroyed its inhabitants with burning sulphur, but spared Lot and his family at the intercession of Abraham. God did however order them not to look back at the burning city. Lot's wife nevertheless turned around and became a pillar of salt. Lot and his daughters withdrew to a cave in the mountains where the young women became pregnant with their father's children, giving birth to Moab, the progenitor of the Moabites, and Ben-Ammi, the forefather of the Ammonites (Genesis 19). Jordan and Israel give different answers to the site of Sodom and Gomorrah. Both claim that the cities were on their territory.

Bathing in the Dead Sea is a memorable experience that virtually no one passes up on. The high salt content makes it almost impossible to submerge; instead, drift around comfortably while reading the papers. After bathing do not forget to rinse off with fresh water.

★
Bathing in the Dead Sea

The Dead Sea is not just the saltiest body of water on earth, it is also the most mineral-rich. It has an unusually high concentration of bromine, magnesium, potassium and iodine. Even in Antiquity people were convinced of the healing powers of the Dead Sea. Allegedly Cleopatra came here to benefit from them. Today a lot of people come to the Dead Sea hoping to alleviate skin problems, lung problems, fibromyalgia syndrome and rheumatism. Ein Bokek, Neve Zohar (► Ein Bokek) and ► Ein Gedi have developed into **spa centres** on the Dead Sea. In recent times several beauty farms have opened in the spa resorts, but there are also plenty of options on offer for tourists seeking more active pastimes. The programmes range from mountain biking to Jeep tours and desert trekking.

Spas, sports

Eilat

E 8

District: Southern
Population: 70,000

Altitude: 20m/65ft

Eilat means almost 365 days of sunshine and warmth, sea, swimming, relaxation and entertainment, both day and night. It is Israel's holiday machine.

▶ VISITING EILAT

INFORMATION

8 Beit Hagesher St.
Tel. (08) 630 91 11
Fax 633 91 22
jody@tourism.gov.il
www.eilat-today.com
Sun–Thu 9am–5pm, Fri, Sat, holidays.
8am–1pm

www.eilat-guide.com
Commercial, but quite in-depth information

TRANSPORT

Coaches: there are several buses a day between Eilat and Tel Aviv / Eilat and Jerusalem (4.5 hrs), as well as to Beersheba and Haifa; number 15 goes to the Egyptian, number 16 to the Jordanian border.

ACTIVE HOLIDAY

Beaches: see p. 230

Diving: Eilat has just one coral reef, the Coral Beach Nature Reserve. Diving bases organize trips to Aqaba / Jordan and to Sinai. The providers hardly differ in their prices. A 5-day PADI Open Water course costs around US$ 360, including the equipment, teaching materials and certificate, e.g. with Lucky Divers (North Beach, www.luckydivers.com).

Bird watching: especially worthwhile in spring when the migratory birds stop around Eilat. Guided walks with the SPNI Field School (HaArava Street, opposite Coral Beach; International Birdwatching Center, tel. 08 / 633 53 39).

Jeep safaris to the natural spectacles of the surrounding area (also organized by hotels).

EVENTS

Red Sea Jazz Festival
Outstanding jazz festival in August (www.redseajazzeilat.com)

Red Sea Classical Festival
This wintertime festival featuring classical music for everyone has been held since 1993.

SHOPPING

Eilat is a free-trade zone, which means no VAT on clothes, linen, shoes and cosmetics. The best places for shopping are Shalom Mall, the *Mall Hayam Shopping Center* with the largest selection, and the *Mall Hakenyon Hahadash*. *Royal Beach Promenade* and *Herods Promenade*, once smart and expensive, are becoming a little run-down.

ENTERTAINMENT

Eilat is famous for its night life, which only gets going in the pubs, bars and night clubs from 10pm. Two pubs can be recommended in the new tourist centre in Downtown: *Underground* with a cool, lively atmosphere and *Unplugged*.

Three Monkeys
Royal Promenade
Tel. (08) 636 88 00
Daily from 9pm, cool drinks and cool live music. Dress code: no shorts or flip flops!

Platinum
King Solomon's Palace
Tel. (08) 636 34 44
Daily 10pm–4am
The in-disco with its laser show mostly plays music from the local charts. Thursdays is for over-25s, Fridays for gays.

Eilat Map

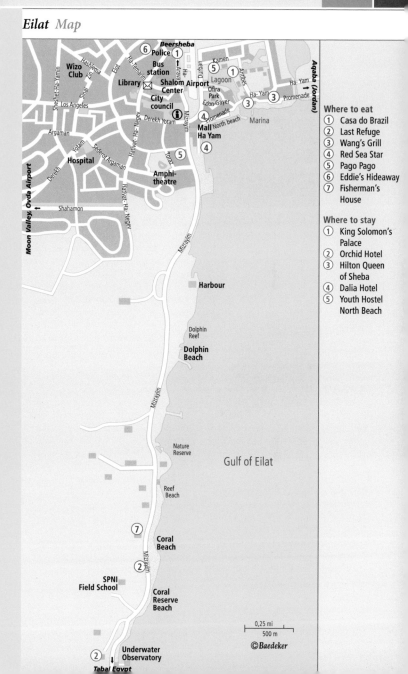

Where to eat
1. Casa do Brazil
2. Last Refuge
3. Wang's Grill
4. Red Sea Star
5. Pago Pago
6. Eddie's Hideaway
7. Fisherman's House

Where to stay
1. King Solomon's Palace
2. Orchid Hotel
3. Hilton Queen of Sheba
4. Dalia Hotel
5. Youth Hostel North Beach

© Baedeker

WHERE TO EAT

There are lots of snack stalls for falafel, McDonald's, pizzas and sandwiches around the Shalom Center. The situation is somewhat more expensive and higher-class along the waterfront promenade, with Indian, Italian, French and American cuisine. There are also lots of tasty fish options.

▶ Moderate

① *Casa do Brazil*
3 Hativat Golani
Tel. (08) 632 30 32
Top-quality Brazilian cooking. Here that means grilled food, be it beef, lamb, pork, fish and poultry – all you can eat or from the menu.

② *Last Refuge*
Coral Beach
at Yam Suf Hotel
Tel. (08) 637 24 37
Fish and seafood restaurant also frequented by locals. The good food makes up for the somewhat florid kitsch interior.

③ *Wang's Grill*
Royal Beach Hotel
Tel. (08) 636 89 89
Specialities from China in an elegant ambience; often better than the fare served in typical Chinese restaurants.

④ *Red Sea Star*
Southern Sq, opposite Le Meridien
Tel. (08) 634 77 77
www.redseastar.com This futuristic underwater restaurant has stolen the show from its rivals. Diners enjoy their meal 5m/15ft below the surface of the water, surrounded by an artificial coral reef, under the beady eyes of real fish on the other side of armoured plate glass. The Underwater Bar and Observatory is open until 3am.

Pago Pago
North Beach near Crown Plaza Hotel
Tel. (08) 6 37 66 60
www.pagopagorest.com
This bar-café-restaurant ship moored in a picturesque location in the lagoon exudes an atmosphere of the South Pacific, while offering good cocktails and fresh sushi.

▶ Moderate / Inexpensive

⑤ *Eddie's Hideaway*
68 Almogim St.
Tel. (08) 637 13 37
Eddie's is one of the most popular restaurants in Eilat, because it is imaginative while still being excellent value for money. The name stems from the fact that the restaurant is not easy to find: up Hatmarim St, turn right after the bus station into Almogim St, around house no. 68 to the back entrance.

▶ Inexpensive

⑥ *Fisherman's House*
Coral Beach
Tel. (08) 637 98 30
All you can eat, little service, very relaxed, but a good buffet selection with several fish dishes, poultry and meat.

WHERE TO STAY

▶ Luxury

① *King Solomon's Palace*
North Beach
Tel. (08) 638 77 97
Fax 633 41 89
www.isrotel.com
420 rooms. Relatively expensive since it is located right on the lagoon and has lots of activities for children, such as the indoor playground Kid's Kingdom.

② *Orchid Hotel*
Almog Beach

Tel. (08) 636 03 60
Fax 637 53 23
www.orchidhotel.co.il
164 rooms, 10 villas. Eilat's most
enchanting hotel complex is situated
opposite the underwater observatory;
it is built in the style of a Thai village.
The bungalows have Far Eastern
interiors and are built along a hillside
with breathtaking views of the sea and
the mountains.

③ Hilton Queen of Sheba
8 Antib / North Beach
Tel. (08) 630 66 66
www.hiltonworldresorts.com
479 rooms. This huge hotel pretends
to be historical, and is decorated with
scenes from ancient Egypt.

► Budget
④ Dalia Hotel
North Beach
Tel. (08) 633 40 04
Fax 633 40 72
www.daliahotel.co.il
62 rooms. Pleasant, clean and inexpensive – the Dalia is a recommend-
able alternative for the tighter budget.

⑤ Youth Hostel North Beach
HaArava St./Elot St.
Tel. (08) 637 00 88
Fax 637 58 35
www.iyha.org.il
Because of the lack of inexpensive
hotels close to the beach, this hostel is
always busy.

The young holiday paradise on the Red Sea attracts visitors with its
hot, dry climate. It only has around eight days of rain each year, and
winter temperatures do not drop below 10°C/50°F, while in summer
they can climb to more than 40°C/104°F. Eilat draws holidaymakers
from Israel and abroad. Every year new hotels are built, even though
Eilat is just an 11km/7mi strip of coastline on the Gulf of Aqaba,
nestling between the mountains of Sinai in the west and those of
Edom in the east. Besides **tourism**, the main source of income for
the country's southernmost town, the large international port also
plays an important role for the Israeli economy.

Holiday paradise on the Red Sea

Although there are no ancient sites in Eilat, the region has a long history. When the Israelites left Egypt, following Moses, they crossed
the Sinai peninsula. »And when we passed ... through the way of the
plain from Elath (Eilat), and from Ezion-gaber, we turned and
passed by the way of the wilderness of Moab« (Deuteronomy 2:8).
However, the site of Elath mentioned was probably that of modern-
day Aqaba in Jordan, just a few miles east of modern Eilat. In the
10th century BC Solomon built ships in Ezion Geber – at the same
time as the queen of Sheba went ashore at this harbour, before going
to Jerusalem for a meeting with Solomon (1 Kings 10:1 ff.). In the
8th century BC the Israelites lost the harbour, which later belonged
to the Ptolemaic dynasty, then the Nabataeans and finally the Romans, who called it Aila. The crusaders built a castle on the offshore
island in 1116. After the state of Israel was founded, a new Jewish
settlement was built in 1949, the kibbutz of Elot, which was later

Even Moses came through here

moved 3km/2mi further inland. With the construction of the **international port** in 1956, Eilat embarked on its development into a city and tourist centre.

What to See in Eilat

Townscape Eilat is a modern and not very attractive town that keeps spreading further up the surrounding hillsides. The airport lies at its centre and has a frighteningly short runway. There have long been plans to construct a new airport in cooperation with Aqaba in Jordan and to use the present site as building land. HaTemarim Street begins at the roundabout at the airport building. It goes all the way to the centre of Eilat and is lined by shopping centres with restaurants, cafés, banks, car rentals and shops, as well as the station. To the south, along Mizrayim St, further shopping centres were built with restaurants and pubs for every taste. Most of the hotels (quite luxurious compared to the rest of Israel) can be found at the north beach or beyond on the big lagoon with the promenade and marina. A second lagoon has been created further to the east.

! **Baedeker TIP**

Aqaba, Jordan

Anyone wishing to make an excursion into neighbouring Jordan is advised to consult the tourist information office, which will have the relevant bus connections and know about the latest visa regulations and the costs involved in crossing the border in both directions.

✳ **Beaches**
North Beach ► The beaches of Eilat are not remote or tranquil – especially not North Beach, the stronghold of sun worshippers, where snacks and drinks are served to loud music. Lifeguards patrol the 5km/3mi beach, which is managed and serviced by restaurants and hotels. Access to Eilat's most-visited beach is free; however, it costs from NIS 20 and upwards for one deck chair for anyone not staying in one of the relevant hotels. It gets quieter further east on North Beach, a sand and pebble beach lined with plenty of cafés and kiosks. North Beach is no good for snorkelling; the beaches in the south are far better for that.

Beaches in the south ► Here too there are several sections that can be accessed free of charge; however, the beaches that require an entry fee because they have cafés, showers, parasols and deckchairs, are nicer and more comfortable (e.g. **Palm Beach, Dolphin Beach, Coral Beach Nature Reserve**). The reef here gives snorkellers and divers what they are looking for. Diving and snorkelling equipment can be hired on most of the beaches.

King City A biblical attraction in Eilat, sited between the inner and the eastern lagoon, is King City (tel. 08.634 44 44, http://www.kingscity.co.il/), an amusement park that aims to use a big multimedia effort to bring

Israel's no. 1 holiday machine is not necessarily a beauty.

the times of King Solomon to life, and also demonstrates all kinds of physical experiments (daily from 9am).

Dolphin Reef

Around 3km/2mi south of Eilat, just behind the harbour, is Dolphin Reef (tel. 08 630 01 00, www.dolphinreef.co.il), where **dolphins are kept in their natural habitat**. The complex has a comparatively small beach, a restaurant, a souvenir shop and a diving school. It is also possible to swim with the animals, but only for a hefty fee.

Underwater observatory

The Red Sea coast between Eilat and Sharm el Sheikh is known for its wonderful **coral reefs**. The beach of Coral Beach Nature Reserve is worthwhile in itself. The upper half of the underwater observatory rises out of the water like a UFO around 100m/100yd offshore; the observation room built around a central stairway tower lies 6m/20ft below the surface, displaying filigree coral reefs and colourful, shimmering fish through large windows (daily 8.30am–5pm, Fri and before holidays until 4pm; www.coralworld.com/eilat).

! *Baedeker* TIP

Diving down

One speciality among Eilat's beaches is **Coral Reserve Beach**, 6km/3.5mi south of Downtown Eilat, which is part of Coral Beach Nature Reserve (tel. 08 66 42 00, www.coralworld.com). Visitors go along walkways over the reef and watch the fish, swim between the coral banks (beware: sea urchins), and go diving or snorkelling.

Yellow Submarine ► At the jetty of the Underwater Observatory is the »**Yellow Submarine**«, which takes visitors to a depth of 60m/200ft to see the coral reefs. Those who prefer to remain above the water can also get to know the underwater world of the Red Sea on a trip in a glass-bottom boat. The boats depart from Eilat Marina.

Around Eilat

Har Yoash, Ein Netafim One excellent viewpoint is the 734m/2408ft Mount Yoach (Har Yoash) to the northwest of Eilat. After driving for around 10km/6mi on road 12 (taxi or rental car), there is a track to the summit. Quite nearby, north of Route 12, is the spring Ein Netafim. Leave the car at the first car park by the road or somewhat further down and walk to the spring. The descent to the spring is very narrow and steep in places, so good footwear and a bit of scrambling experience would be beneficial.

Moon Valley Drive past the turning to Ein Netafim for another 5km/3mi to get to the bare Moon Valley with its granite outcrops at 800m/2625ft.

Red Canyon Around 12km/7mi after the turning to Ein Netafim there is a right-hand turning to the Red Canyon (track). The hike through the **lovely red canyon landscape**, which narrows to a width of just 50cm/20 inches at times, starts at the car park and takes around an hour.

Yotvata Approx. 40km/25mi north of Eilat is the date-palm oasis of the kibbutz of Yotvata, which was founded in 1951 and gets its water from the Ein Yotvata (Arabic: Ain Radian) spring. The visitor centre has an audio-video show that gives an insight into what the region is like, while an exhibition informs visitors about the local flora and fauna as well as the desert's geology and history.

✱
Hai Bar Every day (but only in the mornings!) tours to the nearby **animal reserve** Hai Bar (tel. 08 637 30 57) are organized by the Yotvata visitor centre. The reserve was created in order to give a habitat back to the desert animals which lived in the region during biblical times. Today it is possible to observe antelopes, onagers, ostriches, leopards, wolves, foxes, hyenas and other animals in their natural habitat.

Trip to the Sinai

Organized tour Many hotels and local travel agencies in Eilat run trips to the eastern Sinai. The most popular excursion is to the famous St Catherine's Monastery, which can easily be combined with an ascent of Mount Sinai. The east coast of the Sinai Peninsula, between Taba and Sharm el-Sheikh (240km/150mi south of Eilat), is known for its beautiful **sandy beaches** and especially for stunning **coral reefs**. The Sinai

East coast of the Sinai Peninsula ►

coastline has almost perfect conditions for swimming, surfing, snorkelling and diving. A good road connects the coastal towns. There is a bus connection between Taba and Sharm el-Sheikh, the rapidly growing tourist centre at the southern tip of the peninsula.

Taba

Taba is the first town beyond the Israeli-Egyptian border. There are regular buses between Taba and Eilat. The disagreement between Egypt and Israel about this enclave 8km/5mi to the southwest of Eilat was ended in 1989: the 1km/0.5mi strip, including the luxury hotel and holiday village, has since belonged to Egypt.

Coral Island

Just beyond Taba, on the left-hand side of the road, near the shores of the Red Sea, is Coral Island or Pharaoh's Island. It possesses a small, sheltered harbour on the south side and is equated with the port of Ezio Geber mentioned in the Old Testament. The island has probably been inhabited since the 20th Egyptian dynasty and was probably a significant port for exporting copper from the mines in the Arava and Timna Valleys. The ruins of a 12th-century crusader castle can be seen from afar.

Nuweiba

Nuweiba, around 80km/50mi south of Taba, is an excellent base for trips into the mountains of eastern Sinai. The town centre has shops, restaurants, a post office and a bureau de change, while the larger (and more expensive) hotels can be found to the south of the actual town. There are daily ferries to Aqaba departing from the harbour.

✳
Coloured Canyon

The impressive canyon landscape extends around 30km/18mi north-west of Nuweiba (the last 10km/6mi are on a track). The track ends on a plateau. Climb down into the canyon landscape from here. Sturdy footwear is a good idea for this one-and-a-half-hour hike, which is not otherwise challenging. At the lowest point the canyon narrows into a ravine bordered by high rock walls. The reddish sand-stone makes some very lovely patterns here.

✳ ✳
St Catherine's Monastery

Just outside Nuweiba the largely well-surfaced road branches off to St Catherine's Monastery. This famous place of pilgrimage, which was declared a World Heritage Site by UNESCO in 2002, is located amid the fascinating mountain landscape of the Sinai Peninsula at the foot of the 2285m/7497ft Mount Sinai (Jabal Musa). Emperor Justinian had the fort-like monastery built between 548 and 565, in the location where Moses is believed to have seen the **Burning Bush** (Exodus 3:2 ff.). It was home to up to 400 monks at times. The monastery obtained its name from Saint Catherine, the Alexandrian martyr whose body was, according to legend, carried by angels to the summit of Mount Sinai. The diplomatically skilled monks managed over the centuries to ensure that their monastery was always protected by whoever was in power. More than 100 letters of protection are evidence of this. There is even one from Napoleon.

🕐
Opening hours:
Mon–Thu and Sat 9am/9.30am–noon, closed Fri, Sun and Greek Orthodox holidays

In addition to the church it is also possible to view the site of the Burning Bush, Moses' well and the monks' ossuary. None of the other buildings, the library in particular, are open to the public. A small selection of the most important treasures of the monastery are exhibited in the church's atrium.

◀ Exterior view

From outside the monastery resembles a fort, because the almost square area is surrounded on all sides by a **12–15m/40–50ft-high wall of granite blocks**. The wall section in the southwest dates back to the monastery's foundation. Like the other entrances, the original main gate on the northwest side was walled up by the monks for safety reasons. The only way to get into the monastery's interior was via a hoist. A French expedition built the massive gate tower on the north side and created a small access point in this place, which is still the main entrance to the monastery today.

Saint Catherine's Monastery lies at the foot of Mount Sinai in complete seclusion.

The **monastery area** resembles a labyrinth of interlacing buildings, corridors and stairways. Apart from the abbey and the residential and business wings, there is also an 11th-century **mosque** within the walls. It was built by Muslim Bedouins and is a simple concrete building with a separate minaret. To the northwest, outside the monastery walls, are pleasant gardens with cypresses and olive trees. The monastic compound is dominated by the **Church of the Transfiguration** with its bell tower that in turn dominates all else. Since the church is relatively small and the number of tourist groups relatively large, an in-depth viewing is only possible in exceptional cases. Enter the church through a carved portal from the Fatimid period (11th century). Some of the famous icons and manuscripts from the 12th–16th centuries for which the monastery is known are on display in the narrow anteroom (narthex). Beyond the narthex is the 6th-century basilica with a gilded iconostasis, made by artists from Crete in 1612. It covers the magnificent mosaic in the apse, which was made at the same time as the church was built and depicts Christ's Transfiguration on ►Mount Tabor. The chapel, built in 1216 on the site of the Burning Bush, features silver reliefs under the altar, where, according to tradition, it stood; the Syrian bladder senna on the outside wall of the chapel is believed to be its offshoot.

◄ Inside the monastery

? DID YOU KNOW ...?

- The Church of the Transfiguration is the only place of worship in which mass has been read every day for almost 1500 years.

★ ★ Mount Sinai

Climbing Jabal Musa, a trip offered by almost all of the tour operators, has its reason: the view from the summit down onto wild, barren landscape is magnificent, particularly at sunrise and sunset. In front of this beautiful backdrop Moses is said to have received the **Ten Commandments** from God (Exodus 20:1–17).

There are two main routes up the mountain: the shorter but harder one via the pilgrims' staircase with around 2500 (!) steps, and the unfinished surfaced road started by »Abbas Pasha«. In addition a large portion of the way can be completed riding a camel, so that only the last third has to be done on foot. It takes around two hours to get to the summit.

The town of **Dahab** around 50km/30mi north of Nuweiba got its name from the golden yellow beach (dahab = gold in Arabic). The most expensive hotels are located on the southern bay, while the budget travellers meet in the Bedouin village of Assalah, where

! *Baedeker* TIP

Wrap up warm

Watching the sun rise on Mount Sinai is wonderful, but early in the mornings it gets very cold. That is why it is vital to take a jacket and a thick pullover, even though the temperatures in Eilat and Sharm el-Sheikh are summery. Also, be aware of the fact that despite setting off at such an early hour, there will be lots of other people on the summit!

The early wake-up call and the hard work were all worth it: sunrise on Mount Sinai.

cheap hotels, camps, restaurants and cafés in the Bedouin style, diving schools and shops all line the long waterfront promenade. The infrastructure is tailored to a young clientele with tight purse strings. There are more than half a dozen internet cafés, and in addition to the usual souvenirs for sale also a few original and inexpensive shops. The narrow and not very clean beach in the Bedouin village, on the other hand, is not very attractive. There are far better places, both for swimming and snorkelling, elsewhere in the surrounding area.

Sharm el-Sheikh

No other town on the Sinai Peninsula has focused so obviously on tourism as Sharm el-Sheikh. With its airport and port, which connects the town with Hurghada, the second large tourist centre, Sharm el-Sheikh has the best conditions for such development thanks to its beaches and especially its **fantastic coral reefs**. There is a bazaar with a pedestrian area, countless diving schools, cafés, restaurants, night clubs, shopping and leisure facilities along the wide Naama Bay, around 10km/6mi north of Sharm el-Sheikh's centre. Most of the hotels lie directly by the well-tended beach, only separated from it by the promenade. Shark Bay, around 6km/3.5mi north of Naama Bay, is perfectly suited for snorkelling and diving, because the reef drops away very close to the beach here. Travel agencies and hotels in Sharm el-Sheikh run one-day trips to Ras Mohamed Marine National Park, **the first national park in Egypt**. The protected area, which covers around 200 sq km/75 sq mi, can only

Naama Bay ▶

Shark Bay ▶

Ras Mohamed Marine National Park ▶

be accessed for a fee. Around 140km/90mi of marked trails and maintenance paths have been created from which visitors can enjoy the park's natural beauty. Collecting corals and fossils is strictly prohibited, visitors are only allowed to access the beaches on foot, and diving and snorkelling is allowed in specific sections. The park cannot be reached by public transport. Taking a taxi there is relatively expensive.

✷ Ein Bokek

F 5

District: Southern   **Altitude:** 400m/1310ft below sea level

Ein Bokek, a tourist and resort centre on the southwestern shores of the ►Dead Sea, has a hot mineral spring which has been used for healing since ancient times.

Because of the unusual climatic conditions and the unique water properties of the Dead Sea, surprising results are achieved here, par-

Spa on the Dead Sea

This is only possible in the Dead Sea.

▶ VISITING EIN BOKEK

INFORMATION
In the shopping centre
Tel. (08) 658 41 53

GETTING THERE
Buses several times a day from and to Jerusalem, Beersheba and Eilat.

SHOPPING
Petra Shopping Center: cafeteria and supermarkets, lots of shops with therapeutic creams, ointments, salts and oils from local production.

WHERE TO EAT
Dining here is like accommodation: expensive. One alternative is the Petra Shopping Centre, where it is possible to buy snacks and sandwiches on the ground floor. The BBQ restaurant on the first floor serves hearty shewarma (mutton or chicken on a vertical spit, similar to doner kebabs).

WHERE TO STAY
► Luxury
Lot Spa Hotel
www.lothotel.com
Tel. (08) 668 92 22
With the crowds of tourists, the hotels of Ein Bokek have a tendency towards neglect and surliness, from which the chefs are not exempt. They seem to think they have a captive clientele for whom it is not worth taking too much trouble in the kitchen. An honourable exception is the Lot Spa Hotel. It has indoor and outdoor pools with salt water, and direct access to a nice beach.

Crown Plaza
Tel. (08) 659 19 11
www.afi-hotels.com
Attractive rooms, all with views of the Dead Sea, spa, entertainment for adults and a Kids Club.

ticularly with skin problems. The extremely salty deeper layers of water of the lake in the town are used as a reservoir for the sun's heat.

What to See in Ein Bokek and Around

In Ein Bokek Hotels and spas dominate the scene in Ein Bokek. It is possible to go for a dip in the Dead Sea and publicly accessible spots, such as the southern end of town or near the hotel Grand Nirwana, where visitors will find showers and parasols. To the north of Ein Bokek are the ruins of the castle Metzad Bokek, which the kings of Judah built to defend themselves against the Moabites.

8km/5mi south of Ein Bokek at **Neve Zohar**, several hot sulphurous springs are popular because of

❓ DID YOU KNOW ...?

■ The special properties of the water of the Dead Sea were already known in Antiquity: Cleopatra used it for her body. It is scientifically confirmed that this water has the world's highest mineral content: around 300 grams per litre.

their healing and relaxing properties. Here too there is a public beach (Hamei Zohar).

Follow the gorge or the Zohar River, which flows into the sea at Neve Zohar. Metzad Zohar, a Nabataean castle that was later used by the Byzantines, lies 3km/2mi up this gorge atop a narrow rocky elevation amid a stunning mountain scenery. Another way to get a lovely view of this castle is by driving from Neve Zohar towards ► Arad to the second, upper viewpoint (on the right). The lower viewpoint has a **wonderful view** of the Dead Sea and the mountains of Jordan.

◄ Metzad Zohar

✳ Ein Gedi

F 5

District: Southern
Population: 50,000

Altitude: 400m/1300ft below sea level

Lavish green, streams, springs, waterfalls and cool ponds, exotic plants and rare animals in the wild, hiking trails and idyllic spots to sit and relax – all of these things make the oasis and nature reserve of Ein Gedi one of the most beautiful destinations in the country.

The **nature reserve**, which is equally popular among foreign tourists and locals, is situated between the rivers Nahal David in the north and Nahal Arugot in the south and extends along the western shores of the Dead Sea, around 20km/12mi north of ► Masada. At the southern end of the oasis, the kibbutz with the same name has a well-tended guesthouse. Nearby, on the shores of the Dead Sea, the Ein Gedi Spa offers rest and relaxation. The name of the oasis, already praised by Solomon as a place of great beauty (Song of Songs 1:14), means Kid Spring, though the Kid Spring is just one of four to which Ein Gedi owes its plentiful water supply.

Oasis on the Dead Sea

Ein Gedi can look back on a long history of settlement. The temple above the Shulamit Spring dates back to the 4th millennium BC. The precious temple treasure, which includes 240 heads of sceptres and five ivory carvings, was not found here but in a cave by Nahal Mishmar, 12km/7mi to the south; the inhabitants presumably brought it to safety there. Between the 7th century BC and the 5th century AD five settlements in succession were built on Tell Goren. The first was destroyed in 582 BC by Nebuchadnezzar, but the town was rebuilt and flourished in the 5th and 4th centuries BC. The Hellenistic town of the Hasmoneans was built above these two settlements (2nd–1st century BC). Herod the Great built the fourth settlement, which fell victim to the Jewish War in AD 68. The last settlement was located to the north of the tell (by the remains of the synagogue) and was abandoned in the 5th century.

6000 years of history

▶ VISITING EIN GEDI

INFORMATION
Kibbutz Ein Gedi
Tel. (08) 659 42 21
Fax 658 43 28
www.ein-gedi.co.il

GETTING THERE
Buses run to and from Tel Aviv via
Jerusalem and Eilat several times a day.

WHERE TO STAY
▶ **Budget**
Youth Hostel
www.iyha.org.il
The youth hostel offers inexpensive
accommodation in dorms and the
plentiful kosher breakfast buffet is
included in the price.

A place of refuge in
uncertain times ▶

The caves in the Ein Gedi region were always used as hiding places.
David sought refuge from the anger of the aging King Saul »in the
wilderness of En Gedi« (1 Samuel 24:1–23), which is why the river is
named Nahal David. During the Bar Kokhba revolt, Jewish rebels hid
in the valley of the Nahar Hever, 5km/3mi to the south of Ein Gedi.
Some of the items discovered in the caves were letters by Simon bar
Kokhba, a psalm fragment, metal containers, house keys and clothing.

Ein Gedi Nature Reserve

Orientation

The nature reserve consists of two areas that lie next to each other:
Nahal David and Nahal Arugot. The network of trails has walks of
different lengths; it is easy to spend an entire day in the oasis
(summer daily 8am–5pm, winter daily 8am–4pm).

Hikes

Most visitors choose the car park at the entrance (Nahal David) as
the starting point because this is the fastest way to get to the **David
Falls**, where the water from Nahal David plummets into a pool. The
trail follows the densely vegetated river channel and only climbs
gradually at first, while later it becomes steeper and steeper. Time
and again the water tumbles over rocks into small pools, where it is
at least possible to cool off arms and legs. Thanks to the many

A mud bath in the Dead Sea is supposed to be healthy... →

En Gedi Map

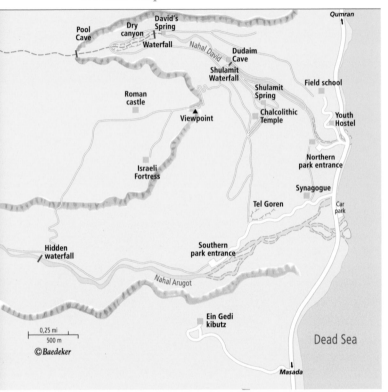

springs that provide water all years round, the plants growing here are not just desert plants, but also reeds and tropical plants such as moringa and the apple of Sodom, which flowers purple. With a bit of luck ibexes can be seen, but the chances of **spotting a rare leopard** are extremely slim. It takes around an hour to walk from the park entrance (Nahal David) to David Falls and back.

There is a trail, sometimes rough, up to the **Shulamit Spring**. The remains of an old water mill have been discovered nearby. To the northwest are the remains of a **Chalcolithic temple**, which served the moon cult and the spring cult. The round moonstone still lies at the heart of the building; the two gates of the cult site point to the **Ein Gedi Spring** on the one side and the Shulamit Spring on the other. Continue further northwards from Shulamit Spring to get to **Dodim Cave** above the David Falls. Plan about five hours for this hike. From the Chalcolithic temple it is possible to continue onwards to the **Dry Canyon**, which takes a further two hours there and back.

On the slopes above the park entrance, SPNI (The American Society for the Protection of Nature in Israel) provides information about the flora and fauna of the Jewish desert and the region around the Dead Sea.

SPNI Field School

Just 1km/0.5mi to the south of the park entrance is the car park where the trail along the Arugot River begins. It leads to the **Hidden Falls** 5km/3mi inland. The hike there and back takes around three hours. Before the road turns right onto the trail, there are the remains of a **synagogue** with attractive mosaics. A few metres beyond the junction are the inconspicuous remains of the former settlement of **Tell Goren**.

Nahal Arugot, Tell Goren

Around 3km/2mi to the south of the park entrance to Nahal David is a road to the Ein Gedi kibbutz, which was founded in the early 1950s. The kibbutz guesthouse towers above the Dead Sea in a magnificent location and is surrounded by a paradise of tropical plants. The Botanical Garden is home to **more than 900 plant species** (there are botanical historical guided tours).
Many guests come to enjoy the Ein Gedi Spa on the beach of the Dead Sea, 5km/3mi from the kibbutz and to bathe in the 38ºC/100ºF sulphur springs, which emerge at the foot of the mountains. The **black mud** from the Dead Sea is also said to have great healing properties.

Kibbutz Ein Gedi, Ein Gedi Spa

Gaza · Ğabaliya

D / E 4 / 5

Area: Gaza Strip
(Palestinian territory)
Altitude: 30m/100ft

Population: 368,000
(1.33 million in the entire Gaza Strip)

The Palestinian city of Gaza is the centre of trade and business of the Gaza Strip, which is 40km/25mi long and up to 10km/6mi wide.

Gaza has a 4000-year history. Fortifications and tombs from around 1750 BC were found 7km/4mi to the southwest, on the Tell al-Ajjul. The Great Mosque in the town goes back to a 13th-century crusader church. The remains of a 5th-century synagogue have been found at the harbour. Its floor mosaic depicts King David as Orpheus.
During the Six-Day War Israel occupied the region. In 1994 the Gaza Jericho Agreement gave Palestine self-rule. Since then it has been the seat of the Palestinian president. However, since Hamas seized power, he has had to do his job from Ramallah. Since October 1999 a 53km/33mi transit route has connected the Gaza Strip with the

Hamas rules here

West Bank, allowing Palestinians from the Gaza Strip to work in the West Bank as long as Israel does not close the border crossings, which it often does after attacks. Many of the Palestinian inhabitants live in refugee camps in terrible poverty. Resistance against reconciliation with Israel has a strong foundation in this economically exploited region.

Recent history The Arab population of southern Palestine fled during the Palestine War of 1948–49 to the area around the city of Gaza, which was occupied by Egyptian troops. After the ceasefire of February 1949 this region went to Egypt.

During the Suez Crisis (1956–57) Israel occupied the Gaza Strip, but gave it back to Egypt in 1957. After the Six-Day War of 1967, Israel put the area under military administration. Following failed negotiations in 1979 and 1982 some autonomy was given to the Gaza Strip and Jericho as a result of the Gaza Jericho Agreement signed in May 1994. Ignoring this, Jewish settlements were built in the Gaza Strip, which, over the course of 2005, when Israel withdrew from the Gaza Strip, were broken up by the Israeli police, in some cases in the face of severe resistance. The Palestinians continue to shoot missiles at Israel from the Gaza Strip, which regularly results in Israeli military action.

The situation came to a head in 2003–04 when Arafat's official residence was surrounded and partially destroyed. After Hamas came to power, fighting broke out in March 2006 between the Hamas and Fatah militias, until Hamas took power in the Gaza Strip (see info box).

After that the Israelis completely sealed off the Gaza Strip; Egypt, which under no circumstances wants to take back responsibility for the territory, built a border wall after Hamas bulldozed the border structures in January 2008 in order to allow the population to shop in Egypt. The Israeli military operation in late 2008 and early 2009 made the situation even more hopeless for the people living in the Gaza Strip (see p. 81).

In 2010 Israeli troops boarded a flotilla of six ships bound for Gaza from various European ports, which claimed to be carrying humanitarian aid. In June 2010 the blockade was relaxed to allow almost all non-military and dual use goods into Gaza.

---

i **Fraternal Conflict**

■ In June 2007, despite constant avowals by both parties to stop fighting, the struggles between the Hamas and Fatah militias escalated into downright war. Hamas attacked the Fatah-controlled security forces and gained control of the Gaza Strip. This came after the treaty that was signed in Mecca in February by the PLO and Hamas, which excluded the crucial questions of disbanding the militias, setting up a single security force and integrating Hamas into the PLO. The civilian population was not of interest to either side, quite the opposite in fact: several hundred civilians who were protesting against the violence were fired on. Those who speak out against Hamas are, it is said, persecuted and denounced as traitors; revenge murders are said to have taken place.

Golan

G 1/2

Area: Golan   **Altitude:** up to 2224m/7297ft

The scenically diverse mountain range to the east of Jordan and the Sea of Galilee between Mount Hermon in the north and Yarmouk River in the south is worth visiting for its harsh beauty, despite the troubled associations its name often triggers.

For decades the area was the **site of violent confrontations** between Syria and Israel and, as a result, a blind spot on the tourist map. The southern section of the Golan Heights consists of a fertile plateau at an altitude of around 1000m/3300ft, which dips down into a few wadis. Grazing land, meadows and fields, interspersed with grey-brown basalt rock, dominate the scene. Towards the north the terrain rises all the way to Mount Hermon, whose summit on Syrian soil lies at an altitude of 2814m/9232ft. It rains comparatively often on the Golan Heights, and in winter the area sees so much snowfall that it is even possible to go skiing here!

Disputed territory

In ancient times the area of the Golan Heights was populated by Jewish settlements. In the 1st century AD, the Golan was part of the territory of Philip the Tetrarch, who founded Caesaera Philippi (►Banias). Gadara (►Hammat Gader) in the south of the Golan on the Yarmouk was a centre of Greek culture and a significant resort. After the First World War, the Golan was first given to Palestine, then in 1923 to Syria. After 1948 the Israeli-Syrian border ran along the Jordan, and the Golan region was turned into a military zone by Syria. In 1967 Israel occupied the area, and in 1981 annexed it. In order to avoid further confrontations, a **UN buffer zone** was set up between Syria and the Golan. Since the Israeli conquest, more than two dozen Jewish settlements have sprung up here next to the villages of the approx. 15,000 local Druze people. In contrast to the Druze

History

Don't get careless!

■ Even today large parts of the Golan are littered with **mines**. Never leave the roads during hikes and do not enter any of the fenced-off areas! Hikes have to be agreed with the SPNI Golan Field School in Katzrin or in the Nahal Hermon Reserve. These places will provide good information and maps. To get an idea of the situation, including bunkers and tank wrecks, go to the **viewpoint Ben Tal** on Route 98 near Manusra.

people in the Carmel, they do not want to be integrated into the state of Israel and are thus hoping that the Golan will be returned to Syria. For Israel the area is extremely important from a strategic perspective: a large part of its drinking water comes from the Golan Heights, indirectly via the Jordan and the Sea of Galilee.

View of the Golan and Nimrod Fortress

What to See in the Golan Heights

Starting points The following places make good starting points for the Golan Heights region: ► Tiberias on the Sea of Galilee, ► Safed or Kiryat Shemona (► Hule Plain). A much-visited destination in the north of the Golan Heights is the Banias nature reserve, as well as the neighbouring crusader castle Nimrod, which lies in a stunning setting (► Banias).

Neve Ativ Around 5km/3mi above Banias, on Route 989, is Moshav Neve Ativ, which has developed into a much-visited holiday resort. The **ski resort with around 35 pistes** is situated at an altitude of 2225m/7300ft on the slopes of Mount Hermon; the summit is on Syrian territory.

Druze villages, Birket Ram In Majdal Shams, 4km/2.5mi beyond Neve Ativ, this road meets Route 98, which heads south. Majdal Shams is the largest of the four Druze villages on the Golan Heights and the highest settlement in Israel and Israeli-occupied territory. Just outside the Druze village of Mas'ada, to the left of the road, is the lake Birket Ram, where it is possible to swim, take out a boat and even windsurf during the summer months. There is a restaurant and a falafel kiosk by the lake as well.

The young administrative capital, which was only founded in 1977, lies in the heart of the Golan Heights, approx. 32km/20mi south of Mas'ada (19km/12mi on Route 98, then another 13km/8mi to the intersection with Route 9088, which turns left to Katzrin). The **Golan Archaeological Museum** in the centre of Katzrin is worth visiting. It addresses the settlement history on the Golan Heights.

Katzrin

On a rocky mountain ridge, which resembles a camel's back, hence the name Gamla (Hebrew gamal = camel), around 15km/9mi to the south of Katzrin, archaeologists discovered the ruins of the ancient city of Gamla (Route 9088 until it joins Route 87, after 3km/2mi east on Route 808; from there it is another 10km/6mi). Gamla's fate is popularly compared to that of Masada, because the Jewish town was also besieged for months by Roman troops in AD 67, finally being conquered after a battle in which both sides suffered heavy losses. The commander of the Jewish fort was Flavius Josephus, who, in his history of the Jewish War, also described the defence of Masada. Visiting the excavation site requires a little time because the steep walk up takes around an hour. Archaeologists have uncovered residential buildings, a synagogue, water channels and baths, oil presses as well as the remains of a town wall. A marked path also leads from the car park to **Israel's highest waterfall**, the 51m/167ft Mapal Gamla in the middle of a national park in which visitors can watch large birds of prey, such as griffon vultures, eagles and buzzards.

✷ Gamla

! *Baedeker* TIP

Golan wine
One of Israel's best-known winegrowing regions is situated on the Golan Heights. Those who wish to sample and buy good quality local wines should visit the Golan winery in Katzrin (to the left of Route 9088 after the archaeological park and the industrial estate; Golan Winery, tel. 04/ 969 84 35, www.golanwines.co.il).

✷ Haifa · Hefa

E 2

District: Northern
Population: 267,000

Altitude: 0–300m/985ft

It is said in Israel that people pray in Jerusalem, live in Tel Aviv and work in Haifa. Some Israelis also claim that Haifa is the most beautiful and cleanest city in the country.

Of course these clichés also contain a grain of truth, because Haifa (Hefa) is indeed an attractive city with lots of parks and well-tended gardens, and at the same time Israel's main port, a significant hub for exporting the country's products and importing oil. Furthermore it is an important industrial location as well as the site of a technical college and a university.

Israel's main port

From fishing village to port

The city's name, Haifa, was mentioned for the first time in the 3rd century AD. The settlement, known for its shipbuilding and Talmud school, was conquered by the crusaders in 1100, and they remained in possession, almost without a break, until 1265. Under the Mamluks and the Ottomans Haifa was an insignificant fishing village. In 1740 Daher el-Omar, the ruler of Galilee, built a new settlement here, which is now the old town, and had a harbour built for grain transports to Egypt.

Haifa's significance grew because the harbour of neighbouring ►Akko turned out to be too small for the new steamboats. Joining the Jewish population in 1868 there came German settlers, Templers from Württemberg (a Protestant sect not to be confused with the medieval Knights Templar). Later Christians from Lebanon and Arabs came here, while the sects of the Baha'i and the Ahmadiyya, which had broken away from Islam, chose Haifa as their main base. In honour of the visit of **Kaiser (Emperor) Wilhelm II** of Germany in 1898 a second jetty was constructed, which pushed forward the development of the harbour. At the Kaiser's suggestion, the city also decided to connect to the railway line between Damascus and Medina.

Haifa – Israel's most important port

▶ VISITING HAIFA

INFORMATION

48 Ben Gurion Blvd.
(German Colony)
Tel. (04) 853 56 06
www.tour-haifa.co.il
Sun–Thu 9am–5pm, Fri 9am–1pm,
Sat 10am–3pm

TRANSPORT

Within the city: buses and the *Car-melite underground funicular railway* every 10 minutes; Sun–Thu 6.30am–midnight, Fri until 3.30pm, Sat from half an hour after the end of Sabbath until midnight.
Outside the city: Haifa Central, 1 Ha'Atzmaut St. / Palmer Sq.; bus station Bat Galim; Sherut to Tel Aviv from 157 Jaffa Rd., Hahalutz St.

SHOPPING

For shopping stay in the area around *Havenim Street*. Other good options are the large *Haifa Mall* in the south of the city, where it is possible to get absolutely anything, as well as *Castra Mall* (4 Fliman St.): apart from being a shopping centre for handicrafts, jewellery and a colourful array of designer goods, this place is also home to what is claimed to be the biggest »painting« in the world: the Austrian-Israeli artist Arik Brauer depicts scenes from the Old Testament on hundreds of painted ceramic tiles, a unique approach.

ENTERTAINMENT

Haifa has a small nightlife scene. Good bars, such as Danni Hadom (5 Ben Gurion Blvd., tel. 04 / 852 32 86), Café 29 (29 Moriah Blvd.), Hamartef (2 Bankim St., tel. 04 / 853 23 67), Batzir Wine Bar (44 Jaffa St., tel. 04 / 853 56 68) or Hasandk (30 Kdoshi Bagdad St., tel. 04 / 853 56 58). Those who feel like dancing should go to the Hit Club (27 Kibbuz Galyut St.) after midnight.

WHERE TO EAT

There are lots of restaurants with many different cuisines to choose from in Ben Gurion Street.

▶ Expensive

① *Hashmura 1872*
15 Ben Gurion Ave.
Tel. (04) 855 18 72
The food served is based on French cuisine, fish and meat in a unique building built by the Templers. The restaurant is considered to be one of the best in Haifa.

▶ Moderate

② *Fattoush*
38 Ben Gurion Blvd.
Tel. (04) 852 49 30
The restaurant has the atmosphere of an Arab tavern, used only in the cooler seasons. Otherwise you can sit outside in the pleasant garden and enjoy Arab cuisine, including Lebanese starters and grills. Fattoush is a good place for breakfast too.

WHERE TO STAY

▶ Luxury

① *Leonardo Hotel Haifa*
10 David Elazar St.
Carmel Beach
Tel. (04) 850 88 88
Fax 850 11 70
www.leonardo-hotels.com
Pleasant deluxe hotel right on the coast with its own beach.

▶ Luxury/Mid-range

Templars Boutique Hotel
36 Ben Gurion Blvd.
Tel. (077) 500 31 10, (050) 520 96 95

www.templars.co.il
Right next to the Fattoush restaurant, where hotel guests take breakfast, in the heart of the German Colony, this stylish little hotel occupies a 150-year-old Templer house. The rooms are not only spacious, but have kitchenettes for self-catering. The only downside: the noise of the street outside.

② ***Dan Panorama***
107 Ha-Nasi St.

Haifa Map

Where to eat
① Hashmura 1872
② Fattoush

Where to stay
① Leonardo Hotel Haifa
② Dan Panorama
③ Templars Boutique Hotel
④ Beth Shalom Carmel

Tel. (03) 835 22 22
Fax 835 22 35
www.danhotels.com
The twin towers dominate the entire Carmel; the room interiors cannot, however, quite keep up with the fantastic views. The hill station of the Carmelite funicular is nearby.

► **Mid-range**
③ *Beth Shalom Carmel*
10 HaNassi Blvd.
Tel. (04(837 34 80, fax 837 24 43
www.beth-shalom.co.il
This very clean and tidy hotel, favoured by pilgrims, lies 250m/800ft above Haifa on Mount Carmel and offers a view to match the location. It was founded by Swiss Christians and is still Swiss-run.

On 23 September 1918, British forces occupied the city and connected it to Egypt via a railway line through Gaza.
After the proclamation of the state of Israel in 1948, Haifa became significant as an arrival port for immigrants from Europe; it developed into the most important industrial site of the country.

Haifa is characterized by mountains and the sea because the port lies on a wide bay on the slopes of ► Mount Carmel. The urban area is divided into three zones that lie one above the other and are connected to each other via **countless flights of steps**. The harbour and the Arab quarters (Wadi Nisnas and Wadi Salib) form the lower town, while the Hadar HaCarmel quarter is the central zone or the main commercial centre of the city, and the upper town, Central Carmel, at an altitude of 250–300m/800–1000ft, consists of generously proportioned houses surrounded by gardens, some hotels, souvenir shops and restaurants.

Mountains and the sea

What to See in Haifa

The 68m/223ft Dagon Silo, an enormous angular box, towers above the surrounding buildings. It is the most remarkable structure in the harbour area and can hold **100,000 tons of grain**. The oldest exhibits in the interesting Grain Museum on the ground floor are millstones and other equipment from Jericho from the 8th millennium BC (only guided tours: Sun–Fri 10.30am, tel. 04 866 42 21).

Dagon Grain Silo and Museum

⊕

Opposite the Dagon Grain Silo is the start of Ben Gurion Avenue, in whose continuation the Bahai Gardens climb steeply up the slope. The former main street of the German Templer Colony (Hamoshava Hagermanit, founded in 1868) and its homes with their typical red tiled roofs was recently restored. Street cafés and wide walkways under shady trees make Ben Gurion Avenue a lively boulevard and a tourist point of interest. In the Templers' former assembly house the Haifa City Museum puts on changing exhibitions. The Templers'

Templer Colony (German Colony)

cemetery, along with the one in Jerusalem, is the only one of its kind still extant and lies to the northwest of the colony (150 Jaffa St., next to the British military cemetery).

Haifa Museum of Art ⊕

Walk along Hagefen Street, past Chagall Artists' House, to get to the Haifa Museum of Art at 26 Shabtai Levi St. It exhibits art from the 18th century to the present with a focus on Israeli art, Jewish and Islamic sacred art and archaeological exhibits (Mon–Wed 10am–4pm, Fri until 1pm, Sat until 3pm, Thu 4pm–9pm).

Herzl Street, Nordau Street

These two streets, linked by steps, lie in the Hadar HaCarmel neighbourhood and are perfect for **strolling around**. Nordau Street is pedestrianized and has lots of cafés and restaurants. Two parallel streets below Herzl Street, Sirkin Street is right back in the Arab quarter with a colourful food market.

! **Baedeker TIP**

Old Technion

The Old Technion, Haifa's former technical college, is located in Abba Khushi Avenue. It was built between 1914 and 1924 using plans drawn up by Alexander Baerwald, an architect from Berlin. Today the striking building houses the National Museum of Science, Technology and Space, in which visitors can make experiments themselves (Sun, Mon, Wed, Thu 9am–6pm, Tue until 7.30pm, Fri until 3pm and Sat until 5pm).

The view of the city is particularly attractive from **Louis Promenade**, which runs behind the two skyscrapers of the Dan hotels. **Impressive views** can also be had from the panoramic Yefe Nof, which runs down into the city. In the former home and studio of the Jewish painter **Emanuel Katz** a small museum with works by contemporary Israeli painters and sculptors has ⊕ been set up (Yefe Nof St. 89; Sun, Mon, Wed, Thu 10am–4pm, Fri until 1pm, Sat and in the holidays until 2pm, Tue 2pm–6pm).

Gan Ha'em Park

Gan Ha'em, the »garden of the mother«, which has a small zoo and the M. Stekelis Museum of Prehistory (Hatishbi St.) is located in the Central Carmel neighbourhood. The museum also displays archaeological exhibits from Galilee and Carmel as well as dioramas about the native flora and fauna.

Tikotin Museum of Japanese Art ⊕

The Tikotin Museum of Japanese Art is home to a significant collection; at 89 Hanassi Avenue (Mon, Tue, Wed 10am–4pm, Fri and in the holidays until 1pm, Sat until 3pm, Thu 4pm–9pm, closed Sun).

Sculpture garden

Walk along Hanassi Boulevard and back into Yefe Nof Street, which in turn opens onto Hazionut Street further down. One place to take a small break on the way down is the pretty garden with sculptures by the artist **Ursula Malbin**.

The Bahai shrine thrones high above the city. →

✱
Baha'i Shrine, Persian Gardens
Shrine daily 9am–noon
The gardens can only be viewed after booking in advance
Tel. 04 831 3131 ▶

Also on Hazionut Street is the entrance to the Persian Gardens, a magical park with some ancient trees. Steps between green lawns and artistically arranged flower beds (only the gardens in the immediate vicinity of the shrine can be visited without advance booking). The focal point of the complex is the Baha'i Shrine, which as been a UNESCO World Heritage Site since 2008. It can only be entered in discreet clothing.

This is the **Tomb of the Bab**, the prophet of the Baha'i religion. He was shot in Tabriz in 1850; followers secretly brought his mortal remains from Persia to Palestine and built a burial site in Haifa in 1909. The monumental domed structure was completed in 1953. Four years later the neighbouring neo-Classical archive building of the Baha'i religious community was built.

? DID YOU KNOW …?

■ The Carmelite Order, founded by the French hermit Bartoldus of Calabria, was born on Mount Carmel in Haifa in 1155.

Outside the Centre

✱
Beaches

Even though it seems unlikely, given that Haifa is a port and an industrial city, it does possess excellent beaches. The most beautiful ones, to the south of the city, are called Zamir, Dado and South Dado Beach (can be seen from Route 2; freely accessible). These long, clean sandy beaches are perfectly equipped with shady seats, showers and toilets, phone booths, restaurants and kiosks, as well as lifeguards of course.

Carmelite Monastery

The Carmelite Monastery lies on Cape Carmel on Haifa's western city beach, immediately next to the Stella Maris lighthouse. To get to it from the city centre, head down Allenby and Stella Maris Street or down Hanassi Boulevard and Tchernikovsky Street. The monastery is dedicated to the **prophet Elijah** and his disciple **Elisha**. Pictures in the dome of the abbey depict their lives. The abbey also contains a statue of Mary made of cedar wood with a porcelain head (1820): the Madonna of Mount Carmel. Steps lead into a grotto with the home and tomb of Elijah.

! Baedeker TIP

Beautiful sounds

The Haifa Symphonic Orchestra puts on a concert in the abbey of the Carmelite Monastery on the last Thursday of every month; those who wish can also participate in a dinner afterwards (information and booking via the tourist information).

The room next to the monastery entrance houses a small museum. In front of the monastery are the tombs of the French invalids from Napoleon's army killed by Ahmed al-Jazzar in 1799.

Elijah's Cave

The path down to Elijah's Cave, where the prophet is believed to have taught, starts opposite the monastery. According to legend, Elijah hid from the kings of Israel in this cave at the foot of the cape. It is the most sacred Jewish site in Haifa. The synagogue there is a destination for pilgrims. The faithful pray behind the red curtain which screens off the cave on the long wall of the synagogue. Elijah is also venerated by Muslims, to whom he is known as el-Khidr.

The upper station of the cable car is sited opposite the Carmelite monastery. It goes down to the sea (daily 10am – 7.45pm).

Cable car

Just 200m/200yd to the south of the lower cable car station is the Clandestine Immigration & Naval Museum. The ship *Af Al Pi Chen* on the roof of the museum building broke through the British blockade during the British Mandate and secretly brought immigrants to Palestine.
The museum belongs to the army; there is an identity check at the entrance (Allenby St. 204; Sun–Thu 8.30am–4pm).

Clandestine Immigration & Naval Museum

🕐

The National Maritime Museum is right next door. **5000 years of maritime history** are presented using ship models, maps, prints and other exhibits (Allenby St. 198; Sun–Wed 10am–4pm, Fri until 1pm, Sat until 3pm, Thu 4pm–9pm).

National Maritime Museum

🕐

The University of Haifa, founded in 1972, is in the south of Haifa, on the road that runs along the ridge of the Carmel mountains. The 30-storey Eshkol Tower, designed by the Brazilian architect Oscar Niemeyer, is quite the eye-catcher. The views from the top floor are fantastic.
The university complex is also home to the **Reuben and Edith Hecht Museum** with archaeological discoveries on the subject of »the people of Israel and its country« as well as a collection of Impressionist and Jewish painting.

University

Around Haifa

It is possible to see the ruins of Atlit Crusader Castle on a peninsula 16km/10mi to the south of Haifa from the coast road. Unfortunately it can only be admired from afar, because it sits in a military training zone.
The castle of the Knights Templar, built in 1218 was abandoned in 1291 after the fall of Akko and the end of the crusader kingdom, whereupon it fell into ruin. When the German emperor Wilhelm II stopped at the ruins of Atlit during his journey through the Holy Land in 1898, the fortress was inhabited by two Arab families. The land around Atlit was already owned by Baron Edmond de Rothschild at the time. In 1903 he founded the Jewish village of Atlit just half a mile to the south of the castle. An agricultural test station was set up in the marshy terrain, in which salt was obtained by evaporating sea water.

Atlit Crusader Castle

Hamat Gader · Hammat Gadér

G 2

District: Northern

The Romans built stately baths on the warm, sulphurous springs of Hamat Gader, 6km/3.5mi from the southeastern shores of the ▶Sea of Galilee. Today the ruins of the old baths have been merged with modern facilities.

Baths and Roman ruins ⏲

The ruins have been integrated into a bathing and leisure park with a spa, restaurants, a small zoo and an alligator farm (daily from 7am; www.hamat-gader.com). The park grounds, which have an oasis-like feel, are surrounded by bare mountains in the valley of the Yarmouk River, a tributary of the Jordan, right on the Israeli-Jordanian border. The water in the large pool from a slightly radioactive mineral spring is particularly appreciated. At 42ºC/108ºF it is good for rheumatism.

What to See in Hamat Gader

Synagogue

The remains of a 5th-century synagogue were uncovered near the pools, at the highest point of the complex. Parts of a mosaic depict simple geometric patterns as well as plant and animal motifs.

✳ Roman baths

The Roman baths are unusually well preserved. An entrance hall leads through a reconstructed columned portal from the 4th century to the various pools. The first pool, in what is the most splendid room in the entire complex, was filled with warm water (tepidarium). There is a small pool to the south of it, which could have been a facility for lepers. The hot-water pool (caldarium) has an oval shape. It got its water from the neighbouring spring, which bubbles up from the ground at 52ºC/126ºF. Also part of the Roman baths is a further small hot pool, as well as a large, partially uncovered cold pool (frigidarium), which was in a hall open to the sky. Little is left of the Roman theatre near the park entrance, which could accommodate 2000 spectators. Today it is used as an outdoor enclosure for

Hamat Gader Plan

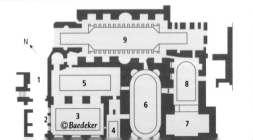

1 Entrance hall
2 Portico
3 Tepidarium
4 Bath for lepers
5 Small tepidarium
6 Caldarium
7 Spring pool
8 Small caldarium
9 Frigidarium

©Baedeker

50 ft

gazelles, sheep and goats. There are plans to open an archaeological museum in the former mosque.

The main attraction for the younger generation is undoubtedly the alligator farm, where Nile crocodiles from Africa, along with alligators and caimans from North and South America, can be seen close up. The extensive enclosure is home to around 2000 of these reptiles. The alligator farm also has a zoo with tropical birds and desert animals as well as a theatre for animal shows.

Alligator farm and zoo

Hazor · Tel Hazor

G 1

District: Northern   **Altitude:** 330m/1080ft

In biblical times Hazor was a lively place. During excavations on the settlement hill Tel Hazor, 21 settlement layers from around 2600 BC to the 2nd century BC were found.

Tel Hazor rises above the road from ► Tiberias to Metulla further north, where it leaves the mountains and reaches the Hule Plain, an ideal location for the early settlers. The Canaanite town flourished for the first time in the 18th and 17th centuries BC. The inhabitants of Hazor maintained trading relations with Mari (modern-day Syria), in whose archives it is listed together with Qatna, Babylon and other significant cities of that period. When the Israelites under Joshua took possession of the land in the 13th century, conquering the Canaanite cities, Hazor burned down (Joshua 11:13). Around 100 years later the first Israelites settled in the depopulated city. Under King Solomon, but especially under **King Ahab** (9th century BC), who resided in Samaria, Hazor once again became a magnificent city. However, in 732 BC the Assyrian king Tiglath-Pileser III destroyed the city again. It continued to exist until the 2nd century, but no longer had any political significance.

Royal city

✳ Excavation Site

Hazor consisted of the upper town (acropolis), which was 600m/650yd long and up to 200m/200yd wide, as well as of the lower town to the north and east, which was around 700m/750yd by 1000m/1100yd in size, but not much of it is left. The upper town on the tell, on the other hand, has been excavated. There are large informative panels at the individual excavation sections.

🕐 Opening hours:
Daily 8am–4pm, in summer until 5pm

Visitors are guided to a viewing platform for an overview of section A, where the Canaanite **royal palace** stood with its wide ceremonial stairs. After its destruction by Joshua in the 13th century BC, Solo-

Upper town

mon created a gateway that was typical of that period, with three chambers on each side of the passageway as well as casemate walls (to the left of the steps) and barracks. In the following century King Ahab built a portion of his large **warehouse** with imposing rows of columns above the barracks. At the western end of the upper town are the remains of the **citadel** (section B), which was extended to monumental proportions under King Ahab.

Water-supply system

The water-supply system was uncovered in section L. As an engineering feat from the time of Ahab (9th century BC), it is no less amazing than the water tunnel of ►Migiddo. The complex consists of a shaft, which was dug through older settlement layers and then also through rock, and has a depth of 30m/100ft. Stairs 3m/10ft wide lead down into it; the fifth, lowest flight of steps takes up the entire shaft and opens out into a 25m/27yd-long tunnel, which ends in a reservoir at groundwater level. This secured the water supply for Hazor even when the spring outside the town was not accessible in the event of a siege.

Lower town

A three-part temple was uncovered in section H, above the remains of three older temples. It dates back to the time of the Canaanite king Jabin. It consisted of an anteroom, a hall and the sanctum in an axial alignment. Discovery of an incense altar, libation tables, a bronze bull and discs with rays led to the belief that the temple was dedicated to the weather god Hadad. The Israeli archaeologist Yadin believed that this temple was the **prototype for Solomon's Temple** in Jerusalem, whose appearance is only known through descriptions. A temple was also discovered in section F, as well as an altar stone weighing 5 tons (15th century BC). Section C contains a temple for the lunar god from the 14th century BC, with several steles.

Ayelet HaShahar, Hazor Museum

Some of the discoveries from Hazor, such as clay objects, weapons and ivory jewellery, can be admired in Hazor Museum in the kibbutz of Ayelet HaShahar 1km/0.5mi away. The small but interesting exhibition is supplemented by copies of finds that are kept in the Israel Museum in ►Jerusalem and a model of ancient Hazor.

Hebron · Hevron · Al-Halīl

F 4

Area: West Bank (Palestinian territory)	**Altitude:** 926m/3038ft
	Population: 160,000

Hebron is the largest Palestinian city in the southern part of the West Bank as well as the centre of industry and commerce for more than a hundred villages and communities in the surrounding area. It is also the location of Abraham's Tomb.

Hebron Map

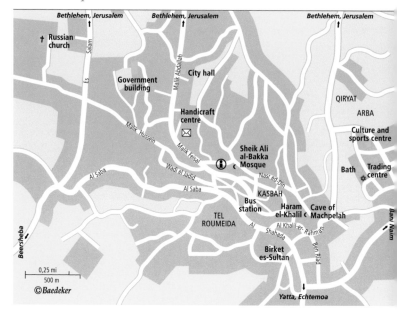

Both the Hebrew name for Hebron, Hevron, and the Arabic name, El Khalil , come from the word for friend, a reference to Abraham (Arabic: Ibrahim), whose tomb is visited by Muslims as well as Jews and Christians.

Abraham's Tomb

Hebron is a **very ancient city**, which has been continuously inhabited ever since it was founded by the Canaanites. The religious significance of the place goes back to Abraham, the progenitor of the Jews and the Arabs. When his wife Sarah died, he acquired the field of Machpelah together with a cave, in which he and his family were buried (Genesis. 23:17–20). After the death of King Saul, 30-year-old David was anointed king of Judah. He resided here for seven and a half years until the conquest of Jerusalem. Herod the Great developed the city further and Emperor Justinian built a church by the cave in the 6th century, which is now the Ibrahim Mosque. After the Mamluk sultan Baibars seized the city in 1267, Jews and Christians were prohibited from entering the sacred precinct. The prohibition remained in place until 1960. After the Six-Day War, Jews were given access to the Cave of Machpelah for the first time in 1967.

Hebron is still divided: »H 1« is home to some 120,000 Palestinians under Palestinian administration, »H 2« is home to approximately 30,000 Palestinians and around 500 fanatical Jewish settlers, protected by an equal number of Israeli soldiers, a constant source of unrest.

The Old City

In the orient   Hebron's Old City still has very much of an oriental feel: the muezzin does not call Muslims to prayer through loudspeakers, the delicious tea in the tea houses costs only a third as much as in Jerusalem and, although some of the restaurants don't look reassuring, the food is always splendid. In addition to food, it is also possible to purchase pots and glassware in the small market streets around the Haram el-Khalil.

Al-Haram al-Ibrahimi ✷   Hebron's cityscape is dominated by the magnificent **tomb above the Cave of Machpelah**, al-Haram al-Ibrahimi (Sanctuary of Abraham). For Muslims Abraham is known as »al-Khalil el-Rahman«, the **Friend of the Lord**. A high wall, built by King Herod, surrounds the sanctuary, which covers an area of around 65 x 35m/70 x 40yd. The top of the wall with the battlements dates back to the Islamic period, as do the two minarets.

Strict security checks! ▶   Since a Jewish doctor perpetrated a devastating massacre in the mosque in 1994, in which 29 people were killed and more than 100 were wounded, access to the sanctuary has been strictly regulated. Jews and Muslims enter via separate entrances into their apportioned area, while Christians are allowed to enter both sections. Despite the rigorous security controls, it is still worth looking around the inside. The Muslim section, i.e. the former crusader church and Ibrahim Mosque, is more impressive from an architectural perspective, whereas the other section is interesting because visitors can see orthodox Jews practising their faith.

Mausoleums ▶   The four mausoleums with cenotaphs for Abraham, Sarah, Jacob and Leah are in the sanctuary courtyard, while the actual tombs are in the cave below.

 VISITING HEBRON

GETTING THERE · SECURITY

No direct bus connection from and to Jerusalem, just a sherut via Bethlehem or Ramallah from Jerusalem's Damascus Gate or organized through a tour operator in Jerusalem. Since there are frequent conflicts in Hebron between Palestinians and Jewish settlers, it is best to ask about the current security situation before visiting.

SHOPPING

The city's souk has a charming Arab atmosphere in quiet times. Smiths, potters etc. produce hand-made goods. However, the mood can change very rapidly when a group of orthodox Jews is escorted around town with heavy military protection.

WHERE TO STAY

Hebron is so close to Bethlehem and Jerusalem that it is currently best to find accommodation in either of those two cities.

Access to the Ibrahimi Mosque is via the courtyard. It was built as a church by Justinian, then altered by the crusaders and in the 14th century turned into a mosque by the Mamluks. The two cenotaphs in this room are dedicated to Isaac and Rebecca. The elaborately carved minbar at the southeastern wall was commissioned by Saladin in 1191. In the right-hand part of the room, the Jewish prayer room since 1967, there is an opening in the floor, through which devout Jews drop notes of supplication. Leave the mosque through the western entrance to get to a long corridor which serves as the women's mosque. On the left-hand side of this corridor there is a hole through Herod's exterior wall so that a square room could be added. Muslims venerate the sarcophagus inside it as the tomb of Joseph (the son of Jacob), while according to Jewish opinion Joseph's mortal remains lie in Shechem near ►Nablus (Joshua 24:32).

◄ Ibrahimi Mosque

It has not always been so peaceful in Ibrahim Mosque.

Around Hebron

Mamre:
Abraham's Oak

Before Abraham acquired the Cave of Machpelah, he had settled in the grove of Mamre. »And built there an altar unto the Lord« (Genesis 13:18). It was here that his wife Sarah died and he »... buried [her] in the cave of the field of Machpelah before Mamre« (Genesis 23:19). The biblical Mamre was west of Hebron,. Taking the information stated in the Bible into account, the most likely location is the Russian Orthodox site of Moskabia with the church (1871) at the »Oak of Rest« (Balut el-Sebat), which is often called Abraham's Oak.

Mountains of
Galilee

Bani Na'im ►

The mountains to the south and east of Hebron are rich in archaeological sites, which confirm that even after the destruction of Jerusalem in AD 70 there were many Jews, including wealthy Jews, who lived not just in Galilee as previously believed, but also in Judaea. Some of their settlements were taken over by the Byzantines, and others continue to exist as Arab towns to this day, for example Bani Na'im, 5km/3mi to the east of Hebron at an altitude of 951m/3120ft. According to local tradition, the mosque, built over a Byzantine church, contains the **tomb of Lot**.

✳ Herodium

F 4

Area: West Bank (Palestinian territory)   **Altitude:** 758m/2487ft

At the height of his reign Herod the Great built a number of fortresses and structures. He had a fort built in the desert as a place of refuge not far from ►Bethlehem, where he himself was buried. His tomb was discovered there in May 2007.

Tradition

Excavations have confirmed the description of the Herodium by Flavius Josephus in his account of the Jewish War. Herod had the summit removed. The plateau thus created was then surrounded by a powerful double wall, reinforced by towers. Inside the walls he built »palaces, which were not just glorious to behold from within, but were also lavishly ornamented from the outside on the walls, battlements and roofs«. There were a garden, apartments, baths and a synagogue on the plateau. The king's tomb had presumably already been destroyed during the Jewish War (AD 66–70).

✳ Excavation Site

Herod's Palace
Floor plan p. 84 ►

A mountain visible far and wide towers above the surrounding hills 11km/7mi to the south of the town where Jesus was born. It ob-

Herod the Great had himself buried high above the desert. →

Herod's tomb was discovered on the northern flank of the Herodium below this spot.

tained its characteristic shape from King Herod's building activity. Here he built a fortified palace, which he determined shortly before his death would be his mausoleum.

Ascent

A wide footpath starting at the car park leads up to the castle grounds in a large curve. However, a more interesting way to get to the castle is via the underground corridors that were built over old cisterns more than a hundred years after Herod, during the Bar Kokhba revolt. From the top there is a magnificent view of the Judaean mountains to the north, all the way to the towers on the Mount of Olives near Jerusalem, and east to the Dead Sea, 1150m/ 3770ft below sea level.

Double wall

The double wall that surrounded the castle complex can still clearly be seen. It was reinforced by three semicircular towers and a round tower in the east (exterior diameter 63m/70yd). The spaces between the two walls were used as corridors and store-rooms. The eastern round tower, originally probably 45m/148ft tall, rises in the inner castle area.

Eastern castle area

The area within the walls is divided into two areas of equal size. To the east was a garden surrounded on three sides by Corinthian columns, while pilasters line the exterior wall. To the north and south the garden was bordered by semicircular niches (exedrae).

Western castle area

The western part of the castle complex consisted of apartments that were mostly single-storey but quite high. The 15 x 10m/49 x 33ft triclinium, the dining room, which opened on to the garden via a large door, can still be made out. The columns and benches along the room's three sides were added in AD 70, when the Jews turned the room into a synagogue. There were bedrooms on both sides of the cruciform courtyard to the north. In Byzantine times there was a chapel here, part of a small monastery which had been built on the ruins of the fortress. That in turn was bordered to the north by the baths with a caldarium and a domed tepidarium on a round floor plan.

---

i **Found!**

■ A sensation in May 2007: the archaeologist Ehud Netzer announced that he had discovered the tomb of Herod the Great. He had been searching for it since 1972 and had finally found remains of a huge podium, urns and a magnificent sarcophagus on the slopes of the Herodium hill, which can undoubtedly be taken to be tomb of Herod.

Lower town

At the foot of the mountain the lower town, built by Herod for his court, was uncovered. Like the castle complex it was laid out on a north-south axis and was divided into three areas: a further large palace, of which little few remains today, bordering it to the north had a large, artificial pool and even further north was the district with residential buildings. The 70 x 46m/77 x 50yd pool at its centre can still be seen easily. It probably served as a reservoir and for swimming and boating.

Herzliya · Herzliyya

E 3

District: Tel Aviv
Population: 100,000

Altitude: 10–40m/30–130ft

Since its foundation in 1924, Herzliya has grown from being an agricultural settlement to a sought-after and expensive residential district just outside of the city of Tel Aviv, which is only 15km/9mi away.

As late as 1948 Herzliya, named after the founder of the Zionist movement, Theodor Herzl, had a population of just 500. Today that figure has grown to around 100,000. Herzliya is popular and famous, not just for being a **residential area for the well-heeled**, but also as a seaside resort. The wonderful sandy beaches are popular with Israelis searching for sea and sun, especially on the Sabbath. The large hotels are located on the waterfront promenade.

Popular residential area and seaside resort

What to See in Herzliya

The town is known for its fine beaches, which run on for more than 5km/3mi in the district of Herzliya Pituah. However, unlike the beaches in Tel Aviv and Haifa, these are not free of charge. Of course visitors get all kinds of creature comforts in return, such as showers, changing rooms, toilets, plenty of beach cafés and restaurants. The most beautiful beaches are Zebulon Beach, Sharon Beach at Sharon Hotel and Accadia Beach.

✳ ✳
Beaches

Herzliya has grown to an expensive residential district

▶ VISITING HERZLIYA

GETTING THERE
Bus connection from Tel Aviv / Allenby St.

WHERE TO EAT
The snack bars and restaurants on Kikar De Shalit are good and not too expensive.

► Moderate
Erez
52 Berekit St.
Tel. (09) 955 98 92
www.lehemerez.co.il

Praised in the whole country for serving imaginative, modern cuisine which is still rooted in regional products.

WHERE TO STAY
► Mid-range
Tadmor Hotel
38 Basel St.
Tel. (09) 952 50 00, fax 957 51 24
www.tadmor.co.il
58 rooms. Not right on the beach but with a nice garden and pool. Very popular with Israelis.

Sidna Ali Mosque	North of the town, directly above the beach, is Sidna Ali (Our Lord Ali) Mosque. The Islamic saint to whom the mosque is dedicated fell fighting the crusaders.
Tell Arshaf	The ruins of the ancient port of Rishpon lie immediately to the north of the Sidna Ali Mosque. Tell Arshaf was already mentioned in Assyrian texts; it was dedicated to Resheph, the Canaanite fire and fertility deity. The Greeks who settled here in the late 4th century BC equated Resheph with their sun god Apollo and changed the town's name to Apollonia. In 1191 the King Richard the Lionheart defeated Sultan Saladin here; in 1265 the Mamluks destroyed the town. Since 1950 several buildings of the Roman town, including a theatre, have been uncovered in Tell Arshaf.

Hula Valley

F 1/2

District: Northern

The Hula Valley (Emek HaHula) in northern Israel is one of the largest drainage and farming areas in the country.

Marshes became farm land	It stretches from Dan on the Lebanese border to ► Hazor in the south, while it is bordered in the east by the ►Golan Heights and the Lebanese mountains in the west. From a tourist perspective the valley is of interest where the original marsh landscape has been preserved, particularly in Hula Nature Reserve.

The rivers Hazbani, Dan and Banias come together at the town of Sde Nehemya to form the River Jordan. This area was marshland for centuries and contaminated with malaria. After the Egyptian grand vizier Ibrahim Pasha took Palestine from the Turks between 1830 and 1840, he had some of the volcanic rock to the south of the Benot Ya'aqov bridge blown up, thereby allowing the water from the Jordan to drain better, which meant it flooded less land. However, political developments prevented him from implementing his plan to cultivate the land with the help of relocated Egyptian fellahin. Jewish immigrants founded the village of Yesud MaMa'ala 15km/9mi to the northeast of Rosh Pinna in 1883. **Baron de Rothschild** supported the settlers by planting eucalyptus trees to help with drainage in 1890. The area was cultivated on a larger scale after the Jewish National Fund acquired the land in 1934; in the 1940s planned settlement began. In connection with the construction of the large water pipe to supply the southern parts of the country, the area was increasingly drained in the 1950s until the marshes were dry and had been transformed into fertile land. In addition to agriculture this region now sustains fish farming.

Towns and Sites in the Hula Valley

Kiryat Shemona

The small town of Kiryat Shemona was founded in 1949 as an immigrant camp on the ruins of a destroyed Arab village at the northwestern end of the valley. Today it has a population of more than 20,000, but its proximity to the Israeli-Lebanese border and associated dangers limit its attractiveness. Kiryat Shemona is a good starting point for trips to the national parks and nature reserves to the south.

Horeshat Valley National Park

There is an extensive national park with a camp site and a cool little lake fed by the River Dan around 5km/3mi to the west of Kiryat Shemona, in the Horeshat (or Hurshat) Valley. Some of the huge oak trees in the park are said to be up to 1500 years old. According to legend they were planted by ten of Mohammed's soldiers. They were camping in this area and, for lack of trees, drove posts into the ground in order to tether their horses. Overnight, the posts turned into large oaks.

★
Hula Nature Reserve
⊙

The most significant nature reserve in the Hula Valley and the oldest in the country extends 15km/9mi to the south of Kiryat Shemona to the left of Route 90 towards Rosh Pinna, in a marsh landscape that is characteristic of the entire area (Sat–Thu 8am–4pm, Fri until 3pm).

After passing the picnic sites at the entrance, it is possible to stroll through this unique biotope on a surfaced path, which at times is supported by wooden stilts (suitable for wheelchairs). Lots of **waterfowl** such as grey herons, cormorants and pelicans nest in the reeds.

With a bit of luck visitors will be able to watch wild boar, water buffalo and even beavers. In spring and autumn storks and other migratory birds gather here. From the observation tower at the heart of the area the entire region can be surveyed. Films screened in the visitor centre give a more in-depth understanding by providing information about the park's flora and fauna.

▶ Dubrovin Farm

Dubrovin Farm was founded by the Russian immigrant Christian Dubrovin and his family in 1904. It has belonged to the Jewish Fund since 1986. The small exhibition gives an insight into the settlers' lives, which was full of privations as they performed pioneering work cultivating the Hula Valley.

✳ Tell Dan Nature Reserve

Around 10km/6mi east of Kiryat Shemona is Tell Dan Nature Reserve, where the River Dan has its source. The river begins at the foot of an ancient tell and is **one of the Jordan's three headwater streams**. There are circular walks of different lengths through the reserve. The longest goes through dense vegetation, across wooden bridges and past caves, to the springs of the Dan, which have been left in their natural state, and up to the tell.

▶ Tell Dan

This was originally the location of the Canaanite settlement of Lais (Layish), which was conquered by the Jewish tribe of Dan. The Danites set up an idol and built a temple for it. Here Jeroboam I, from 933 BC the first king of the northern realm of Israel, built a palace and another temple that was not part of the Jahwe cult. Lais was destroyed 200 years later by Tiglath Pilesar III.

✳ Jericho · Arīhā

F 4

Area: West Bank
(Palestinian territory)

Altitude: 260m/853ft below sea level
Population: 25,000

At the sound of its name it seems as if trumpets should start playing: Jericho. It is the lowest-lying city in the world and probably also the oldest continuously inhabited settlement.

Possibly the oldest settlement in the world

The fertile oasis lies 36km/22mi northeast of ▶Jerusalem and 15km/9mi northwest of the Dead Sea. Thanks to plentiful freshwater springs and a mild climate, bananas, dates, oranges and other fruits flourish here; in the springtime Jericho (Yeriho) reveals a magnificent display of flowers. Visitors mainly come here for the excavation sites.

10,000 years of history

The settlement layers on Tell Jericho go back all the way to **around 8000 BC**. In the Middle Stone Age nomads constructed a striking building, probably a temple, measuring 3.50 x 6.50m/11 x 21ft at the northern end of the tell. Between 8000 and 7000 BC the hunters and gatherers stopped being nomadic, built houses out of bricks and worshipped a fertility and death cult by covering the heads of their dead with a layer of stucco and placing them in their homes. Visible proof that this settlement was already an early town is the construction of a defensive wall, which also included a 9m/30ft stone tower. Somewhat later they dug a trench 8m/27ft wide outside the wall and raised the wall to 7.60m/25ft.

After the destruction of this town by war or earthquake, another tribe inhabited the place in the 6th millennium. Its members already knew about pottery, but they had quite basic homes. In the 5th millennium the settlement was moved westwards to the entrance to ► Wadi Qelt, but soon returned to its old site. Archaeologists have found clay vessels in the shape of human faces dating back to around 2000 BC. During the Hyksos period (18th–16th century BC) a new town wall of stamped earth was built. This town was destroyed in around 1400 BC. ◄ Destruction and rebuilding

The Bible describes the conquest and destruction of Jericho through infernal noise under Joshua in the 13th century BC in great detail (Joshua 6:1–21): »... and it came to pass, when the people heard the sound of the trumpet, and the people shouted a great shout, that the wall fell down flat...« The city was rebuilt under King Ahab. ◄ Trumpets of Jericho

The Babylonians took the last king of Judah, Zedekiah, captive near Jericho in 586 BC, blinding him and taking him to exile in Babylon (2 Kings 25:7). Hellenistic Jericho was built after 332 BC somewhat further south, at the entrance of Wadi Qelt. It was taken by the Maccabees in 161 BC. King Herod made the town his winter residence (what is now the Hasmonaean fort) and secured it by the fort of Kyrpos. Hellenistic-Herodian Jericho was destroyed by the Romans in AD 70. In the subsequent period a settlement grew again to the south of the tell. Several Christian churches and a synagogue are known from the Byzantine period. A new period began in 634 with the Arab conquest. The Umayyad caliphs built a fort and a mosque; Caliph Hisham commissioned a magnificent palace in 724, which was, however, destroyed just a few years later in an earthquake. ◄ From the Babylonians to the Umayyad dynasty

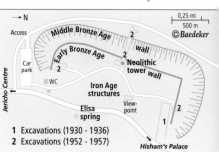

Tell Jericho Map

→ N
Access
Car park
Jericho Centre
WC
Middle Bronze Age
Early Bronze Age
Wall
Neolithic tower Wall
Iron Age structures
Elisa spring
Viewpoint
0,25 mi
500 m
©Baedeker
1 Excavations (1930 - 1936)
2 Excavations (1952 - 1957)
Hisham's Palace

After that Jericho lost significance and was merely a modest village. Since 1994 the town has been under Palestinian administration, but is suffering from the ongoing conflict with Israel. ◄ Modern era

▶ VISITING JERICHO

INFORMATION

**Sultan Tourist Center &
Télépherique**
Tel. (02) 232 15 90, fax 232 15 98
www.jericho-cablecar.com
Daily 8am – 9pm
Information available from the cable-
way on the Mount of Temptation

GETTING THERE · SECURITY

Taxis and sheruts from the Damascus
Gate in Jerusalem, Bethlehem, Nablus
and Ramallah or with an organized
tour. Since Jericho is in Palestinian
territory, check the current political
climate before entering the city.

WHERE TO EAT

Simple grilled dishes can be bought
everywhere. Popular options include:
Al Issawi / Abu Nabil on the marketplace in the city centre; the safest
choice is to order shawerma along
with Arab starters.
Sultan Restaurant
 Mount of Temptation, top end of the

Télépherique
Tel. (02) 232 15 90, daily 9am – 6pm.
Splendid view from the terrace. The
cuisine ranges from snacks to Asian
specialities.

▶ Inexpensive
Al-Rawda
Tel. (02) 232 25 55
Garden restaurant, right at the edge of
town when approaching from the
south (signposted to the left).

WHERE TO STAY
▶ Mid-range
Jericho Resort Village
P. O. Box 162, Jericho
Tel. (02) 232 12 55, fax (02) 232 21 89
www.jerichoresorts.com
60 rooms. The current trump card in
the hotel industry in Palestine. Fantastic, large complex with a huge pool,
tasteful rooms in the hotel and in the
bungalows around the pool, outstanding food. At the northern end of
town right behind Hisham's Palace.

✳ Old Jericho

Jericho today   There are lots of cafés and tea houses, restaurants, falafel stalls and
other kinds of stalls all along the road radiating out of Jericho's central square. Fruit and vegetables from Jericho are considered to be
particularly tasty.

Tell Jericho   Around 2.5km/1.5mi to the northwest of the central square is the tell
of ancient Jericho. Archaeologists started exploring it as far back as
the 1860s. On this hill (Arabic: Tell es Sultan), which covers an area
of around 4ha/10 acres, there are 23 settlement layers one above the
other. Not too much can be seen, however. The most striking aspect
is a deep trench that the archaeologists have laid through the hill,
from which it is possible to see the Stone Age remains from around
7000 BC. Another feature that can be made out is the 2m/6ft-thick

town wall, besides which stands a 9m/30ft stone tower, **one of the oldest monumental stone structures in the world**, around 4000 years older than the Pyramids of Giza!

The spring Ein as-Sultan emerges on the opposite side of the road. It is the largest spring in the oasis. It is also known as Elisha's Spring because the prophet transformed bad spring water into drinking water (2 Kings 2:19–22). Go north from the spring and turn right after around 1km/0.5mi into an avenue lined by cypresses to get to a house in whose cellar the floor mosaic of a 5th or 6th-century floor mosaic has been preserved. At the centre is a medallion with a menorah, a palm branch, a ram's horn (shofar) and the Hebrew inscription »Shalom al Israel« – peace for Israel.

Ein as-Sultan

The ruins of Hisham's Palace (Arabic: Khirbat al-Mafjar) can be found around 2km/1.25mi to the north of Elisha's Spring on the other side of a dried-up river bed. It was begun in 724 by Hisham, the 10th Umayyad caliph and last significant representative of this dynasty. The ruler's winter residence remained uncompleted and was destroyed in 746 by an earthquake. Sand covered the complex, whereupon it fell into oblivion until English archaeologists rediscovered it in 1937. Numerous discoveries from Hisham's Palace, whose figurative depictions are characteristic of early Islamic art, are now on display in the Rockefeller Museum in Jerusalem.

✶ Hisham's Palace

The palace, which is surrounded by gardens, consisted of a residential wing with four sections that were originally two storeys around a square courtyard, as well as a mosque and a large bath, which adjoined this wing to the north. The spacious forecourt, which was once covered by a dome, was decorated by a square pool; today there is a round, very finely ornamented tracery window in the courtyard. Steps in the west wing lead down to an underground bath. Turn northwards (to the right) and walk past the remains of a mosque to get to the magnificent bath hall, which was once supported by 16 columns. The gem is the small rest room in the northwestern corner. It is equipped with an elevated podium, benches to the sides and an excellently preserved mosaic featuring three gazelles and a lion under an orange tree.

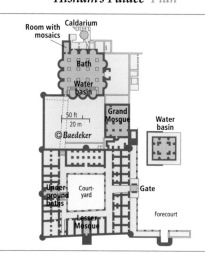

Hisham's Palace Plan

Room with mosaics
Caldarium
Bath
Water basin
50 ft
20 m
©Baedeker
Grand Mosque
Water basin
Under-ground baths
Court-yard
Gate
Forecourt
Lesser Mosque

✶ ◄ Mosaic

This mosaic in the baths is evidence of the magnificence of Hisham's Palace.

Qasr el Yehud Baptism site A 15-minute drive towards the Jordanian border will bring you to the place on the River Jordan near El Maghtas where John the Baptist baptized Jesus. Today it is a restricted military zone. After the Jordanians on their side developed the »Qasr el Jehud« (Arabic: Fortress of the Jews) into a tourist attraction with a church, Israel followed suit on its own side, and here too pilgrims plunge into the sometimes murky waters.

Mount of Temptation A steep mountain to the northwest of ancient Jericho is equated in Christian tradition with the **Mount of Temptation**: after Jesus had been baptized by John the Baptist in the Jordan, he fasted in the desert for 40 days. This caused the devil to hatch a plan. In the third (fruitless) temptation, he led Jesus to a high mountain and showed him all the kingdoms of the world, promising to give them all to Jesus if He would bow down and worship him (Matthew 4:8–11). Saint Chariton built a chapel on the summit in 340. A further one was built by a grotto in which Jesus is said to have stayed. The Greek Orthodox church acquired the land in 1874 and built the Holy Monastery of Sarandarion half way up it in 1895. There is a steep path from the monastery to the summit with the remains of Chariton's chapel and the Hasmonaean fortress of Dok. The summit can be reached in a good 40 minutes on foot (fairly strenuous when it's hot), or in comfort by cable car.

Hasmonaean fortress Around 2.5km/1.5mi to the west of Jericho, ►Wadi Qelt opens out into the Jordan Valley. The expansive palace that was uncovered here was probably commissioned by the Hasmonaean king, Alexander Jannaeus (103–76 BC). It was inhabited by the last Hasmonaeans and subsequently by Herod, who extended it into a magnificent structure and died within its walls. The showy palace, revealing Hellenistic influences, lay in a park with terraces and canals and was constructed symmetrically around a wide courtyard. A large reception hall, rooms decorated with frescoes, and Roman and Jewish ritual baths are among the features discovered. The 32 x 18m/35 x 20yd swimming pool, 4m/13ft deep, is striking, and was also the **scene of a gruesome murder**: it was here that Herod had his 18-year-old brother-in-law Aristobulus, whom he had made a high priest the previous year, drowned (Flavius Josephus I 22:2).

★ Jerusalem · Yerushalayim

F 4

District: Jerusalem
Population: 760,800

Altitude: 606–826m/1988–2710ft

Another name for Jerusalem is »Holy City«, because this was the location of Solomon's Temple, while Christians associate it with the Passion and Resurrection of Christ, and Muslims believe it was where Mohammed's Mi'raj (ascent to heaven) took place. All this is manifested in a wealth of cult sites of the world's three major monotheistic religions, which attract hundreds of thousands of pilgrims every year.

Jerusalem (Arabic: Al-Quds) is the capital of Israel, the country's top tourist destination and a small kaleidoscope of the country, its different inhabitants and its many problems: in the streets of old Jerusalem visitors encounter modern Israel as well as traditional, ultra-orthodox Jews, Greek Orthodox believers as well as Franciscan friars, Arabic market women, Armenian children and of course tourists and pilgrims from all around the world.

Between traditional and modern

Jerusalem lies on several hills on the eastern slopes of the highlands of Judaea, on a limestone plateau above the Kidron Valley in the east and the Hinnom Valley in the south. The heart of the religious city and the main attraction for visitors is the walled Old Town with the Church of the Holy Sepulchre and the very visible Temple Mount. Until East Jerusalem was conquered in 1967, the modern city mainly grew to the west. Since the unification new satellite towns have sprung up on the hills around the old town and the newer West Jerusalem. The most important administrative institutions, ministries and the Knesset, but also parks, museums and the modern shopping quarters, are in the New Town.

Orientation

? DID YOU KNOW …?

■ The Hebrew name Yerushalayim means »place of peace«, the Arabic name al-Quds »the holy one«.

City History

Jerusalem was already inhabited in the **Early Stone Age**. The settlement core developed on the Ophel Mound to the south of the Temple Mount from the 3rd millennium BC onwards. An early Canaanite town grew here, which was called Salem in Abraham's time.

The holy city: view from the Mount of Olives over the Jewish cemetery and beyond, of the Old City and Temple Mount

David conquered the town in around 1000 BC and made it the centre of the Israelite kingdom. His son **Solomon** (around 969–930 BC) built a palace and a temple to the Lord (1 Kings 6–8). After Solomon's death the kingdom split into the northern Kingdom of Israel and the southern Kingdom of Judah, whose capital was Jerusalem. In 628 BC Josiah made **Jerusalem the only legitimate Jewish cult site** (2 Kings 23). In 587 BC the new Babylonian ruler Nebuchadnezzar took the city, destroyed it and took away a large part of the population into the Babylonian captivity. After around 50 years the inhabitants of Jerusalem were allowed to return, building the Second Temple in 520 BC.

Maccabaean revolt

Under Greek rule, from 332 BC onwards, Jerusalem became increasingly Hellenized. From 198 BC the Seleucids began ruling the city. When Antiochus IV Epiphanes defiled the Temple and prohibited the Jewish cult, he triggered the Maccabaean revolt in 167 BC. The Maccabees or Hasmonaeans then ruled the city until the Roman conquest in 63 BC, during which time it grew westwards to Mount Zion.

Roman rule

Herod, who ruled the country from 37 BC, developed the temple site to grand proportions and gave the city palaces, citadels, theatres, a hippodrome, an agora and further buildings, using the Hellenistic-Roman style as a model. When the Jews rebelled against Roman rule,

Titus destroyed Jerusalem in AD 70. The population was either driven out or taken captive. The few who continued living in the city rebelled once more against Rome in AD 135 under Simon Bar Kokhba, but this revolt was also brutally put down and the city was rebuilt by Emperor Hadrian as Aelia Capitolina, which Jews were not allowed to enter.

The Christian era began with **Emperor Constantine**. Both under his government and under that of his successors many churches were built, not least the one above the site where Jesus was buried (Church of the Holy Sepulchre). The rule of the Byzantine emperors ended in 614 with the Persian conquest.

Byzantium and Christianity

Islamic armies conquered Jerusalem in 638, whereupon the Umayyad caliphs had the Dome of the Rock and the al-Aqsa Mosque built here. The crusaders, who were in possession of the city for just under 100 years from 1099, left several churches, palaces and hospices. When the city was taken by Saladin in 1187, Islam became dominant again and Jerusalem remained under the control of the Mamluks and Ottomans, who ruled from the 16th to the 20th century.

Islam

In the 19th century the Christian powers in Europe became more and more influential in Palestine after supporting the Turkish sultan against the Egyptian Ibrahim Pasha. The pope re-established the Latin Patriarchate of Jerusalem, which had been set up in 1099 and abandoned again in 1291. A Protestant German sect known as Templers founded a settlement in 1873, while four years later the American Colony was founded to the north of Damascus Gate. **Jews from all around the world settled in Jerusalem again** after they had been

19th century

prevented from doing so for centuries. In 1855, Sir Moses Montefiore created the first Jewish settlement outside the Old Town. In 1874 the Mea Shearim quarter was built, which is now inhabited by strict orthodox Jews.

20th and 21st centuries On 11 December 1917 the British under General Allenby occupied Jerusalem, making it the seat of the British High Commissioner for the **Mandate of Palestine**. The United Nations resolved in 1947 to internationalize Jerusalem. The Israelis made the western part of the city the capital of their state and conquered East Jerusalem in the Six-Day War of 1967.

New unrest arose when they declared Jerusalem, including the Arab Old Town, the »eternal capital of Israel« in 1980. In 1996 Jerusalem held countless events in honour of its **3000th anniversary**. The city remains a site of frequent bloody confrontations: in October 1990 21 people died in a massacre on Temple Mount and ten years later almost to the day the Likud politician and future prime minister Ariel Sharon triggered the most severe unrest in years, the Second Intifada, as a result of his provocative visit to the same site in the company of journalists and military personnel.

3rd millennium BC	First settlement to the south of Temple Mount
approx. 1000 BC	King David conquers Jerusalem. His successor Solomon builds the First Temple.
587 BC	Nebuchadnezzar conquers the city and destroys the Temple.
around 520 BC	The Second Temple is built.
167 BC.	Maccabaean revolt against Greek rule begins in 332 BC.
AD 70	Emperor Titus destroys the Second Temple and drives out the Jews.
from AD 313	Many Christian churches are built under Emperor Constantine and his successors.
AD 638	Muslims conquer Jerusalem. The Dome of the Rock and al-Aqsa Mosque are built.
19th century	After almost 1900 years Jews are allowed to settle in Jerusalem again.
1950	Israel declares (West) Jerusalem its capital.
1967	Israel conquers Arab (East) Jerusalem.
1980	Israel declares the whole of Jerusalem, including the Arab eastern part, to be its eternal capital.
2012	Ultra-orthodox Jews seek to enforce their strict everyday rules (e.g. separation of the sexes) through insults and violence.

Highlights Jerusalem

Old Town
3000 years of history are present in the Old Town.
► page 285

Western Wall
What remains of the Second Temple, destroyed in AD 70, is a sacred site for Jews.
► page 289

Dome of the Rock
The third most important site of pilgrimage in Islam after Mecca and Medina.
► page 296

Church of the Holy Sepulchre
Several Christian denominations share this

site of Christ's Resurrection.
► page 305

Mount of Olives
The Garden of Gethsemane plays an important role in Christ's Passion.
► page 312

Israel Museum
Archaeological discoveries, Judaica, modern art and, the highlight, the Dead Sea Scrolls.
► page 326

Yad Vashem
Memorial to the victims of the Holocaust.
► page 330

Ancient Jerusalem Map

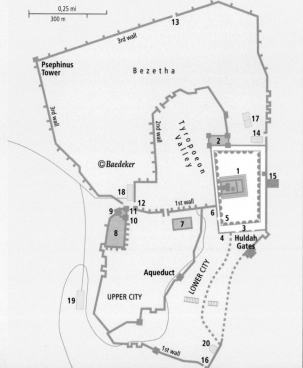

1 Temple
2 Antonia Fortress
3 Stoa Basileios
4 Robinson's Arch
5 Barclay's Gate
6 Wilson's Arch
7 Hasmonaean Palace
8 Herod's Palace
9 Phasael Tower
10 Mariamne Tower
11 Hippicus Tower
12 Garden Gate
13 Women's Gate
14 Birket Israel
15 Gate of Susa
16 Essene Gate
17 Sheep's Pool
18 Hezekiah's Pool
19 Snakes' Pool
20 Pool of Siloam

▶ VISITING JERUSALEM

INFORMATION

Municipal Tourist Information
Jaffa Gate
Tel. (02) 6280 38 202
www.jerusalem.muni.il
Sun–Thu 8am–5pm, Fri 9am–1pm

Christian Information Center
Jaffa Gate, Tel. (02) 627 26 92.
www.cicts.org.
Mon–Fri 8.30am – 5.30pm, Sat
8.30am–12.30pm

TRANSPORT

City buses from 6am–midnight, every
minute during the day. No buses from
one hour before the start of the
Sabbath to the end of the Sabbath.
Coaches, to Ben Gurion Airport etc:
Egged buses, Central Bus Station, 224
Jaffa Road, tel. (03) 694 88 88,
www.egged.co.il.
Palestinian buses depart from Dam-
ascus Gate and go to places such as
Bethlehem, Nazareth, Hebron, Na-
blus, Ramallah and Jericho.
Train: train station at David Remez
Square, central reservations tel. (03)
577 40 00, www.israrailorg.il

SHOPPING

The most lively place to shop is the
bazaar at Damascus Gate, a picture-
perfect Arab souk. Jerusalem's Old
Town is the largest bazaar for devotional objects in the world. The
Kenion Yerushalayim, a shopping
mall measuring 12 ha/30 acres with
200 shops, eight cinemas and more
than 20 restaurants (Sun–Thu
9am–9pm, Fri until one hour before
the start of the Sabbath) is a good,
modern shopping facility outside
town (clothes by Israeli designers,
cosmetics, CDs, books etc).

ENTERTAINMENT

Between Ben Yehuda and Yo'el Salo-
mon Street there is not only a lively
restaurant scene, but also many bars
and pubs. In spite of the orthodox,
supply here is regulated by demand,
so bars still tend to ignore the
Sabbath, but the number doing so is
decreasing. One attractive street with
cafés, restaurants and bars is Emeq
Refa'im St in the German Colony. In
the Industrial Zone of Talpiot in the
south there are numerous in discos
with ever-changing names, where life
really only starts at 11pm.

Haoman 17
17 Haoman St.
Hip-hop, acid jazz, techno – the city's
top club often features international
guest DJs and there are also fashion
shows from time to time
(10pm–6am).

Mike's Place
37 Jaffo, near Zion Square
Tel. (052) 267 07 53
Often live music and the parties
always go on until long after
midnight.

Mirror Bar
11 Shlomo Hamelech St., Mamilla
Hotel
Tel. (02) 548 22 30
www.mamillahotel.com
The Mirror Bar is the rendezvous of
Jerusalem's in-crowd. On Mondays
there's jazz and wine, Tuesdays 1980s
Night Fever, on other days a mix of
music chosen by the DJ (Sun–Tue
from 8pm, Sat from 9.30pm).

The Gossip
12 Shimon Hatsadiq St
Tel. (02) 581 19 22, (052) 5069723

The hotspot of Jerusalem's night life: Ben Yehuda Street

On the wall of fame portraits include Arafat, Einstein, Sadat and Michael Jackson. Many students of the Hebrew University have made this their regular haunt. Numerous Palestinians and expats from the UN and other bodies turn up here, mostly after 10pm. On Thursdays live music, jazz, blues, rock (daily from 6pm to very late).

Hakatzeh

4 Shushan St, Mamilla
www.hakatze.com
This popular, somewhat hard-to-find bar, also known as »The Edge« is the rendezvous for the gay community. On Saturdays and Sundays there's live music, on Mondays drag comedy shows, on other days DJ music (daily 8pm till late).

New Izen

30 Hebron Road
Tel. 02 673 32 16
Crowded, noisy, the drinks ok – the Izen, between Baka and the German Colony is also a restaurant with a classically cool menu (fruits de mer, salads). Music from live bands and DJs (Mon–Thu, Sat from 9pm).

Hataklit

7 Heleni HaMalka St
Tel. (02) 624 40 73
www.myspace.com/hataklit
The name means gramophone record, in other words the good old vinyl disc. The place was founded by three vinyl fans, who found a large clientele with a weakness for scratchy music where the pick-up sometimes jumps (daily from 8pm).

Yellow Submarine

13 Harechavim St, Talpiot
Tel. (02) 679 40 40
www.yellowsubmarine.org.il
This dance club organizes live music evenings (jazz too) which provide a stage for promising artists, and has its own sound studio – a concept that goes down well with the public (daily from 10pm).

Jerusalem Map

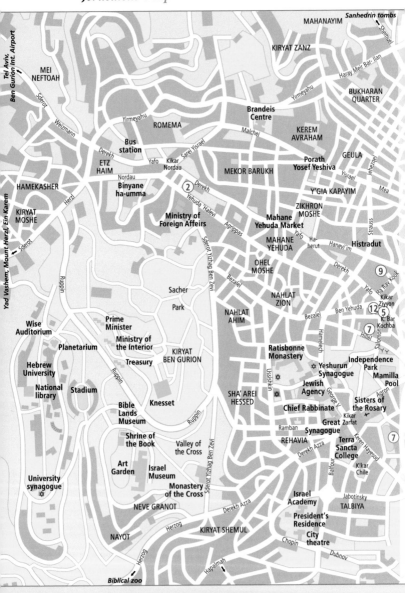

Where to eat
①	La Regence	④	Askadinya	⑦	Spaghettim	⑩	Abu Shukri
②	Arcadia	⑤	Barood Bar Restaurant	⑧	Village Green	⑪	Panoramic Golden City
③	Armenian Tavern	⑥	Pasha's	⑨	Little Jerusalem/ Ticho House	⑫	Tmol Shilshom

Atarot Airport, Ramallah, Nablus

British military cemetery

Hadassah Medical Center

SHEIK JARRAH

NAHLAT SHIMON

Olbergstrasse

Simon's tomb

National Library (Hebrew University)

BEIT ISRAEL

Tombs of the Kings

MEA SHEARIM

Mount Scopus

WADI EL-JOZ

AMERICAN COLONY

Mandelbaum Gate

Ethiopian Church

St Stephen's Church

Rockefeller Museum

RUSSIAN QUARTER

Garden Tomb

Russian Cathedral

Jeremiah's Grotto

Damascus Gate

Herod's Gate

Court-house

Notre-Dame de France

St Anne's

MUSLIM

St Stephen's Gate (Lions' Gate)

City hall

New Gate

CHRISTIAN QUARTER

Tariq al-Mujahedeen

St Stephen's Church

Mary's Tomb

Church of All Nations

Church of the Holy Sepulchre

Temple

Golden Gate

Chapel of the Ascension

EL-TUR

Lutheran Church of the Redeemer

Dome of the Rock

Church of St Mary Magdalene

Dominus Flevit

Jaffa Gate

Western Wall

Mount

Tomb of Absalom

Tombs of the Prophets

Church of the Pater Noster

MERKAZ MIS'HARI

Citadel

ARME-NIAN

Christ Church

JEWISH

al-Aqsa Mosque

Grotto of St James

Tomb of Zechariah

Herodian tomb

Cathedral of St James

QUARTER

Dung Gate

OPHEL

Jewish cemetery

Mount of Olives

YEMIN MOSHE

Zions Gate

Gihon Spring

Montefiore-Windmill

Hagiah Maria Sion Abbey

St Peter in Gallicantu

Cinematheque

David's Tomb

Mount Zion

Pool of Siloam

SILWAN

St Andrew's Station

Hinnom Valley

Bethlehem, Hebron

Khan

0,25 mi

500 m

©Baedeker

Sira
4 Ben Sira St.
Tel. (02) 623 43 66
You can rely on cramped conditions on the dance-floor, and plenty of opportunities to hear live music, sometimes from newcomers, sometimes from well-known Israeli bands (daily from 8pm).

Focaccia Bar
4 Rabbi Akiva St.
Tel. (02) 625 64 28
www.fucaccia-bar.rest-e.co.il. The bar has a restaurant, which attempts to serve Mediterranean-Italian cuisine, not always successfully. The drinks are fine (daily 9am–2am).

Underground
2, Yoel Salomo St.
The city's oldest night club, good rock music, young partygoers. The owner does not mind if everyone dances on the tables and the bar until the morning (daily 9am–morning).

WHERE TO EAT

The selection is not comparable to Tel Aviv, but the quality is. Many restaurants are closed on the Sabbath. Those who would just like a snack on the go will find plenty of falafel and shawerma stalls. Recommended and also praised by the locals: the *falafel stalls*at the corner Hanevi'im St. and Havatzelet St. and 70 Jaffa St.; bagels and bagel sandwiches in many variations are sold by Bagel's Corner, 41 Jaffa Road.

► Expensive
② Arcadia
10 Agrippas St.
Tel. (02) 624 91 38
Good French-Mediterranean cuisine, one of the city's top restaurants. Those who wish to try something more unusual should go for the goose liver with vanilla. Outstanding wine list.

① La Regence
King David Hotel
23 King David St.
Tel. (02) 620 88 88
High-class ambience, modern Israeli cuisine with a Mediterranean touch – a spot for special occasions.

► Moderate
④ Askadinya
11 Shimon Hazadik St.
Tel. (02) 532 45 90
International cuisine not far from the American Colony Hotel. Sit out in the courtyard during the summer and in the cosy guestroom in the winter. On Thursdays a live quartet plays everything from the Bolero to Take Five.

③ Barood Bar Restaurant
Jerusalem Courtyard
31 Jaffa Road, Feingold Court.
Tel. (02) 625 90 81
This place serves delicious oriental dishes from falafel and labneh to »sutlach« (rice pudding). Beware! Smoking is permitted everywhere, so non-smokers should eat outside.

⑥ Pasha's
12 Shimon Hatsadik St, Sheikh Jarrah
Tel. (02) 582 51 62, www.shahwan.org
Pasha's, which specializes in fine Arabian cuisine, opened near the American Colony Hotel in an old Arab mansion with a wonderful garden. Guests have a go smoking the hookah after their meal.

⑦ Spaghettim
Beit Agron, 35 Hillel St.
Tel. (02) 623 55 47
Spaghetti sauce heaven: more than 50 different kinds to choose from – everyone can find their favourite here.

It is even possible to get sweet spaghetti for dessert.

⑨ *Little Jerusalem / Ticho House*
Anna Ticho House
9 Harav Kook St.
Tel. (02) 624 41 86
A green oasis in the city. The gem in this café-restaurant in the former home of Anna Ticho (now a museum) is the terrace with seating under trees and views of the garden. The food is kosher. The sandwiches and Anna's strudel are particularly tasty.

⑧ *Village Green*
33 Jaffa Road
Tel. (02) 625 30 65
The whole range of vegan and vegetarian culinary delights, from lentil soup to organic rye, served in a central location. The clientele is mainly drawn from tourists and resident foreigners (Sun–Thu 9am–10pm, Fri 9am–3pm); there's another branch in the German Colony, 5 Rachel Imenu St, tel. (02) 650 01 06)

► **Inexpensive**
⑩ *Abu Shukri*
79 Al Wad St.
Tel. (02) 627 15 38
Very good Arab restaurant in the old town, right on the Via Dolorosa. The best place in Jerusalem to try hummus, which is why it is always packed. But meat dishes are also served here.

⑪ *Panoramic Golden City Restaurant*
64 Aftimos St, Old Town, Muristan
Tel. (02) 555 78 89
Walk from Jaffa Gate down Souk Street and take the first on the left into Aftimos Market: the Arab restaurant has a fantastic panoramic view of the old town and its back yards from an atmospheric roof terrace. It can get quite chilly at night. Mon–Sat 12 noon–10pm, Sun 12 noon–5pm

⑫ *Tmol Shilshom*
5 Solomon St, tel. (02) 623 27 58
Bookshop, simple restaurant, café, a »home from home«. Fine vegetarian cuisine, meeting place for students and the in-crowd. There are often readings in Hebrew and English in the evenings. Daily 9am –1am, closed on the Sabbath.

WHERE TO STAY

Jerusalem is largely booked out during the important Jewish and Christian holidays, so it is a good idea to reserve well in advance. The Christian hospices are generally a less expensive alternative to the hotels. They have basic rooms and are usually centrally located, which is why they too need to be booked well in advance.

► **Luxury**
① *American Colony Hotel*
Nablus Road (East Jerusalem)
Tel. (02) 627 97 77
Fax 627 977 79
www.americancolony.com
84 rooms. The hotel, built in 1840 for a pasha, is a small gem. The generously sized rooms and all reception rooms are decorated in the oriental style with a lot of taste and attention to detail. The restaurant in the magical courtyard is a popular meeting place for journalists.

② *David Citadel Hotel*
7 King David St.
Tel. (02) 621 11 11, fax 621 00 00
www.tdchotel.com
384 rooms. One of the best hotels in town in a central location with wonderful views of the Old Town and the town walls.

③ *King David Hotel*
23 King David St.
Tel. (02) 620 88 88, fax 620 88 82
www.danhotels.co.il
237 rooms. One of Israel's two
Leading Hotels of the World, the
choice of Israeli state visitors. Very
upmarket clientele.

▶ **Mid-range/Luxury**
④ *Dan Boutique Hotel*
31 Hebron Road
Tel. (02) 568 99 99, fax 673 40 66
www.danboutiquejerusalem.com
128 rooms. Mid-range hotel with a
bar and restaurant at a convenient
distance from the Old Town and the
station. Make sure you do not get a
room facing the busy and noisy
Hebron Road

⑤ *Jerusalem Hotel*
Nablus Road (East Jerusalem; entrance on Antara Ben-Shadad St.)
Tel./fax (02) 628 32 82
www.jrshotel.com
14 rooms. Pleasant mid-range hotel
just a few metres from Damascus
Gate. Cosy atmosphere. Ask for a
room out to the back for a quieter
option. Atmospheric restaurant in the
Arab style in the vaulted cellar; the
Lebanese starter plate is highly recommended.

▶ **Mid-range/Budget**
⑥ *St. Andrew's Scottish Guest House*
1 David Remez St.
Tel. (02) 673 24 01, fax 673 17 11
21 rooms. This Scottish institution,
situated between the Old Town and
the station, feels a little bit like a castle
– at least there is a flag hoisted over
the tower. Basic, but cosy rooms,
small restaurant.

⑦ *YMCA Three Arches Hotel*
26 King David St.

Tel. (02) 569 26 92, fax 623 51 92
www.ycma3arch.co.il
56 rooms. The rooms are not large,
and the breakfast is somewhat meagre, but the building, almost a cathedral, has an enchanting atmosphere.
A central location with views of the
King David Hotel opposite. It is just a
short walk to the Old Town.

▶ **Budget to mid-range**
⑧ *Christ Church Guest House*
Jaffa Gate (at the post office)
Tel. (02) 627 77 27, fax 627 77 30
christch@netvision.net.il
Pleasant rooms and a quiet terrace in
front of the church of the Protestant
hospice, where guests can enjoy tea
and coffee under a pergola.

⑨ *Mount of Olives Hotel*
53 Mount of Olives Road
Tel. (02) 628 48 77, fax 626 44 27
www.mtolives.com
61 rooms. Basic, family-run pilgrimage hotel in a nice setting on the
Mount of Olives. Room 317/318
(panorama room) has the best view of
the Old Town.

Baedeker recommendation

⑩ *Austrian Hospice*
37 Via Dolorosa
Tel. (02) 626 58 00, fax 627 14 72
www.austrianhospice.com
27 rooms and several dorms. A piece of
Vienna in Israel and one of the best
addresses for exploring the Old Town since
it is located right on Via Dolorosa, and yet it
is quiet and inexpensive. It has its own,
secure car park and a small garden. From
the roof terrace of the oldest national house
of pilgrimage, founded in 1857, guests have
a nice view of old Jerusalem. The room
furnishings are spartan, but very clean. The
cafeteria serves Viennese apple strudel!

From Jaffa Gate to Temple Mount

Walking through the Old Town of Jerusalem, with its narrow streets, **★★** many historic sites and different ethnic groups, mixed in with pil- **Old Town** grims and tourists, feels like being in a different age. As a result it was declared a UNESCO World Heritage Site in 1981. The **city within the city** is surrounded by a wall 12m/39ft high, 4km/2.5mi long and guarded by towers, built by Suleiman the Magnificent between 1532 and 1539. Of the six gates that Suleiman built, Jaffa Gate, Zion Gate and Damascus Gate are still extant in their original form. David Street, which runs eastwards from Jaffa Gate, and Suq Khan ez-Zeit, which runs southwards from Damascus Gate, cross in the middle of the Old Town, dividing it into **four quarters**, of which each has its own character: the Christian quarter in the northwest, the Ar-menian quarter in the southwest, the Muslim quarter in the north-east and the Jewish quarter with Temple Mount in the southeast.

> **!** *Baedeker* TIP
>
> ### Above the rooftops
>
> A walk along the city wall of Jerusalem provides interesting insights into the winding streets of the Old Town. As the tour is interrupted at Temple Mount, there is a north tour (starting from the Jaffa Gate) and a south tour (starting from the Citadel). Opening times: Apr–Sept daily 9am–5pm, Oct–Mar 9am–4pm; all year round Fri and holidays 9am–2pm. Duration: Jaffa Gate to Lion Gate: approx. 90 min, Citadel to Dung Gate: approx. 1 hour. The north tour is more interesting if you only want to do one.

Jaffa Gate, named after the trading, pilgrimage and military road that **★** started here and ran to the port of Jaffa, is the interface between the **Jaffa Gate** Old Town and the Jewish new town, and alongside Damascus Gate the most important entrance into the Old Town. It is called Bab el-Khalil (Hebron Gate) by the Arabs and Shaar Yafo by the Jews. The gap to the right next to the narrow gateway was made by the Turks in 1898 in order to give the German imperial couple a suitably majestic entry into the city.

The citadel is located immediately to the south of Jaffa Gate. It is **★** popularly called the Tower of David. It does not, however, go back to **Citadel** King David's time, but to **Herod**, who had a magnificent palace built in 24 BC, which he secured by fortifications. He named the three towers after his brother, his friend and his wife – Phasael, Hippicus and Mariamne. After the city was taken by Titus in AD 70, the Romans moved a garrison into the fort, which later fell into ruin and was then conquered by the crusaders, the Mamluks and the Turks. The Tower of David was built on the foundations of the Tower of Phasael in the 14th century; the Northwestern Tower stands on the site of the Tower of Hippicus.

The citadel is both an interesting excavation site and a museum for **◄ Museum** the history of Jerusalem (Tower of David Museum). Using modern

Jerusalem · Old City *Map*

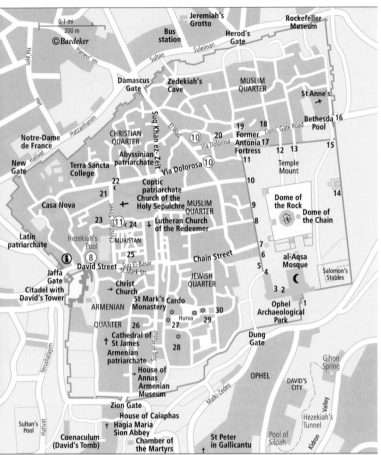

0,1 mi
200 m
©Baedeker

1 Double Gate
2 White Mosque
3 Islamic Museum
4 Maghreb Gate
5 Western Wall (Wailing Wall)
6 Western Wall synagogue
7 Chain Gate
8 Cotton Merchant's Gate
9 Iron Gate
10 Bab al-Nadhir
11 Bab al-Ghawanima
12 Bab al-Atim

13 Bab Hitta
14 Golden Gate
15 Bab al-Asbat
16 Lions' Gate
   (St Stephen's Gate)
17 al-Omariye School
18 Church of the Flagellation
19 Church of the Condemnation
   and Imposition of the Cross
20 Convent of the
   Sisters of Zion
21 Greek Patriarch's Palace

22 al-Khanqah-Mosque
23 Constantine's church
24 Mosque of Omar
25 Church of
   John the Baptist
26 Old Yishuv Court Museum
27 Ramban and
   Hurva Synagogues
28 Sephardi Synagogues
29 Wohl Archaeological
   Museum
30 Burned house

Where to eat

⑩ Abu Shukri

⑪ Panoramic Golden
   City Restauarant

Where to stay

⑧ Christ Church
   Guest House

⑩ Austrian hospice

exhibition technology, interesting models (e.g. the Temple at different times) and dioramas, the history of Jerusalem's Old Town is brought to life. The 4 x 4m/13 x 13ft model of 19th-century Jerusalem in the vaulted underground rooms is particularly interesting. The city's development is presented in an audiovisual show (tel. 02 626 53 33, www.towerofdavid.org.il; Sep–Jun Sun–Wed 10am–4pm, Thu 10am–6pm, Fri only pre-booked groups, Sat and days before holiday 10am–2pm, Jul–Aug Sat–Thu 10am–5pm, Fri 10am–2pm. The Night Spectacular (sound and light show) is worth seeing.

Now turn south to the Armenian Quarter and follow Armenian Patriarchate Road to the monastery of the Armenian Patriarchate. It is the **largest monastery in the city** and the spiritual centre of the Armenians.

Armenian Quarter

The Cathedral of Saint James is a 12th-century building from the crusader era. The attractive portal on the south side of the narthex still dates back to that time. A chapel to the left of the entrance is believed to be the place where **St James the Great** was executed on the orders of Herod Agrippa I in AD 44 (Acts 12:2). According to tradition, his mortal remains were taken to Spain after the Arab conquest, where they have been attracting pilgrims to Santiago de Compostela since the 11th century. Under the cathedral altar is the tomb of James the Just, the first bishop of Jerusalem, brother of the Lord, to whom the Epistle of James in the New Testament is attributed. He was stoned to death in AD 62 (Mon–Fri 6am–7am, 3pm–3.30pm).

◄ Cathedral of Saint James

> ! **Baedeker TIP**
>
> ### Panorama Tour Line 99
>
> Line 99 goes to all of Jerusalem's most important attractions, such as Jaffa Gate, the Knesset and Yad Vashem – either via a single ticket (2-hour city tour) or a day ticket that allows passengers to get on and off at will (tickets available in hotels and on the buses; information tel. 050/842 24 73 and www.citytour.co.il).

Steps near the entrance of the compound lead up to the **Armenia Museum of Art and History**. It presents the history of the Armenian people as well as cult and art objects such as the sceptre of the last Armenian king from the 14th century, liturgical vestments and crowns. In addition this museum houses around 4000 manuscripts from the 10th to the 17th century (currently closed).

Walk back a little along Armenian Patriarchate Road, then turn right into St James Road to get to the Syrian Monastery of St Mark. According to tradition, this richly ornamented 12th-century church stands on the site of the house where, after an angel had freed him from Herod's prison, St Peter revealed himself to the congregation that was praying for him (Acts 12:12–17). Behind the church portal there is an Armenian inscription on the right and in the church there is a font coated in silver. Above it is an icon of Mary, which the

Monastery of St Mark

Remains of the Cardo, one of the main roads in ancient Jerusalem

monks attribute to Luke the Evangelist. In the Eastern church, Luke is believed to have been the **painter of the first and therefore authentic likeness of Mary**. The richly carved patriarch's throne is also worth seeing.

Old Yishuv Court Museum Where St James Road becomes Or Hayim Street there is a small museum on the right-hand side. It provides an insight into the living culture of Ashkenazi and Sephardi families in the second half of the 19th century (Sun–Thu 10am–5pm, Fri 10am–1pm).

Jewish Quarter Walk eastwards to get to the Jewish Quarter. The city's Jewish population already started congregating in this area in the 8th century. There was an influx of Sephardi Jews from Spain in the 15th century and of Ashkenazi Jews from Poland in the 18th century. The quarter was destroyed during the Israeli-Arab fighting in 1948 and rebuilt after the Six-Day War in 1967.

Cardo ▶ Between the Armenian and Jewish quarters is the Cardo, one of the city's main roads during Roman and Byzantine times. The road, uncovered over an area of around 200m/200yd, is now 6m/20ft under the level of the quarter and runs underground in places. The avenue was once lined by covered colonnades and shops, as the replica of a 6th-century floor mosaic on display here shows. This section of the Cardo is once again an up-market shopping street with wine, antique, jewellery and souvenir shops.

Ramban and Hurva Synagogues ▶ Walk up the steps to get to the Jewish Quarter and Ramban Synagogue. It is believed to be the **oldest Jewish place of worship in the**

Old Town, built in 1267 by Rabbi Moshe ben-Nahman Ramban (Nahmanines), who had come to the Holy Land from Spain.

Immediately adjoining Ramban Synagogue is Hurva Synagogue, once Jerusalem's largest synagogue. It goes back to Rabbi Yehuda he-Hasid, who came from Poland with 500 Ashkenazi followers in 1701, whereupon the Jewish community in the city split and the Ashkenazi built their own synagogue. It was not completed by the time of the rabbi's death, however, hence the name Ha-Hurva (ruin). In 1856 it was finally completed, but was destroyed in 1948. Immediately after 1967 several suggestions to rebuild it were made, but never implemented. Only a monumental arch built in 1977 recalled its former grandeur. Reconstruction works finally began in 2006 and it was inaugurated in 2010.

To the south of Ramban Synagogue, there is a street to the left leading to the Sephardic Synagogues. The four houses of worship were rebuilt in 1967 true to the original plans. The Yochanan ben Zakai Synagogue, originally built in around 1610, is particularly impressive. It was named after a rabbi who lived during the Roman period. The neighbouring Eliahu Ha'navi Synagogue (late 16th century) commemorates the stay (Hebrew: Ha'navi) of the prophet Elijah. The Emtsai Synagogue was built in the early 18th century. It is the smallest of the four and originally just the anteroom to other prayer rooms. The interior of the newest synagogue is comparatively plain. This is the Istanbuli Synagogue, built by Turkish Jews in around 1750.

★
◄ Sephardic
Synagogues

The Herodian residential quarter lay to the northeast of this complex. The **Wohl Archaeological Museum** features excavated houses that were built during the reign of Herod (40–4 BC) and destroyed during the Jewish War of AD 70. The size and interiors, especially some well-preserved floor mosaics, and the bath are evidence of the wealth of the inhabitants (Sun–Thu 9am–5pm, Fri and before holidays 9.30am until 1pm).

★
Herodian quarter

The nearby Burnt House was also destroyed by the Romans in AD 70. Although the archaeological discoveries presented here are sparse, there are slide shows several times a day, bringing to life the history of the quarter at the time of Herod and the destruction by the Romans (combined ticket with the Herodian quarter possible, Sun–Thu 9.30am–4.30pm, Fri until 1pm or 12.30pm). Opposite the Burnt House are the ruins of the main Hasidic synagogue, Tiphereth Israel (Israel's Glory).

◄ Burnt House

★ Western Wall

The Western Wall (also Wailing Wall or Kotel) is 48m/52yd long and 18m/59ft high; at the southwestern end of the temple precinct, it is all that remains of the Second Temple and is therefore the most significant sacred site for Jews. The once built-up area has been cleared

The most significant sacred site of the Jews

Baedeker TIP

Respectful

Non-Jewish tourists are allowed to come right up to the Western Wall, but should not talk or have mobile phones switched on out of respect for those praying there. Smoking is as inappropriate as the lighting of candles. Those who wish to can place a prayer note in the Western Wall's crevices. All of these »kvitels« are removed once a month and then buried on the Mount of Olives. A kippa, provided free of charge at the entrance, must be worn. Photo-graphy is banned on the Sabbath.

since 1967 so that there is now sufficient room for tourists, pilgrims and pious Jews, who pray at the Wall or insert **prayer notes** between its large limestone blocks. The eleven regular rows of blocks date back to the time of Herod the Great, while the remains above them – smaller, irregular blocks – mainly date back to the time of Suleiman the Magnificent.

Since it is believed that the Holy of Holies was in the western part of the Temple, it is also believed by Jews that God's presence can still be felt at the Western Wall. Major religious festivals such as Bar Mitzvahs are celebrated at the Western Wall, and this is also the place where recruits of the Israeli army are sworn in. The area immediately in front of the wall is considered a synagogue (so men must cover their heads) which is why it is divided by a fence. The right-hand side is for women, the left-hand side for men.

There are large crowds of believers at the Western Wall on important Jewish holidays.

The walk along the 500m/550yd Western Wall Tunnel (Kotel Tunnel) begins at the square's northern side in front of the Western Wall (by the toilets). It runs below the Western Wall and emerges again at the Via Dolorosa. When the tunnel was uncovered in the mid-1990s, Muslims feared that the Temple Mount would be undermined and become unstable. Works on the tunnel and the discussion about its opening were therefore accompanied by vehement demonstrations. The tunnel is now open to the public as part of a **guided tour** (advance telephone bookings at the tourist information office at Jaffa Gate, ►p. 278). The walk through the tunnel, taking approximately one hour, is impressive. Booking: tel. (02) 627 13 33, www.thekotel. org, Sun–Thu 7am to evening, depending on demand, Fri and before holidays 7am–12 noon, guided tour compulsory. Officially it is recommended to book two months in advance, credit card number needed. Individual tickets are nearly always available at short notice, however.

★ Western Wall Tunnel

An arched passageway in the northeastern corner of the Western Wall leads to Wilson's Arch (named after Sir Charles William Wilson, who uncovered it between 1867 and 1870). It is part of a viaduct that once connected the Temple Mount with the upper city via the Tyropoeon Valley. Under Wilson's Arch, look down into the square shaft. The 14 layers of blocks below the current street level, down to the bedrock, give an impression of the massive nature of this wall. The space is used as a splendid synagogue, which is open to visitors. It is nice just to sit on one of the white plastic chairs and simply watch the goings-on, the ritual preparations and the prayers.

Wilson's Arch

The Archaeological Park lies to the south and southeast of the Western Wall, below the southern wall of the temple district. Not far to the south of the Western Wall is Robinson's Arch, named after its discoverer, the Biblical scholar Edward Robinson. It was a huge overpass that led to the temple square. This was the main entrance to the entire compound. In 1971 a stone, 2m/6.5ft high, from the square's southwestern corner was found. It had collapsed when the Temple was destroyed in AD 70. This cornerstone mentioned by Flavius Josephus had a niche. It is likely that the priest who declared the beginning and the end of the Sabbath stood in it.

Archaeological Park

The Davidson Center houses a **virtual reconstruction of the Temple Mount**, depicting what it probably looked like in the 1st centuries BC and AD until its destruction (Sun–Thu 8am–5pm, Fri until 2pm; www.archpark.org.il).

◄ Davidson Center

★ Temple Mount (Haram ash-Sharif)

Generally speaking Temple Mount is open to non-Muslims daily in summer, except Fridays, 8am–11.30am, and likewise in winter 7.30am–10.30am. Exception: Ramadan. Non-Muslims have to use

Access

Bab el-Magharibeh (Maghreb Gate) to the right of the Western Wall. The access gates on the western side, the Gate of the Chain (Bab es-Silsileh), the Cotton Merchants' Gate (Bab el-Qattanin), the Iron Gate (Bab el-Hadid) and Bab en-Nadhir, are reserved for Muslims. The Israeli authorities are in charge of monitoring visitors to the site, while the administration lies with the Waqf, a kind of Muslim charitable trust. **Visitors should always be aware that access could be restricted or denied entirely for a period of time. For that reason it is advisable to inquire about the current situation at the Temple Mount**. The Dome of the Rock and Al-Aqsa Mosque are currently only open to tourists with written permits issued by the Waqf.

Shrine for three religions
There is no other place on earth where Judaism, Christianity and Islam are so closely connected as here. Israel's old temple square, called Haram al-Sharif, »Noble Sanctuary«, by the Arabs, is the **most significant Islamic site after Mecca and Medina**. According to Islamic belief, the prophet Mohammed ascended to heaven on his mare Al-Burak from the rock on which the Dome of the Rock now stands. The Second Temple, the only legitimate Jewish temple, stood here from the 7th century BC. It was here that Christ was presented to the Lord (Luke 2:22–24) as a baby, debated with teachers (Luke 2:46) as a twelve-year-old, that the Devil had Jesus stand on the highest point (Matthew 4:5), that Jesus drove out the moneychangers (Matthew 21:12) and himself taught in the Temple (Matthew 4:23).

History of the Temple
First Temple ▶
This site's history starts with **Abraham**. He lived with his clan in Beersheba, when God ordered him (Genesis 22) to sacrifice his son Isaac on **Mount Moriah**. This mountain, it is generally assumed, is the site where the Temple was later built. Abraham followed the order, but the human sacrifice was prevented by divine intervention. A ram was sacrificed in Isaac's stead. This event, which probably occurred in the 18th century BC, sanctified the summit between the Kidron Valley and Tyropoeon Valley for all time. In around 1000 BC, David took the city, erected an altar on Mount Moriah and also brought the tabernacle with the Ten Commandments here (2 Samuel 6). His son **Solomon** had the First Temple built on this site (1 Kings 6). It was completed in 950 BC. The preciously adorned house of God was used by the priests appointed by Solomon to pray and

i **Political Problems**

■ In 2004 the wooden pedestrian bridge leading to the Maghreb Gate collapsed as a result of weathering. Non-Muslims then gained access to the Temple Mount via a ramp in the same place. Plans to rebuild the pedestrian bridge led to bitter resistance by Muslims in late 2006 and early 2007: Israeli law requires, for construction on archaeologically significant sites, that precautionary excavations be undertaken in order not to damage any historical remains. The Muslims of Jerusalem protested, fearing for the stability of Al-Aqsa Mosque and the Dome of the Rock. They believed Israel had a political motivation: to emphasize its claim to East Jerusalem. In 2012 the city council once more planned to remove the ramp.

Temple Mount *Plan*

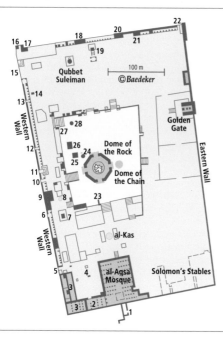

1 Double Gate	17 Madrasah al-Malakiyeh
2 White Mosque	18 Bab al-Atim
3 Islamic Museum	19 Sebil es-Sultan Suleiman
4 Dome of Jussef	20 Bab Hitta
5 Bab al-Magharibeh	21 Madrasah al-Gahdiriyeh
6 Bab al-Silsileh (Chain Gate)	22 Bab al-Asbat
7 Qubbet Musa	23 Pulpit
8 Fountain of Qayt Bay	24 Prophet's prayer niche
9 Madrasah	25 Dome of the Ascension (Qubbet al-Miraj)
10 Bab al-Mastarak	
11 Bab al-Qattanin	26 Hebronite (Qubbet al-Khalili)
12 Bab al-Hadid (Iron Gate)	27 Dome of St George (Qubbet al-Qadr)
13 Bab al-Nadhir	28 Dome of the Spirits (Qubbet al-Aruah)
14 Sebil Ala ed-Din al-Basir	
15 Bab al-Ghawanima	
16 Minaret	

make sacrifices. The main room housed the altar, while the inner sanctum housed the Ark of the Covenant, guarded by two gold cherubim. The walls were panelled with cedar wood and then gilded. The summit of Moriah, which had been incorporated into the Temple, was used as the altar for burnt offerings. Solomon's building stood for almost 400 years until its destruction by the Babylonian **Nebuchadnezzar** in 587 BC.

After the return from the Babylonian captivity the ruins were cleared and the Second Temple (of a more modest size) was built by around 520 BC. **Herod**, Jewish king by grace of the Romans, wanted to appear particularly pious and law-abiding to the people, which is why he refurbished the Temple. At first he expanded it to its current dimensions of around 300 x 480m/330 x 530yd. This required extra earthworks and the construction of pillared substructures (»Solomon's Stables«), since the terrain drops away to the south. The extra terrain thus obtained was surrounded by powerful walls, atop which stood colonnades. Several entrances led into the temple precinct: in the east there was an entrance at the site of the Golden Gate, in the south the Huldah Gates under the royal hall, and in the west Warren's Gate and Barclay's Gate, both of which were named after their discoverers. In addition there are Wilson's Arch and Robinson's

◄ Second Temple

Arch. Everyone was able to access the external forecourt. The inner forecourt, located higher up, was only accessible to Jews and was divided into three: the courtyard for women, the courtyard for Israelites (for men) and the courtyard for priests. The actual Temple, exactly described by Flavius Josephus (*The Jewish War* V, 4–6) had a façade 50m/165ft high and equally wide, made of white marble. The first room housed the seven-armed candelabra and the censer. A curtain (the »veil of the Temple«) separated it from the empty Holy of Holies – the Ark of the Covenant was probably burned during the destruction of the First Temple in 587 BC. Herod's Temple was **destroyed in AD 70 by the Romans**. Since then there has not been another Jewish temple. The sacrificial cult was abandoned and priests were replaced by rabbis, while synagogues took over as prayer rooms. Justinian had a church to the Virgin Mary built on the temple site.

Muslim period ► During the time of the Umayyad caliphs the temple square got the two buildings that have been the city's landmarks ever since: Abd al-Malik built the Dome of the Rock on Moriah, and his son Al-Walid I turned Justinian's church into Al-Aqsa Mosque.

The Dome of the Rock, which was damaged during the Israeli-Arab fighting in 1948, was rebuilt between 1958 and 1964 with financial assistance from Jordan, Egypt and Saudi Arabia, during which it was given a new gold dome. Since the Six-Day War in 1967 the Western Wall has been accessible to Jews again.

✱
Al-Aqsa Mosque Al-Aqsa Mosque (Masjid al-Aqsa), along with its adjoining buildings, including the Museum of Islamic Art (see below), takes up the majority of the southern side of the Temple Mount. Its direction of prayer points to the south, towards Mecca. The crusaders saw in it the Temple of Solomon, and set up their palace in the mosque. The Jews call it Solomon's School (Midrash Selomo). The building was

al-Aqsa Mosque Plan

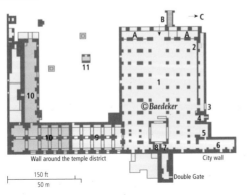

A Atrium
B Steps to the underground room
C Steps to »Christ's cradle«

1 Prayer room
2 Well
3 Elijah's Gate
4 Zechariah's prayer niche
5 Mosque of the 40 Martyrs
6 Mosque of Omar
7 Prayer niche (mihrab)
8 Pulpit
9 White Mosque (women's mosque)
10 Islamic Museum
11 Dome of Jussuf

Wall around the temple district
City wall
Double Gate
150 ft
50 m
©Baedeker

It all seems calm from up above. But there are often arguments between Jews and Muslims on the Temple Mount.

refurbished several times, most recently between 1938 and 1943, when the white Carrara marble donated by Mussolini and the ceiling gifted by the Egyptian king Farouk were fitted.

Jerusalem's largest mosque has room for 5000 believers. The prayer room with its wooden pulpit – a gift from Saladin, who also donated the fine gold-ground mosaics inside the dome – has correspondingly generous proportions. The prayer niche with its small, elegant marble columns, dates back to the same time.

The White Mosque, reserved exclusively to women, adjoins the transept in the west. It dates back to the Knights Templar.

◀ White Mosque

Even further to the west is the Islamic Museum (currently closed) with impressive objects of art: masterly Koran manuscripts and written documents from the time of the Mamluks, clothes, faiences, coins and weapons, but also architectural fragments that were replaced during renovations on the Dome of the Rock and al-Aqsa Mosque.

Islamic Museum

Al-Aqsa Mosque and the Dome of the Rock lie on an axis but not at the same height. Before ascending the stairs to the Dome of the Rock, visitors walk past the large, round ablution fountain (al-Kas). The steps here, like those on the other side of the platform, are covered by attractive Mamluk pointed arch arcades. They are called scales because, according to Muslim belief, this is where the scales with which people are weighed are hung at the Last Judgement.

Ablution fountain, scales

PLACE OF PRAYER

✴ ✴ **The most significant Islamic building in Jerusalem is not a mosque (but it is a place of prayer). It is a shrine, built by the fifth Umayyad caliph, Abd al-Malik, above the holy rock where Mohammed is said to have ascended to heaven (after which he then returned to Mecca).**

① Construction principle
Two (smaller) squares inscribed in an imaginary inner circle at an angle of 45 degrees to one another. The extensions of the sides of the squares intersect in eight places: the supporting columns of the inner octagon. The extensions of the octagon's sides in turn produce two larger squares. There is another circle around these. If the sides of the inner octagon are increased (in parallel) until they meet the outside circle, the result is a large octagon: the 20.5m/22.5yd exterior walls (according to K. A. C. Creswell).

Dome of the Rock Plan

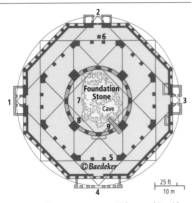

1 Western Gate
  (Bab al-Gharb)
2 Gate of Heaven
  (Bab al-Jannah)
3 Chain Gate
  (Bab al-Silsileh)
4 South Gate
  (Bab al-Qibleh)
5 Prayer niche (mihrab)
6 Slab said to have
  covered Solomon's
  tomb and into which

Mohammed is said to
have hammered 12 gol
nails
7 Fingerprints of the
  archangel Gabriel, whc
  is said to have held ba
  the rock at Mohammec
  Ascension
8 Footprint of the prophe
9 Steps to the
  »Well of Souls«
  (Bir el-Arweh)

② Rugs
The entire interior is beautifully adorned with rugs that were donated in 1964 by Mohammed V, King of Morocco.

③ Holy Rock
The holy rock is the tip of Mount Moriah, which David bought from the Jebusite king Aruauna for 50 silver shekels. This is where Abraham prepared to sacrifice his son Isaac, and where the Ark of the Covenant is said to have stood in the First Temple. A channel in the rock is believed to have been used to drain sacrificial blood into a depression below.
For Muslims this is the place where Mohammed, accompanied by archangel Gabriel, ascended to heaven. On display are an alleged hoof-print made by his mare al-Buraq, some hairs from the prophet's beard and a hand-print said to have been made by the archangel.

④ Inscriptions
Bands of inscriptions with Arabic letters run around the building, both inside and out. They contain excerpts from the Koran and always start with Basmala (»In the name of God, Most Gracious, Most Merciful«), the introductory phrase for the Koran suras 113 and 114. The dome above the inner arcade circle contains quotes from Sura 17 (»The Night Journey«), in which Jerusalem is mentioned. There are also inscriptions about the builders.

⑤ The dome on the inside
Floral ornaments, acanthus plants, wings and gilded arabesques are interpreted as being depictions of paradise.

⑥ The dome on the outside
The roof, which was originally made of lead, was replaced by gilded aluminium sheets in the 1960s: 8 kg/18lb of 24-carat gold was used.

The Dome of the Rock is ranked third amongst the holy sites of Islam after Mecca and Medina.

© Baedeker

Mohammed, guided by archangel Gabriel, rides al-Buraq (depicted here as a fabled creature) to heaven (Persian miniature from around 1540).

The faiences on the outside were commissioned by Sultan Suleiman the Magnificent in the 16th century.

Muslim women pray at the Well of Souls, the cave under the Dome of the Rock, where the souls of the dead are said to gather for prayer on two days a week.

The marble summer pulpit immediately to the left of the top of the stairs also dates back to the Mamluk period.

★ ★
Dome of the Rock (Masjid Qubbat as-Sakhrah)

The most significant Islamic shrine in Jerusalem was built by Abd al-Malik (685–705), the fifth Umayyad caliph. He had an octagonal, domed structure built on the sacred rock of Moriah. Its harmonious effect is the result of exactly calculated proportions. The magnificent façade was adorned with artistic faiences in the 16th century by the Ottoman sultan Suleiman. The elegant, 33m/108ft dome has shone in gilded aluminium since its restoration between 1958 and 1964. King Hussein of Jordan paid for the dome's gilding to be renewed in 1993: around 8 kg/18lbs of 24-carat gold leaf was used. The dome is topped by a 3.6m/12ft crescent.

Interior ▶

The Dome of the Rock has four gates whose copper plates were donated by Qaitbay in the 15th century. The interior is exquisite: richly ornamented wooden ceilings in the two ambulatories, the precious marble of the pillars and columns, whose ancient capitals are gilded, bicoloured round arches between the columns, the way the light comes through the stained glass windows, as well as the gold-base mosaics in the ambulatories and especially in the inner rotunda, above it the lavishly ornamented vault of the dome itself.

Foundation Stone ▶

At the centre of the inner gallery is the Foundation Stone (Sakhrah), which emerges 1–2m/3–7ft from the ground. The crusaders surrounded it with a lattice fence to prevent relic collectors from removing pieces of the rock. According to the Jewish faith, the rock marks the site **where Abraham prepared to sacrifice Isaac**. According to Islam it is the place **where Mohammed ascended to sky on his mare Al-Burak**. Muslims call the cave under the rock Bir-el-Arweh (Well of Souls) because according to their faith the souls of the dead gather here to pray.

Dome of the Chain

Immediately to the east of the Dome of the Rock is a small, round domed structure, known as David's Place of Judgement (Mehkemet Daud) or Dome of the Chain (Qubbat al-Silsila), because according to Jewish tradition Solomon had a chain hung up at his father David's place of judgement. When perjurers took an oath here, a link fell out. According to Islamic tradition, on the other hand, the just and unjust will be separated by a chain here on Judgement Day. The pavilion had allegedly been earmarked by Calif Abd al-Malik as a treasure chamber. As the structure is open to the sides, the dome was the only suitable place to store treasures. As with the Dome of the Rock, the faience ornamentation was commissioned by Suleiman the Magnificent.

Further structures near the Dome of the Rock

The Prophet's Dome (Mihrab al-Nabi), built in 1538, the Hebronite (Qubbat al-Khalili), built in the 19th century by the sheikh of Hebron as a prayer room, and the Dome of the Ascension (Qubbat al-Miraj), which stands on the spot where Mohammed, according to Islamic tradition, prayed before ascending to heaven, can all be found in the northwestern section of the platform around the Dome of the Rock. In front of the arcade of the stairway at the northwestern corner are the Dome of St George (Qubbat al-Qadr) and the Dome of the Soul (Qubbat al-Arwah) from the 15th century, where the souls of saints are said to gather at night. The well to the west of the Dome of the Rock next to the wide stairs is adorned with beautiful arabesques and was donated by the Mamluk Qaitbay in 1455.

Golden Gate

The Golden Gate marks a break in the temple precinct's eastern wall, which was erected in the 7th century on the site of Herod's Shushan Gate. Arabs call the more southerly of the two gateways Bab el-Rameh (Gate of Mercy) and the northern one Bab el-Tobeh (Gate of Repentance), a reference to the Jewish and Muslim expectation that the Kidron Valley and the Mount of Olives will be the **site of the Last Judgement**. According to Christian tradition it was through this gate that Jesus rode on Palm Sunday.

Solomon's Stables

In the southeastern corner of the holy precinct a stairway leads down to Solomon's Stables (usually closed). These are the underground structures that Herod built for the inauguration of the temple square. The crusaders believed the vaulted space had been Solomon's Stables. 88 massive arches, connected by pillars form 12 parallel corridors, which – along with the rings affixed to some of them – make it seem likely that animals were tethered here, and the crusaders also used them as stables. The Islamic administration had a mosque built here. According to the Israeli archaeologists this mosque threatens the entire stability of the Temple Mount.

The scent of the orient wafts through the souks in Jerusalem's Old City.

From Lions' Gate to the Church of the Holy Sepulchre

Muslim Quarter

The walk from Lions' Gate to the Church of the Holy Sepulchre takes visitors into the Muslim Quarter, a fascinating, **labyrinthine mass** of narrow streets, many of which are covered by roofs and vaults, the likes of which are only found in the old towns of Damascus and Cairo. Orientation is a tricky business here, but the residents are more than happy to give directions. There are three covered parallel **souks** where David Street meets the Cardo, the meat bazaar Souk el Lahhamin, the spice bazaar Souk el Attarin and the gold bazaar Souk el Khawajat. There are also souks where the locals buy fresh bread, fruit and vegetables, household goods, but also electronic goods and clothes, where a scent of spices and grilled lamb is in the air and Arab music drowns out the market sounds.

Lions' Gate

The walk begins at Lions' Gate in the eastern city wall. It got its name from the lion reliefs on the outside. As, according to Christian tradition, St Stephen suffered his martyrdom here, it is also known as St Stephen's Gate. In Arabic it is called Bab Sitti Maryam, Gate of Mary.

✳ Church of St Anne

After just a few metres, on the right-hand side, is the Church of St Anne, **the best-preserved structure from the time of the crusaders**. Arda, the widow of Baldwin I, the first Christian king of Jerusalem, had the church built in 1142 at the site where, according to Christian and Islamic tradition, the **house of Mary's parents** stood. The church owes its good condition to the fact that it served as a mosque for around 700 years from Saladin's time. The neighbouring Benedictine convent was turned into a Koran school. In thanks for French support during the Crimean War, Sultan Abdul Mejid gave it to Napoleon III in 1856.

A pointed arch portal between two buttressed pillars marks the entrance. The interior of the basilica, with the typical structure of a nave and two aisles separated by pillars, has a groin vaulted ceiling and is characterized by austere monumentality. Its adornment is limited to the capitals, which feature people and animals as well as plant ornaments. The entrance to the stairs into the crypt lies in the right-hand aisle. This crypt contains the grotto in which the crusaders believed the Virgin Mary was born (Mon–Sat 8am–11.45am, 2pm–6pm, in winter 2pm–5pm).

> ❗ *Baedeker* TIP
>
> **Wonderful acoustics**
>
> The acoustics of the Church of St Anne, which is perfectly suited for Gregorian chants and other singing, still attracts groups of pilgrims, who perform various kinds of choral music. Soloists are also welcome. It is definitely worth going to the church to listen in. For all those visitors who would like to sing there, please be advised that only religious music is permitted.

The Pool of Bethesda lies in the excavation site in front of the **Pool of Bethesda**
church. Jesus healed a lame man here (John 5:8–9), but he did so on
the Sabbath, which angered pious Jews.

The Pool of Bethesda consists of two huge 2nd or 3rd-century cisterns measuring 50 x 50m/55 x 55 yd with a depth of 13m/43ft. They
were separated by a dam and enclosed by high colonnades. The cisterns were originally designed to supply the temple precinct with
water, but in Christ's time they were sought out by the sick hoping
to be cured (John 5:2–5). In the wake of the temple extension, Herod
had the double cistern lavishly adorned with colonnades. In the 5th
century the Byzantines built a basilica here. Its western section stood
on the dam, which was widened by tall foundations for this purpose,
while the eastern section was constructed on solid ground. This
church was destroyed in the early 11th century. The crusaders built a
chapel in the ruins of the northern aisle in the 12th century. The
front arch of the Byzantine church and a mosaic with cruciform ornaments are still clearly visible (opening times as the Church of St
Anne).

The Lions' Gate Street or St Mary's Gate Street (Tariq Sitti Maryam) **Antonia Fortress**
crosses the area where Antonia Fortress once stood. Almost every
ruler built a castle or fortress here,
because this was where practically
all attacks on the city occurred. In
addition it was an excellent vantage
point from which to watch over
the Temple Mount. Herod extended the Seleucid castle into a
magnificent palace and named it
after Mark Antony, who ruled the
eastern part of the Roman Empire
at the time.

The complex, measuring 100 x
160m/110 x 175yd, was probably
Pilate's residence and therefore
the place where (with his sentence) Christ's suffering began. This is
also why the Via Dolorosa begins here. Titus razed the fortress after
the conquest of Jerusalem in AD 70, but large sections survived, because a triumphal arch was erected behind the main entrance for
Emperor Hadrian's visit in AD 135. Known as the Ecce Homo Arch, ◄ **Ecce Homo Arch**
after Pilate's words »Behold the man!« (John 19:5), it still spans Via
Dolorosa.

> **!** **Baedeker TIP**
>
> **Via Dolorosa procession**
> Those who are unwilling or unable to be in
> Jerusalem for Good Friday can nevertheless
> witness a Via Dolorosa procession: every Friday
> at 3pm, and in summer at 4pm, the Franciscans,
> followed by many believers, walk with a cross
> along the Via Dolorosa to the Church of the Holy
> Sepulchre.

In 1838, Ibrahim Pasha left the ruins of the Church of the Flagella- **Church of the**
tion, which dates back to the time of the crusaders, to the Francis- **Flagellation**
cans. The current chapel in the neo-Gothic style was donated by
Duke Maximilian of Bavaria in 1929. Its windows depict the biblical
events centring on Pontius Pilate, Jesus and Barabbas.

Via Dolorosa Map

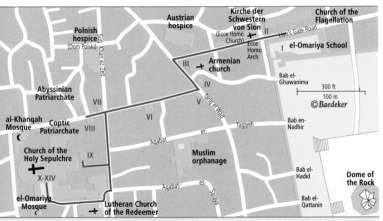

I ——— XIV 14 Stations of the Cross

I Jesus is condemned to death by crucifixion by Pontius Pilatus	VI Veronica wipes the face of Jesus	X Jesus is stripped of His garments
II Jesus carries His cross	VII Jesus falls the second time	XI Crucifixion: Jesus is nailed to the cross
III Jesus falls the first time	VIII Jesus meets the women of Jerusalem	XII Jesus dies on the cross
IV Jesus meets His mother	IX Jesus falls the third time	XIII Jesus is taken down from the cross
V Simon of Cyrene helps Jesus carry the cross	In the Church of the Holy Sepulchre	XIV Jesus is laid in the tomb (Holy Sepulchre)

Convent of the Sisters of Zion

The Convent of the Sisters of Zion (French: Basilique des Dames de Sion) is on the right-hand side of the road. Inside it a model of Antonia Fortress is on display along with explanations. The northern arch of what used to be Hadrian's triple-arch triumphal arch has been incorporated into the convent's choir, which produces an incredible spatial effect. According to Christian tradition, the floor of the crypt, which lies beyond a Herodian cistern, is the **Lithostrotos** and allegedly belonged to a courtyard in Antonia Fortress, in which Pilate's judgement of Jesus took place. This theory has however been refuted, because the floor has been proved to date back only to the 2nd century AD. Nevertheless a closer look is worthwhile, because Roman legionaries carved games into the pavement (Mon–Sat 8.30am–12.30pm, 2pm–5pm).

Via Dolorosa

Sincere piety and profane money-making exist side-by-side in the Via Dolorosa. Right through the souk, past Israeli guards, Arab souvenir dealers and a number of restaurants, groups of pilgrims make their way to the Church of the Holy Sepulchre, all while carrying their cross from station to station and reciting their prayers.

According to tradition, the »**Road of Pain**« refers to the stretch that Jesus had to walk from his sentencing to where he was crucified at Golgotha. There are 14 stations of the cross along this way, some of which are based on the Passion accounts in the gospels, others on tradition. Every year, thousands of people participate in the Good Friday procession along the Via Dolorosa. Stations I–IX lie along the road, stations X–XIV within the Church of the Holy Sepulchre. They should **not be understood as historical locations**. Instead they are markers for the procession. The current road does not follow exactly the same course as it did in the time of Jesus. As a result the route was altered several times and the original seven stations have become 14. The current route mainly dates back to the 18th century, while stations I, IV, V and VIII were only set up in the 19th century.

◀ Stations of the Cross

Station I (Jesus is condemned to death) lies on the south side of Via Dolorosa in the courtyard of the Islamic madrasa al-Omariya on the grounds of the former Antonia Fortress.
Station II (Jesus accepts the cross) lies on the other side of the road at the entrance to the Church of the Condemnation and Imposition of the Cross (built in around 1903). By the way, the condemned »only« had to carry the cross-beam to the crucifixion as the vertical post was already erected there. Station III (Jesus falls the first time), a small chapel built by Jerusalem's Polish community in 1947, is located diagonally opposite the Austrian Hospice, where the Via Dolorosa meets Tariq al-Wad. A short way along Tariq al-Wad is Station IV (Jesus meets His Mother) on the left-hand side of the Armenian Catholic Church of Our Lady of the Spasm, whose floor mosaic depicts this encounter. Turn right again immediately afterwards. The

Way of the Cross
◀ Station I
◀ Stations II–VI

Many pilgrims carry a cross and make their way along the Via Dolorosa.

next station is Station V (Simon of Cyrene carries the cross). This station is marked by a small Franciscan chapel from 1881. Station VI (Veronica wipes the face of Jesus) is also there. The result of this act of compassion was the »Veil of Veronica«, on which the face of Jesus appeared.

Church of the Holy Sepulchre Plan

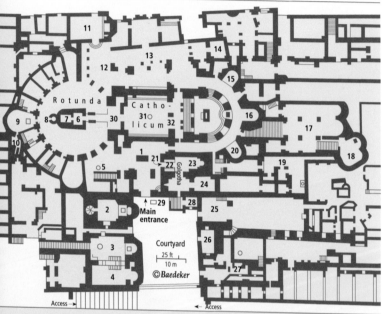

1 Stone of the Unction
2 Chapel of the 40 Martyrs and Belfry
3 Chapel of St John and Baptistery
4 Chapel of St James
5 Site of the Three Marys (Armenian Orthodox)
6 Chapel of the Angel
7 Holy Sepulchre
8 Coptic Chapel
9 Jacobite Chapel (Syrian Orthodox)
10 Tomb of Joseph of Arimathaea (Abyssinian)
11 Franciscan chapel (RC)
12 Altar of Mary Magdalene (RC)

13 Arch of the Virgin Mary
14 Holy Prison (Greek Orthodox)
15 Longinus Chapel (Greek Orthodox)
16 Holy Division of Robes (Armenian Orthodox)
17 Saints Helena Chapel (Armenian Orthodox)
18 Chapel of the Invention of the Cross (RC)
19 Medieval cloister
20 Derision Chapel
21 Adam Chapel (Greek Orthodox)
22 Former tombs of Godfrey of Bouillon and Baldwin I

23 Crucifixion Altar and Stabat Mater Altar (Greek Orthodox)
24 Nails of the Cross Altar (RC)
25 Michael's Chapel
26 Chapel of St John (Armenian)
27 Chapel of Abraham
28 Chapel of St Mary of Egypt
29 Tomb of Philippe d'Aubigny
30 Latin choir (RC)
31 Omphalos (Navel of the World)
32 Greek choir

Stations VII (Jesus falls the second time), a small Franciscan chapel from 1875, and VIII (Jesus meets the women of Jerusalem) are at the intersection of the bazaar street Suk Khan ez-Zeit with Via Dolorosa. Turn back here because the direct route to Golgotha has been blocked by buildings since the Middle Ages. Instead, turn right into the above-mentioned bazaar street. After around 60m/65yd there is a wide staircase on the right leading to the Coptic monastery. Station IX (Jesus falls the third time) can be found to the left of the entrance.

◄ Stations VII–IX

✳ Church of the Holy Sepulchre

The Church of the Holy Sepulchre (Arabic: Keniset el-Qiyame = Church of the Resurrection) stands on the site where Jesus was crucified and laid in his tomb. It is **one of the holiest places in Christianity**.

A visit to the Church of the Holy Sepulchre is one of the most impressive experiences in Jerusalem, for believers and non-believers alike. The Church of the Holy Sepulchre is not really a church, but more a **labyrinthine conglomerate** of sacred sites, dark aisles, smaller chapels, narrow stairs and corridors from different building periods, marked by centuries of use. Groups of pilgrims from all kinds of different nationalities crowd around the tomb. Deeply moved, they touch or kiss the holy sites, while handkerchiefs and ornaments are placed on the Stone of Anointing, and candles are lit. Notwithstanding the crowds in the church, there are many quiet, contemplative places to which believers withdraw to pray.

This house of God is shared by six religious communities: they all share the Stone of Anointing in the entrance area, and the Tomb. The Greek Orthodox church is in charge of the Catholicum (nave), the northern part of Golgotha, the Chapel of Adam below it and the »Holy Prison«. The Roman Catholic church oversees the southern part of Golgotha, the choir between the rotunda and the Catholicon, the Chapel of the Apparition with the Franciscan priory, the Altar of Mary Magdalen and the Chapel of the Invention of the Holy Cross. The areas reserved for Armenians are the Place of the Three Marys, the eastern chapel in the ambulatory and the Chapel of St Helena. The Copts own the chapel at the rear of the Holy Tomb, the Syrians the western chapel in the rotunda and the Abyssinians the Tomb of Joseph of Arimathaea.

🕑
Opening hours: 5.30am–9pm, in winter 4.30am–7pm
Don't miss the door-locking ritual!

Again and again it has been questioned whether Christ's tomb was really located in the place now marked as such in the Church of the Holy Sepulchre. As graves were considered unclean and were always outside Jewish towns, the authenticity of this one was doubted, because it lay inside the Ottoman city wall. The establishment of the exact site of the city walls in the time of Jesus, however, revealed that the Crucifixion took place outside the walls, meaning outside the

Authenticity of the tomb

THE TOMB OF JESUS

★★ »When the even was come, there came a rich man of Arimathaea, named Joseph, who also himself was Jesus' disciple: He went to Pilate, and begged the body of Jesus. Then Pilate commanded the body to be delivered. And when Joseph had taken the body, he wrapped it in a clean linen cloth, and laid it in his own new tomb, which he had hewn out in the rock: and he rolled a great stone to the door of the sepulchre, and departed.« (Matthew 27:57–60)

🕐 Open:
5.30am–9pm, in winter 4.30am–7pm

① Golgotha
In the (Greek Orthodox) Chapel of the Crucifixion, a near life-size depiction of the crucified Jesus can be seen between Mary and his disciple John above the altar. The site where the cross is said to have stood has been protected by bulletproof glass since 1989. To the right of the altar, a metal bar covers the crack in the rock that formed when Jesus died (Matthew 27:52). According to tradition, the place where Mary stood when her son was crucified is now the site of the (Catholic) Stabat Mater Altar. The copper reliefs on the (Catholic) Nails of the Cross Altar date back to 1588. The mosaics of 1937 show how Jesus was nailed to the cross in this location.

② Chapel of the Franks
Looking through a window in the right-hand wall from the Chapel of the Nails of the Cross, there is the Chapel of the Franks (also Catholic), below which lies the Chapel of Mary of Egypt (4th century, Greek Orthodox)

③ Holy Sepulchre and Chapel of the Angel
After the fire of 1808, the Chapel of the Holy Sepulchre was rebuilt in the Turkish Rococo style. There are 43 lamps hanging above the portal, 13 belonging to the Greeks, 13 to the Latins, 13 to the Armenians and 4 to the Copts. The Chapel of the Angel in front of the actual Holy Sepulchre was named after the stone on which the angel who announced the Resurrection to the three women is said to have sat. The current stone is presumably a piece of the round stone that covered the tomb. In the Holy Sepulchre a marble slab on the right covers the remains of the bench where Jesus was laid to rest. Caliph al-Hakim ordered the destruction of the tomb in 1009.

④ Debre Sultan Monastery
Since 1875 the Ethiopian Orthodox church has had a small monastery on the roof of St Helena's Chapel.

The Holy Sepulchre has been covered a chapel in Turkish rococo style since 1808.

urch of the Nativity in
e the various denomina-
he Holy Sepulchre. Left:
monks during a religious
ht: Roman Catholic
ont of the Nails of the
. The Holy Sepulchre
ithout denominations.

Since the Middle Ages pilgrims
have carved crosses into the
wall by the stairs leading down
into St Helena's Chapel.

© Baedeker

As in
Bethle
tions
Church
Armen
service
priests
Cross
remain

Christ's body was laid out
and anointed on the Stone
of the Anointing.

The Holy Sepulchre

city. Another fact in favour of the **authenticity of the site** is that the place was remembered by the Christian community and revered as a holy site from the 1st century AD until the construction of the Church of the Holy Sepulchre by Emperor Constantine, even though Hadrian removed all Christian churches in Jerusalem in the 2nd century and had a temple built on the site.

Construction history
Constantine's church ▶ When Helena, the mother of Emperor Constantine, visited Jerusalem and was shown the holy sites, Constantine had the temple pulled down and the area levelled, so that only Golgotha and the Holy Tomb remained as lumps of rock. The Church of the Holy Sepulchre was built above them. This church combined the two types of church customary in those days, namely the basilica and the centrally-planned rotunda, whose form is derived from the baptistery or funerary chapel. The latter was built around the rock with the tomb of Christ. Adjoining it to the east was a basilica with a nave and four aisles, which in turn was adjoined by an atrium. The rock of Golgotha stood in the open space between the basilica and the rotunda, above which stood the Holy Cross. Construction on this building began in AD 326 and was completed in around AD 335, but it was destroyed when the Persians conquered the country in AD 614. After it was re-conquered by the Byzantines, the church was rebuilt following the old plans in AD 629.

The Fatimid caliph Al-Hakim destroyed the church almost completely in 1009. It was rebuilt in 1048, but on a significantly smaller scale, by the Byzantine emperor Constantine IX Monomachos. The rotunda remained. The only thing now adjoining it to the east was a courtyard surrounded by small rooms.

Time of the crusaders ▶ The crusaders started rebuilding the compound in 1099. Their church was completed in 1149. The French architect Jourdain built a shorter nave on the site of the original basilica. It ended with a semicircle in the east and was vaulted, according to the style of that time. Once again the grave rotunda was preserved. The rock of Golgotha, which had been free-standing until then, was incorporated into the closed nave as an elevated side chapel. In a cave below the rock, tombs were created for the conqueror of Jerusalem, Godfrey of Bouillon, and Baldwin I, the first king of the crusader state. As a result, the layout of the Church of the Holy Sepulchre, with two sacred focal points and two parts to the building, has largely survived until today. The two domes that can be seen from the outside already point to this.

Modern era ▶ Since the church had become unattractive over the centuries and was badly damaged in an earthquake in 1927, the Christian communities who have a holding in the church decided in 1958 to restore it. It was not until March 1995 that the representatives of these religious communities signed an agreement about the renovation of the large dome, after decades of negotiations. These works have not yet been completed.

For generations the Muslim Nuseibeh family have been the guards at the Church of the Holy Sepulchre. Here they are accompanying the orthodox patriarch in their uniforms.

The façade of the entrance, the southern side of the church, is dominated by two pointed arch portals from the time of the crusaders. The right-hand one was walled up by Saladin in 1187. The lavishly ornamented Corinthian corbels above the arches are probably a relic from Constantine's building. The coat of arms between the two portals identifies the tomb of Philippe d'Aubigny, the tutor of King Henry III of England. The epitaph of this knight, who fell in 1236, is the only survivor of many tombs that once lay all around the church.

Front elevation

The church's interior is accessed via the left portal, past the chapel (left) for the **Muslim Guards** from the Nuseibeh family, who for centuries have had the privilege of being in charge of the church's keys. Continue straight on to the stone slab on which Christ's body is said to have been anointed after being taken down from the cross (John 19:40).

The Stone of Anointing

To the right of the entrance is a staircase to Calvary (Golgotha), whose 10m/30ft rock rises 5m/15ft above the floor level. In this spot, where Jesus is said to have been crucified, people come to pray at the Crucifixion Altar, the Stabat Mater Altar and the Nails of the Cross Altar.

✱ **Golgotha**

Climb back down via the northern stairs. The Greek Orthodox Chapel of Adam lies below Golgotha, from where the crack in the rock can also be seen. According to legend, the **skull of Adam** was found here during Christ's crucifixion. Stone benches at either side of the entrance mark the former tombs of Godfrey of Bouillon and Baldwin I.

Chapel of Adam

✶✶
Sepulchre of Jesus

Past the Stone of Anointing and the Place of the Three Marys (Armenian), visitors enter the rotunda with the Sepulchre of Jesus at its centre. The rock of the tomb cannot actually be seen, however. It is hidden in a high, box-like enclosure, which detracts from the architecture of the rotunda, rather than enriching it. Since only a few people are allowed into the Sepulchre at any one time, there is usually a long queue outside the entrance, which often even runs the whole way around the tomb. The small burial chamber is accessed via a low door. By the wall on the right-hand side a marble slab covers the place where the body rested. If one imagines the marble slab were not there, this is a tomb typical of the time of Jesus. The rock in front of it was a boulder whose diameter also determined the height of the entrance. On **Easter eve**, the Greek Orthodox patriarch of Jerusalem lights the »Holy Fire« in the Chapel of the Angel, which was sealed on Good Friday. It is a light from the darkness of the tomb as a symbol of the Resurrection.

Chapels in the rotunda

Behind the Sepulchre of Jesus is the Coptic Chapel. Opposite it, in the outer ring of the rotunda, the Jacobites (Syrian Christians) have a chapel. In this chapel there is an entrance into a rock tomb on the left-hand side, said to be that of **Joseph of Arimathaea**, who buried Jesus (Matthew 27:60, see p. 296).

North aisle

To the north of the rotunda is the Latin section of the complex. There is a Franciscan Church as well as an adjoining priory and the **Altar of Mary Magdalen** here. This is the north aisle. With its high pillars from the time of the crusaders and architectural fragments from different periods, it feels a little neglected, but also more original than other parts of the Church of the Holy Sepulchre. The richly adorned Corinthian columns from Constantine's church are called »Arches of the Virgin Mary«, because it is said that the risen Jesus appeared to His Mother here. The small room at the eastern end of the aisle is known as the Holy Prison.

✶
Chapel of St Helena

The stairs leading down to the Armenian Chapel of St Helena can be found through a round corridor at the eastern end of the nave, past the chapels of Longinus and Division of Holy Robes. Pilgrims from the time of the crusaders carved small crosses into the wall on the right-hand side. Four low columns from the Byzantine period support the high arches on which the vaulted ceiling of the Chapel of St Helena rests. The scant daylight penetrating the dome, the many oil lamps and the large chandelier give this space a powerful atmosphere.

Chapel of the Invention of the Cross ▶

To the right of the main apse, steps lead down into the Chapel of the Invention of the Cross, the former cistern in which Empress Helena allegedly found the cross of Christ. The rocky walls of the chapels still reveal their original purpose. A statue commemorates the pious empress.

From the Church of the Holy Sepulchre to the Citadel

Not far from the Church of the Holy Sepulchre to the east is the Lutheran Church of the Redeemer (Mon–Sat 9am–1pm, 2pm–5pm). Inaugurated by Emperor Wilhelm II of Germany on Reformation Day (31 October) 1898, it stands on a spot that is steeped in tradition: the area had been awarded to **Charlemagne** by the ruler at the time, Caliph Harun al-Rashid, and the church of St Maria Latina was built here. This was destroyed in 1008 by al-Hakim, then rebuilt in the 11th century. The church and the cloister fell into ruin over the centuries. After the area was acquired by Prussia in 1868, the foundation stone of a new church was laid in 1893. It was intended to continue the old Western tradition as close as possible to the Holy Sepulchre, now as the spiritual centre of Protestantism in the Holy Land. Since then the church and adjoining buildings have been the seat of the Lutheran presence in Jerusalem.

There is little worth seeing on the inside, but it is interesting to climb the tower (door to the right behind the entrance), since it is a great vantage point from which to see the entire Old Town and the Mount of Olives.

Lutheran Church of the Redeemer ⏲

◄ View

The entrance to the Muristan, the quarter south of the Church of the Holy Sepulchre, between Christian Street and the three bazaar streets, is next to the Lutheran Church of the Redeemer and is the extension of the Suq Khan ez-Zeit. Muristan is the Persian-Arabic word for hospital and refers to the former pilgrims' hospice of the Knights Hospitaller in this quarter. This bazaar sells a wide range of **leather goods** and is also the location of the Omar Mosque, built in 1216, and of several small restaurants.

Muristan

◄ Greek bazaar

The Church of St John the Baptist can be found in the southern part of the Muristan. It was built by crusaders in 1170. Its façade features Roman spolia. The three-apse complex, which does not have a nave, is now used by the Greek Orthodox community. The building that stood here before this church, a 5th-century chapel consecrated to John the Merciful, Patriarch of Alexandria, is now the crypt. The Church of St John the Baptist was part of a pilgrims' hospice that was founded in 1073 by merchants from the southern Italian port of Amalfi. Later, the spiritual order of the **Knights Hospitallers** was founded here and confirmed by Pope Paschal II in 1113. As a result, John the Baptist took the place of the church's original patron saint. The church is regarded by the Venerable Order of St John, the parent body of the St John Ambulance as its mother church (March–Sept Mon–Sat 8am–noon, 2.30pm–6pm, Oct–Feb Mon–Sat 9.30am–1pm, 2pm–5pm).

Church of St John the Baptist

⏲

Just before the northern end of Christian Street, the Street of the Greek Orthodox Patriarchy turns off to the left. It is named after the

Monastery of Constantine

Museum ▶

Greek patriarch's palace on the right-hand side. The worthwhile little museum in the Greek Orthodox Monastery of Constantine (opposite) displays Roman and Byzantine discoveries and the **sarcophagus of Queen Mariamne**, who was killed in 29 BC by her husband Herod the Great.

Palace of the crusader kings ▶

To the north of the monastery stood the palace in which the crusader kings of Jerusalem resided after handing over their first residence, al-Aqsa Mosque, to the Knights Templar.

Back to Jaffa Gate

Why not continue walking westwards and explore the Catholic (Latin) district? Behind the church of Terra Sancta (right) and after the turning to the New Gate, the Latin Patriarchate lies immediately outside the city walls. From here walk through some narrow streets towards David Street, which you will reach right by the Jaffa Gate opposite the citadel.

On the Mount of Olives

Mary's Tomb

The walk over the Mount of Olives (Arabic: et-Tur, Hebrew: Har Ha-Zeitim) starts at the bend in Jericho Street below Lions' Gate (Stephen's Gate). Walk past a monument, erected for Israeli paratroopers who fell here in 1967, to get to Mary's Tomb (12th century) to the left of the street. It has a Gothic façade.

Marble steps lead into the underground tomb, past two niches. On the right-hand side there is a niche with the tombs of Joachim and

The Church of All Nations on the Mount of Olives

Anne, Mary's parents, and to the left there is one with an altar above Joseph's tomb. At the bottom an elongated room to the right with Mary's Tomb was carved straight from the rock. To the left in front of it is an Armenian altar, to the right a medieval Islamic prayer niche. Daily 5am–12 noon (6am–12 noon in winter), 2pm–5pm). ⏲

Turn left at the portal of Mary's Tomb and walk through a corridor to the Grotto of Gethsemane (opening times as Mary's Tomb). Adjoining at its southern end is the garden of Gethsemane with its ancient, gnarled olive trees. The name Gethsemane comes from the Hebrew Gath-Shamma, which means something like **oil press**. After Jesus had sat with his disciples (on the day we now call Maundy Thursday) on the eve of the Friday before Passover, he went with them »to a place called Gethsemane« (Matthew 26:36), where, plagued by the fear of death, he prayed while his disciples slept. A short while later he was betrayed by Judas Iscariot and arrested by the soldiers of the high priest.

★ Gethsemane

In the 4th century, Emperor Theodosius I built a basilica above the rock in Gethsemane where **Jesus prayed in anguish** (Luke 22:41–44). Its ground plan can still be made out on the floor of the modern church, which was built between 1919 and 1924 with the help of donations from many countries, hence its name Church of All Nations. The pediment mosaic above the main portal depicts Jesus as the mediator between heaven and earth. The interior, which has a murky feel, stands in stark contrast to the colourful façade with its gold-shimmering pediment mosaic. Six columns support the roof, which consists of twelve small domes adorned with mosaics. Reddish-brown columns symbolize the olive trees of Gethsemane. The low lattice around the window is a reference to the crown of thorns (daily 8am–12 noon, 2pm–6pm, Nov–Mar 5pm). ⏲

◄ Church of All Nations

The Church of Mary Magdalen lies to the right. It is a magnificent Baroque structure with **seven gilded domes**. Tsar Alexander III had this church built in 1885 in memory of his mother Maria Alexandrovna. Grand Duchess Elizabeth, sister of the last Russian empress and wife of Grand Duke Sergei Alexandrovich, who was murdered in 1918, was buried in the crypt in 1921. The painting above the iconostasis depicts Mary Magdalen telling Emperor Tiberius of Christ's Resurrection (Tue and Thu 10am–11.30am). ⏲

Church of Mary Magdalen

Around 200m/200yd further up on the left-hand side is the entrance to a compound that is also home to the Franciscan Domus Flevit (»the Lord wept«) Church. It was built in 1955 in the shape of a tear, above the foundations of a 5th-century church from which a mosaic survives (to the left of the entrance). The church's name commemorates the report that Jesus, when he came to Jerusalem for the last time, wept over the future fate of the city (Luke 19:41–44). During construction work for the church, Bronze Age, Roman and Byzan-

Dominus Flevit Church

⊙ tine tombs were found in the surrounding area (daily 8am–noon, 2.30pm–5pm).

Tombs of the Prophets

After a further 200m/200yd, there is a larger area to the right with the Tombs of the Prophets. According to tradition, this is the final resting place of the prophets Haggai, Zechariah and Malachi, 6th and 5th centuries BC).

★ ★
Viewing terrace

The viewing terrace (photo p. 274–75) to the right behind the Tombs of the Prophets offers stunning views of Jerusalem. Look out for the Temple Mount and the Old City with domes, minarets and church towers as well as the skyscrapers of West Jerusalem. Hawkers at the car park offer short camel rides, postcards and souvenirs. The large Jewish cemetery lies below the viewing terrace (see p. 315).

Church of the Pater Noster

Returning from the viewing terrace, the path turns right to the Church of the Pater Noster. This was once the site of the Constantinian Sanctuary of the Eleona (AD 333, destroyed by the Persians in AD 614). Later it became a crusader chapel. Princess Aurelie de la Tour d'Auvergne acquired the derelict compound in 1874 and founded a convent for Carmelite nuns. She was buried here in 1957, long after her death. This is where Jesus is said to have taught his disciples the **Lord's Prayer** (Luke 11: 2–4). The prayer can be read in 80 languages on faience panels.

Evangelical Lutheran Church of the Ascension

Further to the north, the Lutheran Church of the Ascension, founded by the German imperial couple Wilhelm II and Augusta Victoria, stands on the highest point of the Mount of Olives. The fantastic view from the tower ranges from Jerusalem all the way to the West Bank (Mon–Sat 8.30am–1pm).

Chapel of the Ascension

The Chapel of the Ascension stands in a complex of mosques in the Arab suburb of El-Tur (please ring). Since this former village lies on the road from Jerusalem to Bethany (► Around Jerusalem), and, according to Luke (24:50–51), this is where Christ ascended to heaven, crusaders built a chapel here in the 12th century. It was originally open to the sky, but was transformed into a domed building by Saladin. A **footprint, allegedly Christ's**, is held to be evidence of the Ascension. The tomb opposite the Church of the Pater Noster is believed by Jews to be the tomb of the prophetess Huldah. She lived in Jerusalem during the time of King Josiah in the 7th century BC (2 Kings 22:14–20). The southern gates to the temple square are named after her. According to Christian tradition – and the two versions need not exclude each other – it is the grotto of Saint Pelagia of Antioch, who lived here as a penitent and died in 280. The Russian Convent of the Ascension of Our Lord lies to the east of the Chapel of the Ascension. Its 60m/200ft tower is the **landmark of the Mount of Olives**, dominating the area.

Convent of the Ascension of Our Lord ►

A little to the south of Gethsemane Church the narrow Siloa Road turns right into Kidron Valley, which continues southwest in the Valley of Josaphat and separates Mount Moriah, the temple site and the Mount of Olives.

✱
Kidron Valley

»Jehoshaphat« means »God will judge«. Prophecies made by Zechariah and Joel refer to this region and its name: » For, behold, in those days, and in that time, when I shall bring again the captivity of Judah and Jerusalem, I will also gather all nations, and will bring them down into the valley of Jehoshaphat, and will plead with them there for my people and for my heritage Israel, whom they have scattered among the nations, and parted my land...« (Joel 3:1–2). »Multitudes, multitudes in the valley of decision! For the day of the Lord is near in the valley of decision« (Joel 3:14).

The Jews also expect the **Last Judgement** to take place here, as do Muslims – according to their tradition a rope will be spanned from the pinnacle of the Temple over the valley to the Mount of Olives, across which the just, supported by their guardian angels, will cross, whereas sinners will fall into damnation.

The desire to be in this place for the Last Judgement is the reason why Jews and Muslims have made cemeteries on both sides of the Kidron Valley – on the Mount of Olives and outside the walls of the

Jewish cemetery

The name is deceptive: the prophet does not lie buried in the Tomb of Zechariah (right).

Temple Mount. The Jewish cemetery goes back to the **2nd millennium BC**. The large burial monuments at the lower edge to the left of the path, carved from the rock, are also connected with this. They are named after characters in the Old and New Testaments, but they date back to Hellenistic or Herodian times.

Tomb of Absalom ▶ The series begins with the Tomb of Absalom, which used to be pelted with stones in memory of Absalom's rebellion against his father, King David. However, the attribution to Absalom is unhistorical, because the tomb dates back only to the 1st century BC. The square burial chamber has a Doric frieze above Ionic half and quarter columns. Beyond it is the tomb of Joshaphat.

Grotto of James ▶ According to Christian tradition, after Jesus was arrested, James hid in the burial chamber with its loggia-like facade that features two Doric columns and a Doric architrave. The Grotto of James is a Jewish family tomb for the priestly Hezir family (1st century BC).

Tomb of Zechariah ▶ Next is the 9m/30ft Tomb of Zechariah, an imposing cube carved from the rock with Ionic columns and a pyramidal roof.

City of David The Jerusalem of King David was built on terraces on the slopes of Mt Ophel, as was later the Arab Silwan opposite. Discoveries confirm that the Jews who returned from Babylonian captivity settled here and that the place was also inhabited during Persian, Hellenistic and Roman times. It was not until the Middle Ages that the city of David was no longer inhabited, since Jerusalem had by then been moved to what is now the Old Town as well as to the elevation known as Mount Zion. The terrain is now known as the »City of David« (Sun–Thu 8am–5pm, Fri 8am–12 noon, tel. 02 626 87 00, www.cityofdavid.org.il), an excavation as interesting as it is controversial. From the visitor centre (tickets, 3D introductory film, refreshment and souvenir kiosk) the way leads through the area along steps, walkways and paved paths past thousands of clay shards and archaeological rubble, beginning with the large stone building, possibly the remains of David's Palace, and the burnt house. The »City of David« is extremely controversial because Elad, an organization supporting Jewish settlements, is behind it. Whether this place really has any connexion with David is considered to be unproven by many experts. The Arab population of the neighbouring Silwan district fear that Bible archaeology, hand in hand with a David myth that may have no scientific foundation, will be instrumentalized to effect a creeping confiscation, in order to occupy land whose status is to be decided eventually by a peace treaty. In the lower region a »Bible Park« is planned, and no one disputes that Arab houses would have to be demolished to make way for it. The first Jewish settlers have already bought or occupied houses in Silwan, and live among 40,000 Palestinians under military guard.

Gihon Spring Around 400m/450yd to the southwest on the City of David terrain is Gihon Spring, at the eastern foot of Mt Ophel, which runs from the southern wall of the Temple Mount to where the Kidron and Hinnom valleys meet. During Canaanite and Israelite times it was used as a water supply. Since it was outside the city wall, the people of Jerusalem built a tunnel between the spring and the city, where they dug a shaft (named Warren's Shaft after its discoverer) in order to get at their vital water supply even in times of siege. However, that gave the city a hiding place that **King David** used during the conquest of Jerusalem (2 Samuel 5:6–8).

Several centuries later King Hezekiah (727–698 BC) had a tunnel built that was 540m/600yd long, up to 4m/13ft high and 1m/3ft wide, which carried water from Gihon Spring to the Pool of Siloam in the city. It is now open to the public (bring a torch). Instead of negotiating this 533m/580yd long Shiloah tunnel, through which spring water flows (duration: 45 min), you can choose instead to walk dryshod through the 120m/135yd cramped Canaanite Tunnel in about ten minutes. The exit at the Pool of Siloam is around 500m/550yd from Gihon Spring – to the right of the road, below the minaret of a mosque. At this pool, now measuring 6 x 17m/6.5 x 18.5 yd, Jesus restored the sight of the man born blind (John 9:7). Some of the columns belonging to the church built here in the 5th century are now in the pool.

Hezekiah's Tunnel, Pool of Siloam

The Valley of Hinnom extends to the southwest of the Pool of Siloam (from Siloam back to the road, then turn right after around 200m/200yd). During Canaanite times it was a **site of the cult of Baal and Moloch**. These cults involved children being permitted to »walk through fire«, meaning they were burned as sacrifices. The Moloch cult also existed during Israelite times. King Manasseh, the son and successor of King Hezekiah, »sacrificed his own son in a fire« (2 Kings 21:6). The location of this event later became the epitome of evil. As a result the word Hinnom comes from the Arabic word **Gehenna**, meaning hell.

Valley of Hinnom

The elevation in the northwest is called the Hill of Evil Council, as it is said to be the place where the high priest Caiaphas held the council at which it was decided that Jesus was to be killed (John 11:47–53). A shuttle bus brings visitors back to the entrance to the City of David.

◄ Hill of Evil Council

However there are also steps dating back to the Roman period that lead from the Pool of Siloam up Mount Zion. The tradition that Jesus celebrated Passover in a house in the upper city is probably correct. After the meal, Jesus probably went down these steps to Gethsemane. Follow them to the Catholic Church of St Peter in Gallicantu (Gallicantu meaning cock crow), which commemorates Peter's triple denial of Jesus (Matthew 26:69–75). The church, built in 1931, contains discoveries from Jewish and early Christian times (Mon–Sat 8.30am–noon, 2pm–5pm).

Church of St Peter in Gallicantu

Ⓛ

Mount Zion (Har Tsion)

Place of the Last Supper and the miracle of Pentecost

During the time of Herod the Great this elevation was part of the upper city. Since the 4th century it has been revered as the site where Jesus celebrated the Last Supper with his disciples (Matthew 26:17–29; Mark 14:12–25; Luke 22:7–20) and where the miracle of Pentecost took place, when the Holy Spirit descended upon the Apostles (Acts 1:12–14, 2:1–4). However, the information in the Bible about this is very imprecise. According to a document by the patriarch Modestos from the 7th century, this is also said to have been the last place where Mary lived. Since the 12th century the tomb of King David has also been venerated on Mount Zion, but it is not actually located here. It is on Mt Ophel in the old City of David.

The churches built during the Byzantine period in memory of the Last Supper and the washing of the feet (John 13:1–15) were derelict when the crusaders arrived in 1099 and rebuilt the church of Zion, which was destroyed again in 1219. In the 14th century the sultan transferred to the Franciscans the area on which the Christian church once stood, while the Queen of Naples built a church that has a room for the Last Supper. The Franciscans expanded their possessions on Mount Zion until Sultan Suleiman evicted them in the 16th century and built a mosque. In 1898 Sultan Abdul Hamid gave the area to the German Emperor Wilhelm II, who in turn transferred it to the Archbishop of Cologne. 1906 saw the building of a round church architecturally reminiscent of Charlemagne's Palatine Chapel in Aachen: this was to emphasize the »spiritual bond« between Charlemagne and the German emperor, who saw himself to be in Charlemagne's tradition, and to create a connection to the Holy Land. Its name, Abbey of the Dormition of the Blessed Virgin Mary, refers to the tradition that Mary died on Mount Zion.

The room of the washing of the feet is now used as a synagogue. The reputed Tomb of David is in the adjoining room (Sat–Thu 8am–5pm, Fri until 2pm). The cenotaph, which is considered the actual tomb of the king, stands in front of the apse, which is aligned with the Temple Mount to the north – evidence of the original synagogue. The cenotaph is ornamented with cloths upon which stand silver keter crowns and Torah scrolls. Jewish pilgrims pray here, especially on Shavuot, the day assigned by tradition to the death of the king.

Tomb of David

To the left of this room a memorial site (**Martet Hashoa**) was set up for the Jews killed by the Nazis (Sun–Thu 9am–4pm, Fri until 1pm).

 Zion

- Zion was the name the Israelites first gave to the City of David, the former Jebusite city in the southeast of Jerusalem (2 Samuel 5–9), then to Solomon's city and especially to the Temple Mount as the religious centre of the Jews (Isaiah 10:12). The Byzantines gave the name Zion to the southwest hill with the upper city, because they incorrectly believed it was the former City of David. Today the term is restricted to the area of this hill to the south of the city walls.

Leave David's Tomb and turn right into alley. Turn right again through an arch and to steps that lead to the Last Supper Room (Coenaculum), above the room of the washing of the feet and David's Tomb. Two Gothic columns support the vaults of the room, which measures 10 x 16m/11 x 18yd. A 16th-century block of stone opposite the Muslim prayer niche is believed to be the site where Jesus held the Last Supper (daily 8.30am–4pm).

★
Last Supper Room

⏲

The Abbey of the Dormition of the Blessed Virgin Mary dominates Mount Zion and is its most striking building. The beautiful **mosaic floor** has three overlapping circles as a symbol of the Holy Trinity. Rays emanate from this centre to the two next (concentric) circles with the names of the prophets Daniel, Isaiah, Jeremiah and Ezekiel (inside) and the twelve apostles (outside). Next come the signs of the zodiac and an inscription (Proverbs 8:22–26). A mosaic in the curve of the apse depicts Mary with the child. The chapels are dedicated to the Three Magi, John the Baptist and Saint Joseph among others. At the centre of the crypt is a sculpture of Mary on her death bed, which stands below a dome ornamented with a mosaic.

★
Abbey of the Dormition of the Blessed Virgin Mary

In the Roman Catholic cemetery is a grave that became a place of pilgrimage after **Steven Spielberg's film »Schindler's List«** in 1993. Spielberg based the film on the true story of Oskar Schindler (d. 1974), who rescued Jewish slave labourers in his Cracow munitions firm from the Nazis. At his own request, Schindler was buried on Mount Zion. A cross marks his grave. The translation of the German inscription reads: »The unforgettable rescuer of the lives of 1200 persecuted Jews«. The grave is on the lower terrace to the right of the

Oskar Schindler's Grave

central path. It is easy to recognize, being the only one covered with stones in the Jewish tradition.

From the Rockefeller Museum to City Hall

Rockefeller Museum ✱

The Rockefeller Museum at Herod's Gate is part of the Israel Museum and one of the country's most significant archaeological collections. It was named after John D. Rockefeller, who paid for its construction in 1927 with a donation of two million dollars. Roman sarcophagi and architectural fragments such as capitals and mosaics are on display in the atrium-style courtyard.

Tour Tower Hall ►

The tour through the exhibition starts in Tower Hall, where significant excavation sites have been used to create a kind of **cross-section of Palestine's long settlement history**. The time span starts with the body of a gazelle from 12,000 BC and ends with the crusader era.

South Gallery ►

Leave Tower Hall and turn left into the Southern Octagon. On display here are Egyptian and Mesopotamian pieces found in Palestine, many of them in Beit She'an. One of the most impressive exhibits is the stele of Pharaoh Seti I. The adjoining South Gallery houses discoveries from the Stone Age to the Bronze Age: skulls and skeletons, worked stones, alabaster containers, jewellery, figurines and other clay objects. Also on display are wooden objects from the 8th century from al-Aqsa Mosque as well as a coin cabinet.

West Gallery ►

The West Gallery contains the discoveries from Hisham's Palace, which the Umayyid caliph Hisham built in Jericho in 724: windows and reconstructed vaults with rich ornamentation and many figurative depictions (animals and people), which are evidence of the high quality of early Islamic art. Ancient jewellery such as the large golden earrings from Roman times are kept in the Jewel Hall. The oldest exhibits go back to 2000 BC. The North Room is reserved for exhibits from the time of the crusaders (12th–13th centuries).

North Gallery ►

One particularly interesting exhibit here is the reconstruction of a Hyksos tomb from Jericho from 1700/1600 BC. The collection features ceramic containers, tools and jewellery from the Iron Age, i.e. from 1200 BC. The Roman period is mainly represented by glassware, amphorae and ceramic figures, while outstanding glasses, metal door knockers and similar fittings, oil lamps and gold jewellery represent Byzantine times. The Northern Octagon exhibits Jewish objects, including a mosaic from the synagogue of Ein Gedi (www.english.imjnet.org.il, Sun, Mon, Wed, Thu 10am–3pm, Sat 10am–2pm).

Solomon's Quarries / Zedekiah's Cave

Before Damascus Gate, there is a park to the right. A gate at the base of the wall leads into what is known as Solomon's Quarries, a branching cave system that spreads below the Old Town. According to ancient tradition, this is where Solomon had the stones for his buildings quarried. Jews call this place **Zedekiah's Cave**, because Zedekiah, the last king of Judah, hid here from the Babylonian troops in 587 before being taken captive and dragged off to exile in Babylon (daily 9am–4pm, in summer until 5pm).

There is a small alley opposite Zedekiah's Cave. At the end of it is Jeremiah's Grotto. This is believed to be the prison where the prophet was incarcerated for predicting the fall of the city, which actually occurred in 587.

Jeremiah's Grotto

The Damascus Gate is not just one of the most beautiful entrances into the Old Town, but also one of the most lively. In front of the gate are collective taxis waiting to take passengers to Ramallah, Hebron and Bethlehem. Right next door there is a food and clothing market. The road leading from Jerusalem to Damascus via Nablus or Shechem (Sekem) starts at Damascus Gate. For that reason the Jews call this gate Sha'ar Shkhem (Shechem Gate), while the Arabs call it Bab al-Amud (Gate of the Column) after the column from where the **distance to Damascus** was measured. Projecting towers and battlements make this gate, constructed in 1537, the most elaborately designed of the city gates. Remains of the Third Wall, which was only completed shortly before Titus's destruction of Jerusalem, and parts of a Roman gate were discovered under the bridge in front of the gate.

✱ Damascus Gate

Leave Damascus Gate and walk a little way along Nablus Road (Derekh Shehkhem). The small Conrad Schick Street turns off to the right and leads to the Garden Tomb. This is a place of pilgrimage for some **Anglicans**, as a few believe it to be the tomb of Christ. This is because General George Gordon thought he had found Christ's tomb here in 1882; in the outline of the hill he saw a depiction of a skull (Golgotha = »place of a skull«). Gordon's theory was not tenable as the tomb dates back only to later Roman or Byzantine times. The entrance is located on the vertical wall of a low rocky elevation; the burial chamber leads off from a rectangular anteroom. The well-tended garden is also popular as a small green oasis of tranquillity in the Arab quarter of Jerusalem (Mon–Sat 8am–12.15pm, 2.30pm–5.15pm).

✱ Garden Tomb

St Stephen's Church is dedicated to the first Christian martyr and is now part of a Dominican priory. It possesses attractive floor mosaics that were part of an earlier church from the Byzantine period.

St Stephen's Church

Back on Nablus Street, continue northwards. The interesting Royal Tombs lie on the right-hand side. It is the largest burial complex of its kind in Jerusalem. Climb down wide steps in the rock – the channels in the rock wall guide the rain water into a cistern – and through a round arch in the rock, then left into a spacious courtyard. The entrance façade of the burial complex has been worked from the

Royal Tombs

rock. Walk through a vestibule and a low entrance to enter the tombs. In the past they could be closed off with a boulder (still there). There are several burial chambers over two floors leading off from a central room. The complex was acquired by a French Jew in 1874. After her death it became possession of the French state. The sarcophagi were taken to the Louvre.

The name Royal Tombs is based on the incorrect assumption that the kings of Judah were buried here. In fact Queen Helena of Adiabene, who converted to the Jewish faith and moved to Jerusalem in the 1st century AD, had the tombs built for herself and her family (Mon–Sat 8am–12.30pm, 2pm–5pm).

American Colony Hotel One of the most famous and magnificent places to stay in the city is the American Colony Hotel. Built by a wealthy Arab in 1860 as a city palace, it came into the hands of the rich American Anna Spafford in 1896 and she made it available to American and Swedish residents of the city. Selma Lagerlöf told the story in her novel *Jerusalem*. In 1902 the grandfather of Sir Peter Ustinov turned it into a guesthouse: Ingrid Bergman, Marc Chagall, Alec Guinness and of course Ustinov himself are just a few of illustrious names on the long guest list.

! **Baedeker TIP**

A small snack …

… in an ambience that is both stylish and cosy can be enjoyed in the garden restaurant of the American Colony Hotel. The interior courtyard is an idyllic place to rest.

Museum on the Seam The Museum on the Seam, at 4 Hel Handassa St, recalls the pre-1967 border between East and West Jerusalem. It is dedicated to dialogue, understanding and co-existence between different religions, cultures and forms of society. There are 90-minute interactive guided tours around this »Sociopolitical Museum of Contemporary Art«. In the context of an exhibition entitled »Heartquake«, 35 artists from all over the world address the theme of fear and trauma. Among the artists represented are Samuel Beckett, Bruce Nauman and Anselm Kiefer (only with advance booking, tel. 02 628 12 78, www.mots.org.il, Sun–Thu 10am–5pm, Fri 10am–2pm).

Mandelbaum Gate Take St George Street to get to Mandelbaum Gate, a busy intersection. Between 1948 and 1967 this was the only crossing between Israeli and Jordanian Jerusalem, and was reserved for pilgrims and tourists. There was never a gate here, just an opening between barbedwire entanglements. The name referred to the owner of a neighbouring house.

Mea Shearim To the northwest of Mandelbaum Gate is the Mea Shearim neighbourhood, founded in 1875 as the second Jewish settlement outside of the Old City. It is **home to ultra-orthodox Jews** with lots of synagogues, mikvehs (ritual baths), Talmud schools and the workshops of

Torah scribes. The men generally still wear the old eastern European style of clothes. They have payot (side curls), and wear a shtreimel (a fur-trimmed hat) and black clothes. Many women have shaven heads and go out with wigs and headscarves. The quarter is picturesque, but not exactly a tourist destination. It is by no means necessary to identify with the religious and secular beliefs of its residents, but visitors should respect the rules of the place and walk around with covered shoulders, arms and legs. It is not done to photograph people here, at the very least ask for permission first. Recently things have got so heated that even women »decently« clothed as requested had insults hurled at them. Tourist groups are definitely unwanted.

Those with a little time for a **detour** can stroll through the **Bukharan Quarter**, in which Jews from Uzbekistan still wear their traditional costumes, especially on feast days. Even further north are the Tombs of the Sanhedrin, rock tombs from the 1st century AD. The pediment above the entrance is adorned by a fine acanthus and pomegranate decoration. It is generally believed that until AD 70 the members of the Sanhedrin, the supreme council of Jews, were buried in this sizable complex. Synedrion is the Greek word for the highest council of judges under Herod the Great (until 37 BC). Although the Romans reserved the right to pass the death sentence for themselves, the Sanhedrin remained the highest religious legal council of the Jews (Sun–Fri 9am–4pm).

Tombs of the Sanhedrin

The Abyssinian or Ethiopian monastery was founded at the end of the 19th century. Its church, a round structure, is covered by a green dome; lion reliefs above the gate are reminders of the title »Lions of Judah«, held by the rulers of the Ethiopian dynasty, who believed themselves to be descended from the **Queen of Sheba**. They assumed that she had also been the Queen of Ethiopia and that Solomon had given her the crest with the lions of Judah during her visit to Jerusalem.

Ethiopian Church

The landmark of the Russian Quarter is the Russian Orthodox Holy Trinity Cathedral, recognizable by its green domes. The quarter was built in around 1860 as a large complex protected by a wall. Its purpose was to provide accommodation for Russian pilgrims, especially those coming to Jerusalem over the Easter period. The buildings on the northeast side served as the consulate and women's hospice. On the southwest side were the hospital, the mission house with rooms for the archimandrite (abbot), the priests and wealthy pilgrims and, on the other side of the cathedral, a large hostel for men. Today authorities such as the police department and courts are based here.
In ancient times there was a quarry at this site. A 12m/40ft column, which was either meant for the Herodian Temple or for a later Theodosian building, is evidence of this. It broke as it was being worked on and therefore remained unfinished. It lies, still connected to the rock, in a depression opposite the entrance to the cathedral.

Russian Quarter

Ticho House Situated in a beautiful garden, two blocks west of the Russian quarter, in the quiet HaRav Kook, is Ticho House, a branch of the Israel Museum **with works by the painter Anna Ticho** (1894–1980) and ancient Hanukkah candelabras from the collection of her husband, a renowned eye doctor. The museum café and restaurant has a garden ☉ terrace and is a wonderful spot for a midday snack (Sun–Thu 10am–5pm, Tue until 10pm, Fri 10am–2pm).

City Hall The extensive walk ends at the imposing, clean-lined city hall, in which Teddy Kollek (1911–2007) determined the destiny of the city for almost 30 years.

West of the Old City

Shopping Jaffa St. (Derekh Yafo) starts at Zahal Square (Kikar Zahal) and crosses the New Town in a northwesterly direction. Together with Ben Yehuda St. it is the **main shopping street** in West Jerusalem – a colourful mix of shops ranging from expensive to very cheap, cafés and restaurants, travel agencies, the main post office as well as banks, both on this road and the side streets. The street acquired new flair after becoming a pedestrian zone as a result of the tram line. The existing traffic chaos all around has only got dramatically worse.

Independence Park Independence Park (Gan Ha'atzmaut), an extensive park with old trees, starts at the end of King Solomon St. to the west of City Hall. According to legend, »a pious lion guarded the mortal remains of martyrs in the lion's cave«. Mamilla Pool, a former cistern, was part of ancient Jerusalem's water-supply system.

King George St. At Zarfat Square (Kirkat Zarfat) to the west of Independence Park, King George St. (Hamelech George) turns right. It is the address of several important buildings of modern Israel, such as the **Great Synagogue**, inaugurated in 1982, a magnificent building both inside and out. Its construction was surrounded by several controversies. Adjoining it is the **Israeli Rabbinate** (Heichal Shlomo), the country's highest religious authority, the seat of the Sephardi and Ashkenazi Chief Rabbis, who are responsible for matters of Jewish law. The front of the building is adorned by a depiction of the seven-armed candelabra (menorah). The building to the north houses the **Jewish Agency**, which was set up by Theodor Herzl in 1897. It also houses the Jewish National Fund (Keren Kayemet), whose task used to be purchasing land and whose job now consists of making this land available for the Jewish people, and the United Israel Appeal (Keren Hayesod). Even further north is Yeshurun Synagogue, behind which is Ratisbonne Monastery of the Fathers of Sion, which was founded in 1874.

Lincoln Street Now go back to Zarfat Square, follow Keren Hayesod St. in a southeasterly direction and then turn left into Lincoln St., which leads to

King David St. Two hotel buildings with history stand opposite each other here: on the right is the Young Men's Christian Association, constructed between 1928–1933 and easy to recognize by its 46m/151ft tower. It was designed by **Arthur Loomis Harmon**, the architect of the Empire State Building in New York. The floor in the atrium of the **YMCA** is decorated by a replica of the oldest map of Palestine from the 6th century. The **Seraphim relief** on the tower refers to a vision of the prophet Isaiah (Isaiah 6:2). Opposite the YMCA is the elegant **King David Hotel**, which opened in 1930 as the Grand Hotel Palestine, Jerusalem's luxury accommodation par excellence. Many kings and queens and elected heads of state resided here, such as Anwar Sadat in 1977 during the conclusion of the peace negotiations with Israel, and mourners at Yitzhak Rabin's funeral in 1995.

? DID YOU KNOW ...?

■ The headquarters of the British Army were housed in the King David Hotel, which is why the Jewish underground organization Irgun, under the direction of **Menachem Begin**, blew up part of the hotel in July 1946. This attack claimed several lives.

Herodian Tomb

Immediately to the south of the hotel is the tomb of Herod the Great's family. He had a monumental tomb built on the Herodium near Bethlehem for himself (► Bethlehem). His son Antipater, his wife Mariamne and her mother as well as other victims of his violent temper and paranoia were probably buried here. A narrow entrance gallery leads into the tomb. The boulder covering the entrance is still preserved. Until the Second World War the sarcophagi stood in their original position. When British forces stationed in the King David Hotel used the tomb as an air-raid bunker, the sarcophagi were taken to the Greek Orthodox Constantine monastery near the Church of the Holy Sepulchre.

Montefiore Windmill

On the left-hand side further south is Montefiore Windmill. It has a small museum dedicated to the life of the Jewish-English philanthropist Sir Moses Montefiore (1784–1885). Montefiore acquired the area near the windmill in the mid-19th century and built the first Jewish quarter there outside the Old Town walls (Mishkenot Sha'anim). At the same time the area to the east, Yemin Moshe, was also built up. It is home to many artists and also to several well-reputed galleries.

Bloomfield and Liberty Bell Garden

Anyone in search of an idyllic spot for relaxing will find just that along King David St.: Bloomfield Garden with the Lion Fountain to the left of the road and Liberty Bell Garden with a **replica of the American Liberty Bell** on the right-hand side.

Monastery of the Cross

The crusader-period monastery (Arabic: Deir el-Musalliba), an imposing fort-like building, rises up from the Valley of the Cross along

Sderot Hayim Hazaz. According to legend, **Lot** settled here after separating from his two daughters. Allegedly **Christ's cross** was made of the wood of the tree that he planted here, hence the name of the monastery. According to Greek Orthodox tradition, Helena, the mother of Emperor Constantine the Great, founded the monastery during her visit to Palestine. A different story tells that Constantine the Great made the land available to the first Christian king of Georgia, Mirian (d. 342), who built this monastery. The monastery remained in Georgian possession until the late 18th century. Then it was taken over by the Greek Orthodox patriarchate of Jerusalem, which still owns it today. The Georgian manuscripts are kept in the patriarchate's library.

The church tower is Baroque. The church itself goes back to the 12th century. A silver ring in the chancel marks the location of the tree of the Holy Cross. The interior painting depicts biblical motifs, Georgian kings and saints as well as one fresco of Shota Rustaveli, author of the Georgian national epic *The Knight in the Panther's Skin*, as a kneeling figure at the feet of Maximus the Confessor and John of Damascus.

Government Quarter and Israel Museum

★ ★
Israel Museum

The pavilions of the Israel Museum stand on top of a hill to the southwest of the city centre. This is the best-known and largest mu-

The Dead Sea Scrolls are kept in the Shrine of the Book

seum in the country. It brings together the »Shrine of the Book«, significant archaeological discoveries, Jewish art and Judaica, ancient and modern Israeli and international art and a sculpture garden. The most famous treasure of the Israel Museum is the **Dead Sea Scrolls**. Usually a replica is on display; but the other wings also house outstanding exhibits displayed in a careful but exciting manner.

◄ www.english. imjnet.org.il

The striking dome of the Shrine of the Book is meant to be reminiscent of the clay containers in which the famous **Dead Sea Scrolls** were found between 1947 and 1956. Next to it is an imposing black wall, symbolizing the Sons of Darkness, who are in conflict with the Sons of Light, embodied by the white dome. The scrolls are **the oldest manuscripts of the Old Testament** in Hebrew, Aramaic and Greek, dating back to between the 3rd century BC and the 1st century AD. The accompanying exhibition reveals how people lived during the time when the scrolls were written. In addition the museum exhibits the Aleppo Codex, a fragment of a Hebrew Bible manuscript from the early 10th century, as well as the Kokhba letters found by the Nahal River near Ein Gedi in 1960 and 1961.

✶ ✶
◄ Shrine of the Book

There is a model of ancient Jerusalem the way it was shortly before its destruction in AD 70 in the open-air complex below the Shrine of the Book. The city's original terrain profile has been accurately replicated on a scale of 1:50 over a 1000 sq m/1200 sq yd area. The model is based on biblical sources, the Mishna, the Talmud and the findings of modern archaeology.

✶
◄ Model of Jerusalem

Silver statuettes of Canaanite deities (1600–1200 BC) in the Israel Museum, found in Nahariya

Archaeological Collection ▶ The extensive archaeological collection exhibits discoveries from excavations since 1948. Discoveries made before 1948 are on display in the Rockefeller Museum. This collection includes a cast of a Canaanite goddess from Nahariya, a reconstruction of the citadel gate of Hazor, column capitals from Ramat Rachel, the inner sanctum of the temple of Arad and floor mosaics from synagogues. Two silver plates found in the Hinnom Valley, on which words from the Book of Numbers are engraved, have been dated back to the 6th century BC. The replica of an approx. 1700-year-old floor mosaic from a Roman villa in ▶Tzippori (the original is still in situ) is impressive.

Judaica ▶ One of the most interesting departments exhibits Jewish sacred art and objects from everyday Jewish life. Many of the exhibits date **from the diaspora** and show stylistic influences from the various countries in which the Jews sought refuge. The outstanding presentation and the artistic quality of the objects on display – Torah scrolls, Hanukkah candelabras, manuscripts, table objects from a synagogue, a Sabbath tablecloth, traditional clothes and ceremonial dress from Morocco, Yemen, Bukhara and other diaspora areas, wedding jewellery and a lot more – give an in-depth picture of Judaism's religious customs. Among the highlights are the Ark of the Covenant from the old synagogue of Cairo and the gates of the Maimonides Synagogue in Cairo (11th century), as well as the sculptures from the first synagogue from Tiberias dating from the 2nd and 3rd centuries. The museum also possesses the complete interior of a 17th-century synagogue from the northern Italian town of Vittorio Veneto, for which a room was especially built so that it could be set up in the way it was originally laid out.

> **ℹ Israel Museum**
>
> - Bus: nos. 9, 17, 24, 24a, 31, 32 and 99
> - Open: Sat, Sun, Mon, Wed, Thu, holidays 10am–5pm, Tue 4pm–9pm, Fri and before holidays 10am–2pm; closed on Rosh Hashana, Yom Kippur and on the eve of Yom Kippur
> - Information: tel. (02) 670 88 11; www.imj.org.il.

Old masters ▶ A further department is reserved for art from the 15th to 19th centuries. Although the museum cannot compete with other major museums in this field, it does possess some worthwhile pieces, such as works by Flemish and Dutch masters from the 17th century. Other noteworthy features include the Rothschild Hall, a grand salon in the style of Louis XV, which was acquired by Baron Rothschild in 1887, as well as the Italian Pavilion with Venetian furniture and an English dining room from the 18th century.

20th-century art ▶ The collections of modern and contemporary painting, sculpture, photography, graphic works and drawings feature artists such as Klee, Dali, Picasso and Chagall as well as Israeli artists such as Agam, Arikha, Aroch, Dagan, Engelsberg, Kupferman, Paldi, Rubin and Zaritsky.

Israel Museum's Youth Wing ▶ The Youth Wing shows exhibitions designed specifically for children and young people. The focus here lies on interactive forms of presentation.

The Art Garden was created on the slopes of Neveh Sha'anan, based on a design by the American sculptor Isamo Noguchi. The sculptures on display are largely modern works, by artists such as Magdalena Abakanowicz, Henry Moore, Pablo Picasso, Jean Tinguely and Menashe Kadishmani.

◄ Art Garden

The Bible Lands Museum is right next to the Israel Museum. It was founded by historian Elie Borowski (1913–2003) from Poland and his wife Batya. In spite of its name, this museum is less about biblical history and more about the cultures of the Middle East in biblical times. As a result, the exhibits range from a 7000-year-old figurine from the Mesopotamian Tell Halaf to mosaics from the Roman province of Syria from the 4th century AD (25 Granot St.; Sun–Tue, Thu 9.30am–5.30pm, Wed until 9.30pm, Fri 9.30am–2.30pm, Sat 10am–3pm, closed holidays, guided tours in English daily 10.30am and Wed 5.30pm, www.blmj.org).

★
Bible Lands Museum

> ! **Baedeker TIP**
>
> **Music, wine and cheese**
> The Bible Lands Museum is known not just for its exhibitions, but also for its concerts on Saturday nights. The musical spectrum ranges from Jacques Brel chansons with a Yiddish flair to Irish folk music (reservations no later than Friday under tel. 02/561 10 66 are strongly recommended).

Around 200m/200yd to the north of the Israel Museum, on Eli'ezer Kaplan Street, which turns off from Ruppin Blvd, is the **Knesset**, a design that goes back to Josef Klarwein. The Israeli parliament is the most striking building in the government district of Hakirya. The menorah near the entrance, a 5m/16ft seven-armed candelabra, a **gift from the British Labour Party**, designed by Benno Elkan and cast in bronze, is a symbol of the state of Israel. The 29 reliefs depict figures and events from Jewish history. The Knesset was inaugurated in 1966; various mosaics and tapestries are by **Marc Chagall**. Guided tours: Sun and Thu 8.30am–3.30pm, after advance booking under tel. (02) 675 34 20 or 675 34 16. Visitor gallery: Mon and Tue from 4pm, Wed from 11am; groups after prior booking, individual visitors are let in directly (do not forget to bring your passport!).

◄ Visiting the Knesset

To the west of Ruppin Blvd is the Hebrew University. The administrative building to the right of the entrance has a worthwhile 5th–6th century mosaic from Jezreel Plain. At the heart of the compound is the Jewish National and University Library; the white dome of the synagogue named after the New York Rabbi **Israel Goldstein** can be seen in the southern section.

Hebrew University

★ **Mount Herzl and Yad Vashem**

Heading out of town, Ruppin Blvd intersects with Herzl Blvd (Sderot Herzl). Take it to get to the military cemetery and to Mount Herzl,

Mount Herzl

A PLACE OF REMEMBRANCE

✳✳ Yad Vashem, the central Israeli place of remembrance and research institution for the Holocaust, was largely built by the Israeli-American architect Moshe Safdie. The heart of the complex is the Holocaust History Museum in the shape of a 180m/200yd shaft or skewer running into the mountain. The majority of the exhibition is therefore below ground in the Mount of Remembrance.

🕐 Open:
Sun–Wed, 9am–5pm, Thu until 8pm, Fri on days before holidays until 2pm

① **Visitor Centre**
Information, ticket office, café

② **Garden of the Righteous among Nations**
Every tree in this garden stands for a non-Jew who risked his or her life to save Jews from the Holocaust.

③ **Children's Memorial**
Place of remembrance for the approx. 1.5 million murdered Jewish children. Their names are continuously read out.

④ **Pillar of Heroism**
This memorial, built in the style of the crematorium chimneys, commemorates the Jewish resistance.

⑤ **Janusz Korzcak Square**
Memorial for the doctor and orphanage director Janusz Korzcak (Henryk Goldschmidt), who accompanied the children of his orphanage to Treblinka Concentration Camp in 1942, even though he could have saved himself.

⑥ **Hall of Names**
The dome is filled with photographs and documents of 600 Jews who were killed. Their portraits are reflected in a pool of water.

⑦ **Viewpoint**
The view of Jerusalem is meant as a symbol of hope.

⑧ **Holocaust Art Museum**
Most of the exhibits were made during the time of the Holocaust

⑨ **Square of Hope**

⑩ **Synagogue**
The objects on display in this modern building have come from destroyed European synagogues.

⑪ **Monument to Jewish Soldiers and Partisans**
A memorial in remembrance of the Jewish soldiers and resistance fighters in the Allied armies and all Jewish partisans who operated in occupied Europe.

⑫ **Swedish Ambulance**
One of the 36 Swedish Red Cross buses with which around 25,000 concentration camp prisoners were taken out of Germany after the intervention of the Swede Count Folke Bernadotte in March and April 1945.

In the Hall of Names

Cattle
were tr
valley.
taken t
this un
was pl

which is dedicated to the **founder of Zionism, Theodor Herzl** (▶Famous People). His mortal remains were brought to Jerusalem on the first El Al flight in 1949., as Herzl had requested in his will. They were buried on Mount Herzl, the highest point of the city (889m/2617ft), in a simple tomb made of dark granite. The park is also home to the tombs of the Herzl family and the prime ministers Levi Eshkol, Golda Meir and Yitzhak Rabin.

▶ Herzl Museum

The Herzl Museum, which re-opened in 2005 with a new design, presents the short life of this visionary with the help of a film and four exhibition rooms that orient themselves on Herzl's living and working places. The tour ends in Herzl's Viennese study, featuring the original furniture (Sun–Wed 8.45am–6pm, Thu 8.45am–8pm, Fri 8.45am–12.15pm, Tel. 02 632 15 15, Sun–Wed 8.45am–6pm, Thu 8.45am – 8pm, Fri 8.45am – 12.15pm, www.herzl.org.il, advance booking essential).

✶ ✶
Yad Vashem

Go from Mount Herzl to the Mount of Remembrance (Har Hazikaron) on which the Yad Vashem memorial site was constructed in 1957. Yad Vashem is a harrowing **memorial to the Jews who were murdered by the Nazis**. In addition it contains an extensive archive with documents about the Holocaust. The site's Hebrew name, »a memorial and a name«, refers to the prophet Isaiah (Isaiah 56:4–5): »For this is what the Lord says: ... to them I will give in my temple and within my walls a memorial and a name ... I will give them an everlasting name that will not be cut off.« The expansive complex contains several memorial sites; the most important are described below.

i Yad Vashem

- Holocaust History Museum: Sun–Wed 9am–5pm, Thu until 8pm, Fri and before holidays until 2pm, ticket office closes one hour earlier.
- Children under the age of ten are not permitted in the museum.

▶ Symbol of Yad Vashem

The **six-armed candelabra** at the entrance to the administrative building is the symbol of Yad Vashem. Its six arms stand for the approximately six million Jews who fell victim to the Nazi genocide.

▶ Garden of the Righteous Among Nations

Beyond the visitor centre the path leads through the Garden of the Righteous Among Nations. It is dedicated to non-Jews who risked their own lives to save the lives of Jews. Israel awards them the honorary title »righteous among nations« and they are given the right to plant a carob tree marked with their name. Well known »righteous among nations« include Raoul Wallenberg and Oskar Schindler.

▶ Holocaust History Museum

Beyond the garden lies the re-designed Holocaust History Museum, which illustrates the suffering and martyrdom of the Jews during the Third Reich by exhibiting personal items, photographs and written documents that put the individuals in the foreground.

At the end of the Holocaust History Museum visitors can look out over Jerusalem.

Once in the museum, visitors first have to make their way around a mountain of books that were written by Jewish authors and burned in Nazi Germany. Further on, visitors find themselves on the original paving of the Warsaw Ghetto, in front of a cattle truck of the wartime German railway, used to transport Jews to the concentration and extermination camps. The exhibit features the trolleys used by forced labourers in the quarries and an accommodation hut from Auschwitz; Zyklon B canisters are piled up, and the glasses, shoes, tooth brushes and diaries seem to have only just been placed there.

The end of the Holocaust History Museum is marked by the Hall of ◀ Hall of Names
Names. This is where the names of the approximately six million victims of the Holocaust are recorded and kept. »**Pages of Testimony**«, short biographical notes, have already been made of around two million people. The missing names are still being compiled today. At the end of the tour the view opens up across the city of Jerusalem.

The Holocaust Art Museum, which has also been re-designed, pos- ◀ Holocaust Art
sesses around 10,000 artworks that were created by concentration Museum
camp prisoners, survivors and artists working on the Shoah.

Next to the Exhibition Pavilion with its changing exhibitions is the ◀ Learning/Visual
Learning Center. It has computer terminals and audio material, al- Center
lowing visitors to pursue their own questions, listen to stories by
Holocaust survivors and to confront comments made about the
events. The Visual Center shows documentaries.

The synagogue contains objects from synagogues that were plun- ◀ Synagogue
dered and destroyed during the Nazi terror, but also serves as a place
of prayer and is used for religious ceremonies.

Hall of Remembrance ► The Hall of Remembrance is a windowless room made of concrete and large boulders. The names of concentration and extermination camps are written on the floor in Hebrew and Roman letters. An **Eternal Flame** burns in remembrance and also as a warning.

Children's Memorial ► One harrowing memorial is the Children's Memorial, created in 1987. The flames of five candles are reflected countless times in the glass walls in the dark underground room. Every flame is a symbol of the soul of one of the 1.5 million children that fell victim to the Holocaust. A woman's voice recites their names, age and place of birth. It was donated by Abe and Edita Spiegel, whose son Uziel was murdered in Auschwitz when he was two and a half.

Janusz Korczak Square ► The Polish Jewish doctor, author and educationist Henrik Gold-schmidt, better known as Janusz Korczak, has a remarkable sculpture dedicated to him. He ran an orphanage in the Warsaw Ghetto. At the beginning of August 1942 he voluntarily went to the Treblinka exter-mination camp with around 200 children.

Valley of the Community ► The monument on the western slope consists of roughly worked layers of stones between which stone slabs have been engraved with the names of more than 5000 Jewish congregations, communities that were erased by the Nazis and their collaborators.

Cattle Car Memorial ► The Cattle Car Memorial is incredibly expressive: a railway track goes out beyond the slope and at the end of it stands one of the **German railways cattle trucks** in which the Jews were transported to the concentration and extermination camps. The truck, which ap-pears to float above the abyss, not only symbolizes the trip to the hell of destruction, but – pointing towards Jerusalem – also the Jewish hope of a life in their country.

Western Suburbs of Jerusalem

Ein Karem The village approx. 4km/2.5mi to the west and once inhabited by Arabs is, according to Christian tradition, the place where Zechariah and Elizabeth lived, where Mary visited her pregnant cousin Eliza-beth, an event known as the **Visitation** (Luke 1:39–56), and where Elizabeth's son, **John the Baptist**, was born (Luke 1:57–66).

St John's Priory ► A road turns off from the main road and leads to the Franciscan Pri-ory of St John the Baptist. The church was built in the 17th century above John's birth grotto. There is a 5th or 6th-century mosaic near the entrance with peacocks and doves. The Greek inscription reads »Hail martyrs of the Lord«. A marble slab in the crypt also has an in-scription reading: »Hic Praecursor Domini natus est« (The forerun-ner of the Lord was born here). Reliefs commemorate events from the life of John the Baptist.

Mary's Spring ► The spring in the middle of Ein Karem has been called Mary's Spring since the time of the crusaders. The mosque of the Arab population that left the town in 1948 still stands next to it. Stone steps lead up to the Franciscan Visitatio Mariae Church (Church of the Visitation), which stands on the site of the house where Mary is said to have visited Elizabeth. The modern two-storey building with a mosaic of the Visitation on the front was built on the ruins of a crusader church.

This is particularly interesting for anyone who likes the Jewish painter Chagall, because the artist created twelve wonderful glass windows symbolizing the tribes of Israel in the synagogue of the Hebrew University's medical centre. To get there, take the road that leaves Ein Karem in a northwesterly direction towards Eitanim. Turn left after 2km/1.25mi.

Medical centre

◀ Chagall windows

The Tisch Family Zoological Gardens in the district of Manhat is, on the one hand, a nice zoo like many others, and at the same time it specifically breeds animals mentioned in the Bible as well as animals at risk of extinction, such as sand cats, Persian fallow deer, Asian lions, Kleinmann's tortoises and birds of prey (bus lines 26, 33 and 99; daily from 9am; www.jerusalemzoo.org.il).

Tisch Family Zoological Gardens

🕐

Around Jerusalem

The **tomb of the prophet Samuel** has been venerated in the Arab village of Nabi Samwil (Nabi Samuil) in the West Bank. In 1948 Nabi Samwil was an Arab base during the Arab-Jewish fighting. Since 1967 Jewish pilgrims have started visiting this site again.
The crusaders called the 885m/2904ft hill near the village »Mons Gaudii« (Mount of Joy) because from here they were able to glimpse Jerusalem for the first time. In the 12th century (like Emperor Justinian in the 6th century) they built a highly visible church here, which was later turned into a mosque. It houses a cenotaph for Samuel, the prophet and last judge of Israel; the actual tomb of Samuel, who probably lived in the 11th century BC, is in a cave under the mosque.

Nabi Samwil

The village of Al-Qubeiba lies to the northwest of Jerusalem. Some believe it to be the biblical **Emmaus**, where the risen Christ appeared to two disciples (Luke 24:13–15). In 1901 the Franciscans built a church on the site of the crusader church.

Al-Qubeiba

The village of Al-Azarieh (Bethany) is located on the eastern slopes of the Mount of Olives. According to biblical tradition the **raising of Lazarus** took place here (John 11:11–45). The village with the house of Mary and Martha is mentioned again in the story of the Passion: Jesus rode on a donkey from here to Jerusalem across the Mount of Olives. In the 4th century a chapel was built above the burial cave attributed to Lazarus. In the 12th century the crusaders restored the derelict chapel and built a monastery in memory of the house of Mary and Martha. Muslims later built a mosque above the tomb.
The Franciscans erected the new Church of Lazarus in 1953 next to remains from the Byzantine and crusader times on land acquired in

Al-Azarieh

◀ Church of Lazarus

1858 immediately below the tomb. The church has the ground plan of a Greek cross and takes the form of a domed mausoleum. The Latin inscription in the interior consists of Christ's words uttered in Bethany according to the gospel of John: »… he that believeth in me, though he were dead, yet shall he live, And whosoever liveth and believeth in me shall never die.« (John 11:25–26).

Bethlehem ►p. 197

Latrun

F 4

Area: Ajalon Valley, between Jerusalem and Tel Aviv

The monastery, built by French Trappists in 1927, is picturesquely situated amid fruit plantations and vineyards and is known for its wine.

What to See in and around Latrun

Monastery The only parts of the monastery open to the public are the church and the attractive monastic garden with its collection of late Antique and early Christian capitals and reliefs. The wine produced by the monks of Latrun is famous and can also be purchased here. The liqueurs and spirits, the honey and the olives as well as the olive oil from the monks' own production are also worth trying.

The ruin of the 12th-century **crusader castle Toron des Chevaliers** can be found on the hill behind the monastery. The Arabs turned this name into al-Torun/Latrun – Christian pilgrims of the late Middle Ages therefore took this to have been the home of the »good thief« (Latin latro = thief) who was crucified with Jesus and confirmed his faith, whereupon Jesus promised him paradise (Luke 23:40–43).

> ! **Baedeker TIP**
>
> ### Israel in miniature
>
> The Mini Israel Park near Latrun exhibits more than 350 models of Israeli buildings, excavation sites and landscapes on a scale of 1:25 over an area of 4.5ha/11 acres: entertainment for young and old alike (wheelchair-accessible, restaurants and a souvenir shop; tel. 08/913 00 10; Sun–Thu 10am–6pm, Fri 10am–2pm, Sat 10am–6pm, www.minisrael.co.il).

Imwas / Emmaus The ruins of the Arab village of Imwas, whose name comes from Emmaus, lies on road 3 to Ramallah. **Emmaus** is the Greek name of several places in Palestine. This town had a Roman village with mosaic floors from the 2nd century, a synagogue with Hebrew and Greek inscriptions from the 3rd century as well as two Byzantine churches from the 4th and 6th centuries. Imwas is in competition with Qubeiba to the northwest of Jerusalem for the honour of being the biblical Emmaus, where the risen Christ appeared to two men (Luke 24:13–15).

A little further to the north is the entrance to the Canada Park nature reserve. The inhabitants of the three Palestinian villages that once existed here were driven out during the Six-Day War and their homes were pulled down. A few years later Canadian Jews helped set up this park, which is why it is called Canada Park. There are several ancient ruins along the road through the park, a Roman reservoir, an ancient burial cave and a 13th-century sheikh's tomb. A small waterway, shady trees and picnic sites make this a great place to take a break in the countryside. **Canada Park**

✱ Makhtesh Ramon (Mitzpe Ramon)

E 6

District: Southern   **Altitude:** 500–840m/1640–2755ft

The sight of this crater landscape from the viewing terrace in Mitzpe Ramon is like looking at a lunar landscape. This place is definitely one of Israel's most breathtaking natural attractions.

With a length of around 35km/22mi and a width of 10km/6mi, Makhtesh Ramon, which lies in two nature reserves, is the largest subsidence crater in the world. There are two other makhtesh craters like this in the Negev, but they are smaller: Makhtesh Hagadol and Makhtesh Haqatan (►Mamshit, around).
Even though the appearance of Makhtesh Ramon is reminiscent of a volcanic crater, that is not what this is. This 300m/1000ft-deep depression formed around 70 million years ago as a result of erosion and the ground caving in above hollow spaces. **Plant fossils and dinosaur bones** 150 million years old were found at the bottom of the crater. Har Ramon rises up to 1035m/3396ft on the western edge and Har Ored (935m/3068ft) rises in the south. Ruins of fortifications have survived in the southern part of Makhtesh Ramon, including those of Mezad Mishhor, which was built by the Nabataeans at around the time of the birth of Christ in order to secure the caravan route from their capital Petra to Avdat. **World's largest pothole**

The otherwise not very attractive little town of Mitzpe Ramon lies right on the edge of the crater, on the road from Beersheba to Eilat. Right beyond Mitzpe Ramon the through-road winds its way down to the base of the crater – a spectacular drive full of wonderful impressions. Those who wish to take some time enjoying the views of the crater can walk along its edge on panoramic trails to the south **Mitzpe Ramon**

Visitors seem tiny as they stand by the world's largest crater, Makhtesh Ramon.

and north of the road. The crater is lined by imposing rocky hills: Har Marpek, Har Katom and Har Ramon in the south, and Har Ardon in the north-east. Givat Ga'ash in the north is an extinct volcano whose lava has hardened into basalt formations. The magnificent landscape is a rambler's paradise. The Albert Promenade is easy; it starts at the visitor centre and leads along the edge of the crater to bizarre stone formations. The trail to the Carpenter's Workshop (Ha-Minsara) is regarded as moderately difficult. It takes about three hours, and leads through spectacular desert landscape; the Carpenter's Workshop is a rock formation called thus from its wood-like appearance. One of the best hikes is quite demanding: the Nahal Gewanim Trail, leading to spectacular rock formations (five to six hours there and back)

Visitor centre ▶ The modern visitor centre in Mitzpe Ramon, towering above the edge of the crater close to the end of town, provides more detailed information about the landscape, how it was formed, and the flora and fauna of the crater. Visitors get lots of useful and interesting information here, such as about hiking trials and other ways of exploring the natural spectacle. However, the entrance fee is relatively steep. The visitor centre also has a model of the crater. The **panoramic view** of the crater from the viewing terrace is priceless! Sun–Thu 9am–4.30pm, Fri until 4pm).

★★ Mamshit

F 5

District: Southern   **Altitude:** 470m/1540ft

Mamshit is the northernmost of the Nabataean towns in the Negev. Since it underwent few changes during the Byzantine period, the original character of the settlement is much more visible here than in other Nabataean excavation sites.

Mamshit (Mampsis; Arabic: Kurnub) is one of a number of towns founded by the Nabataeans, a semi-nomadic Arab people that settled in southern Jordan from around the 5th century onwards. The Nabataeans secured the route from their capital Petra (in modern Jordan) to the Mediterranean with this »outpost« in the Negev. In the 1st century AD Mamshit was a flourishing trading town with a caravanserai, stables, residential and administrative buildings. When the extensive trading that was the basis of Mamshit's wealth declined because of the Roman invasion, the population switched to an equally lucrative business: breeding noble Arabian horses.

Nabataean town in the Negev

?   DID YOU KNOW ...?

■ One of the most mysterious places in Israel is located 12km/7mi to the southeast of the small town of Dimona, the starting point for visiting Mamshit: the Negev Nuclear Research Center. Many believe that Israel makes its nuclear weapons here, which the government neither confirms nor denies.

The Romans built barracks and baths here. Two churches were built in Byzantine times, in which Mamshit, being a border town, was able to rely on the support of the central government. After the Arab conquest, the town went into decline.

◄ ✳ Excavation Site

The extensive ruins, now protected as a national park, are situated conspicuously on a hill 8km/5mi to the southeast of the town of Dimona, on Route 25 from Beersheba to the Wadi Arava. Enter the compound through the north gate in the 900m/1000yd-long Roman town wall (3rd–4th century) and walk on ancient roads past apart-

⊙ Opening hours: April–Sept daily 8am–5pm, otherwise until 4pm

Mamshit Map

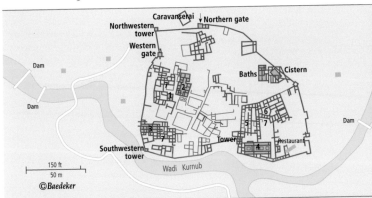

Caravanserai ↓ Northern gate
Northwestern tower
Western gate
Dam
Dam
Baths — Cistern
Tower
Restaurant
Southwestern tower
Wadi Kurnub
Dam

150 ft
50 m
©Baedeker

1 Tower	**3** Western	**4** Eastern Church	**6** House with Frescoes
2 Palace	Nile Church	**5** Market	**7** Residential buildings

ment blocks to a generously sized building, a **palace**, with a courtyard around which rooms of different sizes are located. This was probably the residence of the town governor in the late Nabataean time. Here and for some of the residential buildings, the stone arches that supported the ceilings have been reconstructed. The Nabataeans were sparing with their ornamentation.

Western Church

The 5m/16ft late Nabataean **tower** (late 1st century AD), which had three storeys originally, has excellent views of the excavation site.
Continue straight on to get to the western church by the town wall, a columned basilica. It was built by **Saint Nilus** of Sinai (around 400). An inscription in the nave's mosaic floor commemorates him: »Lord, help your servant Nilus, the builder of this church. Amen.« In addition to this mosaic and the columns, the eastern apses and parts of the marble rood screen, which separates the chancel from the nave, are extant. A small cistern was located below the atrium.

Eastern Church

The Eastern Church, once the town's episcopal church, stands immediately in front of the remains of a police station from the time of the British Mandate, which has been converted into a restaurant with a terrace. It was part of a Byzantine monastic complex. This church is also a columned basilica. Its atrium enclosed a spacious cistern. The mosaic floor from around 400 AD survives in the nave, while a martyr's tomb can be seen in the right apse.

Market

Below the eastern church, accessible via a wide flight of steps, there are three parallel rows with small shops: the town's former market, which was used until Byzantine times. A little to the east of the shops is the largest residential building of the Nabataean town discovered so far. It has a courtyard and stables. The remains of a **fresco** can still be seen in the vaulted ceiling of one of the rooms.
The way back to the north gate leads past the remains of the walls of a **Roman bathhouse**. It had a caldarium, tepidarium and frigidarium. The water for the baths came from the neighbouring cistern, originally covered, which measures 10 x 18m/11 x 20yd.

Nabataean water management

It does not rain a lot in the Negev, but when it does, the rain tends to be torrential and the dry wadis are temporarily turned into raging torrents. This precious water had to be secured. For that reason the Nabataeans built dams (now restored) in the Wadi Kurnub. These dams formed reservoirs in which around 10,000 cubic metres (350,000 cubic feet) of water could be stored. The water was then brought the covered cisterns in clay containers.

Around Mamshit

In addition to ► Makhtesh Ramon there are two further **makhtesh craters** in the Negev: Makhtesh Hagadol (the Big Crater) south of Mamshit and Makhtesh Hakatan (the Small Crater), which extends to the southeast of the Nabataean town. Both of these craters are smaller and less spectacular than Makhtesh Ramon, but they are also more untouched.

Makhtesh
Hagadol,
Makhtesh
Hakatan

Leave Mamshit and drive 4km/2.5mi on Route 25 towards the Arava Valley and then turn on to the southbound Route 206. After 12km/7mi Route 225 turns right towards Yeroham, which leads through the Makhtesh Hagadol. The drive to Makhtesh Hakatan is scenically more attractive. After just 9km/5.5mi on the southbound 206, turn left onto the 227 towards Ma'ale Akrabim. After around 10km/6mi the viewpoint for Makhtesh Hakatan is signposted. The car park lies around 2km/1.25mi to the north of the road; from there it is another half hour to the edge of the crater. The views are ample reward however. At its southeastern side the crater opens up in a deep gorge towards the Zin Desert.

After a further 4km/2.5mi on the 227, the road reaches Ma'ale Akrabim, the Scorpion Pass. The road, which was built under British rule, makes its way steeply down 450m/1476ft into the Zin Desert and then to Hazeva, which lies 137m/450ft below sea level. Here the road meets Route 90 from Eilat to the Dead Sea.

✴ Mar Saba · Mar Saba Monastery

F 4

Area: West Bank
(Palestinian territory)

Altitude: 240m/785ft

The long-established Greek Orthodox monastery of Saint Sabbas (Mar Saba), which is still inhabited by a small community of monks, lies in impressive scenery in the middle of the bare Judaean mountains, just 18km/11mi outside ►Bethlehem.

The Mar Saba Monastery can be reached both from ►Jerusalem and ►Bethlehem on road 398. At Ubeidiya the road turns off to the east. Then it is another 7km/4mi to the monastery. Since Mar Saba is in Palestinian territory, it is best to inquire about the current situation before going or to go with an organized tour.

Approach

Monastery founded under Sabbas

There are countless caves in the near-vertical rock faces in the **Kidron Valley** to the west of Mar Saba, in which hermits settled in the first centuries AD. One of them was the young Sabbas from Cappadocia. He joined a monastery in Jerusalem in 457, then withdrew in 478 to the solitude of the Kidron Valley. Soon further hermits gathered around him and in 492 he founded a monastery on the hillside opposite his first cave. Sabbas enjoyed a high reputation as a theologian, not just in Palestine but also in Constantinople.

John of Damascus

The monastery founded by Sabbas was first destroyed by the Persians in the 7th century, then a little later by the Arabs. In 712 a man withdrew to the abandoned monastery who had no less effect on the world of eastern Christianity than the founder Sabbas: John of Damascus(Iohannes Damascenus). Born in 650, the son of a distinguished Arab Christian family, he achieved high honours at the court of the Umayyad dynasty in Damascus and was the representative of the caliph's Christian subjects. At the age of about 60 he left Damascus and became a monk in Mar Saba. When the Iconoclastic movement began in 726, John of Damascus became the best-known defender of icon worship, which he justified theologically in three famous speeches against the Iconoclasts. When John of Damascus died in around 750 aged 104, he was believed to be the greatest theologian of his time.

Mar Saba and Surroundings

Women's Tower

Only men have access to the monastery. Women are, however, allowed to go to a hill where a tower stands in which female visitors used to be housed. This tower, which contains a chapel and a dormitory, has lovely views of the monastery with its domes, courtyards and buildings arranged above each other on the hillside.

✳
Monastery compound

Enter the monastery compound through a small portal and head into the courtyard down a narrow flight of stairs. There is a small domed building at the centre of this courtyard, in which the mortal remains of the monastery's founder, Sabbas, were kept between 532 and the time of the crusaders. The crusaders took them to Venice. When the Russians rebuilt the monastery in 1838, they took the saint's remains to Moscow. As part of the reconciliation between Rome and the Orthodox Church, Pope Paul VI gave the relics of Saint Sabbas to the monastery in 1965, where they were once again buried in the main church.

The cross-in-square church is richly painted and ornamented with icons, it does not, however, receive much daylight. The interior, which is otherwise only lit by candlelight, lies in a dim half-light. Heavy chandeliers hang from the ceiling. Visitors are led into a chapel that adjoins the cave of Saint Sabbas. As in St George's Monastery in ► Wadi Qelt, the skulls of the monks who were killed by the Persians in 614 are kept here.

Only men are allowed to access the Mar Saba monastery – women may enter the tower at the top left.

The road from Bethlehem to Mar Saba goes right past the Monastery of St Theodosius (after 12km/7.5mi via Beit Sahour), which was founded in 476 by Saint Theodosius from Cappadocia in Asia Minor. During the monastery's heyday it was home to 400 monks. Like Mar Saba and St George's Monastery in ▶Wadi Qelt, it was destroyed by the Persians in 614, while they spared the Church of the Nativity. Greek Orthodox monks rebuilt the monastery in around 1900.

Monastery of St Theodosius

✷ **Masada · Metzada**

F 5

District: Southern (Dead Sea)

Altitude: 60m/197ft
(434m/1424ft above the level of the Dead Sea)

Herod's huge fort, which is one of the most impressive and most visited excavation sites in the country and has been a UNESCO World Heritage Site since 2001, towers on a high mountain plateau within sight of the Dead Sea.

▶ VISITING MASADA

INFORMATION

Masada National Park
Tel. (08) 658 42 07
www.parks.org.il
Open: Apr–Sep
Sat–Thu 8am–5pm, Fri until 4pm;
Oct–March Sat–Thu until 4pm, Fri
until 3pm

GETTING THERE

Turn off from coast road no. 90 on
the Dead Sea about halfway between
▶Ein Bokek and ▶Ein Gedi; from
▶Beersheba via ▶Arad (signposted:
Metzada).
Get to the top (from the eastern side)
via the cable car (daily except Fri
8am–4pm) or on foot on the »Snake
Route« (strenuous, approx. 1 hr).

Herod's fortress
The fact that the Romans were only able to conquer this fortress three years after the fall of Jerusalem in AD 70, and that the remaining rebels escaped Roman captivity by committing mass suicide, caused Masada (Metzada) to become a symbol of modern Israel, demonstrating the desire of the Jewish people and the state of Israel, which have always been threatened from many different sides, to assert themselves and to demonstrate resistance. The slogan **»Masada must never fall again«**, with which army recruits were sworn in at Masada, is founded in this legend.

? DID YOU KNOW ...?

■ ... that 800m/900yd cable car, built in 1971, is the lowest-lying cable car in the world? The upper station near the excavation site on the rock plateau lies at around 10m/30ft below sea level.

Architectural history
A small fortified complex already existed on Masada, which **Herod the Great** then extended between 37 and 31 BC. It possessed all the creature comforts of a residence, but also the strength of a fortified refuge. During the troubles that took place in 40 BC, when the Parthians supported the Hasmonaean Antigonus, Herod brought his family and his fiancée Mariamne to safety here. This happened again when Octavian defeated Mark Antony and Cleopatra, the rulers of the east until then, at Actium in 31 BC; Herod went to Rhodes in order to swear allegiance to the new ruler of Rome.

Masada during the Great Revolt
In AD 66, even before the start of the revolt, a group of Zealots ensconced themselves on Masada, led by **Menahem ben Judah**. These Zealots were members of the radical party that had left Jerusalem during serious conflicts within the Jewish community. These confrontations soon led to Menahem being murdered in Jerusalem. When the Great Revolt broke out, his nephew, **Eleazar ben Ya'ir**, took charge. Even after the fall of Jerusalem in AD 70, the rebels on

Masada Plan

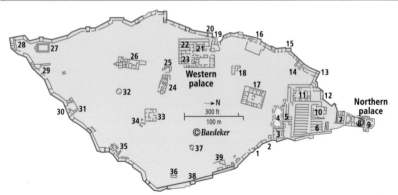

1	Eastern gate (Snake Path gate)	10	Baths	21	Administrative wing of the western palace
2	Casemate walls	11	Administrative buildings	22	Storehouse
3	Buildings	12	Northern gate (Water gate)	23	Royal rooms of the western palace
4	Quarry	13	Tower	24	Small palace
5	Villa with frescoes	14	Synagogue	25	Ritual bath
6	Warehouse	15	Casemate walls	26	Small palace
7	Upper terrace of the northern palace	16	Tower	27	Cistern, pool
8	Central terrace of the northern palace	17	Byzantine building	28	Southern bastion
9	Lower terrace of the northern palace	18	5th-century church	29	Underground cistern
		19	Western gate	30	Southern gate (cistern gate)
		20	Tower		

31	Ritual bath
32	Columbarium
33	Small palace
34	Byzantine-era residential buildings
35	Homes of the zealots
36	Cistern
37	Byzantine-era residential building
38	Tower
39	Homes of the zealots

Masada did not give up. The fortress was still home to 967 men, women and children.

Two years later the Romans decided to end this last resistance with a siege. Their commander, **Flavius Silvus**, constructed a 4500m/ 5000yd wall around Masada, behind which he set up eight camps. The main camp was on the western side and a ramp was built in order to get battering rams and other siege machinery to the walls of the fortress. After eight months the Romans broke through the western wall.

In light of this hopeless situation, Eleazar gave a now famous speech to his comrades in arms, in which he proclaimed that it was better to die than to be taken captive. They burned their possessions except for their food supplies, in order to demonstrate to the Romans that it was not hunger that had forced

! *Baedeker* TIP

Quenching your thirst …

… becomes an expensive business if you buy drinks at the cable car station at the foot of the Masada Plateau. One alternative is to get free drinking water from a tank at the excavation site at the top.

MASADA

✳ ✳ **The huge Masada Fortress near the Dead Sea was extended between 37 and 31 BC by Herod the Great. Just over 100 years later it witnessed the Zealots' fight against and defeat by superior Roman forces. From this event the state of Israel, and especially its army, draws a large part of its sense of identity.**

🕐 Open:
April–Sept, Sat–Thu, 8am–5pm; Fri until 4pm;
Oct–March, Sat–Thu until 4pm, Fri until 3pm

① Upper terrace
The upper part of the Northern Palace consisted of four rooms. According to the latest research, it is believed that the complex was not just Herod's private palace, but also served as an official residence.

② Central terrace
The central terrace 20m/65ft lower, believed to have been the king's pleasure palace, consists of two concentric walls.

③ Lower terrace
Even lower still (14m/46ft) is the square lower terrace, a colonnaded courtyard whose fluted Corinthian columns stand on pedestals with coloured render. It was here that the king received his visitors. The skeletons of three defenders of Masada were also found at this level.

④ Baths
At the centre of the bathhouse was a courtyard surrounded on three sides by columns. This courtyard led into the apodipterium (changing room), whose floor was covered in triangular black and white tiles. Adjoining it were the tepidarium (warm room), which also had a tiled floor, the frigidarium (cold room), which consisted of just one pool, and the caldarium (hot room). The latter is still very impressive because of the surviving hypocaust system. The tiled floor mosaic could be heated by warm air channelled through clay pipes, which is why it was built on more than 200 small pillars.

⑤ Warehouse complex
It consisted of 27 rooms in total. They were used to store all kinds of supplies such as wine, oil, flour, spices etc. in clay containers. Many of them are marked with the owner's name or with the indication that the content is kosher.

⑥ Defensive wall
The huge castle, which would have been difficult to capture because of its site alone, was surrounded by a 1300m/1420yd casemate wall, further fortified by 37 towers. It surrounded the approx. 200 x 600m/220 x 650yd summit plateau with its palaces, administrative buildings, warehouses, barracks and cisterns. Herod built twelve cisterns, each with a capacity of 4000 cu m/140,000 cu ft. Together with the food stores this was meant to guarantee that the fortress could withstand even longer sieges. This is exactly what happened several decades later during the Jewish rebellion against Rome.

⑦ Roman ramp
During the siege the Romans set up eight legionary camps around Masada and surrounded the mountain with a levee 2m/6ft thick and 4km/2.5mi long. The attack took place via a ramp on the western flank, which was around 200m/220yd long. The Romans built a 25m/80ft-high platform on it, and placed a tower that was 20m/66ft high on the platform. From the tower they were able to use a battering ram against the wall.

⑧ Western Palace
After the construction of the Northern Palace, the Western Palace (approx. 4000 sq m/45,000 sq ft) lost its function as the official residence. It is likely that it was merely used as a main supply building after that. Near the southwest corner a pool, 15m/50ft wide and 7.5m/25 ft deep, and stairs were uncovered. It was probably built by the Zealots as a mikvah and pool.

⑨ Pool
A pool measuring 18 x 12m/20 x 13yd is also thought to have been a cistern.

them to choose this end. Then, even though Jewish law forbids suicide, they chose ten men by lot who were to kill everyone there and ultimately themselves. When the Romans arrived for their attack the next morning, they found 960 dead; two women, who had hidden with five children in an aqueduct, survived the mass suicide. The Siege of Masada was documented by **Flavius Josephus** (*The Jewish War* VII 8:6–8).

The myth of Masada
Masada was systematically explored between 1963 and 1965. The archaeologists found human bones believed to have belonged to the rebels. In 1969 they were buried in situ in an act of state. Whether these bones were really the mortal remains of those participating in the Great Revolt is in serious doubt now. There is also doubt about whether Flavius Josephus's report of the events was accurate or heroically inflated. Basically, all that is certain is that more than one interpretation is possible for many facts that can be cited to reconstruct the events. The myth of Masada is therefore unlikely to die out any time soon.

> ! **Baedeker TIP**
>
> **The myth lives on in light and sound**
> The story of the fortress comes alive in an impressive show with light effects and music every Tuesday and Thursday at 9pm between April and October in Masada's amphitheatre on the west side of the excavation grounds, which can only be accessed from Arad.

Excavation Site

Orientation
The fortress takes up the entire expansive plateau, which drops off somewhat towards the south. The tour begins at the eastern gate; turn right and head to the **Northern Palace**, then to the western side to the **Western Palace**. The ruins on the southern half of the plateau are less spectacular.

Depots
On the way to the Northern Palace, the path leads past a small villa with the remains of frescoes and past large depots. It is still possible to make out the walls between the narrow store rooms, which collapsed during an earthquake and have been partially erected again.

★★ Northern Palace
Herod's Northern Palace with the king's private rooms is the fort's boldest structure: it stands in three storeys in the rock's steep northern end.
The top floor with the living quarters ends in a semicircle, from where the views of the two lower floors and the panoramic views of the desert mountains all the way to the ►Dead Sea are spectacular. Climb down to the lower storeys to see the cisterns that were carved into the rock.

Adjoining the Northern Palace are the baths, which are laid out according to the Roman model. The view of the entire fortress from the roof of the baths is excellent.

Baths

It is believed that the buildings that come after the baths were Herod's work chambers; the Zealots installed a ritual bath (mikveh) here.

Administrative buildings

To the south of the baths is a further complex of buildings and a 5th-century church. It was built when Byzantine monks settled here. The church is accessed via an anteroom. The apse in the east exhibits a depression that was probably used for relics. The room adjoining the nave to the north has a **mosaic floor** that is still extant in parts. It depicts plants and fruits. The monks also drew crosses on the walls of the southeastern cisterns.

Byzantine church

Leave the Byzantine church and continue to the western end of the fortress to see the **oldest synagogue in the world** and the only one already in existence during the time of the Second Temple. Its roof was supported by columns; in Herod's time the building was divided by a wall. The Zealots reconfigured it and added several stone benches among other things. Scrolls found here are now on display in the Israel Museum in Jerusalem.

Synagogue

The western gate and the extensive Western Palace are also sited on the western wall opposite the Roman ramp. The Zealots turned these rooms into living spaces. They also set up a further mikveh a bit further to the southeast. A relatively well-preserved mosaic floor was discovered in a room formerly used as a reception room. It is the oldest mosaic floor ever discovered in Israel. In addition to geometric patterns it also has various plant motifs, such as vine and fig leaves and olive branches; animals and humans were not depicted out of religious reasons.

★ **Western Palace**

At the southern tip of the extensive compound are two further large and open **cisterns**, and the **southern bastion**. On the return route back to the eastern gate, along the eastern wall, near the southern gate, visitors can pass by and view a third ritual bath, one more cistern and further residential buildings from Byzantine times and the time of the Zealots.

? DID YOU KNOW ...?

- There are numerous cisterns in the fortress. But in the desert there would not have been enough rainfall to fill them up. So during the time of Herod eight large cisterns were constructed on the western slope 80m/265ft below the peak; another 50m/165ft below them there were four more cisterns with a volume of 40,000 m³ (8.8 million gallons). The rain water that flowed down from the peak and the water of two rivers west of the mountain was diverted into these. Donkeys then carried water barrels up to the fortress to provide water for drinking, washing and irrigation.

** Megiddo

F 2

District: Northern

Altitude: 160m/525ft

20 settlement layers from more than 3500 years confirm the great historical significance of ancient Megiddo, situated 30km/18mi to the southeast of ►Haifa. The excavation site, now a national park, has also been a UNESCO World Heritage Site since 2005.

A strategically important location

Megiddo lay on the **Via Maris**, the most significant trade route of Antiquity. It led from Egypt to Syria, leaving the coast near Caesarea and reaching the Jezreel Valley via the Wadi Ara. Megiddo controlled this important trade route here, at the exit of this valley, at the fork to a western branch to Tyre and Sidon and an eastern branch to Damascus and Mesopotamia.

A Canaanite settlement existed here from as early as the 4th millennium BC until the Israelites seized the land. Still extant from this era are a Chalcolithic temple and a further temple which houses a large round altar. After the battle of 1479 BC, when **Thutmose III** took the pass during his push to the Euphrates, the town was under Egyptian influence. The Amarna archives from the 14th century BC contained letters by the Egyptian governor Biridiya requesting military reinforcements against the Chabiru (possibly the Hebrews).

Joshua ►

In the 13th century, after Joshua's triumph over the king of Hazor, he also defeated the king of Megiddo (Joshua 12:21). However, the Israelites only remained in possession of the town for a short time because in the 12th century the Philistines took Megiddo and the entire Jezreel Valley all the way to Beit She'an.

Solomon ►

A new development occurred when David defeated the Philistines in around 1000 BC. In the 10th century Solomon turned Megiddo into the main town of the 5th administrative district. Under governor Baana it reached all the way to Beit She'an (1 Kings 4:12). A palace for ceremonial purposes, probably the royal residence, stood to the east of the main gate.

Ahab ►

Solomon's city was destroyed by Pharaoh Sheshonk (Sisak in the Bible) in 923 BC. In the 9th century it was rebuilt by **King Ahab**. Megiddo was probably particularly important to the ruler because it lay on the route to the Phoenician home of his wife. Ahab built stables for 450 horses above Solomon's northern and southern palaces. The golden age under Abah ended in 733 BC with conquest by the Assyrians under Tiglath-Pileser III. During the Persian period, after 538 BC, Megiddo was abandoned. It appears again in modern times as the site of important battles: in 1799 Napoleon defeated Turkish

Megiddo was already abandoned in the 6th century AD.

troops here, in 1917 General Allenby did the same, and in 1948 the Israelis defeated Arab alliances threatening Haifa.

✴ Excavation Site

Leave the car park and head to the **museum**, which has a large model of the reconstructed Megiddo. Next, head up a 100m/100yd ramp to the entrance of the northern section of the tell. The first feature that comes into sight is a gate from the 15th century BC. It stands on a bend in front of **Solomon's Gate**. The three chambers on the two sides of the gate are easy to make out.

There are extensive remains of buildings on the adjoining compound to the south, where some 13th-century ivory carvings were found. The path leads past ruins of buildings, possibly stables, which Ahab built over Solomon's Northern Palace, to a viewpoint. There are helpful information panels with reconstructions of the town.

From the platform visitors look down into **Schumacher Trench**, named after the German archaeologist Gottlieb Schumacher, who uncovered this section of the complex as part of the first excavations between 1903 and 1905. Look down on to a Canaanite temple with a

⏱
Opening hours:
April–Sept daily
8am–5pm, Fri
8am–3pm, Oct--
March until 4pm, Fri
until 2pm

Viewpoint

Round altar

Megiddo Map

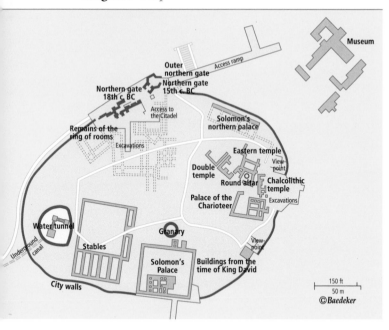

Museum

Outer northern gate
Access ramp
Northern gate 15th c. BC

Northern gate 18th c. BC
Access to the Citadel

Remains of the ring of rooms

Excavations

Solomon's northern palace

Eastern temple

Double temple

View-point

Round altar

Chalcolithic temple

Palace of the Charioteer

Excavations

Water tunnel

Granary

View-point

Underground canal

Stables

City walls

Solomon's Palace

Buildings from the time of King David

150 ft
50 m
©Baedeker

striking, large round altar. Although it dates back to older times, it was restored when the neighbouring eastern temple was built in around 1900 BC. A staircase on the eastern side leads up to the High Square.

Eastern Temple ▸ The Eastern Temple, as is standard for Semitic temples, consists of an anteroom, a main room and the sanctum.

Grain silo, stables On the southern part of the tell a large round grain silo was let into the ground. It dates back to the time of King **Jeroboam II** (8th century BC). Two spacious complexes lie behind it, which Ahab built above Solomon's palace buildings. On the right-hand side is a courtyard with the famous stables, in which there are stable aisles, feeding troughs and pillars with holes to allow up to 450 animals to be tethered.

Water tunnel The path now leads down to the large water tunnel, whose construction still elicits admiration today. The cave with the spring of Megiddo lies outside the tell. In Solomon's day a »gallery« measuring 2m/ 6.5ft in height and 1m/3ft in width was cut into the fortress wall, which lead to the cave with the spring on the tell's southwestern hillside. Ahab, who was also responsible for the water system in ▸Hazor, decided to build a **connection between the castle and the spring**

that would be inaccessible to the enemy in the event of a siege. A 60m/200ft shaft was dug, first through earlier settlement layers, then through rock. Then a horizontal corridor was carved into the rock, reaching the cave with the spring after 120m/400ft. The monumental water supply system has been made accessible to the public through the installation of stairs and raised walkways.

Around Megiddo

Megiddo lies on the edge of the Jezreel Valley, which in turn extends from the bay to the north of Haifa southeastwards to the Jordan Valley. The Arabs call the valley Marg Ibn Amer, while in the Old Testament it is known as the **Plain of Esdrelon**. The Jezreel Valley is one of the most fertile regions in the country and Israel's largest valley, which is why it is also called simply **HaEmek**, meaning valley. In the southwest the Wadi Ara marks the transition between the Jezreel Valley and the Sharon Valley via the Carmel range. The Jezreel Valley was a frequent source of conflict, in the time of Deborah (Judges 5:19) and Gideon (Judges 7:5) for example, because of its fertility, but also because it was a route from one place to another.

Afula is now the main town and central transport hub of the Jezreel Valley. The **kibbutz of Yizre'el** was founded on the road from Afula to Jenin in 1938. It is one of the many Jewish settlements that were founded after the Jewish National Fund began in 1910 to buy up the land, which had been in private Lebanese hands since 1870.

Jezreel Valley

◄ Afula

★ Montfort

F 1

District: Northern   **Altitude:** 200m/655ft

The former French crusader castle of Montfort, the largest ruin in western Galilee, towers imposingly on a forested ridge around 15km/9mi from the Mediterranean coast and the seaside town of ►Nahariya.

The French count Joscelin de Courtenay built the castle in the 12th century to protect Akko, which was then destroyed by Sultan Saladin in 1187.**Hermann von Salza**, Grand Master of the Teutonic Knights, acquired the ruin and the associated domain in 1220: he wanted to turn the castle into a grand master's residence. In 1271 the knights surrendered to the Mamluks led by Baibars after he agreed to let

A French castle

Montfort *Plan*

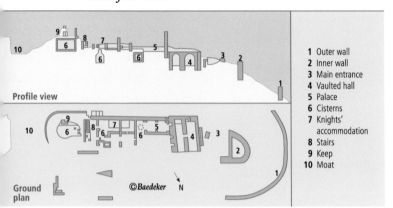

Profile view

Ground plan

©Baedeker N

1 Outer wall
2 Inner wall
3 Main entrance
4 Vaulted hall
5 Palace
6 Cisterns
7 Knights' accommodation
8 Stairs
9 Keep
10 Moat

them leave and take their archives and the treasure of their order. The castle, known by the Arabs as **Qalat Quren**, has been abandoned ever since. Today the ruin is part of the Cochav Hayarden National Park.

✷ Castle Ruins

Opening hours:
April–Sept daily 8am–5pm, Oct–March until 4pm

The fastest way to get to the castle from ►Nahariya is through the Christian Arab village of Mi'ilya on Route 89. Then it is another 3km/2mi uphill all the way to the end of a narrow road. The rocky path, a steady climb, starts beyond the car park. The castle ruin suddenly emerges on a high rocky outcrop above the deep Wadi Quren. The other way of getting here starts in Rosh Hanikra (►Nahariya, Around) on Route 899; after around 10km/6mi, at Elon kibbutz, turn off to Goren Natural Forest. The view from the car park of the forested valley and the castle ruin is lovely. It is a 90-minute walk along a hiking trail to get to the ruin.

Castle complex

The castle, whose rooms are laid out on an east-west axis, was once surrounded by walls, which were reinforced by square and round towers. The castle was most difficult to defend towards the west. For this reason the crusaders dug a deep trench here and built a powerful defensive tower on the other side of it, which was connected to the castle via a drawbridge. One of the towers still stands at its original height of 18m/60ft. The views of the forested landscape from this tower are most impressive.

Yehiam castle

A drive to Montfort Castle can easily be combined with a visit to the fortress of Yehiam, which lies around 6km/4mi to the south of Montfort. Even though the Mamluk sultan Baibars destroyed the castle in 1265, its impressive size can still be made out. Parts of the walls and the eastern tower remain extant.

Mount of Beatitudes

G 2

District: Northern

The Mount of Beatitudes, where Jesus gave his Sermon on the Mount, is located on the northern shore of the Sea of Galilee, above Tabgha and ►Capernaum.

This hill has since ancient times been considered the location of Christ's Sermon on the Mount (Matthew 5–7), a central source of Christian ethics. To get there from the ►Sea of Galilee, drive towards Rosh Pinna from ►Tiberias and ignore the road to Capernaum on the right. The domed chapel, which has an access road, can then be seen on the right-hand side.

Site of the Sermon on the Mount

The Church of the Beatitudes stands at the spot where Jesus gave his Sermon on the Mount.

Church of Beatitudes

🕐 Opening hours:
Daily 8.30am–noon,
2.30pm–5pm

The Sermon on the Mount was once commemorated in a church lower down. The new church, situated in a shady garden on Ospizio Monte di Beatitudine, was built by Antonio Barluzzi in 1937. **Local basalt, white Nazareth stone** for the arches **and Roman travertine** for the columns give the Church of Beatitudes its special character. The view of the Sea of Galilee from the octagonal building's arcade is magnificent. The church's eight sides are, as Latin inscriptions reveal, dedicated to the eight Beatitudes that Jesus proclaimed at the start of the sermon about the poor in spirit, those who mourn, the meek, those who hunger and thirst for righteousness, the merciful, the pure in heart, the peacemakers, and those who are persecuted for righteousness' sake (Matthew 5: 3–10). The dome symbolizes the ninth beatitude (Matthew 5:11f.), in which Jesus promised reward in heaven for those persecuted for his sake.

Mount Gilboa · Har Gilboa

F 2/3

District: Northern   **Altitude:** 508m/1667ft

Mount Gilboa borders the Jezreel Plain around 30km/18mi south of the ►Sea of Galilee as part of the foothills of the mountains of Samaria. There are two national parks here. The significant excavation site of ►Beit She'an is also only 15km/9mi away.

King Saul's death
In Jewish history Mount Gilboa (Har Gilboa) was the site of tragic events: King Saul gathered his army here against the Philistines and questioned the Witch of Endor. As she predicted, the Israelites lost. Saul's sons Jonathan, Abinadab and Malchishua were killed; the king fell on his sword and the victorious Philistines hung his body on the wall of Beit She'an (1 Samuel 31:1–12). David referred to this fate in his lament: »Ye mountains of Gilboa, let there be no dew, neither let there be rain, upon you ... for there the shield of the mighty is vilely cast away...« (2 Samuel 1:21).

What to See around Mount Gilboa

Getting here
A winding road with pretty views leads up to the 508m/1667ft mountain range, which is particularly attractive in spring. This road can be accessed from the road between ►Beit She'an and Afula.

Gan HaShelosha National Park
Gan HaShelosha National Park is situated at the northern foot of Mount Gilboa, between ► Beit She'an and Beit Alfa (see below). It has ponds, natural waterfalls and shady picnic sites. Archaeological discoveries are on display in a small museum.

Ma'ayan Harod National Park is situated 10km/6mi to the northwest, towards Afula, on the forested northern slopes of the mountain range at the source of the Harod. This is a lovely spot for a dip and a picnic. The spring is considered to be the one at which the judge Gideon, at God's behest, chose his warriors to defeat the Midianites (Judges 7:5).

Ma'ayan Harod National Park

The mosaic floor of a synagogue from the 6th century was uncovered near the kibbutz of Beit Alfa (founded in 1921) at the foot of Mount Gilboa, 6km/4mi to the west of ▶Beit She'an and 19km/11mi east of Afula. Together with the mosaic of Tiberias Hamat (▶Tiberias) it is one of the most significant pieces of evidence of synagogue construction during the Byzantine period. Even though the synagogue lies in the grounds of Hefzi Bah kibbutz, it bears the name of the neighbouring Beit Alfa, since the synagogue grounds belonged to the ancient Beit Alfa.

Beit Alfa

The synagogue, now with a roof again, has a nave and two aisles, a semicircular apse for the Torah shrine in the south and surviving floor mosaics in the nave and the right aisle. While the aisle features ornamental patterns, the nave is dominated by figurative depictions (daily 8am–4pm, in summer until 5pm).

◀ Synagogue

The nave's floor mosaic is divided into three fields. The **sacrifice of Isaac by Abraham** is depicted behind the old central portal: two men guide Abraham's donkey to the left, bearded Abraham in a long gown is in the centre, with the sacrificial knife in his right hand, holding little Isaac with his left hand. Behind Abraham a ram is tied to a tree; above it is the hand of God, instructing Abraham to sacrifice the ram instead of his son. The sacrificial altar can be made out to the right. The central field is dominated by a cosmological picture. Its central circle depicts a frontal view of the quadriga of the sun god Helios. The twelve signs of the zodiac are shown around him, the four seasons in the corners. The southern field depicts the closed Torah shrine at the centre, flanked by seven-armed candelabras, censers, two birds and two lions.

🕐
✷
◀ Floor mosaic in the nave

Mount Tabor · Har Tavor

	F 2

District: Northern   **Altitude:** 588m/1929ft

The conical Mount Tabor (Har Tavor), which rises from the Jezreel Plain 21km/13mi north of Afula, is often mentioned in the Old Testament and is also considered to be the site of the Transfiguration of Christ.

Two churches and magnificent views make the drive to the peak worthwhile. The route is signposted. The relevant road turns off in a

Getting there

Far-reaching views of the Jezreel Valley from Mount Tabor

northwesterly direction from the main road between Afula and Tiberias at the southern end of Kefar Tavor.

Site of the Transfiguration of Christ In the 2nd millennium BC the Canaanites had temples which were dedicated to Baal on Mount Tabor as well as on ► Mount Carmel and Mount Hermon. In the 12th century BC the prophetess Deborah and the military commander Barak gathered their troops on the mountain in order to destroy the Canaanite Sisera from here (Judges 4:12–16). According to Christian tradition, Mount Tabor is the site of the Transfiguration of Jesus (Matthew 17, Mark 9:2–13; Luke 9:28–36): »Jesus taketh with him Peter, and James, and John, and leadeth them up into an high mountain apart by themselves: and he was transfigured before them. And his raiment became shining, exceeding white as snow.« This idea, along with the Resurrection, is **one of the central theme in the theology of the Eastern churches**. The first Christian churches on Mount Tabor were built as early as 422, and from 553 the mountain was an episcopal see. The crusaders extended the site, turned it into a place of pilgrimage and built a fort, which withstood Saladin in 1191 but was destroyed by Baibars in 1263. In 1631 the Druze emir Fakhr al-Din gave the summit to the Franciscans, whose monastery is still there today. The northern section of the summit plateau belongs to the Greek Orthodox community, which built the Church of Elijah in 1911.

What to See on Mount Tabor

The path forks behind the Gate of the Winds. The left path leads to the **Greek Orthodox northern section** with the Church of Elijah. The courtyard with the open cistern is surrounded by cell wings on the northern and eastern sides. To the west of the church is the cave of Melchizedek, a king and priest during the time of Abraham (Genesis 14:18–20).

Church of Elijah

Keep right to get to the property of the Catholic Franciscans. Walk through the walled monastery courtyard, between the remains of an older church (left) and the convent garden with a monument commemorating the visit of Pope Paul VI in 1964, to Tabor Church or the **Transfiguration Basilica**, which was built between 1921 and 1923 to plans by Antonio Barluzzi.

✳ *Transfiguration Basilica*

The church, built out of pale limestone, is based on a type of church developed in Syria between the 4th and 6th centuries. This becomes particularly clear from the monumental design of the façade with two projecting towers and the arch between them, crowned by a pediment. Once again following the Syrian model, there are wide arches separating the nave from the aisles on the inside. The apse is decorated by a modern gold base mosaic depicting the Transfiguration of Christ. A few steps go down to a chancel dating back to Byzantine times. Tabor Church possesses three grottoes, which symbolize the three tabernacles that Peter wanted to build: the Grotto of Christ in the eastern part of the church, the Chapel of Elijah in the left façade tower and the Chapel of Moses in the right-hand one. The crosses in the mosaic floor of the Chapel of Moses indicate that it dates from before 422, because in that year Theodosius II prohibited the use of the cross symbol for floors, so that people would not step on the cross with their feet.

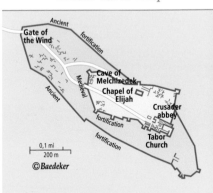

Mount Tabor Map

Gate of the Wind
Ancient fortification
Medieval
Ancient
Cave of Melchizedek
Chapel of Elijah
Crusader abbey
fortification
Tabor Church
fortification
0,1 mi
200 m
©Baedeker

There are still some old walls to the south and north of the church. From here there are far-reaching views of the mountains of Nazareth to the west, the Jezreel Plain and the mountains of Samaria rising in the south, the Jordan Valley and the eastern mountains.

✳ *View*

Nablus · Nābulus · Shechem

F 3

Area: West Bank
(Palestinian territory)

Altitude: 550m/1805ft
Population: 115,000

Nablus lies 63km/39mi to the north of Jerusalem between Mount Gerizim and Mount Ebal. It is the second-largest city and one of the most important centres of trade and industry in the West Bank. For a long time it has been a stronghold of militant Palestinians.

Muslim for 1400 years

The city enjoyed a special strategic significance because of its location on the intersection of two old trade routes: one connected the Mediterranean coast with the Jordan Rift Valley, the other served as a north-south axis across the mountains of Samaria.

In AD 72 Titus founded the settlement of **Flavia Neapolis** 2km/1.25mi to the northwest of the abandoned Shechem or Sichem (▶p. 361). This settlement quickly flourished. The town was mainly home to Samaritans (▶p. 361), but soon a Christian community also established itself here. In 521 the Samaritans killed the bishop and destroyed the churches, whereupon Emperor Justinian had the rebels who refused to convert to Christianity killed or sold into slavery. In

The bazaar in Nablus

636 the Arabs took Neapolis and renamed it Nablus. Apart from a short Christian phase during the time of the crusaders, Nablus has remained Muslim. After the end of the British Mandate in 1948, Nablus fell to Jordan. In 1967 it was occupied by Israel, an occupation which ended in December 1995. The Palestine Liberation Organization (PLO) was able to flourish particularly well in Nablus; to this day the Fatah faction of Mahmoud Abbas, the president of the Palestinian National Authority, remains dominant here. Its security forces have made the city safe again by being tough on every kind of militant action.

Nablus is the home of the Samaritans, a religious group whose only other surviving community is in Holon near ►Tel Aviv. The Samaritans are descended from both Jews and »people from Babylon and Kuthah« (2 Kings 17:24). They are not recognized as Jews by the orthodox. Their holy scripture is a Torah roll (probably 2nd century) that contains the five books of Moses. Since 350 BC the Samaritans have had their temple on the 881m/2890ft Mount Gerizim. Today the community in Nablus has around 300 members. A **museum** on Mount Gerizim provides information about the history and culture of this religious community.

Home of the Samaritans

What to See in and around Nablus

Apart from visits to the archaeological sites – Tell Balata, Joseph's Tomb and Jacob's Well – do stroll through the old **kasbah**. During a walk through the busy streets and alleys, take a look at the **kanaafe factories**, where a famous treat from Nablus is still produced by the ancient method. It is also worth visiting **the traditional soap factories** of Nablus (one in the central al-Nasir Street), which use olive oil as their basic ingredient. Non-Muslims are not permitted to enter the **Great Mosque of Nablus** on al-Nasir Street in the heart of the old quarter. Built as a Byzantine basilica, it was later transformed into a crusader church and then into a mosque.

Also on al-Nasir Street, around 400m/450yd to the west of the mosque, are **Palestine's two oldest bathhouses**, an ideal place to relax. In addition to steam baths there are pretty central lounges with pillows and mattresses on which visitors can rest, drink tea and coffee, and smoke a hookah. The recent history of Nablus is less than glorious. The city became notorious as the haunt of »brigands and bandits«, as one newspaper put it, and the old quarter a sinister underworld. At least, this used to be the case. 60 per cent of all Palestinian attacks on Israel started from here. The walls are plastered with posters mourning the »fallen martyrs in the struggle again Zionism«.

Lively old quarter

The **biblical Sichem** (Hebrew Shechem) was located on Tell Balata. This settlement is associated with many events of the Old Testament. Abraham camped here and built the first altar (Genesis. 12:7), and

Sichem

VISITING NABLUS

INFORMATION

Nablus Municipality
Failsal Street
P. O. Box 218
Tel. (09) 237 93 13
www.nablus.org

GETTING THERE · PERSONAL SAFETY

Take taxis or sheruts from Damascus Gate in Jerusalem, or an organized tour. Since Nablus lies in Palestinian territory, it is important to find out about the current political situation before visiting the city.

WHERE TO EAT

▶ **Moderate**
Zeit ou Zaater
Tel. (09) 238 40 50
Restaurant adjoining the Al-Yasmeen hotel with a smart atmosphere and outstanding cuisine.

WHERE TO STAY

▶ **Mid-range**
Al-Yasmeen Hotel
Tel. (09) 233 35 55, (059) 976 69 44
www.alyasmeen.com
30 rooms; oriental style including a souk; hotel in the heart of Nablus with views of the Manara clock tower, An-Nasr Mosque and Mount Gerizim.

Al-Qasr Hotel
Al-Qasr St.
Tel. (09) 238 54 44
alqasr@netvision.net.il
41 rooms; on the city's western slopes, between the university and the old quarter. Around ten minutes' walk to the centre.

later his grandson Jacob did the same (Genesis. 33:18–20). Since Jacob's sons had killed all the men of Sichem in order to avenge the honour of their raped sister, he had to flee with his family. At the assembly at Shechem, Joshua ruled on how Canaan was to be shared out among the Israelites (Joshua 24). On the field that Jacob had purchased, Joshua had the mortal remains of Jacob's son Joseph buried (Joshua 24:32). In the 10th century Shechem became the capital of the northern kingdom of Israel, but when the residence of ▶Samaria was founded, Shechem lost its significance. The excavated remains of the walls and temple from the time of the biblical Shechem are rather modest.

Jacob's Well On the eastern slopes of Mount Gerizim, around 500m/550yd to the southeast of Tell Balata, stands a church that has recently been rebuilt. It houses a 36m/120ft-deep well, which, according to tradition, was dug by Jacob, and was the place where Jesus asked a Samaritan woman for water (John 4:5–9).
There was already a church with a cruciform floor plan above the well in AD 380. It was destroyed and rebuilt several times. During

the time of the crusaders a church was built above the well. While the church fell into ruin after the 15th century, its crypt and the well have survived.

Joseph's Tomb was located a bit to the north of Jacob's Well. It was destroyed in autumn 2000 during Palestinian unrest. This was allegedly the final resting place of Jacob's son Joseph, who had been sold by his brothers to an Egyptian caravan.

Joseph's Tomb

Nahariya

F 1

District: Northern
Population: 43,000

Altitude: 0–10m/33ft

Nahariya, situated along a nice section of the Mediterranean coastline 30km/18mi to the north of ► Haifa, is a well-kept, quiet seaside town and an ideal base for trips to the scenically attractive hinterland, which features lots of historical sites.

The seaside resort of Nahariya, which is incredibly popular among Israelis, was founded in 1934 by Jews from Germany. It got its name from the river (Nahal) Ga'aton, which flows right through the town – between eucalyptus trees and the two lanes of the main road Sderot Hagaaton, which leads straight to the waterfront. The town hall, home to the tourist information and a museum, lies on the northern side of this road, while the station, cafés, fast-food restaurants and other eateries can be found on the south side. During the war with Lebanon in 2006 the town was hit several times by Hezbollah missiles.

Popular seaside resort

Around Nahariya

Anyone interested in roses should visit the international Christian settlement of Nes Ammim, around 10km/6mi to the southeast. It was set up in 1963 by young Christians, mostly Dutch, and is known for its rose farms.

Nes Ammim

The **Tell Achziv National Park** is located around 5km/3mi to the north of Nahariya, where the Keziv River flows into the Mediterranean. The crusaders called the place Castel Imbert. In more recent times, until the state of Israel was founded, it was inhabited by Arab fishermen.
Today the ruins of Achziv have been incorporated into a national park, which is visited more for its beautiful beach and the extensive green space than for its ruins. On the Sabbath and other holidays, only visit if you don't mind crowds.

Tell Achziv

► VISITING NAHARIYA

INFORMATION

Tourist Office
Municipality Building
19 Hagaaton Blvd.
Tel. (04) 987 98 00

GETTING THERE

Train connections and regular buses
to Haifa

ENTERTAINMENT

The street cafés on Haagaton Blvd are
popular meeting places. The best one
is Penguin (no. 31). At weekends the
expensive nightclub of the Carlton
Hotel is the place to be.

WHERE TO EAT

► Moderate

Penguin
31 Haagaton Blvd.
Tel. (04) 992 00 27
A long-established restaurant
(founded in 1940, eight years before
the state of Israel) that serves pasta,
fish and meat dishes, Chinese food
and burgers. The place is very popular
with locals.

► Inexpensive

Singapore Chinese Garden
17, Jabotinsky Blvd.
Tel. (04) 992 49 52
Very good Chinese restaurant, lovely
ambience

WHERE TO STAY

► Luxury

Carlton Hotel
23, Haagaton Blvd.
Tel. (04) 900 55 11
www.carlton-hotel.co.il
The leading hotel in Nahariya, centrally located, has 200 attractive
rooms and suites; book early. the
hotel also organizes trips into the
surrounding area.

Madison Hotel
17 Ha'ali St., tel. (073) 200 50 00
www. madison -hotel.co.il
Ideal beach location, totally refurbished in 2011, complete with swimming pool, private beach, and free
access to the country club.

► Mid-range

Hotel Frank
4, Haaliyah St., tel. (04) 992 02 78
www.hotel-frank.co.il
Close to the beach; disused pool,
rooms with sea views

BEACHES

The beach promenade runs to the
south of the main road behind the
city beach, which is accessible free of
charge. *Galei Galil Beach*, Nahariya's
central beach with two pools, a playground, showers and lifeguards, lies to
the north of Haga'aton. Another place
to swim is on the beach by the village
of Shave Zion, 3km/2mi to the south
of the town.

Akhzivland ►   Immediately to the north of the fenced-in national park is a wooden
house that looks somewhat obscure. Its owner acquired the plot in
1952 and later declared it the **independent state of Akhzivland**.
Upon »entry«, visitors can have a pretty stamp put in their passports

and take a tour of an interesting private museum that exhibits archaeological discoveries.

The **spectacular chalk cliffs and grottoes** of Rosh Hanikra are at least as popular as Achziv National Park. They can be found 7km/ 4.5mi further north, right on the border to Lebanon. The striking, bright white cliff that abruptly interrupts the flat coastline has been difficult to pass since time immemorial. Lots of caravans and armies, including the army of Alexander the Great during his military campaign in Egypt, have had to pass it. Ever since then the steps he created have been known as »**Scala Tyriorum**«, the Ladder of Tyre. During the Second World War British engineers managed to dig a 250m/ 275yd tunnel for the railway line between Beirut and Haifa. When Western Galilee was cut off from the rest of Israel during the war of independence in 1948, Haganah blew up the tunnel and the bridges because they feared an Arab invasion from Lebanon. Today part of the tunnel is accessible again.

★ Rosh Hanikra

There is a restaurant and a souvenir shop on top of the cliff. Here tickets for the cable car are sold. It goes down to the grottoes 200m/ 655ft below. At NIS 45 it is an expensive pleasure, for a trip of around one minute. The water level in the caves, which formed as a result of soft rock being eroded, varies according to the tide, and the water takes on a different colour depending on the time of day. They are a real experience (summer daily 8.30am–6pm, July and August until 11pm, winter until 4pm).

◄ Cable car

★ Nazareth · Natzrat

District: Northern   **Altitude:** 350m/1150ft
Population: 72,000

Nazareth (Natzrat) lies above the Jezreel Valley on the southern edge of the mountains of Galilee, around 40km/25mi to the southeast of Haifa. The town, in which Archangel Gabriel announced the forthcoming birth of Jesus to Mary, and where Jesus spent most of his life, is one of the most significant places of pilgrimage in Christianity.

Nazareth, an insignificant village in the time before Christ, is mentioned neither in the Talmud nor in the Old Testament. However, the hill on which stand the Church of the Annunciation and the Church of St Joseph's Carpentry has been inhabited since the time of the patriarchs, i.e. since the 2nd millennium BC, as shown by tombs from this period and underground rooms in the tufa, which were used as larders. The name Nazareth appears for the first time in the New Testament in the account of the Annunciation to Mary (Luke

Site of the Annunciation

Nazareth Map

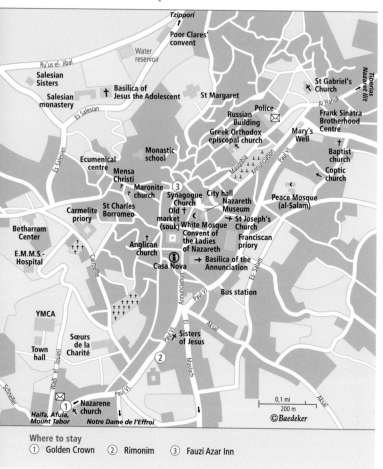

Tzippori
Poor Clares' convent
Water reservoir
Ru'us el-Jibal
Salesian Sisters
Salesian monastery
Es Salesian
Basilica of Jesus the Adolescent
St Margaret
St Gabriel's Church
Police
Russian Building
Frank Sinatra Brotherhood Centre
Greek Orthodox episcopal church
Al Hanuk
Mary's Well
Baptist church
Monastic school
Ecumenical centre
Mensa Christi
Maronite church
Synagogue Church
City hall
Nazareth Museum
Coptic church
Peace Mosque (al-Salam)
Carmelite priory
St Charles Borromeo
Old market (souk)
White Mosque
St Joseph's Church
Betharram Center
Anglican church
Convent of the Ladies of Nazareth
Franciscan priory
E.M.M.S.-Hospital
Carmelite
Casa Nova
Basilica of the Annunciation
Bus station
Paul VI
Afsal
YMCA
Sœurs de la Charité
Sisters of Jesus
Town hall
Wadi el-Jouan
Maslach
Paul VI
Afsal
Schneller
Nazarene church
Notre Dame de l'Effroi
0,1 mi
200 m
©Baedeker
Haifa, Afula, Mount Tabor
Tiberias Nazareth Illit

Where to stay
① Golden Crown ② Rimonim ③ Fauzi Azar Inn

1:26–33). Jesus probably lived in Nazareth until after his baptism by John (Luke 3:21). He later spent most of his time in the area around ►Capernaum. The **Grotto of the Annunciation** subsequently became a place of worship, and Christians settled in Nazareth early on.

In 614 the Persians, together with the Jews, conquered the town and destroyed it. The Christian population dropped as a result. When it was reconquered in 629, the Byzantines took their revenge by destroying the Jewish houses. Rebuilding work only took place under the crusader Tancred, who took Nazareth in 1099 and then ruled it as the Prince of Galilee. The town, which was destroyed yet again in

▶ VISITING NAZARETH

INFORMATION

Tourist Office
Casa Nova St
Tel. (04) 601 10 72, (050) 621 40 29
www.nazarethinfo.org, Mon–Fri
8.30am–5pm, Sat 9am–1pm, closed
Sun

TRANSPORT

There are buses to Tiberias, Afula,
Haifa, Tel Aviv and Jerusalem several
times a day; sheruts and taxis wait at
Paul VI Road.

EVENTS

The Nazareth Festival with Arab
folklore takes place in late summer.

WHERE TO EAT

The restaurants around the Old Town
serve good Arab fare at unbeatably
cheap prices, e.g. Al-Salam in Paul VI
Rd., Astoria, Fahoum and Tishreen in
Annunciation Street to name a few.
Anyone seeking finer cuisine will have
to head up to the restaurant of the
Golden Crown Hotel.

WHERE TO STAY

► Luxury / Mid-range

① *Golden Crown*
2015 Mount of the Precipice
Tel. (04) 650 80 00
www.goldencrown.co.il
353 rooms. The Golden Crown, the
first five-star hotel in town, opened
on the hill above Nazareth. It is worth
checking it out if only for the views of
the Jezreel Valley.

② *Rimonim*
Paul VI Rd.
Tel. (04) 650 00 00,
www.rimonim.com
226 rooms. Pleasant mid-range hotel
in the centre of town.

► Mid-range / Budget

③ *Fauzi Azar Inn*
In the souk, tel. 04 6 02 04 69
www.fauziazarinn.com
Marble floors, ceiling frescoes; a cosy
200-year-old Arab villa, which has a
dorm in addition to the usual single
and double rooms.

1263 by Baibars and the Mamluks, was only settled by Christians
after the Druze ruler Fakhr al-Din had given his permission. In the
19th century, under Ottoman rule, Nazareth grew to the size of a
small town. Today Nazareth, which is called an-Nasira by the Arabs,
is the **largest Arab community in Israel**. In the past the majority of
the population were Christian, while today more than two-thirds are
Muslims. The demographic shift is also reflected in the politically
fraught everyday life of the town. There are periodic attempts by
Muslim extremists to inflame the population against Christian pilgrims, hitherto in vain, even though the Jama'at Ansar Allah, the
Supporters of Allah, have erected a poster wall at the entrance to the
Church of the Annunciation. In Arabic and English, it quotes Sura 3,
Verse 85 of the Koran: »And whoever desires other than Islam as re-
ligion – never will it be accepted from him, and he, in the Hereafter,
will be among the ranks of those who have lost.«

What to See in Nazareth

Townscape The town received a facelift in many places for the holy year of 2000 and the expected influx of visitors. Nevertheless Nazareth was not turned into a thing of beauty. The town centre in the valley, still a mix of modern, unattractive church buildings and rapidly built high-rises interspersed with some Arab souk atmosphere, is plagued by traffic and has no relaxing green spaces or pretty squares.

Down into the Old Town Nazareth is characterized by lots of churches. The route into the centre is easy to find: always head downhill. The main street is Paul VI Road. **Annunciation Street** (El-Bishara, more often known as Casa Nova Rd) turns off from it. It leads to the Church of the Annunciation and the Old Town; almost all the other attractions are easily reached on foot from here. At the lower (northern) end of Annunciation St. there is a small Arabian bazaar as well as several stalls selling devotional objects. The pretty little garden on the left-hand side of the road, diagonally opposite the entrance to the Church of the Annunciation, is owned by the Casa Nova pilgrims' hospice.

✳ Church of the Annunciation

Previous buildings The current church had **four predecessors**. The first modest church, built in the style of the synagogues of the time, was constructed here by Jewish Christians in the 3rd century. The second church, a small structure with a round apse and projecting atrium, was commissioned by Empress Helena, the mother of Emperor Constantine the Great, in the 4th century. It was built by the converted Jew Joseph of Tiberias. Next to it to the south was a small monastery, which the Persians destroyed in 614. The third church was built in the early 12th century by Tancred, the Prince of Galilee. Its dimensions were significantly larger. The basilica with its nave and two aisles was 30m/33 yd wide and 75m/82 yd long. In 1263 when Baibars destroyed it (though he spared the grotto).

It was not until 1730 that the Franciscans were able to build a new, significantly smaller church, which, in contrast to the earlier church was not built on an east-west axis. Instead the choir was at the northern end above the grotto. The building was demolished in 1955 to make room for the current monumental church.

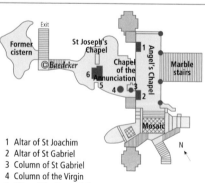

Grotto of the Annunciation Plan

1 Altar of St Joachim
2 Altar of St Gabriel
3 Column of St Gabriel
4 Column of the Virgin
5 Altar of the Annunciation
6 Altar of the Flight into Egypt

The fifth church, designed by the Italian architect **Giovanni Muzio** and inaugurated on 23 March 1969, is the largest modern church in Israel and also a significant example of how difficult it is to find a balance between modern forms and respect for traditions. Despite precious materials and the participation of many artists from around the world, the current building primarily achieves its impact through its colossal dimensions. The floor plan is very similar to that of a basilica. The modern exterior walls were built above existing foundation walls of the long sides and the eastern apses were also incorporated into the new church. The combination of a basilica with a central ground plan is new. A large octagon in the floor spatially links all the layers of the building, from the oldest layers, i.e. the Grotto of the Annunciation and the remains of the earliest church buildings at the very bottom, all the way to the high dome.

Construction principle: basilica and central ground plan

The courtyard is accessed from the entrance gate in the west. Its exterior walls on the western and southern side have a peristyle. The three bronze portals were created by the German artist Roland Friederichsen. The central portal depicts, top left, the birth of Christ. Below it is the flight to Egypt and the adolescent Jesus. His baptism in the River Jordan is portrayed bottom right, above it the Sermon on the Mount and the Crucifixion. The southern portal depicts scenes from the life of Mary.

If entering the Church of the Annunciation via the western main portal, visitors first find themselves in the lower church. At the northern (left-hand) side, the wall of the old crusader church with its half-columns, on which the new walls stand, can still be made out. Then walk eastwards through the church to the octagon below the dome, where the church's original level can be seen. The Grotto of the Annunciation, with the inscription »Verbum caro hic factum est« (»The word became flesh here« cf. John 1:14) on the altar, can be seen to the north (left). The columns immediately in front of the grotto are attributed to the synagogue church of the 3rd century. The modern altar stands at the centre of the octagon, while a nave from the nave with a round apse from the second Church of the Annunciation (4th–5th century) can be seen in the south (right). The copper canopy above the grotto is from Belgium. Past the octagon and further eastwards are the three apses of the crusader church. Some of the rich capitals from the 12th century in the right-hand apse are of note here.

Lower church

The upper church also has a nave and two aisles and the same octagonal opening in the floor through which it is possible to see down to the grotto. The light dome above it forms a lily, the symbol of Mary's purity. The marble floor depicts scenes connected with Mary and the Marian councils. The mosaic in the presbytery depicts the church: Christ with Mary and Peter as well as saints. To the left next to it is a chapel for the saints of the Franciscan order, and the Chapel of Sacraments to the right.

Upper church

Baptistery Leave the upper church via the northern gate to get to a courtyard in which stands the baptistery. Some excavations of ancient Nazareth can be made out below the chapel.

Further Sites in Nazareth

St Joseph's Church, inaugurated in 1914, stands around 100m/100yd further towards town. It was **built above a cave** said to have been used by Joseph as a home and a workshop. The remains of a cistern and several storage pits, which probably date back to the village at the time of Jesus, can be seen.

Right in the souk, just a few metres to the west of St Joseph's Church, is the **synagogue church** in which the Greek Catholic **Melkites** celebrate their mass. Steps to the left of the church portal lead down to the synagogue, which was allegedly visited by Jesus. In fact the meagre remains date back to the 6th century.

Mensa Christi The Franciscan Church of Mensa Christi was built in 1861. It can be found just a few hundred metres to the west of the synagogue church. It houses a rock 3.6m/12ft long and 3m/10ft wide, from which Jesus and his disciples are said to have eaten.

Salesian Church A path zigzags up from the Mensa Christi Church up to the monastery of the French Salesians, which is home to the Church of Jesus the Adolescent. The view of Nazareth from here is attractive. The church was built in 1918; the marble statue above the high altar depicts Jesus at the age of 16.

Nazareth Village »Living History« is the attraction on offer near the hostel: actors in costume make the time of Jesus come alive in recreated houses and workshops in Nazareth Village (tel. 04 645 60 42 www.nazareth village.org, daily except Sun 9am–5pm).

Mary's Well and Church of St Gabriel Around 1.5km/1mi to the northeast of the Church of the Annunciation, on Well Square, is Mary's Well. According to an apocryphal gospel, the archangel Gabriel first appeared to Mary at the village well. Mary's Well is a modern structure, however, and does not stand exactly on the site of the old well. The old well is under the altar of the neighbouring Greek Orthodox Church of St Gabriel, which is worth visiting for its beautiful architecture.

Around Nazareth

The village of **Cana** (Kafr Kanna), 8km/5mi northeast of Nazareth on the road to Tiberias, is known as the place where Jesus performed his first miracle. He turned water into wine at the **»wedding at Cana«** (John 2:1–11). There are two churches commemorating this event in this friendly town inhabited by both Christians and Muslims. One good souvenir option here is »wine from Cana«.

The Franciscan church, inaugurated in 1883, lies in the centre of Cana. According to tradition it was built on the site of the house where the wedding took place. An old jug on display at the church is said to be one of the six jugs in which the water became wine.

◄ Franciscan

Opposite the Franciscan church is the Greek Orthodox church, built in 1556 on the ruins of a mosque. This church also has two stone vessels, which are also associated with this miracle, but they are in fact no older than 300 years.

◄ Greek Orthodox church

The Church of Nathanael on the northern outskirts of town also belongs to the Franciscans. It was built in the late 19th century in honour of Nathanael of Cana, who was initially sceptical about Jesus (»Can anything good come out of Nazareth?«), but then worshipped him as the Son of God (John 1:46–49) and was also present at the »Miraculous Catch of Fish« where the risen Christ appeared to the disciples (John 21:2).

◄ Church of Nathanael

Nebi Musa

F 4

Area: West Bank (Palestinian territory)

According to Muslim belief, the tomb of Moses (Nebi Musa), who is venerated as one of the most significant prophets in Islam, lies 30km/18mi east of ►Jerusalem, in the heart of the Judaean desert in breathtaking landscape.

At the end of the great journey from Egypt through the Sinai, the deserts of Zin and Paran and the land of the Edomites, Moses saw the Promised Land, but was not allowed to set foot in it. From the summit of 808m/2651ft Mount Nebo, he looked down on to the Dead Sea, 1200m/3940ft lower, the Jordan Valley and the oasis of Jericho, which his people under Joshua were to conquer as the first city west of the Jordan. Moses was buried »in a valley of the land of Moab, ... but no man knoweth of his sepulchre unto this day.« (Deuteronomy 34:6). Despite this statement, Islamic tradition says the tomb of Moses lies west of the Jordan at the site of Nebi Musa (Nabi Musa).

The tomb of Moses?

The security situation permitting, it is best to take a taxi from Damascus Gate in Jerusalem or sign up for an organized tour to Nebi Musa.

Maqam al-Nabi Musa

i Nabi Musa Festival

■ The Christian Easter and the Jewish Passover period is also the time when Muslims undertake pilgrimages to the tomb of Moses. Ever since Ottoman times this event has been accompanied by riots against those of other faiths. The first major Arab rebellion during the British Mandate occurred at the festival in 1920. The festival started up again in 1997.

The **main mosque** of the complex, built for the tomb of Moses, lies on the western side of the courtyard. The mosque is divided by a wall, into a larger, eastern side for the men and a smaller one for women. The women's section is slightly lower in order to prevent the two sexes from making eye contact during prayer. To the right of the main entrance there is a doorway into a small room, which houses a **cenotaph for Moses** from the time of Sultan Baibars. The large cemetery outside the complex was established for Muslims who wanted to be buried at this holy site.

✴ **Netanya**

E 3

District: Central
Population: 180,000

Altitude: 20m/65ft

The town of Netanya, situated around 30km/18mi to the north of ►Tel Aviv amid the sand dunes of the Sharon plain, is one of the most popular holiday destinations on the Israeli Mediterranean coast because of its pleasant climate and glorious, long beaches. Israel's Rimini, so to speak.

What to See in Netanya

Herzl Street, Haatzmaut Square

The town's main road, named after Theodor Herzl (►Famous People), is also the most important shopping street, with lots of shops, restaurants and cafés. It runs from Netanya Interchange, the departure spot of the overland Route 2, in an almost dead-straight line towards the coast, where it joins the traffic-calmed **Kikar Haatzmaut**. Despite the cafés and restaurants all around, the large square with its sizable fountain in the middle is not very atmospheric. Starting at the square's seaward side are the green spaces with which the cliffs have been transformed into an attractive pedestrian zone with a waterfront promenade. The modern amphitheatre, open towards the sea, was built to host open-air performances.

Market

Benyamin Blvd or Weizmann Blvd is Netanya's north-south axis. In Zangwill St., which runs parallel to Weizmann Blvd, a daily market is held with a large selection of fresh fruit and vegetables, meat and fish.

▶ VISITING NETANYA

INFORMATION

Tourist Information
Haatzmaut Square
Tel. (09) 882 72 86
www.netanyatourism.org.il

GETTING THERE

Buses (to the Central Bus Station) and sheruts (to Zion Square) from Tel Aviv and Haifa depart approx. every 15 minutes

EVENTS

During the summer there are daily discos, concerts and theatre performances for the Haatzmaut Open Air on Haatzmaut Square.

SHOPPING

There are plenty of good shops in **Kenyon Mall** at the end of Herzl St. and in Hadarim Mall (2 Hacadar St.). The largest shopping centre is **Sharon Shopping City** near the Poleg Industrial Zone (take bus 48).

ENTERTAINMENT

The place to meet in the evenings is **Liberty Square**; visitors enjoy the cool evening air and make their way to the bars and clubs, such as the **Hamakom Club** (11 Haatzamaut Sq., tel. 09 / 833 16 77).

WHERE TO EAT

▶ Expensive

① *Shibolym Restaurant*
1 Hatzoran St.
Tel. (09) 999 99 99
French-oriental cuisine, not exactly cheap but very good.

▶ Moderate

② *Marakesh*
7 David Hamelech St.
Tel. (09) 833 47 97

This restaurant serves Moroccan fish and meat dishes.

WHERE TO STAY

▶ Luxury

① *The Seasons on the Sea*
1 Nice Blvd
Tel. (09) 860 15 55
Fax 862 30 22
www.haonot.co.il
Modern high-rise hotel right on the beach with 100 rooms and suites.

▶ Mid-range

② *Margoa Hotel*
9 Gad Machnes St.
Tel. (09) 862 44 34
www.hotelmargoa.co.il
75 rooms. Family hotel on the garden promenade.

▶ Budget

③ *Orit Guesthouse*
21 Hen St.
Tel. / fax (09) 861 68 18
www.israelsvan.com/orit
Pleasant guesthouse with 7 rooms.

BEACHES

Eight official beaches around 10km/ 6mi long, very clean and well looked after, with lifeguards, restaurants, kiosks and sports opportunities. **Herzl Beach** and **Sironit Beach**, with sunshades, showers and slides for children, have shallow water close to the shore. Those who prefer quieter environs should check out the beaches to the north and south of the centre. There are further attractive beaches in the surrounding area, such as in **Kfar Vitkin** 6km/3.5mi to the north. Although there are no showers, lifeguards, or sunshades, **Poleg Beach**, around 7km/4.5mi south of Netanya, has dunes up to 60m/200ft high.

Netanya Map

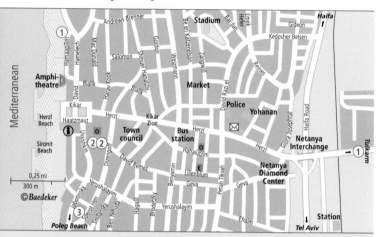

Where to eat
① Shibolym
② Marakesh

Where to stay
① Seasons on the Beach
② Margoa Hotel
③ Orit Guesthouse

Diamond polishing
In the Second World War immigrants from Antwerp brought the art of polishing diamonds to Netanya. Today several thousand people work in the diamond industry and trade. The **National Diamond Center** provides information about diamond polishing, and also sells jewellery of course (90 Herzl St, tel. 09 / 862 04 36).

✳ **Qumran**

F 4

Area: West Bank (Palestinian territory)   **Altitude:** 330m/1085ft below sea level

The Dead Sea Scrolls are more than 2000 years old and world famous. They are the oldest biblical texts and were found in the Caves of Qumran on the coast of the Dead Sea in 1947. The scrolls are on display in the Israel Museum in Jerusalem, while in Qumran visitors can see the excavation site in the barren desert landscape.

Discovery of the scrolls
When a Bedouin boy discovered the first scrolls in a cave in Qumran in 1947, and they proved to be the **oldest copy of the Old Testament**, Qumran, 20km/12mi south of ► Jericho, achieved instant fame. The Bedouin sold the scrolls to an Armenian antique dealer in Bethlehem, after which they went on an adventurous journey. Three of the scrolls found their way into the hands of Professor Eliezer Sukenik at the University of Jerusalem in 1947. The archbishop of the

Syrian St Mark's Monastery took four of them to the United States in 1948, where he offered them for sale in 1954. The Israeli archaeologist Yigal Yadin, son of Professor Sukenik, bought the scrolls, which have been on display together with the others in the **Shrine of the Book** in the Israel Museum in ▶Jerusalem since 1965.

After the sensational discovery, excavation works at the monastery-like complex of the Jewish Essene sect, where the scrolls were found, began in 1952. Archaeologists searched more than 40 caves for further scrolls and were successful in eleven of them. More than 900 manuscripts were found; just four of the caves contained 20,000 fragments, some of them tiny. The manuscripts, **mostly in Hebrew but some also in Aramaic**, are made of parchment and were once stored in clay pots. Some of these pots are still extant and were even filled with intact scrolls when they were discovered.

Many of the texts, most of which were written in the 2nd and 1st centuries BC, are copies of Old Testament books, making them the oldest-known Bible manuscripts to date, and around 1000 years older than previously known copies. One of the two **Isaiah scrolls** is 7.34m/24ft long and contains almost the entire text of the Book of Isaiah. There are also non-biblical scrolls, such as the 2.90m/10ft **War Scrolls**, which address God's victory over the powers of darkness in the end of days, the 1.80m/6ft **Community Rule** and the 9m/29ft **Temple Scroll**, which describes the Temple of the end of days, as well as rules for sacrifices and festivals. The National Museum of Amman in Jordan has two copper scrolls, which were found in Cave 3 in 1953. Copper plates list the locations in the Judaean Desert that the priests selected as hiding places for the temple treasure, shortly before the destruction of Herod's Temple in AD 70 by the Romans.

Biblical and non-biblical scrolls

The oldest copies of the Old Testament were found in the caves of Qumran.

Who were the people of Qumran? Like the Essenes described by the ancient historians Flavius Josephus, Pliny the Elder and Philo of Alexandria, the people of Qumran were members of **Jewish apocalyptic reform groups**, which existed at the time of Jesus alongside the Sadducees and Pharisees. These groups intensively prepared for the apocalypse and saw evidence of its approach in many current events.

Until a few years ago, scholars did not distinguish between the Essenes and the people of Qumran; but today it is known that although they had many similarities, they did not necessarily form a group. The above-mentioned ancient historians contradicted themselves in their description of the Essenes and were probably referring to several different reform groups. Most of these groups rejected the traditional Jewish lunar calendar and used the solar calendar to determine the dates of their Jewish holidays, as did the primitive Christian church. The reform groups also exhibited a very strict interpretation of the Jewish laws and preached non-violence. Their lives were to be stricter and purer than those of other Jews. They lived among fellow believers and wanted to achieve a reform of the whole of Judaism.

Life in Qumran In the approximately 200 years of their existence, the people of Qumran practised a **strictly regulated communal life**. The monastery was probably constantly inhabited by around 200 to 300 men, women and children. Extreme frugality, piety and especially purity (white clothes, ritual baths) were the uppermost principles. It is considered likely that **John the Baptist** was in touch with the community in Qumran. Maybe he was even a member at one time. Those who were accepted via a ritual bath after several years as a novice handed over their fortune. After ritual cleansing the members gathered once a day to eat together. They farmed land in nearby Ein Feshkha, but also on the plateau surrounding the monastery. During the time of Jesus the marl terraces were still intensively cultivated with date palm plantations; the water came from springs in the Wadi Qumran, which have now run dry.

 VISITING QUMRAN

GETTING THERE · PERSONAL SAFETY

Qumran is best reached from Jerusalem by taxi (from Damascus Gate) or via one of the many tour operators in Jerusalem. Buses to the Dead Sea stop here on request.

Since Qumran lies in Palestinian territory, it is best to inquire about the security situation before visiting.

INFORMATION

Qumran National Park
Tel. (02) 994 22 35
www.parks.org.il
Excavation site: April–Sept daily 8am–5pm, Oct–March 8am–4pm

A THREAT TO CHRISTIANITY?

The famous Dead Sea Scrolls created headlines again 40 years after their discovery. There was even talk of a conspiracy by the Vatican, which is said to have held back the publication and deciphering of the Dead Sea Scrolls. What remains of this theory?

The title itself sounded inflammatory: *The Dead Sea Scrolls Deception* is the name of a work by two American journalists, Michael Baigent and Richard Leigh, which was published in 1991. It was allegedly meant to throw light on the conspiracy theory. The authors are said to have come across two crimes in two different eras

during their research. They believed they had discovered in the scrolls that Jesus was an Essene and did not produce any original teachings, but merely developed the existing teachings of the Essenes. Christ's brother James then recorded them in the Dead Sea Scrolls. The interpretations of Saint Paul, which are important

foundations of Christianity, distorted these messages and turned them into »the teachings of Jesus«. James and Stephen are even claimed to be victims of mysterious murders. The second crime, according to the two authors, took place in the more recent past: the Vatican, so their theory goes, used middlemen to prevent the publication of central writings from the Dead Sea Scrolls in order to eliminate the danger that fundamentals of Christianity could be overturned by new insights about events in the time of Jesus.

New insights

Today, almost 20 years after the scandal, the uproar about the bestseller has died down and the two journalists have been exposed as the mouthpiece of the sensationalist US biblical scholar Robert Eisenman. All of the Dead Sea Scrolls have been published now, including the tiniest fragments from Cave 4, which previously spent decades locked up in the scroll room in the Rockefeller Museum in Jerusalem, where they were only accessible to a small international team of scholars. The true scandal, according to the renowned New Testament scholar Klaus Berger, was the lack of interest on the part of scholars to publish the scrolls in their entirety and systematically compare them with the contents of the New Testament. The translation of the texts has indeed revealed much that is new and interesting, especially the **large number of parallels** between religious Jewish reform groups at the time of Jesus and early Christianity. This could in no way shake the foundations of Christian faith, however; quite the opposite in fact. Berger asks provocatively: »Does the Christian religion have to distinguish itself ›against‹ the others or should it rather take shape in their midst?« Early Christianity did not differ from other Jewish groups at the start of the Common Era through having any remarkable new ideas, he states: there were even many parallels. **What is so unique about Christianity, he says, is the work of Jesus**, which is never mentioned in the Dead Sea Scrolls, as they were written earlier.

Common features

The common features between early Christianity and the Qumran community are still of great interest. It is only in the New Testament and in some of the texts from Qumran that we find the concept of the renewal of Israel by a council of twelve men, which ties in with the twelve tribes of ancient Israel. There is a very close relationship between the ritual baths in Qumran and early Christian bap-

tism, even though Christian baptism only occurs once, while the ritual bath in Qumran was performed on a daily basis. In both cases the immersion stands for a turning point.

The **daily meals** that were taken together in Qumran are popularly associated with the Christian Eucharist. More recent research has revealed that the shared meals in Qumran symbolized the daily sacrificial ceremonies in the temple, since communal life was also considered to be a spiritual temple that replaced the material temple in Jerusalem. The Christian Eucharist, which re-enacts the sacrifice of Christ, could have its origin or at least its inspiration in this context.

The **deep piety and the prayer habits** in Qumran reveal the closest parallels to early Christianity. The faith in God that they lived every day was expressed through prayers, blessings, worship and hymns. Early Christianity was similar. Even though there is nothing about early Christianity in the Dead Sea Scrolls, the contents of its faith are much closer to those of the early Christians than to those of other known groups within Judaism at the time, such as the Pharisees and Sadducees.

It is therefore a **new and revolutionary** insight that the spiritual Jewish environment from which Christianity developed 2000 years ago can be recognized in the apocalyptic reform groups of Judaism, which included the Essenes, the people of Qumran and other groups. Christianity is therefore not defined by being different from Judaism; it can also be understood as an intensification of certain Jewish concepts. Thanks to the deciphering of the Dead Sea Scrolls, the Judaism of Christ's day is also accepted as a »context« for early Christianity by a wide Christian population.

What to See in Qumran

The monastery-like complex, built on a terrace above the northern shore of the Dead Sea, was founded in around 150 BC above the remains of a settlement from the 8th and 7th centuries BC. It was destroyed in 31 BC by an earthquake, but partially rebuilt from 4 BC onwards. The final destruction occurred in AD 68 at the hands of Roman troops during the Great Revolt against the occupiers. The inhabitants must have taken their library to safety in the nearby caves shortly beforehand.

✳
The monastery complex

The complex was once surrounded by a high wall. No sleeping quarters were discovered so it is likely the inhabitants slept in the surrounding caves. The remains of a defensive tower stand near the entrance. It affords the best overview. To the east of it were the utility rooms and the kitchen. There is a long, narrow room to the south of the tower, whose upper storey probably housed the writing room, the **scriptorium**, in which many of the discovered scrolls were written – a conclusion drawn from the discovery of long, narrow desks, three inkwells and manuscript samples. The elongated room to the south of the scriptorium, measuring 24 x 4.5m/26 x 5yd, is believed to have been an assembly room or dining room, the **refectory**. Right next to it, in a small larder, piles of tableware were found, around 1700 clay vessels in total. In the western section of the excavation site a canal connects the cisterns to the ritual baths, which were fed from the Wadi Qumran.

Beyond the buildings, further south, is a refuge, which is situated exactly opposite Cave 4. In this cave around 20,000 manuscript fragments were found, some of them only the size of a postage stamp.

Qumran Plan

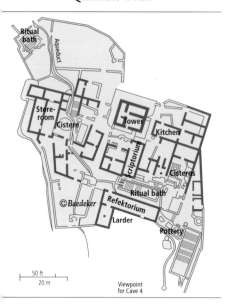

50 ft
20 m

Viewpoint for Cave 4

✳
Caves

Their long-drawn-out publication caused the »Dead Sea Scroll scandal« (▶ Baedeker Special p. 377). Some of the other caves in which scrolls were found lie high up in the mountains, others in the cliffs of the marl plateau where the monastery stands. The first scrolls were found in Cave 1 in 1947 more than a kilometre to the north.

Ramallah · Rām Allāh

Area: West Bank
(Palestinian territory)

Altitude: 870m/2855ft
Population: 61,000

When the West Bank was handed over to the Palestinian National Authority in December 1995, Ramallah became the West Bank's administrative centre and has been the unofficial capital of the Palestinian territories ever since. A large percentage of the Palestinian elite live in and around Ramallah. The Palestinian Legislative Council is based here, as are the official Palestinian radio and television broadcasters and a number of ministries.

The Second Intifada seemed to have put paid to Ramallah. With its restaurants, bars and clubs, the city had been a nightlife outpost for the Jerusalem scene. Rumours, Up Side and the Black Horse, to name just three, were venues for celebrations and dancing all night long. Nothing of this was left after the Intifada, and many feared none of it would return for a very long time. But they were wrong. Ramallah is rocking once more, and is the party hotspot of the West Bank. While Jerusalem's Jews are still leery, tourists and expats are prepared to undergo the checkpoint controls to make their way here.

Capital of the Palestinian National Authority

Orientation is exceptionally easy in Ramallah. The six main roads of the two parts of town emanate from a central square, al-Manarah. The offices of the Palestinian National Authority, the Mukataa, once a British barracks, were partially destroyed by the Israeli military; **Yassir Arafat** lies buried here in a modern mausoleum. The Khalil Sakakini Cultural Centre (4 Raja St, tel. 02 298 73 75, www.sakaki-ni.org) exhibits modern Palestinian art, while the Popular Art Centre exhibits traditional handicrafts.

What to see

✳ Ramla

District: Central
Population: 65,000

Altitude: 70m/230ft

The modern town, 19km/12mi southeast of ► Tel Aviv, possesses several interesting buildings from Islamic and Christian times, including the White Tower and the medieval Great Mosque.

Ramla (Ramle) is a town with a long history. The **Umayyad caliph Suleiman** founded it in 715 with a fortress, palaces and mosques. He named it Ramle (»sand«) after the region's sandy soil. When the

Founded by the Umayyads

Umayyads were replaced by the Abbasids in AD 750, very devout Sufis from the caliph residence of Baghdad came to Ramle. At the end of the 11th century and the start of the 12th century, the armies of the crusaders and the Egyptian Fatimids fought several battles. After the crusaders came the Mamluks in 1267. Today Ramla is a largely Jewish town with a small Arabic and Christian population.

What to See in and around Ramla

Great Mosque
The Great Mosque, originally a 12th-century crusader basilica, is located in the eastern part of town to the south of Herzl Street, in the middle of the oriental market. Its appearance has not changed to any great degree. The current minaret stands on the foundations of the former belfry.

Church of St Joseph
Follow Herzl St. in a northwesterly direction to get to the Franciscan Church of St Joseph. It is dedicated to the biblical **Joseph of Arimathaea**, who made the tomb set aside for himself available for the burial of Jesus.

✳
White Tower, White Mosque
The 27m/89ft White Tower, the main attraction in Ramla, was built by the Mamluk sultan Baibars in 1270 and was completed shortly after 1300. The blind arches and round-arch windows, which are reminiscent of Gothic bell towers, reveal the influence of Western architecture. 120 steps lead up to its **viewing platform**, where the view of Ramla is splendid.

According to Islamic tradition the White Tower is also called the »tower of the 40 companions of the prophet«, while Christians refer to it as the »tower of the 40 martyrs« who are said to lie buried here. It was originally used as the minaret of the White Mosque, which was built by the Umayyads in the 8th century. On the south side, opposite the tower, lay the elongated prayer room with twelve columns; Caliph Suleiman had three huge, vaulted cisterns built in the courtyard. Steps lead down to them. In the courtyard's northwestern corner is the tomb of the Islamic saint **Nebi Saleh**.

> ! *Baedeker* TIP
>
> **Biblical landscape**
> The attraction of the **Neot Kedumim** nature reserve, around 7km/4.5mi east of Lod, is that it is a journey back in time: the plants cultivated here dominated the landscape of biblical Israel. Anyone feeling peckish after a stroll through the »ancient landscape« can regain their strength from a »biblical« menu in one of the two garden restaurants (more information under tel. 08/977 07 77, www.neot-kedumim.org.il).

St Helen's Pool
The road that branches off from the main road to the east of the police station leads to a cistern 9m/30ft deep, which dates back to around 800. The crusaders attributed it to Empress Helena (4th century), who commissioned lots of building works, which is why they called it »St

Helen's Pool«, but the cistern dates back to the era of the fifth Abbasid caliph **Harun al-Rashid** (766–809), of *Arabian Nights* fame.

Ben Gurion International Airport lies near Lod (Lydda), 3km/2mi to the northeast of Ramla. Founded during the time of the Israelites' land seizure and destroyed by the Assyrians in the 8th century BC, Lod was settled by Greeks from the 4th century BC onwards. A Christian community established itself here early on. Peter came to these believers and healed one man who had been bedridden for eight years (Acts 9:32–34). Under Arab rule the town was called al-Ludd. Most Arab inhabitants were forced to leave the town in 1948; today it is largely home to Jewish Israelis, but also a few Arab families.

Lod

Lod is believed to be the **birthplace of Saint George**, whose tomb is the town's most-visited attraction. Saint George, who had served as a tribune in the Roman army, suffered martyrdom under Diocletian in 303. His mortal remains were brought to Lod, where his tomb has been on display since the 5th century. As »el-Chodr«, who will overcome the daemon Dadjal outside of the gates of Lod on Judgement Day, Saint George also became an Islamic saint.

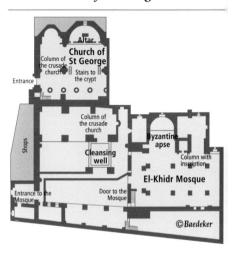

Church of St George Plan

© Baedeker

A first church above the tomb of Saint George, founded in the 6th century, was destroyed several times. During the second half of the 12th century the crusaders built a new church, a basilica with a nave and two aisles This church was destroyed by the Mamluks. El-Chodr Mosque was built on its ruins. After the Greek Orthodox believers had acquired the land in 1870, they built the current church of St George. The separate entrances to the church and the mosque can be found on the western side. The left one leads into the Greek Orthodox church of St George. Above the entrance is a relief of the saint as a dragon slayer. The church stands above the northern parts of the nave and left aisle of the former crusader church. The steps down into the crypt are in front of the iconostasis. The crypt contains the saint's tomb. Saint George is depicted on the sarcophagus lid, which according to the inscription was replaced in 1871 under patriarch Kyrillos.

✳
◀ Church of St George and El-Chodr Mosque

The right-hand entrance leads into El-Chodr Mosque, whose apse in the prayer room still dates back to the Byzantine church of St George.

★ Safed

District: Northern   **Altitude:** 750–834m/2460–2736ft
Population: 28,000

This small artists' town in the mountains of Upper Galilee, 35km/ 22mi from Tiberias and the Sea of Galilee, is one of the four holy Jewish towns and a centre of Kabbala mysticism.

History   In 1102 the crusaders built a castle here, which was acquired by Saladin in 1188. Renovated in 1240 by French Templars, it had to capitulate to the Mamluk sultan Baibars in 1266. Safed became a Jewish town in the 16th century under Ottoman rule, when Jews from Europe and northern Africa settled here. In around 1550 they already numbered more than 10,000. The **first Hebrew book** was also printed in Safed in 1578. In the late 19th century Arab families settled once more in the rebuilt town. At the start of the war in 1948 Safed was home to 12,000 Arabs and 1700 Jews. In the wake of the fighting the Arab population fled from the town.

> ### *i* Strict »Tzfat«
>
> ■ When visiting Safed, which is pronounced »Tzfat«, bear in mind that the rules regarding dress are somewhat stricter here than in other towns in Israel, though miniskirts are seen often enough. Safed is also fairly strict about observing the Sabbath. This means that from Friday evening until Saturday evening many restaurants and cafés are closed.

What to See in Safed

Hametzuda   The districts of Safed are spread over a very hilly landscape. The town is approached via sweeping curves through new housing estates up to the old centre. The heart of the town below Yerushalayim Street nestles on the slopes of Hametzuda Hill in terraces – climbing steps in Safed is almost unavoidable! The 834m/2736ft tell is worth climbing for the **good views**. In the park there are some scanty remains of a crusader fortress and a monument commemorating those fallen in 1948.

Cave of Shem and Ever ▶   The Cave of Shem and Ever lies below the tell. According to Jewish tradition Noah's son Shem and his grandson Ever studied the Torah here.

Rehov Yerushalayim   Rehov Yerushalayim (Jerusalem Street), which is partially pedestrianized, is the **main shopping street**. It has many small street cafés, boutiques, tattoo and body-piercing studios, and also estate agents with numerous adverts for rental properties. Safed is totally geared to spiritual tourism, which got an additional uplift in 2009 with a visit from the pop queen and Kabbala devotee Madonna. Everywhere you can find Kabbala courses (in English), many of them bookable

● VISITING SAFED

INFORMATION

Visitor Centre
17 Alkabez St
Tel. (04) 692 44 27

GETTING THERE

Several bus connections a day from
Akko, Haifa, Tel Aviv and Jerusalem
to the bus station at the entrance to
the town

EVENTS

The Wolfson Community Centre
regularly hosts concerts, matinees and
other cultural events (Hapalmach St.,
tel. 04 / 697 12 22). Another lively
venue is the Yigal Allon Theatre &
Cultural Centre (Hapalmach St., tel.
04 / 697 19 90).

SHOPPING

The artists' quarter in the Old Town
attracts busloads of tourists with its
numerous galleries and craft shops.
There is a respectable exhibition of
artworks in the old mosque, now the
Safed Artists House (tel. 04 6 92 00
87, Sun–Thu 9am–4pm, Fri
9am–2pm, Sat 10am–2pm,
www.artists.co.il/safed)

WHERE TO EAT

► Inexpensive
Art Café
71 Yerushalayim St.
Tel. (04) 682 09 28
Small dishes, snacks and a good
selection of coffees.

Mr. Lachuch
17 Alkabez St
A classic: Ronen, aka Lachuch, serves
Yemeni flatbread with herbs and
cheese, always fresh.

Mul Hahar
70 Yerushalayim St.
Tel. (04) 692 04 04
Restaurant specialized in fish
dishes

Café Baghdad
61 Yerushalayim St.
Tel. 04 692 24 29
Good view over the valley from the
terrace. Menu includes meat, fish and
pizza.

WHERE TO STAY

► Mid-range
Ruth Rimonim
In the artists' quarter
Tel. (04) 699 46 66
www.rimonim.com
81 rooms; the hotel, housed in a
former caravanserai, combines the
charm of its age with modern
amenities.

► Budget
Beit Binyamin Youth Hostel
1 Lohamei Hagetaot St.
Tel. (04) 692 10 86
tzfat@iyha.org.il
Very pleasant accommodation with
20 well-equipped rooms

at short notice. Continue walking past the southern end of the street
to get to the town's artists' quarter, then head northwest to explore
the interesting old town and its many synagogues.

Artists' quarter

✳ Continue southbound down Rehov Yerushalayim to get to the artists' quarter; it was built in the area that had been an Arab residential neighbourhood until 1948. The small, jumbled houses, most of which are surrounded by pretty little gardens, are home to around 60 painters and sculptors. Many of them have their own galleries. The former mosque in this quarter is now used by the artists as a retail space for their work.

Synagogue quarter

✳ The boundary between the artists' quarter and the old town or synagogue quarter to the north is formed by Ma'alot Olei Hagardom, a wide street of steps. Its name means »men who were hungry« and refers to the situation of the Jewish inhabitants during the Arab siege. Narrow streets and houses built out of light-coloured stone give the synagogue quarter a friendly atmosphere with an oriental feel. Attractive handicrafts and souvenirs are for sale in a small bazaar. The synagogues, all of them named after important rabbis, hardly differ at all from the residential buildings in their appearance. The **Yosef Caro Synagogue** stands in the eponymous street near the house in which the rabbi lived. A little further down is **Ha'alsheh Synagogue**, while **Abouav Synagogue** lies a little further to the north. Its wooden shrine still contains the Torah that the Spanish rabbi Abouav wrote in the 15th century. **Ha'ari Synagogue** at the lower western end of town is the oldest synagogue in Safed. Mentioned in documents for the first time in 1522, it was used by the Sephardi, i.e. by Jews who came here from Muslim countries or India. Look out for its artistically designed Torah shrine made of olive wood, which was created at the end of the 19th century by an eastern European wood carver.

The museum, located in a wonderfully restored old house with a garden, contains many interesting details about the history of Safed and Jewish life in the town. It lies relatively far down the hillside near the Olei Hagardom steps (Sun–Thu 9am–2pm, Fri until 1pm).

◀ Hameiri House (Beit Hameiri)

Continue even further down the hill, in a northbound direction, to get to the Jewish cemetery, in which Rabbi Ari (d. 1573) and Yosef Caro (d. 1575) lie buried.

◀ Old Jewish cemetery

Around Safed

The village of Meron, founded north of ancient Meron in 1949, lies 9km/5.5mi west of Safed on the eastern slopes of 1208m/3963ft Mount Meron. It is the site of the tomb of Rabbi **Simeon bar Yochai**, a leader of the Bar Kokhba revolt. He and his son Eleazar hid from the Romans in a cave near Peki'in in the valley of the same name on the western slopes of Mount Meron during the last Jewish revolt. Jewish tradition associates the kabbalistic book of **Zohar** (»Splendour«) with him, but that was only written in Spain in 1270.

Meron

The tombs of Simeon bar Yochai and his son Eleazar lie at the centre of town, in a building surrounded by a high wall. The building with the two tombs is adorned with shallow white domes. The two pipe-like copper containers on the roof are used as flares when processions are held.

◀ Tomb of Simeon bar Yochai

The **synagogue**, whose remains can be found on an elevation to the north of the town centre, is also associated with the name Simeon bar Yochai. Only the south-facing main façade of the building, which once measured 27 x 13.5m/ 90 x 45ft, is extant. Two rows of eight columns each divided the 3rd and 4th-century synagogue into a nave and two aisles.

> ## ! Baedeker TIP
>
> ### Rashbi Hilula
>
> In honour of Rabbi Simeon Bar Yochai, thousands of Jews from all around the world come to Meron every year in late April or early May to celebrate real Jewish »folklore« during the Rashbi Hilula festival, with processions, song and dance.

There are further tombs not far from the Simeon mausoleum, including the rock tomb of **Rabbi Hillel** and his students, as well as the tomb attributed to **Rabbi Shammai** across the valley. Both rabbis founded Mishnah schools in the 1st century; Hillel's teaching were liberal, while Shammai's were strict.

◀ Tombs

Around 40km/25mi to the northwest of Safed, above the kibbutz of Bar'am, is the eponymous excavation site, now a **national park**, with an old synagogue that is worth seeing. According to legend prophet Obadiah and Esther, wife of the Persian king Xerxes, were buried in Bar'am. The restored synagogue, which remains extant up to the second storey, dates back to the 2nd or 3rd century, making it one of the **oldest cultural monuments in the country**.

★ Bar'am

✷ Samaria · Shomron

Area: West Bank
(Palestinian territory)

Altitude: 430m/1410ft

Between 880 and 721 BC Samaria was the capital of the northern Kingdom of Israel. Its extensive ruins lie above the Arab village of Sebastiya, 11km/7mi to the northwest of ▶ Nablus, and around 30km/18mi east of ▶ Netanya.

Capital of the Kingdom of Israel
When the United Monarchy broke up after Solomon's death in 928 BC, the capital of the Kingdom of Israel was first in Shechem (▶ Nablus) and then in Tirzah near Nablus. After a quick succession of kings the fifth ruler of the Kingdom of Israel, **Omri**, founded the new capital, Samaria, in the 9th century. Omri and his son **Ahab**, who also commissioned a lot of building works in ▶ Hazor and ▶ Megiddo, built palaces and temples in Samaria. When Samaria was conquered by the Assyrian **Shalmaneser V** in 722 BC, the kingdom ceased to exist. In the following period Samaria was a military base for the Assyrians, Babylonians and Persians.

The town was revitalized by **Herod**. He had married the Hasmonaean princess Mariamne there in 38 BC and renamed it **Sebaste** in honour of Augustus (Greek »Sebastos«). Sebaste only flourished for a few years. Jewish rebels set fire to the Temple of Augustus and a short while later, in AD 68, **Vespasian** destroyed the fort. When his son Titus founded Neapolis (▶ Nablus) in AD 72, Sebaste's decline was guaranteed. Because **relics of John the Baptist** were found in Sebaste – although he was not killed here but in Machaerus in eastern Jordan – pilgrims have been coming here since the 5th century, and the relics are still venerated in the mosque in Sebastiya village today.

✷ Excavation Site

Approach
There are two access roads to the ruins of Samaria. Either drive through the village of Sebastiya (only for cars) or take the small road a little further to the north and drive through the western gate of the former town, along the colonnaded road to the ruins (also open to buses).

Forum
The ancient forum lies right behind Sebastiya. Facilities include a car park, a restaurant and a souvenir shop. At the western end of the 128 x 72m/140 x 79 yd square was a **market basilica** from the time of Septimius Severus (around AD 200). The foundation walls and an exedra in the north can still be made out and some columns are also still standing.

Acropolis
A footpath leads from the forum's northwestern corner to the acropolis. Visitors first come to an Israelite wall on the hillside, from the

Samaria Map

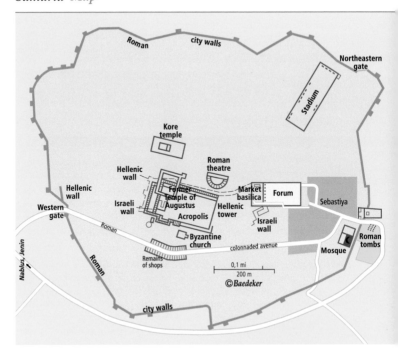

Roman
city walls

Northeastern
gate

Stadium

Kore temple

Roman theatre

Hellenic wall

Market basilica   Forum

Hellenic wall

Former Temple of Augustus

Israeli wall

Hellenic tower

Sebastiya

Western gate

Acropolis

Roman

Byzantine church

Israeli wall

Roman tombs

Remains of shops

colonnaded avenue

Mosque

Nablus, Jenin

Roman

0,1 mi
200 m
© Baedeker

city walls

9th or 8th century BC, in front of which a Hellenistic fortified wall with a powerful round defensive tower (3rd century) was built. To the right next to it are the remains of a Roman theatre. To the left of the tower is a monumental flight of steps. It led to the **Temple of Augustus**, built by Herod, which is completely gone now. It was built above the buried palace of King Omri by his son Ahab and his Phoenician wife Jezebel, which is also why there was a statue of Astarte here. The pieces of ivory discovered here confirm statements by contemporary witnesses about the magnificent ornamentation of this palace and about those »who feel secure on Mount Samaria« (Amos 6:1–4).

A small church built to the south of the acropolis during the Byzantine period occupies the spot where, according to tradition, the head of **John the Baptist** was discovered.

Byzantine church

A road lined by colonnades and shops leads from the forum to the western city gate. This road was built in around AD 200 and can also be seen from the acropolis. Although the city gate dates back to King Omri, in its current form it is more recent.

✶
Colonnaded road

Mosque The mosque in the village of Sebastiya, which is located in the eastern area of the ancient city grounds, emerged from a 12th-century crusader church, which in turn succeeded a 4th-century Byzantine church. It is believed that the tombs of the prophets Elisha and Obadiah as well as the burial site of John the Baptist's head are in niches in the crypt. The remaining relics of John the Baptist can be found in the Umayyad Mosque in Damascus.

★ Sde Boker

E 6

District: Southern   **Population:** 600

The kibbutz of Sde Boker, the »field of the farmers«, is located right in the desert landscape of the ▸Negev, around 50km/30mi to the south of ▸Beersheba and above the Wadi Zin. The flourishing agricultural settlement is a good starting point for hikes into the wild and romantic nature reserve of Ein Avdat.

Sde Boker and Ben Gurion The kibbutz is closely associated with the name of David Ben Gurion, Israel's first prime minister (▸Famous People). When he stepped down from office in 1953, he joined the young kibbutz in order to do »what was really important«, meaning making the Negev fertile. 14 months later he took on another political office, initially that of minister of defence, then that of prime minister again. It was not until 1963, when he was 77, that he withdrew fully to Sde Boker, where he also found his final resting place.

What to See in Sde Boker

★
Ben Gurion's house Around half a mile to the south of the kibbutz, there is a turning off Route 40 to the house that Ben Gurion once lived in. The small house, situated in a pretty garden, is only a little more luxurious than

 VISITING SDE BOKER

INFORMATION
Tel. (08) 653 28 01
www.boker.org.il/english

WHERE TO EAT
▸ **Inexpensive**
Zin Inn
The »desert restaurant« on the university campus serves hearty, honest fare.

WHERE TO STAY
▸ **Budget**
Field School Hostel Hamburg House
Campus
Tel. (08) 653 20 16
orders@boker.org.il
The two guesthouses of the kibbutz's university have 47 and 20 rooms respectively with 2 to 6 beds in each.

Modest accommodation for a great statesman: David Ben Gurion's house in Sde Boker

the other houses in the kibbutz, and the interior has remained almost unchanged (Sun–Thu 8.30am–4pm, Fri until 2pm, Sat 9am–2.30pm). ⏲

Turn east off the main road 3km/2mi to the south of the kibbutz, to get to the University of the Negev (Midreshet Sde Boker), a branch of Ben Gurion University in ▶Beersheba. The university, founded by Ben Gurion, is dedicated to researching arid areas, and especially the ▶Negev.

Ben Gurion University of the Negev

The tombs of Ben Gurion and his wife Paula are in a very well-tended park, immediately beside the library. The two simple tombs, surrounded by trees, are right by the cliffs down to the **Wadi Zin**, which begins at the spring of Avdat. On the way there fairly tame ibexes wait to be fed; it is better not to indulge them.

Ben Gurion's tomb

✴ Ein Avdat

The spring at Ein Avdat – not to be confused with the neighbouring ruins of ▶Avdat – is **one of the most beautiful natural features in the Negev**. Four springs rise amid a landscape of bare (except for a few settlements) mountains of almost oppressive contours. Ein Avdat spring, which rises in a lovely canyon-like gorge, is particularly plentiful. The Nahal Zin emerges from this gorge and goes on to flow through the Zin Desert (Midbar Zin).

Approach and hike to Ein Avdat spring

The canyon in which Ein Avdat spring is located opens up between Sde Boker and Avdat; the access route to the spring begins at the University of the Negev. Take the road out of the kibbutz and drive to the university. Turn right shortly before reaching the first buildings. The narrow road goes down into the valley and ends at a car park. Continue on foot from here. The gorge gets progressively narrower. The white cliffs reflect the sunlight and the water flows between boulders and bushes. The trail then leads to the place where the spring water flows over a rock face and gathers in a pool. Ibexes come to the pool to drink in the mornings and evenings.

! Baedeker TIP

View of the canyon

Not got enough time for a hike to Ein Avdat spring? Then at least take a look down into the canyon. The viewpoint is signposted on Route 40 between Sde Boker and the ruins of Avdat.

★ ★ Sea of Galilee · Yam Kinneret

G 2

District: Northern   **Altitude:** 210m/690ft below sea level

Stunning scenery and varied leisure activities make the Sea of Galilee a popular holiday and day-trip area for Israelis. At the same time the sea is also an important destination for those with an interest in religious history.

Holiday region with biblical sites

Tabgha, the site of the miracle of the multiplication of the loaves and the fish, and ▶Capernaum, where Jesus found his disciples, are just two examples of sites on the lake shores that are associated with Christ's life and influence. **Israel's largest freshwater lake**, set between the Golan Heights in the east and the Galilean mountains in the west, lies 210m/690ft below sea level and is therefore the **lowest-lying freshwater lake in the world**. The body of water, which covers an area of 170 sq km/65 sq mi and is up to 45m/148ft deep, is also Israel's most important drinking-water reservoir: it provides 4% of the country's requirements, which is why fluctuations in the water level are sometimes extreme. On the promenade in Tiberias a striking sculpture in the shape of the lake indicates the current water level.

Tourism is mainly centred around the northern and western shores. The southern and eastern shores are quieter. However, there are several bathing beaches with picnic sites and leisure facilities there too. The largest town and the tourist stronghold on the Sea of Galilee (Yam Kinneret) is ▶Tiberias with the spa resort of Tiberias-Hammat. The climate on the shore of the lake is warm all year round and hot

VISITING SEA OF GALILEE

INFORMATION
Lake Tiberias

BY BOAT
Regular boat connections between Tiberias and the kibbutz of Ein Gev on the lake's eastern shore (trip duration: approx. 45 mins) as well as between Tiberias and Ginosar and the excavation site of Capernaum.

WHERE TO EAT
► Moderate
Ein Gev Fish Restaurant
Kibbutz Ein Gev
Tel. (04) 665 81 368
Well-known restaurant on the lake's eastern shore with a large garden terrace.

WHERE TO STAY
► Mid-range
Nof Ginosar
Ginosar
Tel. (04) 679 21 61, fax 679 21 70
www.ginosar.co.il

170 rooms. Well-maintained hotel complex with its own beach, swimming pool, tennis court and boat rental facility.

Baedeker recommendation

Maagan Holiday Village
Jordan Valley
Tel. (04) 665 44 00
Fax 665 44 55
www.maagan.com
36 rooms and 112 apartments. Extensive complex on the southern shore with a nice, well-kept garden, kids' pool and a mini market. Perfectly suited for families.

► Budget
Ein Gev Holiday Village
Tel. (04) 665 98 00
resort@eingev.org.il
184 rooms. Family-friendly holiday village in the kibbutz of Ein Gev on the eastern shore.

---

in summer, allowing subtropical plants to flourish here. They add to the special appeal of the scenery. Since there are lots of fish in the lake, fishing still has a certain economic significance here. The restaurant speciality here is St Peter's fish, a cichlid.

Northern Shore

Lavish green frames the Jordan just before it flows into the Sea of Galilee. The nature reserve Hayarden Park (Jordan River Park) is a lovely spot to explore the river and the surrounding area as part of a boat trip or a hike (April–Sept daily 8am–5pm, in winter until 4pm). To get to Hayarden from ►Capernaum, take road no. 87 along the waterfront for around 2km/1.25mi in an eastbound direction. Just after Ariq Bridge across the Jordan, Route 888 branches off to the entrance of the nature reserve. The settlement, which is probably 3000 years old and was discovered in the 1990s, is allegedly **the bibli-**

★
Hayarden Park, Bethsaida
⊙

Passengers should feel completely safe on board this boat on the Sea of Galilee.

cal **Bethsaida**, presumably the capital of the king of Geshur, whose daughter Maacah was married to King David. Bethsaida is also the birthplace of the apostles Peter, Andrew and Philip. According to the St Mark's Gospel (Mark 8:22–26) Jesus healed a blind man here.

Two marked hiking trails through the park grounds start at the old mill. Anyone wanting to go down the Jordan by boat can hire a kayak or dinghy.

Further places on the north shore The most interesting sites on the lake's north shore are ►Capernaum and Tabgha. The view from the ►Mount of Beatitudes to the north of Capernaum is priceless.

Western Shore

Ginosar kibbutz The kibbutz of Ginosar, founded in 1937, lies on the shore of the Sea of Galilee around halfway between Capernaum and ►Tiberias. When the lake's water level dropped significantly in 1986 as a result of a long dry spell, a spectacular discovery was made in the mud: a wreck 8.20m/27ft long and 2.30m/8ft wide, which was built between 70 BC and AD 90 and is now on display in the kibbutz's **Yigal Alon Center**. Boats like this were used for fishing during the time of Jesus. The interesting museum also provides information about Galilee's settlement history and the region's special features (Sat–Thu 8am–5pm, Fri until 1pm).

5km/3mi further north is the pilgrimage site of Tabgha (Hebrew: Ein Sheva), the **»site of the seven springs«**. This is the purported site of the **miraculous Feeding of the Five Thousand** by Jesus (Matthew 15:32–38; Mark 8:1–9).

★
Tabgha

The first church in this place, a hall church measuring 15 x 9m/50 x 30ft was built in the 4th century and replaced by a columned basilica in the 5th century. In order to protect the basilica's floor mosaics, which were discovered in 1911 and fully uncovered in 1932, a make-shift wooden church was built next to it in 1936; in 1956 a Benedictine monastery was built. In the early 1980s the provisional church was pulled down as it had become dilapidated. A Byzantine-style church was then built on the foundations of the basilica.

◄ Church of the Multiplication

The largely preserved **5th-century mosaics** are of varying artistic quality. The floors in the nave and the left aisle depict simple geometric patterns, while the mosaics between the columns are more artistic. They depict geese, herons and other birds. The most interesting mosaics can be found in the transepts: the artist, who was evidently familiar with the Nile delta, depicted the flora and fauna of that region, including flamingos, ducks and snakes, lotus blossoms and reeds. The mosaics in the southern aisle also depict a nilometer, with which the river's water level was checked. An altar was built above the stone on which Jesus is said to have laid the bread and fishes to »feed the five thousand«; right in front of it the most famous mosaic of the Church of the Multiplication depicts two fishes and a basket of bread.

★ ★
◄ Mosaics
Photo p. 86

An area to the east is also part of the Tabgha site. Its entrance can be found some 200m/200yd further along the road towards Capernaum. A path leads past the place where the Byzantines tapped a spring and down to the **Church of the Primacy of St Peter**, which stands right on the shores of the Sea of Galilee. The predecessor of the present church, built of black basalt by the Franciscans in 1933, dated back to the 4th century and was destroyed in 1263. The simple hall church is believed to be the place where the risen Jesus appeared to his disciples and Jesus told Peter »feed my lambs ... feed my sheep ... feed my sheep«, thereby handing over the running of the Church to him (John 21:16–16). Jesus and his disciples are said to have eaten together afterwards at the large stone block in the eastern part of the church.

◄ Church of the Primacy of St Peter

There is a complex of ruins between the Church of the Multiplication and the Church of the Primacy of St Peter, immediately to the north of the road. The Church of the Beatitudes was built here in the 4th century, at around the same time as the first Church of the Multiplication and the first Church of the Primacy of St Peter. There are monastic rooms in the south of the complex, while there is a hall church in the north, whose apse projects to the east above the enclosing wall.

◄ Church of the Beatitudes

Eastern Shore

8km/5mi opposite Tiberias as the crow flies is the kibbutz of Ein Gev, which was founded in 1937 and whose residents mainly live off

Ein Gev kibbutz

agriculture and fishing. The late mayor of Jerusalem, **Teddy Kollek** (▶ Famous People), was among its founders. Trippers mainly come here for the popular fish restaurant (p. 393). A small museum in the kibbutz explains the history and development of fishing on the Sea of Galilee; the Esco Music Center stages the Ein Gev Music Festival every year in April.

Southern Shore

Yardenit Baptists created the baptismal site of Yardenit (tel. 04 6 75 91 11, www.yardenit.com) in 1981 near where the Jordan flows into the Sea of Galilee. Even though this is not the place where Jesus was baptized, some 1 million pilgrims annually still come here for baptism in the »holy waters« of the Jordan, and receive a certificate to confirm the same.

A huge souvenir shop and a restaurant look after the worldly needs of the pilgrims: on sale are bottles and canisters of water, also crosses, rosaries, wine, date jam and cosmetics.

Degania Around one kilometre beyond Yardenit is Degania, the **country's oldest kibbutz**, founded by Russian emigrants in 1909. Here a burned-out tank belonging to the Syrian army, which got all the way to the kibbutz during the war in 1948, can still be seen. The museum, named after Aharon D. Gordon, one of the founding members of the kibbutz, exhibits archaeological and natural historical items from the region (Sun–Thu 9am–3pm, Fri 10am–1pm). The kibbutz of Degania Bet, which has a guesthouse, is very close by.

> ❗ **Baedeker TIP**
>
> **Outstanding sea views**
>
> Around 5km/3mi to the north of Ein Gev, Route 789 turns off from Route 92 and reaches the viewpoint of Mitzpe Ofir after 9km/5.5mi. The view of the Sea of Galilee is wonderful from here.

★ ★ Tel Aviv · Jaffa / Yafo

E 3

District: Tel Aviv	**Population:** 390,000
Altitude: Sea level	

»Big Orange«, is the Israeli nickname for Tel Aviv. It is not just the country's second-largest city and the heart of the most important economic region, it is also a city where going out and having fun are given priority. As the »White City« it plays on its splendid legacy of Bauhaus architecture, as »Gay TLV« on its high degree of tolerance and openness, which are not to be taken for granted in Israel.

The political problems and religiosity that are ubiquitous in ►Jerusa-   **Israel's trend city**
lem seem far away here. Not many men wear a kippah or even a
shtreimel here; instead lots of fashion-conscious young people like to
throw themselves into the city's nightlife in »Shabbat Night Fever«,
for which there are plenty of bars and cafés available. There are also
boutiques, malls and unusual shopping venues unlike any to be
found elsewhere in the country. The city also has museums, theatres,
concert venues and galleries, thereby offering an interesting, diverse
cultural life: **Tel Aviv sets many trends** in Israel. In a survey con-
ducted worldwide, Tel Aviv was chosen as the »best gay city«, way
ahead of New York or London.

Just a stone's throw from the centres of culture and commerce, visitors find the long city beaches to which the people of Tel Aviv come
to unwind. Those who prefer an old-town atmosphere should go to
Jaffa, the old port to the south, with which Tel Aviv merged a long
time ago.

Tel Aviv is no beauty; anyone looking down on the city from the   **»White City«**
Shalom Tower or the viewing platform on the 49th floor of the Az-

Tel Aviv's skyline with the Azrieli Towers

▶ VISITING TEL AVIV – JAFFA

INFORMATION

Tourist Information
46 Herbert Samuel St.
Tel. (03) 516 61 88
www.tel-aviv.gov.il
www.visit-tlv.com
www.tel-aviv-insider.com
Sun–Thu 9.30am–5pm, Fri
9.30am–1pm
Hatachana Train Station Building 5
Tel. 03 776 40 05
Sun–Thu 10am–8pm, Fri 10am–2pm

Jaffa Visitor Centre
Kedumim Square
Tel. (03) 518 40 15
www.oldjaffa.co.il

TRANSPORT

From Ben Gurion International Airport: taxi (30 mins.) or sherut (group taxi). The airport shuttle (line 222) departs every 45 minutes and stops at the major hotels on the waterfront promenade, in Allenby Street, at the youth hostel and at the station.
Urban buses: Dan Bus Lines, 5.30am–midnight, every few minutes (not in operation on the Sabbath).

SIGHTSEEING

Themed city tours in English:
Bauhaus in Tel Aviv (Sat 11am from Rothschild St. / corner of Shadal St.)
University of Tel Aviv (Mon 11am from the campus entrance at Syonon bookshop)
Old Jaffa (Wed 9.30am from the clock tower opposite the police station in Jaffa).

SHOPPING

Shops, boutiques and cafés: from Dizengoff Center Mall across Dizengoff Square to almost the end of **Dizengoff Street**. Further shopping streets include **Allenby St.** and **Ben Yehuda St.**, with lots of shops run by Russian immigrants. **Sheinkin St.**, which is not entirely cheap, and **Mercaz Ba'alei Melacha St.** are home to designer stores and the studios of young fashion designers; the choice is similar in the trendy **Shabazi St.** in the Neve Tzedek quarter. A huge, highly modern shopping mall is **Azrieli Towers. Carmel Market**, a fragrant oriental vegetable, fish, meat market as well as a flea market (Allenby St) is an experience.

EVENTS

Tel Aviv has a vast number of cultural events on a near daily basis. Up-to-date information and listings can be found in the English-language daily newspapers.

Cameri Theatre
30 Leonardo da Vinci St
Ticket line tel. (03) 606 19 60
www.cameri.co.il
Many productions at the Cameri have English subtitles.

Cinematheque
2 Sprinzak St.
Tel. (03) 606 08 00
www.cinema.co.il. As well as hosting the Tel Aviv International Documentary Festival every year in spring, the Cinematheque has a discerning daily film programme and lots of film series for cineastes.

Felicja Blumental Music Center and Library
26 Bialik St.
Tel. (03) 620 11 85
www.fbmc.co.il/center
Regular, outstanding classical music concerts

Habima National Theatre
2 Tarsat Blvd.
Tel. (03) 629 55 55
www.habima.co.il
English subtitles on Thursdays

Israel Ballet
4 Har Nevo St.
Tel. (03) 604 66 10
www.iballet.co.il
Classical ballet performances as well
as modern dance shows

Mann Auditorium
1 Huberman St.
Tickets: tel. (03) 621 17 77
www.hatarbut.co.il

Venue of the Israel Philharmonic
Orchestra; the conductor Zubin Meta
also makes the stage available for
musical productions from Broadway.

Israel's best stage: Habima National Theatre

Mayumana Hall
15 Louis Pasteur St.
Jaffa
Tel. (03) 681 17 87
Worthwhile and often unusual music
and performance events

Suzanne Dellal Center for Dance and Theatre
6 Yehieli St.
Tel. (03) 510 56 56
www.suzannedellal.org.il
One day it's *Carmen*, another it's a
tango festival – the programme of the
Suzanne Dellal Center is always good
for a surprise and a fantastic evening.

The Arab-Hebrew Theatre
10 Mifratz Shlomo St.
Jaffa
Tel. (03) 681 55 54
www.arab-hebrew-theatre.org.il
A theatre with two ensembles, one
Jewish and one Arab, which perform
both separately and together.

Wohl Amphitheatre
Hayarkon Park, Yehoshua Gardens
Tel. (03) 642 28 28
Regular open-air theatre performan-
ces and concerts.

NIGHTLIFE

Tel Aviv has an extremely vibrant
nightlife, but it rarely gets going
before 11pm. A wonderful entertainment venue with bars, restaurants,
shops and concert stages can be found
at the Old Port on the area of the 25
Piers. Get there on foot (it's close to
the hotels) along the waterfront
promenade from Hayarkon St. More
and more clubs are charging to get in
and some even have a minimum
consumption requirement. You may
have to queue to get into a restaurant
unless you have a reservation. There is
an unmistakable trend away from
mega-discos with several dance floors
for hundreds of guests and towards
smaller clubs.

Haoman 17
88 Abarbanel St
Tel. 03 681 36 36
Daily from 11pm. A mega-club: five bars and the same number of dance floors, room for 2500 dancers. Top DJs from all over the world appear here; partying until the next morning.

Erlich
Tel Aviv Port
Tel. (03) 546 67 28
Order tapas and shrimps along with drinks. Towards midnight it gets really full around the circular bars and on the dance floor.

Ginga
Bikurei Haitim Center
6 Heftman St.
Tel. (03) 561 11 03
This dance club has managed to hold on to its reputation as being the meeting place for the in-crowd for several years now.

Nanuchka
28 Lilenblum St
Tel. 03 516 22 54
Even by Tel Aviv standards the proprietress Nana has succeeded in creating an unusual bar-restaurant. The red walls of the Georgian establishment are full of her favourite poems. Georgian specialities are served, the bar is well stocked, and dancing often takes place on the bars themselves, not just to Georgian music.

Mish Mish
17 Lilenblum St.
Tel. (03) 516 81 78
A fairly expensive cocktail bar, always well attended.

Lima Lima
42 Lilenblum St

Tel. 03 560 09 24
Get a few drinks, retire to the red sofas or dance to soul, funk or hip-hop on the small dance floor. Monday night is gay night. Lima Lima is popular with a relaxed clientele.

Rivendel
Tel Aviv Port
Tel. (03) 602 31 29
Bar with sea views and a large terrace

Shabul Jazz Club
Tel Aviv Port, Hangar 13
Tel. (03) 546 18 91
www.shabluljazz.com
Live jazz almost every day.

Tel Aviv Brewhouse
11 Rothschild Blvd.
Tel. (03) 516 86 66
Anyone with a taste for speciality beers should go to the Brewhouse. Blondelight, Moonshine, Quantum and Masters are the names of the beers brewed here.

TLV Club
Tel Aviv Port
Tel. 03 576 10 22
Tel Aviv's international airport code was chosen as a name by one of the city's most popular nightclubs. Occasional live music and regular party nights for homosexuals, lesbians and swingers.

Whisky à Go-Go
3 Hataarucha Street, Tel Aviv Port
Tel. (03) 544 06 33
This enormous bar extends over several floors and rooms.

WHERE TO EAT

The gastronomy scene is a bit confusing. The waterfront promenade and the area around Hayarkon Street already offer everything the stomach desires, from kosher Chinese food to Mongolian grilled dishes. Coffee houses such as Café Tamar in Sheinkin St. and Café Basel in Basel St. are both classic places to take a break from shopping and get quite busy from early in the morning.

► Expensive

① *Mul Yam*
Tel Aviv Port, Hangar 24
Tel. (03) 546 99 20, www.mulyam.com
Top-class fish dishes and an extensive wine list. Experimental cuisine is represented by grilled asparagus with Swiss cheese fondue.

② *Orca*
57 Nachalat Binyamin
Tel. (03) 566 55 05
Smart restaurant and interesting European-Levantine cuisine – Orca is considered to be one of the best restaurants in Israel.

► Moderate

③ *Bellini*
Suzanne Dellal Center
6 Yechieli St.
Tel. (03) 517 84 86
Those who fail to reserve in time will miss treats like veal à la masala and spaghetti puttanesca.

⑩ *Vicky Cristina*
Tel. 03 736 72 72
The name is a nod in the direction of is the clue. Here there's wine and tapas. Enjoy the night from the tables in the garden of the historic Neve Tzedek train station. There are more than enough bars in the vicinity to move on to.

④ *Batya*
197 Dizengoff St.
Tel. (03) 522 13 35
Excellent Jewish and eastern European cuisine since 1941. Try the goulash and apple strudel for dessert.

⑤ *Birnbaum & Mendelbaum*
35 Rothschild Blvd.
Tel. (03) 566 49 49
Good, large steaks

⑥ *Keren*
12 Elat St.
Tel. (03) 681 65 65
Seafood tartare and ravioli stuffed with goose pate are just two of the delicious dishes served at Keren.

⑦ *Manta Ray*
Alma Beach
Tel. (03) 517 47 73
The fish starters are very tasty; this is also a good place for a savoury breakfast. The mood is particularly pleasant on the terrace at sundown.

⑧ *Max Brenner Chocolate Bar*
43 Rothschild Blvd., tel. (03) 560 45 70
Almost anything that can be made with chocolate, from drinks to complete meals, is served here. But this restaurant is also a good place for salads and sandwiches and observing what's goings.

⑨ *Stefan Braun*
99 Allenby St.
Tel. (03) 560 47 25
The restaurant's name (Braun was a furrier) does not suggest that this place serves sharira and other Moroccan specialities. Tip: the beetroot salad, flavoured with cinnamon, a secret recipe of the establishment. The bar is a popular rendezvous.

⑪ *Dr. Shakshuka*
3 Beit Eshel St, Jaffa
Tel. 03 682 28 42
Shakshuka is an Arab omelette with tomatoes, parsley and numerous

Tel Aviv Map

Sde Dov Airport
Haifa
RAMAT AVIV
Levi Eshkol
Derekh
Shay' Agnon
Planetarium
Eretz Israel Museum
Harbour
Maccabia Stadium
Sderot Israel Rokach
Yargon
Yehuda Hamakabi
Bene Dan
Ushshkin
Gan Ha'azma ut Ha-Yarqon
Sderot Nordau
Ibn Gvirol
Pinkas D.
Mediterranean
Marina ③
Ben Yehuda
Dizengoff
Sokolov
Bet Ha-More
Jabotinsky
Kikar Hamedina
Ben Gurion House ④
Arlozorov
Bet Ha-Histadrut
Bet Lessin
Sderot David Ben Gurion
Weizmann
Arlozorov
⑥
⑤ City hall
Chief Rabbinate
Derekh Haifa
TEL AVIV
Frischmann
Kikar Zina Dizengoff
Kikar Y. Rabin
David Ham
Tel Aviv Museum of Art
Ichilov Hospital
② Mendele
George
Sderot Shaul Hamelech
Tel Aviv public library
Courthouse
④ Old Cemetery
Pinsker
Dizengoff
Ben Ziyon
Helena Rubinstein Pavilion
Frederic Mann Auditorium
Kaplan
Derekh Hashalom
Opera Tower
⑧
Hist. Museum
Bialik House
Rubin Museum ⑩
Jabotinsky Museum
Habimah Theatre
HAQIRYA
Tivka
Carmel Market
Kikar Magen David
Sheinkin
Rothschild
Halevi
Carlebach
Petah
Wholesale market
Herbert Samuel
Ha-Karmel
Great Synagogue
⑨ ⑧
Sderot Yehuda
Derekh
Sadeh
Yitzhak
‹ Hassan Bek Mosque
⑦
Shalom Tower ② ⑤
Haganah Museum
Allenby
Helen Keller House
Nahalat Binyamin
Independence Hall ③
Ohel Moed Synagogue
Sport Center
La Guardia
Etzel Museum
NEVE TZEDEK
✉ Yafo
Levinsky
Yad Eliyahu Synagogue
Sderot Haha'ayil
YAD ELIYYAHU
Great Mosque
⑩ ⑥
ⓘ Hatachana Train Station
Herzl
Derekh Ha-Hagana
Greek Orthodox monastery
Clock tower ⑦
Elat
Shama
New bus station ⓘ
St Peter's
Derekh
Sderot Har Tsiyon
Artists quarter
Archaeol. Museum ⑫
Siksik Mosque
GIV'AT HERZL
SHEKUNAT SHAPIRA
HATIQWEA
YAFO
Bloomfield Stadium
Levanda
SHEKUNAT
Yehuda Hayamit
Derekh Yizhaq Ben Zevi
Kibuts Galuyot
Golomb
Etsel
GIV'AT 'ALIYYA
† Coptic church
Yerushalayim
Russian church
Holon, Jerusalem
Southern station

Where to eat

① Mul Yam
② Orca
③ Bellini
④ Batya
⑤ Birnbaum & Mendelbaum
⑥ Keren
⑦ Manta Ray
⑧ Max Brenner
⑨ Stefan Braun
⑩ Vicky Cristina
⑪ Dr. Shakshuka
⑫ Puah

Where to stay

① Alexander
② Dan Tel Aviv
③ Hilton
④ Isrotel Tower
⑤ Renaissance
⑥ Leonardo Basel Hotel
⑦ Beit Immanuel
⑧ Metropolitan

spices. It is served at long tables, with bread on the side. Also on the menu: mezze, couscous, lamb, grills etc. The drink speciality is a wonderfully fresh lemonade.

► **Inexpensive**
⑫ *Puah*
Rabi Yohanan, Jaffa
Tel. (03) 682 38 21
Right on Jaffa's flea market, making this a great place to take a break from some strenuous shopping and sight-seeing. Snacks served along with coffee.

WHERE TO STAY
► **Luxury**
① *Alexander*
3 Habakook St.
Tel. (03) 546 22 22
Fax 546 93 46
www.alexander.co.il
Modern, elegantly furnished apartment hotel. All 48 suites have their own kitchen.

② *Dan Tel Aviv*
99 Hayarkon St.
Tel. (03) 520 25 25, fax 524 9755
www.danhotels.com
Tel Aviv's premier address with 286 rooms and suites, a top-quality restaurant and several shops.

③ *Hilton Tel Aviv*
Independence Park
Tel. (03) 520 22 40, fax 527 27 11
www.hilton.com
582 rooms. Top hotel with restaurants, a pool bar, a sushi bar and the large Cybex Spa.

④ *Isrotel Tower*
5 Shalom Aleichem St.
Tel. (03) 511 36 36
Fax 511 36 66
www.isrotel.co.il

The Isrotel has 90 suites and is housed in the striking 30-storey round building near the Opera Tower.

⑤ *Renaissance Hotel*
121 Hayarkon St.
Tel. (03) 521 55 55, fax 521 55 88
www.marriott.com
342 rooms. A hotel that is particularly popular with travel groups; on the coast with nicely furnished rooms; direct access to the beach, sun terrace and swimming pool.

► **Mid-range**
⑥ *Leonardo Basel Hotel*
156 Hayarkon St.
Tel. (03) 520 77 11,
www.atlas.co.il
Centrally located hotel, refurbished in 2011, with well-equipped rooms, a restaurant and a pool. The beach is on the other side of the busy road.

⑦ *Beit Immanuel*
8 Auerbach St, Jaffa
Tel. (03) 682 14 59
www.beitimmanuel.org
60 beds. Anyone preferring to stay in Jaffa rather than Tel Aviv can do so in this renovated Christian hospice, which Baron Ustinov, the grandfather of actor Peter Ustinov, bought from the German Temple Society in 1878. It even accommodated Kaiser Wilhelm II.

⑧ *Metropolitan*
15 Trumpeldor St.
Tel. (03) 519 27 27
Fax 517 26 26
www.hotelmetropolitan.co.il
228 rooms. Three minutes to the Opera Tower, five to the beach, ten to Allenby Street and fifteen to the Dizengoff Center: the Metropolitan has a very favourable location, and is thus popular with coach tours.

rieli Tower will discover that the centre has quite a provincial character: relatively narrow streets, lots of gardens and three or four-storey flat-roofed houses, usually covered in white render, which cannot deny their stylistic connection with European Modernism. For that reason Tel Aviv is also known as the »White City« (►Baedeker Special p. 406).

Skyscrapers can mainly be found on the waterfront promenade and east of the Ayalon. The highest block of the **Azrieli Towers** is the tallest building in Israel at 189m/620ft. Most hotels – all of them establishments of the expensive kind – can be found on Hayarkon Street, which runs parallel to the beach, as well as on its southern continuation, Herbert Samuel Street. The small town of Jaffa is further south again.

Young city The birth hour of Tel Aviv struck in 1909, when emigrants from Russia founded the suburb of Ahuzat Bayit in the dunes north of Jaffa. The settlement was called Tel Aviv, meaning **»spring hill«**. After Arab unrest in 1921, shortly after the end of the Turkish rule, it became an independent town; a short while later, in 1924, Tel Aviv already had a population of 35,000.

New Jewish-Arab tension caused a lot of Jews to leave Jaffa and move to Tel Aviv in 1929. In 1936 Jaffa's harbour was closed. Tel Aviv opened its own harbour at Tell Qasile. The UN Partition Plan for

At the heart of Tel Aviv: the fire and water fountain on Dizengoff Square

Palestine determined in 1947 that Jaffa, a town with a population of 100,000 at the time, 30,000 of them Jewish, should remain Arab, while Tel Aviv, with a population of around 230,000, should become Israeli. In 1948 the Israelis took Jaffa. On 14 May 1948 David Ben Gurion proclaimed the state of Israel in the former house of Tel Aviv's first mayor, **Meir Dizengoff**. In 1950 the old Jaffa was merged with the new Jewish town under the name of Tel Aviv–Yafo.

What to See in the Centre of Tel Aviv

Dizengoff Square is an excellent starting point for strolls through Tel Aviv. It is named after Meir Dizengoff (1861–1936) from Bessarabia. The square consists of two levels; pedestrians use the upper platform, which is adorned by the striking but somewhat dilapidated Fire and Water Fountain, a work by the Israeli artist **Yaacov Agam** (b. 1928). *Dizengoff Square*

Dizengoff St. runs southeast from Dizengoff Square to Habima Square, home to the Habima Theatre, Israel's **national theatre**, built in 1935. It was founded in Moscow in 1917, but moved to Tel Aviv in 1928. *Habima National Theatre*

Immediately to the north of the theatre is the Helena Rubinstein Pavilion for Contemporary Art, a branch of the Tel Aviv Museum of Art. Works by modern artists from Israel and around the world are displayed in changing exhibitions (6 Tarat Blvd.; tel. 03 528 71 96, Mon, Wed, Sat 10am–4pm, Tue and Thu 10am–10pm, Fri 10am–2pm). *Helena Rubinstein Pavilion* ⊙

Adjoining the Helena Rubinstein Pavilion to the east is the Frederic Mann Auditorium (Huberman St, tel. 03 6 21 17 77, www.hatarbut.co.il), the venue of the Israeli Philharmonic Orchestra. It has space for 3000 people, making it the **country's largest concert hall**. *Mann Auditorium*

Just over half a mile northeast of Habima Square, on Shaul Hamelech Blvd. is the Tel Aviv Museum of Art. Built in 1971, it houses an interesting art collection with works by artists from Israel and other countries, including by Degas, Monet, Pissaro, Kokoschka, Léger, Moore and Picasso. One of the most impressive works is a Chagall dating from 1933: *Jerusalem's Fortress*, the church in Chagall's Russian home town, the weeping prophet Jeremiah, sinister forebodings cheered up by a cow playing the fiddle. In 2011 a new, bold annex was opened to a design by the US architect Preston Scott Cohen. Behind a façade of 465 concrete tiles of different shapes and sizes, there are three levels at an angle to each other, connected by a light well in the middle, a total of 18,500 sq m/200,000 sq ft for permanent and temporary exhibitions. The Art Road to Peace in the Herta and Paul Amir Building was conceived as a peace project, an initiative designed to promote mutual understanding between Jews and Arabs *Tel Aviv Museum of Art*

TEL AVIV, THE WHITE CITY

Tel Aviv has the image of a city without history, a city lacking outstanding architectural monuments. Clichés like this are hard to dispel, but they do need to be revised from time to time.

For example when UNESCO declares an ensemble of buildings here to be a World Heritage Site, as it did in 1996. Around 4000 buildings, from detached residences and apartment houses to office blocks and corner shops, testify to the influence of the Bauhaus, a German school of design which was a dominant force in 20th-century architecture from the 1920s onwards and an inspiration for the Modernist movement. Buildings that survive in Tel Aviv make the city a **unique »open-air museum« of modern architecture**. Take a stroll through Tel Aviv, not at night, but in the late afternoon. And not by car, but on foot. It does not really matter what street you choose between Ibn Gvirol Boulevard and Allenby Street, as every one of them has buildings that cannot deny their 1930s origin and their relationship to the Bauhaus, even though their charm has suffered as a result of many subsequent additions, or, more commonly, decades of neglect.

New shapes

The easiest way to recognize the style is the **shape of the balconies**. They wrap around the façades like horizontal brackets. This looks particularly elegant when the corners of the building are rounded, like the bows of a ship. A further unmistakable characteristic are the unique window shapes, which are rarely squares or upright rectangles, as is widespread in Europe. Instead they are either narrow slits or wide bands that run around the entire facade. The penchant for the horizontal is further emphasized by the fact that most buildings are no higher than three, maximum four storeys and, like those of their Arab neighbours, have flat roofs. The white paint, a trademark of the Mediterranean and Levantine as well as modern architecture, earned Tel Aviv the sobriquet **»White City«**.

From Berlin to Palestine

How did Bauhaus get to Israel? The answer is both simple and sad: lots of talented architects with a Jewish background, including famous ones like **Erich Mendelsohn**, had to leave Europe in the 1930s since they were persecuted by the Nazis. Some of

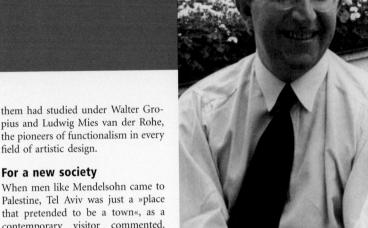

Erich Mendelsohn, one of the pioneers of the Bauhaus style in Tel Aviv

them had studied under Walter Gropius and Ludwig Mies van der Rohe, the pioneers of functionalism in every field of artistic design.

For a new society

When men like Mendelsohn came to Palestine, Tel Aviv was just a »place that pretended to be a town«, as a contemporary visitor commented. For the town planners and architects who moved to Tel Aviv, this was not a flaw. Quite the contrary: the settlement, which had been founded only a few years earlier, proved to be an **ideal place for experiments**.

Even though the disciples of Bauhaus from Europe also implemented projects in Jerusalem and especially in Haifa, the port to the north, Tel Aviv became the »model« **for modern architecture**. The Bauhaus style seemed perfectly suited for expressing the immigrants' view of their own identity, as it was not tied to any traditional language of forms or to a national cultural legacy. Instead it embodied values and ideas such as modernity, world citizenship and the departure into a new society. The fact that the young architects did not merely copy the European model, but found their own solutions, is evident in the balconies, which have brick parapets to provide protection from the sun.

Rediscovered treasures

Anyone walking through the streets of Tel Aviv today will discover that many of these balconies have disappeared visually, since the residents have made them part of their living space by adding glass or blinds. Nor do the countless boxes containing air-conditioning systems and the crumbling render contribute to the attractiveness of the buildings. For decades the city accepted the decay of its Bauhaus architecture and did nothing to conserve this unique cultural heritage, a rethinking began in the 1990s, which has benefited many of the houses.

The **Bauhaus Center** runs **guided tours**. It also sells reading materials, souvenirs and audio guides (99 Dizengoff St, tel./fax 3/522 02 49. www.bauhaus-center.com). Furniture and accessories are on display in a small exhibition in the **Bauhaus Museum** (Bialik Square).

through art (27 Shaul Hamelech Blvd.; tel. 03 6 07 70 20, www.ta-museum.com, Mon, Wed, Sat 10am–4pm, Tue and Thu until 10pm, Fri until 2pm).

Bialik House

Bialik Street with its pretty houses and gardens is a typical example of a traditional residential neighbourhood in Tel Aviv. The street is named after the poet **Chaim Nahman Bialik** (1873–1934), who lived in no. 22 with the striking wooden bay window on the first floor. Both inside and outside, this building, constructed in 1925, is one of the few surviving examples of an architectural style in which Arab elements were combined with European Art Nouveau. The building and its interior were restored with a lot of attention to detail. It has now been made accessible as a museum.

Rubin Museum

Bialik was friends with the painter **Reuven Rubin**, whose former home and studio is just a stone's throw from Bialik House. Rubin, who died aged 81 in 1974, is one of Israel's internationally renowned painters. The museum exhibits paintings and drawings from the 1920s to the 1970s (14 Bialik St.; Mon, Wed, Thu 10am–3pm, Tue until 8pm, Sat 11am–2pm).

Carmel Market

Walk down Bialik Street to get to lively **Allenby Street** and after it to Carmel Market, which begins at Kikar Magen David. The first section of this street market focuses on clothes, but also on other items of everyday use. However, the food market a little further south, which has a very oriental atmosphere, is more interesting. There are lots of nice little shops just a short distance away in **Binyamin Street**, which runs parallel to Allenby Street.

Tel Aviv's currently best-known and most popular shopping and entertainment street, **Sheinkin Street**, begins north of Allenby Street, also on Kikar Magen David. Why not take in the scenery from one of the many small street cafés?

> ## Baedeker TIP
>
> **Photo Prior**
>
> A real treasure lies hidden behind the windows of an inconspicuous photo shop at 30 Allenby St.: Miriam Weissenstein, who left Czechoslovakia for Palestine in 1921, and her husband Rubi documented Palestine and Israel with a camera from the 1930s. Rudi Weissenstein was, for example, the only one to photograph David Ben Gurion when he proclaimed the state of Israel. A quarter of a million negatives lie in the drawers. Since the death of Miriam Weissenstein in 2011, her grandson Ben has carried on the business with great commitment. It is a pleasure to chat to him.

Haganah Museum

Return to Allenby Street and walk south along it to the **Great Synagogue**. The building on the corner of Rehov Ahad Ha'am was built in 1926. The Haganah Museum is nearby. It is housed in the former home of the Haganah commander **Eliahu Golomb**. The museum displays documents and exhibits on the history of the underground or-

A typical example of the Bauhaus style in Havakuk Street

ganization which was founded in 1920 to defend Jewish towns and settlements, and was incorporated into the re-organized Israeli army after the proclamation of the state of Israel in May 1948 (23 Roths- ⏲ child Blvd; Sun–Thu 8am–4pm, tel. 03 560 86 24).

The home of the first mayor of Tel Aviv, **Meir Dizengoff**, can be found near the Haganah Museum. In the Independence Hall David Ben Gurion proclaimed the state of Israel on 14 May 1948. On display are various exhibits, most of them connected to this historic event (16 Rothschild Blvd; Sun–Thu 9am–2pm).

Independence Hall

⏲

The next street is Herzl Street, the first street of Tel Aviv when it was newly founded in 1909. The Hebrew grammar school named after Theodor Herzl (►Famous People) was built at its northern end in 1909 but pulled down in 1958 to make way for **Tel Aviv's first skyscraper**, Migdal Shalom (Shalom Tower). The 142m/466ft tower, still a landmark of the city, was the tallest building in Israel when it opened.

✶
Shalom Tower

Because of its many street cafés, small clothes and jewellery boutiques as well as its trendy shops, Sheinkin Street is often compared to London's Soho or New York's Greenwich Village, but for a place to live, artists and better-off families now choose to move a few streets away, to the city's oldest quarter, Neve Tzedek. Founded in

✶
Neve Tzedek

Skyscrapers line the corniche in Tel Aviv.

1887 as a suburb of Jaffa, it is dominated by winding roads and low Arab-style buildings. Junk dealers have found a home here, as have artisans and small shops. The Suzanne Dellal Dance and Theater Center, known for its modern productions, can be found at the heart of this quarter.

North and East of the Centre

Yarkon

The Yarkon River (yarok = green) is the boundary line to the northern part of Tel Aviv. In Antiquity it was the border between the tribes of Ephraim in the north and Dan in the south. The grassy areas beside the river are a popular destination on the Sabbath, making them often very crowded.

Eretz Israel Museum

The Eretz Israel Museum is an expansive complex with several pavilions and a large excavation site (Tell Qasile). Anyone with an interest in the country's history and culture will have no trouble spending a morning here. The round tour leads through the various pavilions, which are devoted to different subjects and collections, from coins, ceramics and glass to the history of writing and ideas as well as Judaica, Jewish sacred handicrafts and folklore. The museum also possesses a **planetarium**, a building with an ancient oil press and a garden with the typical plants of Palestine.

Tell Qasile ▶

Rising at the heart of the museum compound is Tell Qasile with its excavations and a pavilion in which the excavated discoveries are on display. **Twelve settlement layers** of the small port near the Yarkon that was founded by the Philistines have been excavated on the hill. The lowest dates back to the 12th century BC. A brick building from the earliest period was discovered, as were a strong wall and two copper furnaces from the 11th century. After destruction by the Egyptians, the kings of Israel rebuilt the city in the 9th century BC. In 732 BC it was destroyed again by the Assyrians (2 Haim Levanon St., Ramat Aviv, tel. 03 6 41 52 44, www.eretzmuseum.org.il, Sun–Wed 10am–4pm, Thu until 8pm, Fri and Sat until 2pm, Planetarium shows: Sun–Thu 11.30am and 1.30pm, Sat 11am and 12 noon).

With façades made of exposed concrete and brown limestone, Zvi Hecker gave the Palmach Museum on the slopes above the Eretz Israel Museum a striking appearance. The exhibition about the Jewish underground organization Palmach and the early days of the Jewish state is presented with lots of effects and has a real experiential quality (10 Haim Levanon St, tel. 03 643 63 93, www.palmach.org.il, no admission for children under 6; Sun, Mon, Wed 9am–5pm, Tue until 8pm, Thu until 2pm, Fri until 1pm). **Palmach Museum**

The Museum of Jewish Diaspora (Beth Hatefutsoth), founded in 1979, can be found in the eastern part of the university campus. Film and sound recordings, models and a lot more teach visitors about the life and culture of Jews in various countries and times (Klausner St., entrance: 2 Matatia Gate, tel. 03 745 78 00, www.bh.org.il; Sun, Mon, Tue, Thu 10am–4pm, Wed until 6pm, Fri 9am–1pm). **✶ Museum of Jewish Diaspora**

The suburb of Ramat Gan was built on the hill to the east of the city centre in 1920. Because of its many green spaces it is also known as Garden Heights. Today Ramat Gan is mainly known for being the **centre of the Israeli diamond trade**. The Harry Oppenheimer Diamond Museum can also be found in the Diamond Exchange. The exhibition pieces also include particularly valuable loans. Films explain how diamonds are processed (1 Jabotinsky St, tel. 03 575 15 47; Sun–Thu 10am–4pm, Tue until 7pm). One of the attractions of Ramat Gan is the **Safari Park**, in which African animals can run around freely on an area of 100ha/245 acres (Bernstein Street; Sun–Thu 9am–4pm, Fri until 1pm). **Ramat Gan**

◄ Harry Oppenheimer Diamond Museum

✶ Jaffa · Yafo

Jaffa (Yafo), to the south of Tel Aviv's centre, has a very different feel to Tel Aviv, which has a European atmosphere. Jaffa still holds on to the flair of an old Arab town. Things get particularly lively in the evening hours when the restaurants at the heart of the old quarter get busy. **Lively old quarter**

Jaffa changed a great deal in the 20th century. The British Mandate created wide openings in the labyrinthine streets to gain more control during the unrest of 1921, and extensive renovation works took place after the mass exodus of the Arab population following the foundation of the state of Israel in 1948. Some of the bazaar and the historic buildings on the acropolis, the site of the oldest settlement,

Jaffa Map

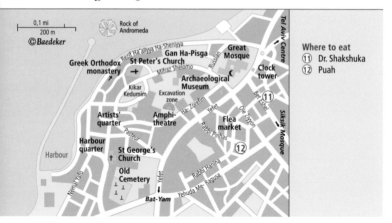

survive. The old quarter was recently renovated. Many of the old houses by the harbour are inhabited again or are used as restaurants, bars, cafés, galleries and handicraft businesses. Many of the houses inhabited by Arab Israelis also attract speculators who harass the long-standing residents.

Mythology and legend
According to Jewish tradition, Noah's son **Japheth** founded the town of Jaffa after the Flood. According to Greek tradition the town goes back to Joppa, one of the daughters of Aeolus, the god of the winds.

Rock of Andromeda ►
The Greeks believed that the rock in the sea in front of the harbour is the one to which Joppa's daughter **Andromeda** was tied and was threatened by a sea monster until Perseus freed her. The story of the **prophet Jonah** dates back to the 8th century BC. Wishing to evade God's order to preach in Nineveh, he went aboard a ship in Jaffa. As he was then believed to be the cause of a great storm, the sailors threw him into the sea, whereupon he was swallowed up by a great fish and spat out again on the coast (Jonah 1 and 2).

The New Testament associates Jaffa with the report about the raising of Tabitha by the apostle Peter, who subsequently spent several days in the house of Simon the tanner (Acts 9:36–43).

History
The best starting point for a sightseeing trip in Jaffa is the 37m/121ft hill above the natural harbour, where a wall from the time of the Hyksos (18th–16th centuries BC) has been discovered. Pharaoh **Tutmose III** conquered the port in 1468 BC. In around 1200 BC the Philistines settled in Jaffa and on Tell Qasile (► p. 404). In around 1000 BC David conquered the city. Nevertheless a Phoenician population dominated in Jaffa in the following centuries, then, from the 3rd century BC, a Greek or Hellenized population. In the 1st century BC Jaffa's harbour became insignificant when Caesarea was founded.

A contrast to Tel Aviv with its European feel: old Jaffa

Jaffa's Christian period began with the **visit of Saint Paul**. In the 4th century Jaffa was a bishop's see, in 636 it was conquered by the Arabs. In the 7th and 8th centuries it flourished under the Umayyad and Abbasid caliphs. After it was conquered by the crusaders in 1099, the settlement was developed into a port for pilgrims going to Jerusalem. In 1267 the Mamluks conquered Jaffa and ended the rule of the crusaders. In 1650 the Ottoman authorities gave the Franciscans permission to build a church and pilgrimage hospice in Jaffa. In 1807 Muhammad, who earned the sobriquet Abu Nabbut (»Father of the Club«) because of his severity, became pasha of Gaza and made Jaffa into his residence.

◄ Christian era

A new development began in the mid-19th century under European auspices. After a capitulation treaty agreed with Turkey had given the European powers great influence in Palestine, the French built hospitals and extended the churches and monasteries. The Russians built a Church of St Peter at »Tabitha's Tomb« by the hill of Abu Kabir. In 1869 German Templers from Württemberg founded the agricultural settlement of Jaffa-Valhalla. In 1871 they founded **Sarona** to the northeast of Jaffa. Sarona is becoming increasingly popular with tourists. In 1887 and 1890 further settlements were founded to the north, such as the Jewish settlement of Neve Tzedek (►p. 409) and Neve Shalom. In 1892 the French built a railway line to ►Jerusalem.

◄ European influence

The Clock Tower in Jaffa's centre was built in 1906 for the 50th anniversary of the reign of the Ottoman sultan Abdul Hamid II (1842–1918). The Great Mosque or **Mahmoudiya Mosque** stands next to the Clock Tower. The Ottoman governor Muhammad Pasha built it in 1810, using ancient columns from Ashkelon and Caesarea. Mistaking their ancient function, he had them placed upside down. An experience for those who just like to potter around is the local Souq Hapishpishim flea market, a good address for antique furniture, but also for books, cheap clothes, utensils and knickknacks of all kinds.

Clock Tower and Great Mosque

Jaffa Museum

A few minutes' walk further the southwest is the Jaffa Museum, nicely situated in pleasant green spaces. Housed in the old Turkish seraglio, it possesses an interesting collection of archaeological finds (10 Mifraz Shlomo St, tel. 03 682 53 75, Sat–Thu 9am–10pm, Fri until 2pm).

St Peter's Church

Just a few hundred metres further, the acropolis is the site of the **Franciscan monastery** of St Peter, which was built in 1654 on the site of a 13th-century crusader fortress. Its name commemorates the apostle's stay in Jaffa.

Excavation site ►

Earlier settlement layers have been uncovered on the square in front of the monastery and on the hill (Gan Hapisga) to the east, such as a 6m/20ft wall from the Hyksos period (18th–16th centuries BC), a city gate with the name of Pharaoh Ramesses II (1290–1224 BC) as well as the remains of a Canaanite town and a Jewish settlement from the 4th century BC.

Kedumim Square
★

Artists' quarter ►

The visitor centre (tel. 03 518 40 15, www.oldjaffa.co.il), which has an interesting exhibition, is located on the central square of Old Jaffa near St Peter's Church. To the south of the square is the artists' quarter. The pretty buildings house art galleries, studios and souvenir shops as well as nice little restaurants.

★
Harbour district
Mosque ►

The hill above St Peter's Church affords nice views of the old harbour. Narrow stepped streets lead up to the lovingly restored houses above the fishing harbour and marina. Continue southwards towards the old lighthouse to a smaller mosque from 1730. It stands on the site where, according to tradition, the house of Simon the tanner once stood, where Peter stayed after his miraculous raising of Tabitha from the dead.

Russian monastery

Around 2km/1.25mi to the southeast of old Jaffa is the slender tower of the Russian monastery, attractively surrounded by palm trees. The Russian Empire acquired the hill of Abu Kabir in 1860 and built St Peter's Church as well as accommodation for pilgrims here. Below the monastery courtyard is a burial cave with several burial niches. The cave belonged to a Jewish cemetery of the 1st–4th centuries; according to Christian tradition this is where Tabitha, who had been resurrected by Peter, was ultimately buried.

Around Tel Aviv – Jaffa

Rehovot

Rehovot, founded in 1890, lies around 20km/12mi to the southeast of Tel Aviv on the coastal plain. It is the centre of orange cultivation in Israel. At the same time the **»city of citrus fruits«** is the seat of one of the most renowned research institutions in the country. More than 2500 scientists, technical staff and students work in the Weizmann Institute of Sciences, named after the country's first president, Chaim Weizmann (1874–1952). Weizmann, who studied chemistry at several western European universities and also worked to promote the Zionist movement, settled in Rehovot in 1920 and founded the Daniel Sieff Research Institute, an agricultural research facility. In 1949 the research institute was renamed **Weizmann Institute of Sciences**.

At the northern outskirts of Rehovot, near the Weizmann Institute of Sciences, stands the house in which Chaim Weizmann lived from 1949 to 1952 and which was designed by the architect Erich Mendelsohn (1887–1953). The famous scientist and politician is buried in the garden.

◄ Weizmann House

The kibbutz of Givat Brenner (Giv'a = hill, mountain), founded in 1928, lies around 5km/3mi to the southeast of Rehovot. It was named after the writer **Yosef Chaim Brenner**, who was killed by Arabs in Jaffa in 1921. The town, now one of the largest kibbutzim in Israel, produces canned foods and irrigation equipment. There is also a timber processing industry. Givat Brenner was home to the sculptor **Jacob Loutchansky** (1876–1978), whose works, inspired by events in Israel's history, adorn the kibbutz's squares and gardens.

Givat Brenner

Herod the Great founded this town at the spring of the Yarkon River (15km/9mi east of Tel Aviv) and named it after his father Antipater. Antipatris is the place where Saint Paul spent a night when the Romans brought him from Jerusalem to Caesarea (Acts 23:31). The town was destroyed by an earthquake in 363; the crusaders built a castle here, which was later also used by the Turks. Most of the ruins date back to that period.

Antipatris

✶ Tiberias · Tverya

G 2

District: Northern **Altitude:** 212m/695ft
Population: 64,000

Tiberias (Tverya) is the undisputed holiday resort on the ►Sea of Galilee. Tiberias, on the western shores, and its spa resort of Tiberias Hammat are popular holiday destinations in spring, when the climate here is already warmer than that of the Mediterranean coast. However, in addition to the many opportunities for leisure and relaxation in the town and the stunning surrounding area, Tiberias – alongside Jerusalem, Hebron and Safed – possesses one of the four sacred sites of the Jews as well as sites and attractions of religious historical interest.

Herod Antipas (20 BC–AD 39), one of Herod the Great's sons and the sovereign at the time of Jesus, founded the town in the year 17

In honour of the emperor

and named it after Emperor Tiberius. Tiberias, which took over from Sepphoris (▶Tzippori) as the royal residence, was located between Hammat and Rakkat, which are cited in the Old Testament as fortified cities in the area of the Naphtali tribe (Joshua 19:35). Since it was built on the cemetery of Hammat, pious Jews considered it »impure«, which is why only »heathens« settled here at first. Jesus, who taught in this area, also appears not to have entered Tiberias.

After Herod Antipas's death, Agrippa II gave the town paved streets and a palace. After Rabbi **Simeon bar Yochai** (buried in ▶Meron) declared Tiberias a »pure« town towards the end of the 2nd century, the Sanhedrin (high council), the highest Jewish political and legal authority, moved its headquarters here. Its leader (prince, chief), the Nasi, was also the highest spiritual authority of the Jews until Emperor Theodosius II abolished the office in 429. From the 3rd century on, Tiberias developed into the religious centre of Judaism. The town was then known as Tverya; the Jews derived this name from the Hebrew word »tabur« (navel) and considered the town to be the »navel of the world«. It was here that the **Mishnah**, a collection of Jewish religious laws, was completed in around AD 200, as was the **Jerusalem Talmud** in around AD 400. Furthermore, this is where the vowel characters of Hebrew writing were devised. After conquest by the Persians in 614 and a few years later by the Arabs, Jewish scholars joined the community in Babylon or went to Jerusalem. From 1099 to 1187 Tiberias was part of the realm of the crusader prince Tancred and the kings of Jerusalem. In 1247 Baibars destroyed the town, which was only resettled in the 16th century under Ottoman rule.

Modern era ▶ In 1561 Sultan Suleiman the Magnificent handed the town to the Jew Don Joseph Nasi, a refugee from Spain, and his aunt Donna Gracia Mendes, who created a Jewish state under Ottoman suzerainty in Galilee. It did not exist for long, however. Not until the 18th century was Tiberias inhabited again, when the Druze emir **Daher el-Omar** rebuilt the town and citadel. In 1765 a first group of Jewish emigrants from Poland settled here. In around 1940 the town had a population of 12,000, half of it Arab, the other half Jewish. In 1948 it became exclusively Jewish.

What to See in Tiberias

Modern holiday resort Before reaching the town centre, visitors coming from Haifa will first drive through modern Tiberias, which is climbing higher and higher up the hillsides on the western shores of the Sea of Galilee. The main

▶ VISITING TIBERIAS

INFORMATION
Tourist Office
23 Habanim Street
Tel. (04) 672 56 66, fax 672 50 62

Go Galilee
1 Jordan Street
IL 14100 Tiberias
Tel. (06) 679 19 81

GETTING THERE
Buses from Jerusalem, Nazareth and Haifa to the bus station in Hayarden Street; Sheruts to Habanim Street.

BY BOAT
Ferries regularly depart from the waterfront promenade for Ein Gev on the other side of the Sea of Galilee as well as to Ginosar and Capernaum.

BEACHES
Although Tiberias possesses several beaches (subject to fees), there are nicer ones on the Sea of Galilee. Those just wishing to take a quick dip can also do this in »wild« spots; however, these places are not very comfortable for an afternoon on the beach.

SPORT AND OUTDOORS
Water ski and boat rentals can usually be found very close to the major beach hotels.
Sailing trips and cruises are run by Kinneret Sailing Company (tel. 04 / 672 18 31) and Lido Cruises (tel. 04 / 672 15 38, decks@barak.net.il)
River rafting on the Jordan is organized by Abukayak (Jordan River Park, tel. 04 / 692 10 78) and Kfar Blum & Beit Hillel Kayaks (tel. 04 / 690 26 16)

ENTERTAINMENT
Life after the beach, be it in a restaurant, a bar or a nightclub, takes place almost exclusively *in the vicinity of the marina*. Cruises on the Sea of Galilee for parties and dancing are both popular and noisy.

WHERE TO EAT
▶ Moderate / Expensive
② Decks
Lido Beach
Tel. (04) 672 15 38
Right on the water at the jetty for cruise ships. Excellent bar-restaurant with a »Biblical Grill« for tasty fish and meat dishes.

① Pagoda
Lido Beach, Gdud Barak St.
Tel. (04) 672 55 13
Chinese, Thai and Japanese cuisine. This beach restaurant has made a name for itself with a Far Eastern culinary triad.

WHERE TO STAY
Hospitality in Tiberias has, in general, seen better days, a result of trying to attract local holidaymakers with rock-bottom prices. But there are exceptions.

▶ Luxury
① The Scots
1 Gdud Barak St., tel. (04) 671 07 10
www.scotshotels.co.il
The 19th-century building once served the Scottish church as a hospital. Today the refurbished structure, with its domes and arches, houses a hotel with »antique rooms« and an atmosphere of bygone days. From the pool, there is a view of the lake on the other side of the road. The Torrance Restaurant in the former clinic vaults serves excellent fish dishes and has a notable list of Galilean wines.

② *Shirat Hayam*
Yigal Alon Promenade
Tel.(04) 672 11 22
www.shirathayam.org.il
Next to the small sculpture park, only separated by the promenade from the lake, guests can stay in a lovingly furnished boutique hotel. In the spa there's a »romantic room« for couples. The bar is well stocked.

► Mid-range
③ *Gai Beach Hotel*
Derech Hamerhazaot (Promenade)
Tel. (04) 670 07 00, fax 679 27 76
www.gaibeachhotel.com
200 rooms. Extensive hotel complex on the road between Tiberias and Tiberias-Hammat, right on the Sea of Galilee. The well-kept beach and the adjoining water park with flumes and a wave pool guarantee plenty of watery fun.

④ *Prima Tiberias*
1 Elhadif St.
Tel.(04) 679 11 66
www.prima.co.il
Many of the 93 rooms of this hotel, which is built on a hill, have wonderful views of the lake.

► Budget
⑤ *Astoria*
13 Ohel Ya'acov St.
Tel. (04) 672 23 51, fax 672 51 08
www.astoria.co.il
Well-kept, family-run mid-range hotel with 88 pretty rooms and a pool.

⑥ *Beit Berger*
25 Neiberg St.
Tel. (04) 671 51 51, fax 679 15 14
Pleasant little family-run hotel with 47 well equipped rooms. Ten minutes walk to the beach.

Tiberias Map

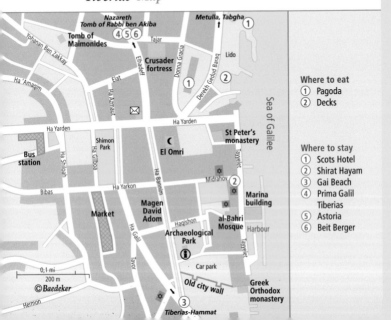

Where to eat
① Pagoda
② Decks

Where to stay
① Scots Hotel
② Shirat Hayam
③ Gai Beach
④ Prima Galil Tiberias
⑤ Astoria
⑥ Beit Berger

©Baedeker

access road is the address of many mid-range hotels. The more expensive ones can be found right on the water. The **old quarter**, where most buildings are still of more recent construction, extends between the waterfront promenade (Tayelet) and Hagalil Street. Most of the restaurants, pubs and cafés can be found in the pedestrian street Midrahov, which runs right towards the lake, and in Haqishon Street, which runs parallel to it.

An art centre and a restaurant were opened above the remains of a crusader fortress, which Daher el-Omar had built out of black basalt in 1738. It can be found at the northern end of the old quarter.

Crusader fortress

Walk from here towards the waterfront promenade to get to the monastery of St Peter, which was built in the second half of the 19th century above the remains of a crusader church. The apse protrudes like a ship's bow, thereby commemorating Peter's fishing boat.

St Peter's Church

Around 200m/200yd to the south of the monastery is El Bahri Sea Mosque, built in around 1880. It now houses the municipal museum, which mainly exhibits archaeological discoveries from the region.

El Bahri Sea Mosque

The small archaeological park and the tourist information centre can be found in Habanim Street, just outside the 18th-century town walls. Here at the Jordan River Hotel, which is right next door, there used to be a Byzantine residential quarter which later became the centre of the crusader town, but there is not much evidence to be seen of that today.

Archaeological park

Several men of significance to Judaism lie buried in the old cemetery in Ben Zakkay Street in the northwest. The most notable is **the philosopher and doctor Maimonides** (Rabbi Mosheh ben Maimon, also known as RaMBaM, that being the acronym for his name). The family of the scholar, who was born in Cordoba in 1135, had to leave Spain because of their faith in 1149. After stops in Fez, Morocco, Jerusalem and Alexandria, Maimonides finally arrived in Cairo, where he became the personal physician of Saladin in 1158. At the same time he was the head of the Jewish community in Cairo. In addition to several medical treatises he also wrote influential mishnah

Cemetery
✳
◄ Tomb of Maimonides

> **!** **Baedeker TIP**
>
> **Fun in the water**
> The water park in Tiberias has a wave pool and seven flumes, some of them steep, some of them bendy. This great attraction is situated right on the beach (free to guests) at the Gai Beach Hotel (open: April–Oct daily 9.30am–5pm).

commentaries. His main philosophical work, *The Guide for the Perplexed* (*Moreh Nevukhim*), influenced people such as Albertus Magnus, Thomas Aquinas and Spinoza. As he requested, Maimonides, who died in Cairo in 1204, was buried in Tiberias.

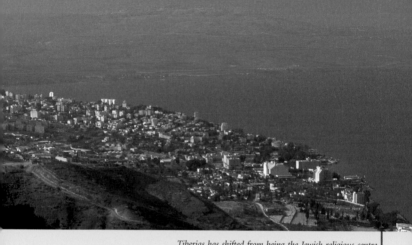

Tiberias has shifted from being the Jewish religious centre to a holiday destination on the Sea of Galilee.

The domed **tomb of Rabbi Akiva** lies above the old cemetery in the middle of a new residential quarter (access via Rehov Trumpeldor). Rabbi Akiva, who was born in around AD 50, saw the prophesied Messiah in Simon bar Kokhba, the leader of the Jewish revolt against the Romans that began in AD 132. After the failure of the revolt, he was killed by the Romans in AD 135.

Tiberias-Hammat

Leave the old town in a southbound direction on the waterfront promenade, past several lidos, to get to Tiberias-Hammat with its hot sulphurous springs. The two spa centres, **Tiberias Hot Springs Health Spa** and **Tiberias Hot Springs Recreation Centre**, whose hot springs are also open to the public, lie right on the through road. Tiberias Hot Springs Health Spa specializes in medical treatments, while the Recreation Centre focuses on relaxation and beauty.

✱
Synagogue ▶

The entrance to an excavation site, whose main attraction is a early medieval synagogue with a well-preserved mosaic floor, can be found immediately to the south of the spa centres. A synagogue was built here as early as the 3rd and 4th centuries. A new one was built on its ruins in the 6th and 7th centuries. There is a square stone structure in the southern section of the older synagogue for the Torah shrine, while the later building possesses a semicircular apse. The **fully preserved floor mosaic** dates back to the older synagogue. It is distinguished by a high artistic standard and figurative depictions. The main mosaic features the sun god Helios at the centre, surrounded by the twelve signs of the zodiac, while the seasons are depicted in the corners. The Torah shrine is depicted at the southern end between two seven-armed candelabras, along with thuribles and shofars. The motifs largely correspond to those in ▶Beit Alfa, but the artistry is more refined.

Above the synagogue is the domed tomb of Rabbi Meir (it cannot be accessed via the park). He was a student of Rabbi Akiva. According to tradition prayers at his tomb are more likely to be answered. Rabbi Meir is also known as **»Baal HaNes«** (»miracle worker«).

◄ Tomb of Rabbi Meir

Around Tiberias

On Route 77, just after a big left-hand curve before leaving town, there is a right-hand turn towards ►Nazareth. This road leads to the Arbel Valley and the kibbutz of the same name. The views of the Wadi al-Hammam, framed by steep cliffs, from the elevation above the kibbutz are impressive.

Arbel Valley

Drive all the way to the end of the road through the Arbel Valley. After around 10km/6mi the road reaches Nabi Shu'ayb at the northern foot of the Horns of Hattin (see below). Nabi Shu'ayb is an important **sacred site for the Druze people**. They venerate the tomb of Jethro, father-in-law of Moses, in a domed building here. In April they celebrate the memory of this man, whom they consider to be the first of their seven prophets.

Nabi Shu'ayb

Leave Tiberias on Route 77 towards ►Nazareth. After around 10km/6mi the Horns of Hattin (Hebrew: Karnei Hittin) can be seen to the right. This mountain, which is not all that high, got its name because of its double summit, which was formed when one of its craters collapsed. The elevation, which can be reached after a half-hour hike, still features some Bronze Age ruins. Even more impressive are the wonderful views of eastern Galilee and the ►Sea of Galilee.

Horns of Hattin

The Horns of Hattin came to fame as a result of the Battle of Hattin on 4 July 1187, when **Saladin** defeated the crusaders under the leadership of **Guy of Lusignan**, the king of Jerusalem. This defeat caused the Kingdom of Jerusalem, founded by crusaders, to lose large parts of its territory and Jerusalem itself after an existence for 88 years. For the next hundred years it was reduced to a coastal strip with ►Akko as its capital.

◄ Battle of Hattin

✶ Timna

E 8

District: Southern

Around 30km/18mi to the north of ►Eilat is Timna Valley Park. It measures around 60 sq km/23 sq mi and is an attractive desert landscape with bizarre rock formations such as the famous King Solomon's Pillars, ancient Egyptian copper mines and ancient rock drawings.

What to See in Timna Valley Park

Opening hours:
Sat–Thu 8am–4pm,
Fri until 1pm
★
King Solomon's
Pillars ►

King Solomon's Pillars can be found a few miles beyond the entrance. This 50m/164ft sandstone wall, which glows red in the light of the sun, formed over millennia as the result of erosion. The feature was named by the archaeologist Nelson Glueck, who explored Timna's copper mines back in the 1930s. Steps lead up to a relief at 30m/100ft. It depicts Pharaoh **Ramesses III** (1184–1153 BC) making a sacrifice to the Egyptian goddess Hathor. On the eastern side of the massive sandstone formation are the remains of a temple dedicated to the goddess Hathor. It was built in the 13th–12th century BC and is now surrounded by a protective barrier.

Hill of Slaves

The Hill of Slaves rises opposite King Solomon's Pillars. This is a **miners' camp** that existed from the 14th to the 12th century BC. Two gate towers secured the entrance. The remains of houses and workshops were found within the area, which is partially surrounded by a wall.

Lake Timna

In order to increase the recreational value of Timna Valley Park, a small lake with a restaurant and picnic sites has been set up nearby, to the east of King Solomon's Pillars.

The Pillars of Solomon, illuminated by the sun in the desert

To get to the »Mushroom«, head back towards the entrance of the park and turn left. The remains of homes, workshops, furnaces and larder pits from the 14th–12th centuries can be seen beside a 6m/20ft mushroom-shaped rock formation.

The Mushroom

Follow the road that leads past the Mushroom to get to a car park. There are signposted trails to the Egyptian copper mines from here. After around 200m/200yd the trail reaches a large sandstone arch, after which the path then heads steeply uphill to ancient galleries and shafts. Head up to the viewing platform to see light-coloured circles on the ground. They are shafts that have been filled in again.

Egyptian copper mines

A little further north of the Egyptian copper mines, rock drawings were discovered in a crevice that can now be accessed via steps. They too date back to the Egyptian period (13th–12th century). The drawings depict ibexes, ostriches, people and carts.

Rock drawings

* * Tzippori

District: Northern

Tzippori National Park, 6km/3.5mi to the northwest of ►Nazareth, is one of the country's most interesting excavation sites because of its fabulous mosaics and also the beautiful surrounding scenery.

In contrast to nearby Yodefat (►Around Akko), this town, which is not mentioned in the Old Testament and was called **Diocaesarea** during Roman times, did not take part in the rebellion of AD 66, which is why it was spared by the Romans. The town grew in significance when the High Council of ►Beit She'arim moved to Tzippori, which was also known by its Greek name **Sepphoris**. **Judah the Prince**, the highest spiritual authority of the Jews at the time, lived here for 17 years until his death. He was buried in Beit She'arim. In around the mid-3rd century the High Council moved to ►Tiberias. The moshav of Tzippori was founded in 1949, one year after the Israeli army had taken the 12th-century crusader castle (renovated in the 18th century) and expelled the Arab population.

Seat of the High Council

What to See in Tzippori National Park

The official tour (tel. 04 656 82 77, www.parks.org.il) of the expansive ruins only starts higher up, but there is already something of interest at the first car park beyond the ticket booth: one of the many synagogues that once existed in Tzippori has been excavated below. At the second car park the waymarked path leads past a kiosk and through a small wood to the ruins on the hill. Right behind the

⏱
Opening hours:
April–Sept daily
8am–5pm, Oct–-
March until 4pm

✳ St George's Monastery

🕐 Opening hours:
Mon–Sat 8am–1pm
and 3pm–6pm

One option is to take the road from ▶Jerusalem towards ▶Jericho and turn left after around 25km/15mi (signposted). Drive to a car park on the left-hand side of the road for a first view of the rocky Wadi Qilt from the somewhat higher northern edge. From the car park, take the track that is only suitable for off-road vehicles and continue northeast to a hill with a cross. On foot this hike takes around an hour and a half. This is a lovely viewpoint from which to see the Greek Orthodox monastery of St George, which, with its cave church, clings imposingly to the rock face. The entrance is a further half-hour hike on the stony track. The other, simpler way is to hire a guide in Jericho (every hotel will oblige), and to access the enchanting monastery from there.

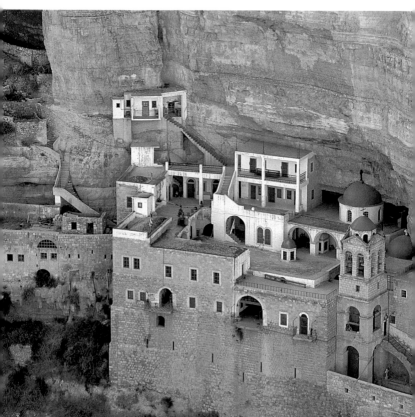

St George's Monastery, which is built into the rock face, can only be reached on foot.

The monastery was founded in around 480. It flourished in the 6th century but it was then destroyed by the Persians in 614. The current monastery was built between 1878 and 1901. St Mary's Church has several fine icons and paintings. The Church of St John and George still has a **6th-century mosaic floor**. In addition the monks show visitors a grotto that houses the remains of their brothers who were killed during the Persian conquest of Byzantine Jerusalem.

<table>
<tr><td>!</td><td>Baedeker TIP</td></tr>
</table>

Holiday snapshot?
Anyone wanting to get a good picture of St George's Monastery should be aware that this is only possible in the morning, because from noon onwards it lies in deep shade.

✴ Zikhron Ya'akov

E 2

District: Haifa
Population: 15,000

Altitude: 50m/165ft

After the ►Golan, ►Carmel is the best-known wine region in Israel and Zikhron Ya'akov, founded by Romanian immigrants in the southern Carmel in 1882, is one of the most important wine towns in the country – an absolute must for wine enthusiasts!

Zikhron Ya'akov sees a particularly large number of visitors on the Sabbath, because the food here is excellent, the atmosphere in the garden and street cafés is lovely, and people-watching on the traffic-calmed Hameyasdim Street is most relaxing. **Baron de Rothschild** had wine and almond plantations set up in Zikhron Ya'akov in 1889, seven years after it was founded, while a bottle factory was built 9km/5.5mi to the west in what is now the kibbutz of Nahsholim. As thanks the settlers named the town 30km/18mi south of Haifa after Edmond de Rothschild's father Jakob (Ya'akov).

Wine town

What to See in Zikhron Ya'akov

The main attraction of the town is Hameyasdim Street, which is lined by old, mostly lovingly restored little houses with gardens. Even though Zikhron Ya'akov patently lives from tourism – almost every other house is a café, a restaurant or a souvenir shop – the road does not have the air of a shopping street. When strolling along Hameyasdim, visitors also come past the **Binyamin Pool** the »head«of the first irrigation system of 1891, which was named after Edmond (Hebrew: Binyamin) de Rothschild. The **old synagogue** from 1885 also dates back to the town's founding days.

✴
Hameyasdim Street

⏵ VISITING ZIKHRON YA'AKOV

INFORMATION
Tourist Office
12 Hameyasdim Street
Tel. (04) 639 03 04

WHERE TO EAT
▶ **Moderate**
Pastoraly
56 Hameyasdim St.
Tel. (04) 639 11 51
Ensemble of very tastefully decorated
restaurant, a café and a cosy wine
cellar in a historic building on a large
farm.

Picciotto
41 Hameyasdim St.
Tel. (04) 629 06 46
Very good place for Italian cuisine in a
lovely Mediterranean-style ambience.

WHERE TO STAY
▶ **Mid-range / Budget**
Maimon
4 Zahal St., tel. (04) 629 03 90
www.maimon.com
Pleasant, inexpensive accommodation
with 25 nicely furnished rooms, a
restaurant, a sun terrace and a garden.

WINE
**Carmel Oriental Wine Cellars
(Carmel Mizrachi)**
At the southern outskirts of town
Tel. (04) 629 09 77
www.carmelwines.co.il
Guided tours: Sun–Thu
8.30am–3.30pm, Fri until 1pm
Israel's largest winery sells its kosher
wines in newly designed premises.

**Ramat Hanadiv
(Tomb of the
Rothschilds)** A road turns right to Ramat Hanadiv (»hill of the benefactor«) on the southern outskirts of town. Baron Edmond de Rothschild requested to be buried here. In 1954 his mortal remains and those of his wife Ada were brought from France to Israel and buried here in a state ceremony. In the west of the well-tended, lavish Memorial Gardens, where the **Rothschild Mausoleum** is also located, a stone map shows all the settlements that Edmond de Rothschild founded in Israel.

Around Zikhron Ya'akov

Jabotinsky Park ⁕ A pretty spot for a picnic under tall, old pine trees: Jabotinsky Park (see below) lies on a hill between Zikhron Ya'akov and Binyamina and is a popular spot for families to spend the Sabbath. Below the park, on the road to Zikhron Ya'akov, is a small, relatively well-preserved Roman amphitheatre.

The town of Binyamina, nestling into the hills 5km/3mi to the south of Zikhron Ya'aokov, is also named after Baron Edmond (Binyamin) de Rothschild. It was founded in 1922. Binyamina, which is surrounded by orange and fig plantations as well as vineyards, also has a winery.

Binyamina

GLOSSARY

Aliyah Jewish immigration to Palestine. The first Aliyah (Jews from Russia and Poland) started in 1882; the second Aliyah (1904 -- 1914) marked the beginning of the Zionist workers' movement.

Ark of the Covenant At the command of Moses Bezalel made a portable shrine out of acacia wood and covered it with gold inside and out, which the children of Israel carried along on the wanderings (Exodus 37). It was the symbol of God's presence for which a golden throne of grace flanked by cherubim was created. According to later traditions the ark contained the stone tablets with the law that Moses had received on Mt Sinai. During the time of the Judges the ark stood in Shiloh. The Philistines stole it, David got it back and brought it to Jerusalem, where Solomon built the temple for it. It has been lost since the destruction of the temple in 587 BC.

Aron Kodesh "holy ark": the cabinet in the synagogue in which the Torah scrolls are kept.

Ashkenazim Jews (or descendants of Jews) from central or eastern Europe, where they had originally migrated to via the Balkans (Ashkenaz = Germany)

Bar Mitzva "Son of the law": formal rite of passage into the congregation for Jewish boys at the age of 13

Bat Mitzva "Daughter of the law": formal rite of passage for girls, like the Bar Mitzva, but at the age of 12

Beth haMidrash House of study and prayer for Talmud

Berakha Blessing, prayer

Brit Mila Circumcision ceremony for boys at the age of eight days

Gabbai Head of the synagogue

Gemara A kind of encyclopaedia that contains explanations and exegesis of the Mishnah, compiled around AD 500.

Haggadah »telling«: Part of the Talmud; edifying, ethical and legendary Jewish writings from late Antiquity expanded during the Middle Ages and then compiled into the Haggadic midrashim.

Halakha »path«: legal part of the Talmud, system of laws mostly derived from the Torah and formulated as individual laws. Basis of religious practice.

Hassidim 1. During the time of the Maccabees (second century BC) the term for a pious Jew (Hasidaean; Hassidim = pious). 2. Name for a follower of Hassidism, a movement that began in the 18th century in the Ukraine and Poland, whose followers honoured Rabbi Israel ben Elieser (1699 to 1760) of the Ukraine as a model, Zadik (holy man) and miracle worker. Their goal was to internalize religion instead of the following the strict Talmudic law.

Hazzan Prayer leader or cantor in the synagogue

Kabbalah »receiving«: in Talmudic times the term for the oral reception that existed alongside of the written law. In the Middle Ages it referred to Jewish mystic philosophy concerned with the nature and work of God, the creation of the world and the end of time. Kabbalah reached its high point in 13th century Spain, when the Zohar was written.

Karaites (Karaim) Jewish sect that was started in the 8th century AD in Persia, which recognizes only the Tanakh (Old Testament) and not the Talmud and the Rabbinic tradition. Around 850 a group moved to Ramla in today's Israel, where it exists until today.

Kashrut All of the laws of purity for food and other areas of human life. They go back to Moses, who was motivated by hygienic and aesthetic aspects in composing them, and who especially wanted to see Israel separated from other nations. The laws of purity for women in childbed and for circumcision can be found in Leviticus 12, for marriage and chastity in Leviticus 18, the law on sanctifying daily life and on the Sabbath in Leviticus 19. Deuteronomy 17 contains the law forbidding worshipping heathen gods; chapter 24 discusses married life. Leviticus 11 and 17 as well as Deuteronomy 14 contain laws on pure or impure animals and foods (► Baedeker Special p. 124).

Kehilah Jewish religious commuity

Kibbutz Autonomous settlement with common ownership

Kosher ►Baedeker Special S. 114

Menorah Seven-armed candleholder made by Bezalel (Exodus 37)

Midrash »exegesis «: Rabbinic literature is collected in the midrashim; explanation of Bible texts from 30 BC to AD 900. Halakhic midrash contains interpretations of religious texts; aggadic midrash contains ethical and contemplative texts.

Mikveh Ritual immersion bath

Minian Prayer quorum of at least ten men

Mishneh »repetition«: Collection of Jewish laws completed around AD 200, divided into six orders (sedarim).

Moshav Settlement organized as a cooperative

Rabbi »my teacher«: Religious teacher called by the congregation (no ordination). His duties include carrying out certain parts of the prayer service – along with the Hazzan – directing and supervising religious instruction, performing religious ceremonies like weddings and so on. The term rabbi comes from the Aramaic and Hebrew word rab = great (in knowledge) and is an honourable title for Jewish scholars. The New Testament contains the even more honourable title *rabbuni* (Mark 10:51 and John 20:16).

Sanhedrin Hebraicised form of the Greek synhedrion: the high council consisting of members of the Jewish aristocracy under the leadership of the high priest (first mentioned under the Hellenistic rulers in the 3rd century BC). During the Maccabean period the Sanhedrin was the highest court; during the time of the Roman procurators it was the highest Jewish office for all legal and administrative matters. After the destruction of Jerusalem and the temple in the year AD 70 Rabbi Yohanan ben Zakkai got permission to move the seat of the Sanhedrin to Jamnia. Around AD 140 the Sanhedrin moved to Usha (Galiliee), later to Tiberias.

Shofar Ram's horn, which is blown on the Day of Atonement and on the Jewish New Year

Shulchan Aruch Summary of religious laws composed in the early modern period.

Sephardim Jews (or their descendants) who lived in Spain and Portugal; after being expelled from there in 1492 they settled in various European countries, in North Africa and the Near East. Today all oriental Jews are (incorrectly) called Sephardim (Sepharad = Spain).Tabernacle According to Exodus 25 – 31 and 35 – 40 while the Israelites lived on the Sinai Peninsula after the Exodus they made a tent out of linen cloth, a kind of portable temple in which the ark of the covenant, the table for the showbread and the seven-armed candleholder (menorah) were kept.

Synagogue Greek term for an assembly, later also for the building in which they assembled. It probably was already conceived during the Babylonian Captivity (587 – 538 BC) and gained significance as time went on. The oldest synagogues have been documented in Egypt from around 250 BC; in the Hellenistic period synagogues were the centres of Jewish life in the entire Mediterranean region. Most of the synagogues found in Palestine and Syria come from the 3rd to the 7th centuries.

Tallit Large, light-coloured cloth with dark edging, which is worn by pious Jews as a prayer shawl.

Talmud »teaching«: most important collection of the teachings of post-biblical Judaism. It was begun in the 6th century BC and it contains religious laws that were transmitted orally until then, and which existed parallel to the written Mosaic law. The Talmud consists of the Mishnah and the Gemara. There is a Babylonian Talmud in the East Aramaic language, which was completed around AD 500 and which has become the definitive version for religious practice, and the Jerusalem (more correctly Palestinian) Talmud from around AD 400.

Tephillin Prayer straps, also sometimes called phylacteries, made of dark leather with a small box that contains texts from the Torah. The tephillin are worn on weekdays during morning prayers.

Torah »teaching, instruction «: the five books of Moses (Pentateuch)

Yeshiva School for the study of the Talmud

INDEX

LIST OF MAPS AND ILLUSTRATIONS

PHOTO CREDITS

PUBLISHER'S INFORMATION

Illustrations etc: 172 illustrations, 62 maps and diagrams, one large map
Text: Dr. Martin Beck, Robert B. Fishman, Dr. Otto Gärtner, Annekathrin Kleefeld, Wolfgang Liebermann, Karin-Lucke-Huss, Georg Rössler, Thomas Volkmann, Andrea Wurth, Reinhard Zakrzewski
Editing: Baedeker editorial team (John Sykes)
Translation: John Sykes■
Cartography: Christoph Gallus, Hohberg; MAIRDUMONT/Falk Verlag, Ostfildern (map)
3D illustrations: jangled nerves, Stuttgart
Design: independent Medien-Design, Munich; Kathrin Schemel

Editor-in-chief: Rainer Eisenschmid, Baedeker Ostfildern

1st edition 2013
Based on Baedeker Allienz Reiseführer »Israel« 12. Auflage 2010

Copyright: Karl Baedeker Verlag, Ostfildern
Publication rights: MAIRDUMONT GmbH & Co; Ostfildern

Printed in China

BAEDEKER GUIDE BOOKS AT A GLANCE
Guiding the World since 1827

- Algarve
- Andalusia
- Australia
- Austria
- Bali
- Barcelona
- Berlin
- Brazil
- Budapest
- Cape Town •
  Garden Route
- China
- Cologne
- Dresden
- Dubai
- Egypt
- Finland
- Florence
- Florida
- France
- Gran Canaria
- Greek Islands
- Greece
- Iceland
- India
- Ireland
- Israel
- Italian Lakes
- Italy
- Japan
- Jordan
- London
- Madeira
- Mexico
- Morocco
- Naples • Capri •
  Amalfi Coast
- New York
- New Zealand
- Norway
- Paris
- Portugal
- Prague
- Rome
- Sicily
- South Africa
- Spain
- Thailand
- Turkish Coast
- Tuscany
- Venice
- Vienna
- Vietnam

DEAR READER,

We would like to thank you for choosing this Baedeker travel guide. It will be a reliable companion on your travels and will not disappoint you.
This book describes the major sights, of course, but it also recommends hotels in the luxury and budget categories, and includes tips about where to eat or go shopping and much more, helping to make your trip an enjoyable experience. Our authors ensure the quality of this information by making regular journeys to Israel and putting all their know-how into this book.

Nevertheless, experience shows us that it is impossible to rule out errors and changes made after the book goes to press, for which Baedeker accepts no liability. Please send us your criticisms, corrections and suggestions for improvement: we appreciate your contribution. Contact us by post or e-mail, or phone us:

▶ **Verlag Karl Baedeker GmbH**
  Editorial department
  Postfach 3162
  73751 Ostfildern
  Germany
  Tel. 49-711-4502-262, fax -343
  www.baedeker.com
  www.baedeker.co.uk
  E-Mail: baedeker@mairdumont.com